CIM
STUDY TEXT

Advanced Certificate

Management Information for Marketing Decisions

New in this July 2001 edition

- New material on continuous assessment

- Reflects recent exams

BPP Publishing
July 2001

First edition 1999
Third edition May 2001

ISBN 0 7517 4117 5 (previous edition 07517 4105 1)

British Library Cataloguing-in-Publication Data
A catalogue record for this book
is available from the British Library

Published by

BPP Publishing Limited
Aldine House, Aldine Place
London W12 8AW

www.bpp.com

Printed in Great Britain by
WM Print Ltd
Frederick Street
Walsall
West Midlands WS2 9NE

We are grateful to the Chartered Institute of Marketing for permission to reproduce in this text the syllabus, tutor's guidance notes, and past examination questions.

HOW TO USE THIS STUDY TEXT (v)

SYLLABUS (x)

TUTOR'S GUIDANCE NOTES (including Website links) (xiv)

THE EXAM PAPER (xvi)

STUDY CHECKLIST (xviii)

CONTINUOUS ASSESSMENT (xix)

• Introduction • Structure and process • Preparing for Assignments • Presentation of the Assignment • Time Management for Assignments • Tips for Writing Assignments • Writing reports • Personal Development Plan for Management Information for Marketing Decisions • Core and option Assignments (examples: finance and forecasting; marketing research)

ORDER FORM

REVIEW FORM & FREE PRIZE DRAW

HOW TO USE THIS STUDY TEXT

Aims of this Study Text

To provide you with the knowledge and understanding, skills and applied techniques required for passing the exam

The Study Text has been written around the new CIM Syllabus (reproduced below, and cross-referenced to where in the text each topic is covered) and the CIM's Tutor's Manual.

- It is **comprehensive**. We do not omit sections of the syllabus as the examiner is liable to examine any angle of any part of the syllabus - and you do not want to be left high and dry.

- It is **on-target** - we do not include any material which is not examinable. You can therefore rely on the BPP Study Text as the stand-alone source of all your information for the exam.

To allow you to study in the way that best suits your learning style and the time you have available, by following your personal Study Plan (see below)

You may be studying at home on your own until the date of the exam, or you may be attending a full-time course. You may like to (and have time to) read every word, or you may prefer to (or only have time to) skim-read and devote the remainder of your time to question practice. Wherever you fall in the spectrum, you will find the BPP Study Text meets your needs in designing and following your personal Study Plan.

To tie in with the other components of the BPP Effective Study Package to ensure you have the best possible chance of passing the exam

Recommended period of use	Elements of BPP Effective Study Package
3-12 months before exam	**Study Text** Acquisition of knowledge, understanding, skills and applied techniques.
1-6 months before exam	**Practice & Revision Kit (9/2001)** Tutorial questions and helpful checklists of the key points lead you into each area. There are then numerous Examination questions to try, graded by topic area, along with realistic suggested solutions prepared by marketing professionals in the light of the Examiners Reports. The September 2001 edition will include the December 2000 and June 2001 papers.
1-6 months before exam	**Success Tapes** Audio cassettes covering the vital elements of your syllabus in less than 90 minutes per subject. Each tape also contains exam hints to help you fine tune your strategy.

BPP PUBLISHING

Settling down to study

By this stage in your career you may be a very experienced learner and taker of exams. But have you ever thought about *how* you learn? Let's have a quick look at the key elements required for effective learning. You can then identify your learning style and go on to design your own approach to how you are going to study this text - your personal Study Plan.

Key element of learning	Using the BPP Study Text
Motivation	You can rely on the comprehensiveness and technical quality of BPP. You've chosen the right Study Text - so you're in pole position to pass your exam!
Clear objectives and standards	Do you want to be a prizewinner or simply achieve a moderate pass? Decide.
Feedback	Follow through the examples in this text and do the Action Programme and the Quick quizzes. Evaluate your efforts critically - how are you doing?
Study Plan	You need to be honest about your progress to yourself - don't be over-confident, but don't be negative either. Make your Study Plan (see below) and try to stick to it. Focus on the short-term objectives - completing two chapters a night, say - but beware of losing sight of your study objectives.
Practice	Use the Quick quizzes and Chapter roundups to refresh your memory regularly after you have completed your initial study of each chapter.

These introductory pages let you see exactly what you are up against. However you study, you should:

- **Read through the syllabus and teaching guide** - this will help you to identify areas you have already covered, perhaps at a lower level of detail, and areas that are totally new to you

- **Study the examination paper section,** where we show you the format of the exam (how many and what kind of questions etc)

Key study steps

The following steps are, in our experience, the ideal way to study for professional exams. You can of course adapt it for your particular learning style (see below).

Tackle the chapters in the order you find them in the Study Text. Taking into account your individual learning style, follow these key study steps for each chapter.

Key study steps	Activity
Step 1 *Chapter topic list*	Study the list. Each numbered topic denotes a **numbered section** in the chapter.
Step 2 *Setting the Scene*	Read it through. It is designed to show you **why the topics in the chapter need to be studied** - how they lead on from previous topics, and how they lead into subsequent ones.
Step 3 *Explanations*	Proceed **methodically** through the chapter, reading each section thoroughly and making sure you understand.
Step 4 *Key Concepts*	**Key concepts** can often earn you **easy marks** if you state them clearly and correctly in an appropriate exam.
Step 5 *Exam Tips*	These give you a good idea of how the examiner tends to examine certain topics – pinpointing **easy marks** and highlighting **pitfalls**.
Step 6 *Note taking*	Take **brief notes** if you wish, avoiding the temptation to copy out too much.
Step 7 *Marketing at Work*	Study each one, and try if you can to add flesh to them from your **own experience** - they are designed to show how the topics you are studying come alive (and often come unstuck) in the **real world**.
Step 8 *Action Programme*	Make a very good attempt at each one in each chapter. These are designed to put your **knowledge into practice** in much the same way as you will be required to do in the exam. Check the answer at the end of the chapter in the **Action Programme review**, and make sure you understand the reasons why yours may be different.
Step 9 *Chapter Roundup*	Check through it very carefully, to make sure you have grasped the **major points** it is highlighting
Step 10 *Quick quiz*	When you are happy that you have covered the chapter, use the **Quick quiz** to check your recall of the topics covered. The answers are in the paragraphs in the chapter that we refer you to.
Step 11 *Illustrative question(s)*	Either at this point, or later when you are thinking about revising, make a full attempt at the **illustrative question(s)**. You can find these at the end of the Study Text, along with the **Answers** so you can see how you did.

BPP PUBLISHING

Developing your personal Study Plan

Preparing a Study Plan (and sticking closely to it) is one of the key elements in learning success.

First you need to be aware of your style of learning. There are four typical learning styles. Consider yourself in the light of the following descriptions. and work out which you fit most closely. You can then plan to follow the key study steps in the sequence suggested.

Learning styles	Characteristics	Sequence of key study steps in the BPP Study Text
Theorist	Seeks to understand principles before applying them in practice	1, 2, 3, 7, 4, 5, 8, 9, 10, 11 (6 continuous)
Reflector	Seeks to observe phenomena, thinks about them and then chooses to act	
Activist	Prefers to deal with practical, active problems; does not have much patience with theory	1, 2, 8 (read through), 7, 4, 5, 9, 3, 8 (full attempt), 10, 11 (6 continuous)
Pragmatist	Prefers to study only if a direct link to practical problems can be seen; not interested in theory for its own sake	8 (read through), 2, 4, 5, 7, 9, 1, 3, 8 (full attempt), 10, 11 (6 continuous)

Next you should complete the following checklist.
Am I motivated? (a) ☐

Do I have an objective and a standard that I want to achieve? (b) ☐

Am I a theorist, a reflector, an activist or a pragmatist? (c) ☐

How much time do I have available per week, given: (d) ☐

- The standard I have set myself
- The time I need to set aside later for work on the Practice and Revision Kit
- The other exam(s) I am sitting, and (of course)
- Practical matters such as work, travel, exercise, sleep and social life?

Now:

- Take the time you have available per week for this Study Text (d), and multiply it by the number of weeks available to give (e) (e) ☐
- Divide (e) by the number of chapters to give (f) (f) ☐
- Set about studying each chapter in the time represented by (f), following the key study steps in the order suggested by your particular learning style

This is your personal **Study Plan**.

Short of time?

Whatever your objectives, standards or style, you may find you simply do not have the time available to follow all the key study steps for each chapter, however you adapt them for your particular learning style. If this is the case, follow the Skim Study technique below (the icons in the Study Text will help you to do this).

Skim Study technique

Study the chapters in the order you find them in the Study Text. For each chapter, follow the key study steps 1-2, and then skim-read through step 3. Jump to step 9, and then go back to steps 4-5. Follow through step 7, and prepare outline Answers to the Action Programme (step 8). Try the Quick Quiz (step 10), following up any items you can't answer, then do a plan for the illustrative question (step 11), comparing it against our answers. You should probably still follow step 6 (note-taking).

Moving on...

However you study, when you are ready to embark on the practice and revision phase of the BPP Effective Study Package, you should still refer back to this Study Text:

- as a source of **reference** (you should find the list of key concepts and the index particularly helpful for this)

- as a **refresher** (the Chapter Roundups and Quick Quizzes help you here)

A note on pronouns

On occasions in this Study Text, 'he' is used for 'he or she', 'him' for 'him or her' and so forth. Whilst we try to avoid this practice it is sometimes necessary for reasons of style. No prejudice or stereotyping accounting to sex is intended or assumed.

BPP PUBLISHING

SYLLABUS

Aims and objectives

- To develop students' understanding of the need for and place of an integrated management information system in supporting marketing decisions and to be able to develop appropriate MkIS structures by applying basic concepts

- To emphasise the importance of forecasting in the planning process and to apply forecast information in a variety of contexts relating to marketing decisions

- To apply financial concepts in order to make effective marketing decisions together with an ability to apply financial analysis to a variety of marketing management problems

- To explore the sources of marketing research information, how they are obtained (strengths and weaknesses) and be able to apply marketing research information to a range of marketing problems in a variety of contexts

- To develop a practical and applied understanding of developments in information and communication technologies that impact upon marketing management decisions and how management information is gathered, stored and communicated both within and across organisational boundaries

Learning outcomes

Students will be able to:

- Apply their understanding of management information systems in designing appropriate marketing information systems (MkIS) and management control systems

- Recommend appropriate changes to management information systems to achieve specific objectives in a specific context

- Demonstrate their understanding of the importance of forecasting information in a range of marketing contexts and be able to apply this to forecast at a variety of levels, eg organisational, departmental, product level, and service level

- Apply their knowledge and understanding of financial management to make appropriate marketing decisions and recommendations and to work within predetermined budget limits using appropriate financial controls

- Apply their knowledge and understanding of management information structures to design and implement appropriate systems to collect a variety of data and market intelligence in order to provide improved decisions making. In so doing students will be able to identify benefits to internal and/or external customers

- Design and implement appropriate marketing control systems through effective use of management information from a variety of sources that will include internal and external data

- Analyse, evaluate and apply a range of quantitative and qualitative data and make appropriate recommendations that lead to effective marketing decisions in specific marketing contexts

- Understand the place of information and communication technologies in the process of generating, storing and retrieving a variety of sources of management information for marketing decision making

BPP PUBLISHING

TUTOR'S GUIDANCE NOTES

The following is BPP's summary of the Tutor Manual produced by the CIM for this subject.

The syllabus is designed to reflect the new focus on information as it is applied to marketing decisions, and contributes to understanding developed at Certificate level as well as underpinning the Planning and Control and Analysis and Decision papers at Diploma level. It is important that students appreciate the links both between the syllabus areas for this subject and with papers at other levels. It is strongly recommended that students have previously completed the Advanced Certificate module Marketing Operations or are studying that subject in parallel with this one.

Financial analysis, forecasts, marketing research activities, external sources and information and communication technologies all contribute information to marketing decision making and are therefore a necessary part of a marketing manager's competence.

The emphasis is now upon application of knowledge rather than the testing of knowledge alone, and the examination will test the ability of candidates to apply their knowledge to a variety of marketing problems in a variety of contexts.

Specific aspects of the syllabus

Management Information Systems – Basic Concepts (10%)

The examining team is keen to receive scripts that relate MkIS to a specific context. You should think about how you use information in your own organisation as a way of achieving this. You might find you never have enough information, or that you have too much!

Information and Communication Technology Supporting Marketing Decisions (20%)

This is an ever-expanding field, so you should read widely in order to supplement this Study Text with other sources. The technology pages and supplements of the broadsheet newspapers provide up to date information, as do many Internet websites. You need to be able to show that you understand how technology is influencing the way in which data is accessed, processed, analysed and evaluated when making marketing decisions.

Forecasting Information for Marketing Decisions (10%)

You need a knowledge of the range of forecasting methods and tools that are available when putting forecasts together. These are listed in the syllabus. You will need to be able to apply simple forecasting techniques particularly in the area of sales forecasting.

Financial Information to Support Marketing Decisions (40%)

This is now the most heavily weighted area of the syllabus and you will need to demonstrate understanding of basic financial concepts as applied to marketing decisions in a number of different contexts.

Marketing Research Information Applied to Marketing Decisions (20%)

You will need an understanding of appropriate marketing research methods that generate information for specific contexts. This part of the syllabus, in common with the others, is also sharply focused towards the use of marketing research information in making marketing decisions, so it is the application of knowledge to a variety of situations that will be tested.

WEBSITE LINKS

Extracted from the CIM's online Tutor Manual, these websites are specific to this paper.

Syllabus Section	Web Address	Description
Management Information Systems: Basic Concepts	**www.mckinseyquarterly.com** (see 'information technology' section)	Free full text articles on information technology issues from one of the world's premier business journals.
	www.whatis.com/tour.htm	A useful illustrated introduction to how the Internet works, with explanations of the associated terminology.
Information and Communication Technology Supporting Marketing Decision	**www.e-envoy.gov.uk**	Regular monthly updates detailing progress in the Government's efforts to make the UK 'the best place in the world for eCommerce.
	www.mckinseyquarterly.com (see 'electronic commerce' section)	Free full text articles on electronic commerce issues from one of the world's premier business journals.
	www.forrester.com	Provides free summaries of the latest research reports on the growth of eCommerce.
	www.theecademy.com	UK based daily email news service on the latest ebusiness developments and local networking events.
	www.wilsonweb.com	An exhaustively-detailed reference on the full range of Internet marketing issues, available as a free monthly newsletter. American in origin, but still a valuable resource and often light years ahead of UK developments.
	www.ecommercetimes.com	Another useful and comprehensive daily email news service on the latest ebusiness developments. Again, a US perspective.
Forecasting Information for Marketing Decisions	**www.cyberatlas.com**	Latest statistics and projections of Internet growth.
	www.statistics.gov.uk	Detailed information on a variety of consumer demographics from the Government Statistics Office.
	www.nw.com	Latest statistics and projections of Internet growth.
	www.gbn.org	The Global Business Network which encourages collaborative exploration of the future using forecasting tools such as scenario planning.

THE EXAM PAPER

Assessment methods and format of the paper

Number of marks

Part A: one compulsory case study, with two questions	40
Part B: three questions from six (equal marks)	60
	100

Time allowed: 3 hours

Analysis of past papers

The analysis below shows the topics which have featured in past papers.

June 2001

Part A (compulsory case study question worth 40 marks)

A conglomerate is considering offering a new product and has commissioned a market research report.

1(a) Evaluate quality of marketing research report
1(b) Further information before pilot of new product
1(c) Forecast profit for new product
1(d) Using the web site

Part B (answer three questions worth 20 marks each)
2   Use of Internet in the marketing mix
3   Budgeting for an event
4   Types of marketing research
5   Methods of apportioning overheads
6   Preparing a sales forecast
7   Investment appraisal techniques

December 2000

Part A (compulsory case study question worth 40 marks)

Four-week money-off coupon promotion for a consumer magazine

1(a) Direct product profitability statement for promotion period
1(b) Direct product profitability statement covering post-promotion period
1(c) Discuss reducing risks and improving effectiveness of promotion
1(d) Recommendation on whether promotion should go ahead

Part B (answer three questions worth 20 marks each)
2   Use of marketing information to develop long-term customer relationships
3   Costing of customer support service; ways of charging customers for the service
4   Difficulties in combining internal data sources with external databases
5   E-commerce and security of data transmitted via Internet
6   (a) Using market research information as part of the marketing information system
      (b) Marketing research techniques to develop the organisation's knowledge base
7   Variances of sales, cost of sales and gross profit based on budget for a product

June 2000

Part A (compulsory case study question worth 40 marks)

Data given on three products: sales promotion and price discounts planned

1(a) Effect of promotion on sales and gross profit
1(b) Effect of discounting
1(c) Effect of promotion and discounting run simultaneously
1(d) Alternatives to promotion and discounting
1(e) Further information before making recommendations

Part B (answer three questions worth 20 marks each)

2 Merits of different forecasting techniques
3 Report on new customer services investment
4 Reasons, methods and information for pricing research
5 *Either:* Activity based costing and its merits
   or: The marketing budget; financial variances, budgeting for overheads
6 Statement of direct product profitability per unit, and its merits
7 Define, explain and discuss limitations of key performance indicators

December 1999

Part A (compulsory case study question worth 40 marks)

A retailing company is deciding on marketing strategies to open up new channels of distribution.

1(a) Budgeted financial statements
1(b) Discuss assumptions used in (a)
1(c) Explain reservations in development of channels of distribution
1(d) Discuss policy of charging customers for a catalogue

Part B (answer three questions worth 20 marks each)

2 *Either:* Activity based costing systems
   or: Budgetary control systems
3 Website development: critical path analysis and costs
4 Preparation of budgeted financial statement
5 Market research, sampling and use of external agency
6 *Either:* Features of MkIS
   or: Implementing new management information systems
7 Application of ICT in an organisation

STUDY CHECKLIST

This page is designed to help you chart your progress through the Study Text, including the Action Programme and illustrative questions. You can tick off each topic as you study and try questions on it. Insert the dates you complete the chapters Action Programme and questions in the relevant boxes. You will thus ensure that you are on track to complete your study before the exam.

	Text chapters Date completed	Action programme Number	Date Completed	Illustrative questions Number	Date Completed

PART A: MANAGEMENT INFORMATION SYSTEMS

1 Management information for marketing decisions		1,2		-	
2 Developing a marketing information system		1,2		1,2	

PART B: INFORMATION AND COMMUNICATION TECHNOLOGY

3 Technology supporting marketing decisions		1,2,3,4		3	

PART C: FORECASTING INFORMATION

4 Forecasting information for marketers		1,2,3,4		4	

PART D: FINANCIAL INFORMATION

5 Financial information and marketing		1		5	
6 Introducing cost behaviour		1,2,3,4		-	
7 Costing techniques and their application to marketing		1,2,3,4		6	
8 Decision making for marketers		1,2,3		7	
9 Pricing and profitability		1,2,3,4,5		8,9	
10 Cost/volume/profit analysis		1,2,3,4,5		10,11	
11 Budget preparation and control		1,2,3		12,13,14	
12 Ratio analysis		1,2		15	

PART E: MARKETING RESEARCH INFORMATION

13 Market intelligence		1,2,3		16,17	
14 The marketing research process		1,2,3		18	
15 Marketing research applications		1		19	

GUIDE TO CONTINUOUS ASSESSMENT : MANAGEMENT INFORMATION FOR MARKETING DECISIONS

Aims and objectives of this *Guide to Continuous Assessments*
*   To understand the scope and structure of the Continuous Assessment process
*   To consider the benefits of learning through continuous assessment
*   To assist students in preparation of their assignments
*   To consider the range of communication options available to students
*   To provide assistance in the development of the Personal Development Portfolio (PDP)
*   To look at the range of potential assessment areas that assignments may challenge
*   To assist with time-management within the assessment process

Introduction

It is now over five years since the Chartered Institute of Marketing (CIM) introduced continuous assessment (ie assignment based assessment) as an alternative to the examination process.

At time of writing, there are over 80 CIM Approved Study Centres that offer the Continuous Assessment option as an alternative to examinations. This change in direction and flexibility in assessment was externally driven by industry, students and tutors alike, all of whom wanted a test of practical skills as well as a knowledge-based approach to learning.

At the Advanced Certificate level, *Management Information for Marketing Decisions,* the basis of this particular module, and Effective Management for Marketing can be assessed through an assignment route as opposed to the examination due to the practical nature of both syllabuses, which cover marketing in practice as well as marketing theory.

Clearly, both of these subject areas lend themselves to assignment-based learning, due to their practical nature. The assignments that you will undertake provide you with an opportunity to be **creative in approach and in presentation.** They enable you to give a true demonstration of your marketing ability in a way that perhaps might be inhibited in a traditional examination situation.

Continuous assessment offers you considerable scope to produce work that provides existing and future **employers** with **evidence** of your **ability.** It offers you a **portfolio** of evidence which demonstrates your abilities and your willingness to develop continually your knowledge and skills. It will also, ultimately, help you frame your continuing professional development in the future.

It does not matter what type of organisation you are from, large or small, as you will find substantial benefit in this approach to learning. In some cases, students have made their own organisation central to their assessment and produced work to support their organisation's activities, resulting in subsequent recognition and promotion: a success story for this approach.

So, using your own organisation can be beneficial (especially if your employer sponsors you). However, it is equally valid to use a different organisation, as long as you are familiar enough with it to base your assignments on it. This is particularly useful if you are between jobs, taking time out, returning to employment or studying at university or college.

To take the Continuous Assessment option, you are required to register with a CIM Accredited Study Centre (ie a college, university, or distance learning provider). **Currently you would be unable to take the Continuous Assessment option as an independent learner.** If in doubt you should contact the CIM Education Division who will provide you with a list of local Accredited Centres offering Continuous Assessment.

Continuous assessment

Structure and process

The **assignments** that you will undertake during your studies are set **by CIM centrally** and not by the study centre. This standardised approach to assessment enables external organisations to interpret the results on a consistent basis.

There are three assignments per module.

- Assignment 1: Personal Development Portfolio Assignment
- Assignment 2: Core assignment
- Assignment 3: Optional Assignment

The purpose of each assignment is to enable you to demonstrate your ability to research, analyse and problem-solve in a range of different situations. You will be expected to approach your assignment work from a professional marketer's perspective, addressing the assignment brief directly, and undertaking the tasks required. Each assignment will relate directly to the syllabus module and will be applied against the content of the syllabus.

Assignment 1

The Personal Development Portfolio will run for the duration of your module, maximising your potential to show your own personal development through your learning. This assignment is singularly about **you** and how, through a range of activities, you **develop your strengths** and start to **address your weaknesses**. We will be looking at your overall approach to this assignment later in this unit.

Assignment 2

Assignment 2 is a core assignment. It is mandatory, so all students will be taking this assignment.

Assignment 3

However, Assignment 3 enables students to choose from four assignment options. In doing this, students will be able to select the assignment most appropriate to their individual needs, of a greatest personal benefit.

You will typically have six weeks to complete Assignments 2 and 3, from the time the assignment brief is issued until the submission date. This is a national standard set by CIM, and is a maximum period for the assessment work to be undertaken. Clearly, time management will be an issue with these two assignments in particular. Again, we will be looking at this issue shortly.

Whilst we can focus clearly upon the Personal Development Portfolio in Assignment 1, the bases of **Assignments 2 and 3 are not known in advance** (like an examination situation). This has been established as good practice so that no one student or study centre is advantaged over another. Therefore, all students will receive the assignments 2 and 3 as 'unseens'. Although we do not know what the themes for the Assignments 2 and 3 will be, we can look at **potential** themes in order to focus your minds on typical approaches that you might take.

All of the Assignments clearly indicate the links with the syllabus and the assignment weighting (ie the contribution each assignment makes to your overall marks).

Once your Assignments have been completed, they will be marked by your accredited centre, and then **moderated** by a CIM External Moderator. When all the assignments have been marked, they are sent to CIM for further moderation. After this, all marks are forwarded to you by CIM (not your centre) in the form of an examination result. Your **centre** will be able to you provide you with some written feedback on overall performance, but **will not** provide you with any detailed mark breakdown.

Preparing for Assignments: a guide

Before looking at the Personal Development Portfolio and potential assignment themes and approaches, it might be helpful to consider how best to present your assignment. Here you should consider issues of detail, protocol and the range of communications that could be called upon within the assignment.

Presentation of the Assignment

You should always ensure that you prepare two copies of your Assignment, keeping a soft copy on disc. On occasions assignments go missing, or second copies are required by CIM.

- Each Assignment should be clearly marked up with your name, your study centre, your CIM Student registration number and ultimately at the end of the assignment a word count. The assignment should also be word-processed.

- The assignment presentation format should directly meet the requirements of the assignment brief, (ie reports and presentations are the most called for communication formats). You **must** ensure that you assignment does not appear to be an extended essay. If it does, you will lose marks. In many of the assignments, marks are awarded for presentation and coherence.

- The word limit may not always be included in the assignment brief. However, you should not exceed 3000 words unless otherwise specified. For the Personal Development Portfolio, more than 2000 words is unnecessary.

- **Appendices** should clearly link to the assignment and can be attached as supporting documentation at the end of the report. However failure to reference them by number (eg Appendix 1) within the report and also marked up on the Appendix itself will lose you marks. Only use an Appendix if it is **essential** and clearly adds value to the overall Assignment. The Appendix is not a waste bin for all the materials you have come across in your research, or a way of making your assignment seem somewhat heavier and more impressive than it is.

Time management for Assignments

One of the biggest challenges we all seem to face day-to-day is that of managing time. When studying, that challenge seems to grow increasingly difficult, requiring a balance between work, home, family, social life and study life. It is therefore of pivotal importance to your own success for you to plan wisely the limited amount of time you have available.

Step 1: Find out how much time you have

Ensure that you are fully aware of how long your module lasts, and the final deadline (eg 10 weeks, 12 weeks, 14 weeks etc). If you are studying a module from September to December, it is likely that you will have only 10-12 weeks in which to complete your assignments. In other words, one assignment spans the **duration** of the course, and **two** assignments, to be completed within six weeks to complete, also run through the course. This might sound challenging, but it is manageable.

Step 2: Plan your time

Essentially you need to **work backwards** from the final deadline, submission date, and schedule your work around the possible time lines. Clearly if you have only 10-12 weeks available to complete three assignments, you will need to allocate a block of hours in the final stages of the module to ensure that all of your assignments are in on time. *Failure to submit your assignments on the due date could mean that your marks are capped at 50%.*

Step 3: Set priorities

You should set priorities on a daily and weekly basis (not just for study, but for your life). There is no doubt that this mode of study needs commitment (and some sacrifices in the short term). When your achievements are recognised by colleagues, peers, friends and family, it will all feel worthwhile.

Step 4: Analyse activities and allocate time to them

Consider the **range** of activities that you will need to undertake in order to complete the assignment and the **time** each might take. Remember, too, there will be a delay in asking for information and receiving it.

- Preparing terms of reference for the assignment, to include the following.

1	A short title
2	A brief outline of the assignment purpose and outcome
3	Methodology – what methods you intend to use to carry out the required tasks
4	Indication of any difficulties that have arisen in the duration of the assignment
5	Time schedule
6	Confidentiality – if the assignment includes confidential information ensure that this is clearly marked up and indicated on the assignment
7	Literature and desk research undertaken

This should be achieved in one side of A4

- A literature search in order to undertake the necessary background reading and underpinning information that might support your assignment

- Writing letters and memos asking for information either internally or externally

- Designing questionnaires

- Undertaking surveys

- Analysis of data from questionnaires

- Secondary data search

- Preparation of first draft report

Always build in time to spare, to deal with the unexpected. This may reduce the pressure that you are faced in meeting significant deadlines.

Warning!

The same principles apply to a student with 30 weeks to do the work. However, a word of warning is needed. Do not fall into the trap of leaving all of the work on your Portfolio assignment to the last minute. If you miss out important information or fail to reflect upon your work adequately or successfully you will be penalised for both. Therefore, time management is important whatever the duration of the course.

Tips for writing Assignments

Everybody has a personal style, flair and tone when it comes to writing. However, no matter what your approach, you must ensure your assignment meets the **requirements of the brief** and so is comprehensible, coherent and cohesive in approach.

Think of preparing an assignment as preparing for an examination. Ultimately, the work you are undertaking results in an examination grade. Successful achievement of all four modules in a level results in a qualification.

There are a number of positive steps that you can undertake in order to ensure that you make the best of your assignment presentation in order to maximise the marks available.

Step 1 – Work to the Brief

Ensure that you identify **exactly what the assignment asks you to do**.

* If it asks you to be a marketing manager, then immediately assume that role.

* If it asks you to prepare a report, then present a report, not an essay or a letter.

* Furthermore, if it asks for 3,000 words, then do not present 1,000 or 5,000 unless in both instances it is clearly justified, agreed with your tutor and a valid piece of work.

Identify if the report should be **formal or informal**, who it should be **addressed to**, its **overall purpose** and its **potential use** and outcome. Understanding this will ensure that your assignment meets fully the requirements of the brief and addresses the key issues included within it.

Step 2 – Addressing the Tasks

It is of pivotal importance that you address **each** of the tasks within the assignment. **Many students fail to do this** and often overlook one of the tasks or indeed part of the tasks.

Many of the assignments will have two or three tasks, some will have even more. You should establish quite early on, which of the tasks:

* Requires you to collect information
* Provides you with the framework of the assignment, ie the communication method.

Possible tasks will include the following.

* *Compare and contrast.* Take two different organisations and compare them side by side and consider the differences ie the **contrasts** between the two.

* *Carry out primary or secondary research.* Collect information to support your assignment and your subsequent decisions

* *Prepare a plan.* Some assignments will ask you to prepare a plan for an event or for a marketing activity – if so provide a step by step approach, a a rationale, a time-line, make sure it is measurable and achievable. Make sure your actions are very specific and clearly explained. (Make sure your plan is SMART.)

* *Analyse a situation.* This will require you to collect information, consider its content and present an overall understanding of the actual situation that exists. This might include looking at internal and external factors and how the current situation evolved.

* *Make recommendations.* The more advanced your get in your studies, the more likely it is that you will be required to make recommendations. Firstly **considering and evaluating your options** and then making justifiable **recommendations**, based on them.

* *Justify decisions.* You may be required to justify your decision or recommendations. This will require you to explain fully how you have arrived at this decision and to show why, supported by relevant information, this is the right way forward. In other words, you should not make decisions in a vacuum; as a marketer your decisions should always be informed by context.

- *Prepare a presentation.* This speaks for itself. If you are required to prepare a presentation, ensure that you do so, preparing clearly defined PowerPoint or overhead slides that are not too crowded and that clearly express the points you are required to make.

- *Evaluate performance.* It is very likely that you will be asked to evaluate a campaign, a plan or even an event. You will therefore need to consider its strengths and weaknesses, why it succeeded or failed, the issues that have affected it, what can you learn from it and, importantly, how can you improve performance or sustain it in the future.

All of these points are likely requests included within a task. Ensure that you identify them clearly and address them as required.

Step 3 – Information Search

Many students fail to realise the importance of collecting information to **support** and **underpin** their assignment work. However, it is vital that you demonstrate to your centre and to the CIM your ability to **establish information needs,** obtain **relevant information** and **utilise it sensibly** in order to arrive at appropriate decisions.

You should establish the nature of the information required, follow up possible sources, time involved in obtaining the information, gaps in information and the need for information.

Consider these factors very carefully. CIM are very keen that students are **seen** to collect information, **expand** their mind and consider the **breadth** and **depth** of the situation. In your *Personal Development Portfolio,* you have the opportunity to complete a **Resource Log,** to illustrate how you have expanded your knowledge to aid your personal development. You can record your additional reading and research in that log, and show how it has helped you with your portfolio and assignment work.

Step 4 – Develop an Assignment Plan

Your **assignment** needs to be structured and coherent, addressing the brief and presenting the facts as required by the tasks. The only way you can successfully achieve this is by **planning the structure** your Assignment in advance.

Earlier on in this unit, we looked at identifying your tasks and, working backwards from the release date, in order to manage time successfully. The structure and coherence of your assignment needs to be planned with similar signs.

In planning out the Assignment, you should plan to include **all the relevant information as requested** and also you should plan for the use of models, diagrams and appendices where necessary.

Your plan should cover your:

- Introduction
- Content
- Main body of the assignment and then
- Summary
- Conclusions and recommendations where appropriate

Step 5 – Prepare Draft Assignment

It is good practice to always produce a **first draft** of a report. You should use it to ensure that you have met the aims and objectives, assignment brief and tasks related to the actual assignment. A draft document provides you with scope for improvements, and enables you to check for accuracy, spelling, punctuation and use of English.

Step 6 – Prepare Final Document

In the section headed 'Presentation of the Assignment' in this unit, there are a number of components that should always be in place at the beginning of the assignment documentation, including **labelling** of the assignment, **word counts**, **appendices** numbering and presentation method. Ensure that you **adhere to the guidelines presented**, or alternatively those suggested by your study centre.

Writing reports

Students often ask 'what do they mean by a report?' or 'what should the report format include?'.

There are a number of approaches to reports, formal or informal: some report formats are company specific and designed for internal use, rather than external reporting.

For Continuous Assessment process, you should stay with traditional formats.

Below is a suggested layout of a Management Report Document, as recommended by the CIM Training Division. Prepared by the Senior Moderator and Delegate Mentor, it is presented to for delegates on a broad range of sales and marketing programmes.

- ***A Title Page*** – includes the title of the report, the author of the report and the receiver of the report
- ***Acknowledgements*** – this should highlight any help, support, or external information received and any extraordinary co-operation of individuals or organisations
- ***Contents Page*** – providing a clearly structured pathway of the contents of the report – page by page
- ***Executive Summary*** – a brief insight into purpose, nature and outcome of the report, in order that the outcome of the report can be quickly established
- ***Main body of the report divided into sections, which are clearly labelled***. Suggested labelling would be on a numbered basis eg:
  - 1.0 Introduction
  - 1.1 Situation Analysis
  - 1.1.1 External Analysis
  - 1.1.2 Internal Analysis
- ***Conclusions*** – draw the report to a conclusion, highlighting key points of importance, that will impact upon any recommendations that might be made
- ***Recommendations*** – clearly outline potential options and then recommendations. Where appropriate justify recommendations in order to substantiate your decision
- ***Appendices*** – ensure that you only use appendices that add value to the report. Ensure that they are numbered and referenced on a numbered basis within the text. If you are not going to reference it within the text, then it should not be there
- ***Bibliography*** – whilst in a business environment a bibliography might not be necessary, for an **assignment-based report it is vital**. It provides an indication of the level of research, reading and collecting of relevant information that has taken place in order to fulfil the requirements of the assignment task. Where possible, and where relevant, you could provide academic references within the text, which should of course then provide the basis of your bibliography and your Resource Log for the PDP. References should realistically be listed alphabetically and in the following sequence
  - Author's name and edition of the text
  - Date of publication
  - Title and sub-title (where relevant)
  - Edition 1st, 2nd etc
  - Place of publication
  - Publisher
  - Series and individual volume number where appropriate.

Assignment One – the Personal Development Portfolio

On the following three pages you will find your Personal Development Portfolio for *Management Information for Marketing Decisions*.

The **six** tasks that you will undertake will highlight the scope of your existing skills and your future continuing professional development.

Firstly read the assignment through and look at each of the tasks. Then we will discuss at how you can best approach it.

The resources you will need for this assignment are: a lever arch file, folder dividers and plastic wallets.

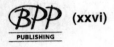

The Chartered
Institute of Marketing

Continuous Assessment
Assignment

Academic Session 2001 - 2002

Management Information For Marketing Decisions

Assignment No. 1 - Personal Development Plan (PDP)

This assignment is the Personal Development Plan, which is compulsory.

Candidates must complete this assignment in order to complete their portfolio which will also include the core assignment and an optional choice assignment

July 2001

ASSIGNMENT 1 – PERSONAL DEVELOPMENT PLAN (PDP)

Assignment Brief

The purpose of this assignment is to enable and encourage you to reflect upon how applicable the learning on your CIM Advanced Certificate has been within your professional development process. Furthermore it aims to illustrate how the learning process has allowed you to develop different attitudes and styles of working, over your period of study.

The format that the PDP will take is entirely up to the individual, as long as the main headings shown below are covered. It is recommended that you commence the PDP approximately three weeks into your module, and you should continue to evaluate your learning up to the end of your CIM Certificate.

The purpose of the PDP is for you to evaluate how the CIM Advanced Certificate course has benefited you, perhaps with reference to certain specific situations, rather than great detail on one particular aspect of your learning.

Part of your learning on any CIM course\module is reading around the subject or accessing other information sources. The CIM workbook is just a basis on which to develop. Evaluation of other resources should be part of your personal development.

It is suggested you work to a maximum of 2,500 words; supporting evidence must be kept to a minimum. This assignment is designed to be reflective, and perhaps less structured, than the others you will be completing for this module.

There are proformas attached if you wish to use them to complete the tasks, (for example keeping a resource log), but nothing is compulsory and it maybe best for you to develop your own individual style.

A skills analysis sheet for Management Information for Marketing Decisions is attached and should be completed as a start point to enable you to focus on the skills you may wish to evaluate.

Assignment tasks:

Tasks to be covered within this assignment are:

Task 1

- A personal assessment of your strengths and weaknesses. This could take the form of a personal SWOT. Someone else completing a SWOT analysis showing his or her views of you could also be included.

- Examine and evaluate any other forms of personal assessments you may have undergone, such as work-based appraisals, Belbin or other personal profiling.

- From this analysis, select areas that you feel would personally benefit from developing from new, or, existing skills to be developed further.

Task 2

- Write a Career Development plan, which includes
  - A description of your present role and attach a recent job description.
  - A brief Career History showing how you arrived at this point.
  - How you see your career developing over the next five years.

Task 3

- Refer back at your analysis for Task One and Task Two. Select one recognized strength and one weakness, which you think is key to you achieving your career plan. Give reasons for your choice.

Task 4

For each of the two skills selected show:

- Your evaluation of your present skills in this area.

- How you believe you could develop \ develop further within that area. What actions would be required? What time scale \ costs would be involved.

- How often would you need to review your progress?

- A learning diary detailing specific learning occasions, which occur during the module, relevant to developing these skills. This should be contained in a maximum of 5 A4 sheets.

Task 5

- A reflective statement on your experience of the learning process. How does this compare with your expectations? Evaluate how your CIM Advanced Certificate studies have helped you to develop, and how you could plan your next stage of development.

Task 6

- What resources have you accessed as part of your CIM Certificate, and how helpful were they.

- Which would you recommend to others, give reasons for your recommendations?
    This Assignment carries 30% of the marks for your final assessment

Role of the PDP

The Personal Development Portfolio (PDP) assignment is designed to develop your own personal and individual skills. Each Continuous Assessment module available from CIM has the same assignment, but requires you to look at the **context of the module that you are studying for**. For example, this particular module focuses on *Management Information for Marketing Decisions*. However, you might also be studying for Effective Management for Marketing at this time. If this is the case, you will see that **both assignments are identical in terms of the tasks that should be undertaken, but the differences come in terms of the skills audit that you undertake, as the skills audit** frames the basis of your assignment.

The PDP has in the past been described as a 'powerful learning vehicle'. The process of developing the log is developmental and allows for dialog and self-reflection to take place.

The activities involved in the PDP process have been designed to enable you to evaluate your progress in meeting the learning outcomes of the syllabus and using them as your own development objectives. To reflect the important nature of this, the PDP assignment equates to almost one third of your examination grade, ie 30%.

Self-reflection is deemed an important part of the process, whereby you are given the opportunity to reflect on your current abilities, and then on the various development activities undertaken. You will reflect on how you approach the work, how the work turned out and perhaps what you could improve in the future. Essentially you should look at the self-reflection process as one that could ultimately improve your future performance.

Task 1 – The SWOT analysis and skills audit

In the table on the page after next you will see a skills audit. You will find this document very helpful in managing Task One of this PDP Assignment. The assignment asks you to undertake an **analysis** of your **strengths** and **weaknesses**, and also a consideration of the **opportunities** and **threats** that face you in your everyday environment.

A good starting point for this is to look at the skills audit below and assess your ability in each of the areas listed. You will see that you can grade the areas in terms of importance. Clearly if you skills level is **below 2**, then this can be categorised as a **weakness** and could potentially be subject to further development. If it is above 2 then either there is room for improvement, or indeed your could find that you are actually quite confident in this area. In addition to this, you are asked about the importance of this area to your role currently and **in future**. This is where **strengths** and **opportunities** come into play. Where you establish that you are currently doing something successfully, this could be determined as an overall strength. This could then present opportunities for you in the future, as your strengths enable you to develop your role and move towards a promotion or a new role altogether.

From this skills audit, you are to select key areas that you feel would be personally beneficial to you. You will see that, within the grid, there are some areas that have been **filled** in to provide you with an insight as to what this means. The comments in this instance show that the person completing the PDP has a number of areas that need development in connection with a new role, that of a marketing assistant.

When undertaking the skills audit you should think carefully about your existing role and your future potential roles: not just about improving yourself in the immediate future, but also about the potential scope of a five-year career plan, which you will be developing in task 2.

You may have undertaken a range of similar assessments within your own organisation, or your may have recently been through a performance appraisal with your employer. If so, use these processes to assist you in considering your existing position in relation to the skills audit; the comments in your appraisal feedback will help you determine your performance to date, and areas of future training and development.

From your personal perspective, you should consider using your appraisals and skills audit as part of your learning process. As well as meeting your learning objectives for your CIM qualifications, you could be going some way towards meeting your work based objectives. This approach presents an opportunity for you to involve your line manager in your self assessment and the project, thereby showing how PDP process might move you closer towards meeting your appraisal objectives.

BPP PUBLISHING

INSERT INTO PORTFOLIO DEVELOPMENT AREAS	Syllabus Ref MIMD	Current Skill Level (None / High)	Importance to Current Role (Low / Vital)	Likely Future Importance (Low / Vital)	YOUR COMMENTS
Identify Mgt/Mkt Information needs	1.1/2	0 - 1 - **2** - 3	[ ] [ ] [ ] [ ] [X]	[ ] [ ] [ ] [ ] [X]	I have been working as a Market Research Manager for a Business to Business heavy engineering company and this has been a major part of my role and will continue to do so, as the organisation expands due to a takeover, my role has also expanded, this will be vital to my ongoing success.
Design or specify a MkIS/MIS	1.2/3	0 - 1 - 2 - 3	[ ] [ ] [ ] [ ] [ ]	[ ] [ ] [ ] [ ] [ ]	
Identify improvements to a MkIS/MIS	1.4/5	0 - 1 - 2 - 3	[ ] [ ] [ ] [ ] [ ]	[ ] [ ] [ ] [ ] [ ]	
Identify ICT solutions to manage customers	2.1	0 - 1 - **2** - 3	[ ] [X] [ ] [ ] [ ]	[ ] [ ] [ ] [ ] [X]	As a result of the take over, there is now a heavy influence on ICT to manage customers, this will become increasingly important to my role. Whilst I do have some experience of this area, there is plenty of scope for it to improve and add value to my role.
..... inform/support mktg decisions	2.2	0 - 1 - 2 - 3	[ ] [ ] [ ] [ ] [ ]	[ ] [ ] [ ] [ ] [ ]	
..... improve mktg processes	2.3	0 - 1 - 2 - 3	[ ] [ ] [ ] [ ] [ ]	[ ] [ ] [ ] [ ] [ ]	
..... gather and manage mkt information	2.4	0 - 1 - 2 - 3	[ ] [ ] [ ] [ ] [ ]	[ ] [ ] [ ] [ ] [ ]	
..... restructure mkts and offerings	2.5	0 - 1 - 2 - 3	[ ] [ ] [ ] [ ] [ ]	[ ] [ ] [ ] [ ] [ ]	
Use quantitative techniques to forecast sales	3.1	0 - 1 - 2 - 3	[ ] [ ] [ ] [ ] [ ]	[ ] [ ] [ ] [ ] [ ]	
Use decision trees to assess options	2.3	0 - 1 - 2 - 3	[ ] [ ] [ ] [ ] [ ]	[ ] [ ] [ ] [ ] [ ]	
Use critical path analysis to plan projects	2.4	0 - 1 - 2 - 3	[ ] [ ] [ ] [X] [ ]	[ ] [ ] [ ] [ ] [X]	I am capable of developing a critical path analysis, although my experience of this is fairly limited, it is something that will be essential to my broader role if I am going illustrate SMART working practices.
Interpret balance sheets/ financial reports	4	0 - 1 - 2 - **3**	[ ] [ ] [ ] [ ] [X]	[ ] [ ] [ ] [ ] [X]	Competitor analysis and comparisons have been an essential part of my role so has establishing the position of potential clients. As Market Research Manager, I have been responsible in essence for all information search and information management. This is an area of tremendous importance, on for which I have significant experience.
Calculate contribution and break-even	4.1/2	0 - 1 - 2 - 3	[ ] [ ] [ ] [ ] [ ]	[ ] [ ] [ ] [ ] [ ]	
Apply a variety of costing techniques	4.4	0 - 1 - 2 - 3	[ ] [ ] [ ] [ ] [ ]	[ ] [ ] [ ] [ ] [ ]	
Use financial data to inform price decisions	4.3-6	0 - 1 - 2 - 3	[ ] [ ] [ ] [ ] [ ]	[ ] [ ] [ ] [ ] [ ]	
..... inform product decisions	4.3-6	0 - 1 - 2 - 3	[ ] [ ] [ ] [ ] [ ]	[ ] [ ] [ ] [ ] [ ]	
..... inform distribution/channel decisions	4.3-6	0 - 1 - 2 - 3	[ ] [ ] [ ] [ ] [ ]	[ ] [ ] [ ] [ ] [ ]	
...... inform promotional decisions	4.3-6	0 - 1 - 2 - 3	[ ] [ ] [ ] [ ] [ ]	[ ] [ ] [ ] [ ] [ ]	

..... inform market/expansion decisions	4.3-6	0 - 1 - 2 - 3	[ ] [ ] [ ] [ ]
..... inform investment decisions	4.11	0 - 1 - 2 - 3	[ ] [ ] [ ] [ ]
Apply and interpret common financial ratios	4.7	0 - 1 - 2 - 3	[ ] [ ] [ ] [ ]
Prepare and manage a marketing budget	4.9/11	0 - 1 - 2 - 3	[ ] [ ] [ ] [ ]
Gather secondary data on mkt/customers	5	0 - 1 - 2 - 3	[ ] [ ] [ ] [ ]
..... on competitors or distributors/channels	5	0 - 1 - 2 - 3	[ ] [ ] [ ] [ ]
..... on an overseas market	5	0 - 1 - 2 - 3	[X] [ ] [ ] [ ] This has now been part of my role to date, however, my organisation has been just been taken over, and my role is changing to include market research for international markets.
Plan and manage primary research projects	5	0 - 1 - 2 - 3	[ ] [ ] [ ] [ ]
Design/apply questionnaire research tools	5	0 - 1 - 2 - 3	[ ] [ ] [ ] [ ]
Conduct qualitative research	5	0 - 1 - 2 - 3	[ ] [ ] [ ] [ ]
Analyse and interpret data	5	0 - 1 - 2 - 3	[ ] [ ] [ ] [ ]
Graphically present research findings	5	0 - 1 - 2 - 3	[ ] [ ] [ ] [ ]
YOUR OWN CHOICE (discuss with tutor)			Please ensure that you note the syllabus reference.
		0 - 1 - 2 - 3	[ ] [ ] [ ] [ ]
		0 - 1 - 2 - 3	[ ] [ ] [ ] [ ]

When you have completed your skills audit, put it in your lever arch file at the front, as it will be a constant source of reference and reminder to you whilst you are progressing through the course.

Task 2 – Career Development Plan

This task requires you to write a Career Development Plan. This is quite an interesting concept and might for many provide the first real opportunity for you to sit down and really consider where do you go from here. It is quite often an interesting activity for students to undertake. Think along the following lines:

- Where am I now?
- Where do I want to go in the future?
- How am I going to get there?

These three questions will form the basis of your career development plan.

Step 1   Firstly, in order for you to analyse where you are now, it is helpful to open a section within your PDP file titled **Career Development**. In this particular section, insert your Curriculum Vitae, existing job description and a brief career history. Think about where you started off, your first job, where you are now (ie your existing job), how many job changes you have had and career changes. You should also think about any promotions have you encountered in your career history. What was the nature of the promotion? What strengths assisted you in achieving the promotion? What opportunities did it provide you with?

Step 2   Secondly, consider where you want to go in the future. Why are you taking the CIM qualifications, what are you expecting them to achieve for you? Are you moving into new business areas, new business sectors or using these qualifications as a tool to assist you promotion prospects within your own organisation? Whatever the reason, start to analyse them, and map out potential stages you might embark upon in the next five years, both in terms of career and training and education to aid your prospects of career progression.

You will probably find this quite a challenging task. You may find that you cannot complete it early on in the course, and you may wish to take time to think it over. Your PDP assignment should be ongoing throughout the duration of your module, which gives you time to sit back and think about the future, areas of interest that have arisen as a result of the course, or areas of interest that you know the course can develop for you. However, you should establish some framework of career development by the time you are a third of the way through your module.

Task 3 – Selection of Key Development Points

This task is very brief and requires you to review your skills audit and career plan, and select the areas of development most appropriate to you. The task requires you to select **one** particular **strength** from the skills audit and SWOT analysis, which you can further develop and enhance in order to exploit career opportunities, and one **weakness**, that reduces effectiveness in your existing role. Dealing with this could aid future roles and promotion prospects.

If you look back at the grid in figure 1.2, you might select *Using critical path analysis to plan projects, or gather information on overseas markets.* These are registered as a weakness, and could both also add significant value as to how you manage your role.

For the strength, it is likely that you might select the area relating to *identifying management and marketing information needs* as this is vital to your ongoing success in your expanded role. Currently this appears to be an overall strength in your current role, important to your current role, and vital to the future market research management role. Therefore you would, in this

instance, think about how you might develop this further and exploit your abilities to gain recognition for your skills in this area, with a view to personal promotion.

Whichever point you select, you must be able to **justify your choice**, explaining why it is important to you to address these two key areas and how they might help you achieve your career development plan. This essentially acts as your rationale for development.

Task 4 – Action Plan and Learning Diary

This task sees you starting to prepare for action. Now that you have identified your **key development points** and justified your selection, you need to define some sense of direction, action and outcome.

In order to do this, you should consider what your development pathway is going to consist of.

Continuing with the example we have used so far, to develop your role in identifying management and marketing information needs, which you have highlighted as strength, you could-

Find new ways for both known and unknown organisations of identifying key issues / drivers; state what they are and how they influence your organisation and how you might best measure their importance.

You now need to plan your approach, for example:

- Develop an action plan on a **week-by-week basis**, which predetermines how you are going to develop your activities throughout the duration of the module.

- The action plan should include **date** of action, **description** of the action, proposed **outcome** and **proposed date** of outcome. Action plans, like objectives should be SMART (Specific, measurable, achievable, realistic and timed), provide direction directive and should propose clear outcomes. Give the actions a **reference** number so that your tutor can cross-reference your actions with the learning diary.

- Your action plan should include **key review points.** (When are you going to review your development? Reviews will take place at the end of each activity or indeed activities will be reviewed half way through and at the end.) Ensure that you put in **progression measurement points** to ensure that you remain on target. This action plan should provide the basis of a development strategy.

- Develop a 'success criterion' for each action. For example, define a new criterion establishing information needs in relation to a particular customer group or indeed a particular market sector. Use this to guide you in collecting the right information. Refer to the marketing research planning process, ensure your research objectives are SMART and that the criteria you define has clear purpose.

- This success criterion provides you with an **opportunity to consider what you have done**, how it could be improved, and then develop the work further to meet the required standard. This approach shows progression, development and improvement.

  Regular **feedback** from your tutor and employer, if you have involved them in the process, is essential to give you a clear insight into your progression.

- **Keep a learning diary.** This learning diary should be a record of your activities, including how the activity went, how successful it was, the benefit of the activity and proposing further action. Clearly divide your pages so that your tutor, when marking your assignment, can see how the learning diary records your actions in line with your action plan. Ensure that you cross-reference your actions, so that it is clear how the actions and the learning diary interlink. (This should be no longer than 5 pages of A4 – remember the word limit is 2000 words.)

When you do decide the basis of the development points, and are considering how to formulate your action plan and what activities you should undertake, please be aware that you can use elements of your other assignment work to support your development. Should you do this, it should be by negotiation with your tutor and your work should be cross-referenced in order to provide evidence.

Whilst previously a standard approach to recording this information was provided by CIM, it is now entirely up to you and your tutor to decide the best way of presenting this information. However, we recommend develop key headings for each activity (ie your action plan and learning diary) so that the two are compatible. (You will note that this is stated in the introductory part of the assignment.)

Task 5 – Reflective Statements

You are required to **reflect upon your activities** and your personal development in the selected areas for the duration of your course. Students often underestimate this part of the assignment, and fail to address it effectively. It is this part of the assignment that actually brings all of your work together, gives it purpose and future direction.

Here are the key components that you should always include:

- Where did you start of (ie why did you choose the particular elements of the key skills unit as your development points?)

- What activities have you undertaken?

- How do you think that they might help you in your career plan?

- How effective were you in improving your performance and behaviour in respect of your selected development points?

- How have you improved and why?

- How will you continue to develop this area in the future, how do you anticipate you might use it?

- The reflective statement is not just reflecting on what has been, but is developmental considering what is to come!

Task 6 – Resource Log

The CIM are very keen that you **read broadly** to support your learning and personal development. Reading, surfing the Internet, working through journals and newspapers is a critical aspect of your professional, vocational and academic development. In order to **prove** that you have looked at each of these areas, and that you have **applied** the theory in the context of your learning and personal development **you are required to make a record of your resources**.

Here you should look at the following:

- Provide a list of books and journals you have read – this could of course include this BPP Management Information for Marketing Decisions in Practice Study Text, but should also include others (for example as suggested in the CIM's reading list).

- Explain the basis of your reading in summary format and how it helped you in progression your action plan and the key development points within it.

- Would you recommend this text to others? If so, why? Justify your recommendations overall.

Students' **failure** to address the resource log, use resources and indeed provide evidence of their use and their benefits is significant and can often be the dividing line between a good pass and a average pass, or indeed a pass and a fail.

Resources are **essential** to your development; you have to broaden your horizons, explore new theories and practices and apply them. Take a futuristic and developmental approach to your learning.

Conclusion

You will see that the process is quite structured. It should and should be designed in an ordered way, that can measure your successful professional development. The process need not to be arduous, if don't leave it until the last minute. You should complete it as you go through the duration of the module. This is the only way in which you can show true evidence of successful development.

Your folder should have six compartments to it, each one representing the assignment task. Ensure that you provide your tutor with a contents page, clearly headed sections. Ensure that you name, study centre name and student registration is clearly marked on each section, so that they do not get lost or mixed up with other work. This is essential.

Core and optional Assignments

As suggested earlier in this unit, we cannot give you specific guidance on the core or optional assignments, as this goes against the grain of fairness and equity across the study centre network. However it might be useful to consider two potential themes, and how you might approach the subject areas, in terms of research, a questioning approach and meeting the requirements of the brief. It is usual that the presentation format is predetermined by CIM and usually takes the form of a report of presentation.

For the purpose of Management Information for Marketing Decisions therefore, we will look at **finance and forecasting** and market research. These are two key areas in relation to this module.

You will need to assume an operational management stance in your response to the assignment. However, it is likely that the assignment may give you a role. You must look at your assignments from a management context you are after all, through these studies, being prepared for marketing management at an operational level.

Do not forget to read through the relevant chapter in your BPP Study Text in conjunction with these assignments, in order that you ensure that you are practically applying successfully, concepts, theories and skills that have been highlighted in your texts.

Finance and forecasting

This particular area of the syllabus is the one that seems to cause most **discomfort to students.** It focuses on your ability to understand the nature of finance in the context of marketing, and how financial data can be used to forecast future events.

For the purpose of this particular syllabus area, and the BPP Study Text, you need to consider the importance of company accounts, of your clients, your competitors and your own organisation? What do they say about your organisation? How are they presented? Are they readable?

For the purpose of **this** exercise, you are to **prepare a report** that looks at the purpose and nature of company accounts, and what should be included. In addition to this you will be **expected to discuss the relevant ratios** an organisation should use when reading company accounts. You should then present the accounts of your own company or one you know well, and provide a

report on the company, with ratios presented, explaining the basis of the information you have provided. In particular, the reader of your report is interested in the **liquidity** and **sales potential** of your company.

In future, your **role** will include **project management** of the production of the annual accounts, for which you are to prepare a **critical path analysis**. In doing this you will need to consider a breadth of information, and fully explain the stages you will go through in preparing the accounts.

The following approach might be useful

- Provide a situation analysis, who is your company, what is their role, what is their product or service offering

- Explain the purpose and benefits of annual company reports, and give a brief overview of the details provided within you annual report, putting your organisation in context of this assignment

- Provide a brief insight into how your company report might compare against that of your direct competitor, and consider what improvements might be made

- How well do you think the organisations are portrayed within the accounts? What improvements can be made? (qualify and justify your comments)

You will now need to move onto the next stage of the report. This requires you to use a range of **ratios** in order to provide an insight into the current position of your organisation, in particular the liquidity.

You will benefit from re-reading the financial information section in relation to ratio analysis within your BPP Study Text. You might find that helpful.

- Now provide a step-by-step walk through the accounts, and with worked ratios shown in your text, provide an overview of the current financial situation of the organisation. **NB: Make sure you illustrate the ratios fully and accurately within the report.**

- Ensure that you comment on existing company performance. Try to draw out any conclusions about future stability, liquidity, sales performance and overall financial performance. If you see scope for developing a financial forecast from this information and previous accounts, show how you might do so, justifying your assumptions and approach.

  (As a marketer, you should be able to use financial accounts as a source of information to aid forecasting)

- Next is your **critical path analysis**. Ensure that you are fully conversant with the principles of the critical path technique. Many students fall down on this task as they provide a chart or a grid, where as you are to produce a critical path analysis.

- Carefully **illustrate** your critical path analysis, explaining its function, direction and outcome carefully underneath it. This is essential to your success.

- Finally, you are asked to clearly explain the stages that you, on behalf of the organisation, might work through, if you are to prepare the annual accounts, what they would include, and why. You might benefit from taking a step-by-step approach to this also, clearly linking it with your critical path and its supporting narrative, to illustrate, that from a project management perspective and as a marketer you understand the importance of financial data in forecasting the future performance of your company.

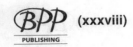

This might appear on the surface to be quite easy and mechanistic, however do not be fooled by this, as many students fail to pass this type of assignment as a result of their inability to understand the nature and value of annual accounts in terms of forecasting future financial performance, and analysing current financial performance.

NB: Remember this is not a 'real' assignment, but an approach you could take if a similar assignment should arise. Remember to refer to the early part of unit for guidance on preparing for the assignment.

Marketing research

For the PDP, the role of Market Research Manager was used. Well, as regards this final section on assignment approaches, you should consider adopting the role of Market Research Manager as you are charged with preparing a two research briefs and undertaking associated research projects for your organisation. You are also tasked with consider how Information Communication Technology has contributed to your research project and the definition of your criteria for information search.

The previous CIM Assignment actually asked you to select two areas for research application, the list is presented below:

- Developing a promotional campaign
- Developing new products or services
- Developing new or existing markets
- Establishing or developing customer service relationships
- Improving customer service
- Changing channels or improving channel efficiency
- Improving category management
- Pricing Decisions
- Sales Decision

Remember to read the relevant chapter of your BPP Management Information for Marketing Decisions Study Text. You will find the coverage on marketing research very helpful indeed.

Assignment Approach

- For this assignment you are required to select two from the above list and explain why they are important to the future development of your organisation. To this end provide a situation analysis, showing how these issues fit into context in your organisation. An overview of the organisation in terms of product/service offerings, size, scope, turnover etc, would help the marker tremendously.

- If it is helpful for your organisation to develop existing markets, then prepare a research brief around it, highlighting the necessity for the information you require, what information you require, your research objectives, and proposed outcomes. You must do this for each of your selected areas. Therefore what is important is closely defining your research problem, justifying your selection of problem as being important, and outlining the nature and scope of the involvement in solving the problem. **NB: Writing research briefs has proven to be a difficult task for many students, ensure that you familiarise yourself with the content and structure that research briefs can involve.**

BPP
PUBLISHING

- You will be aware from your experience that research is an expensive activity. You may be given a budget amount, ensure that the subsequent steps you are about to take, are reflect of the budget amount dedicated to research, is reflective or your chosen approach.

- In order to meet your research objectives, you should now consider the nature of the data you will require, ie the level of primary and secondary data to be used in your research project. In addition to this you must identify the techniques you are going to use for data collection and clearly outline and explain their purpose. If you choose questionnaires, then you should design a questionnaire, ensuring that it adheres to the principles of questionnaire design.

- Consider the balance of primary and secondary data that you might use, particularly as secondary data is perhaps less specific to the actual problem that you might like. Consider the validity of the information you are collecting, how important is it that the information is absolutely accurate, or without bias. How important are these issues?

- Ensure that the techniques you use are appropriate to your organisation and its needs. As a Market Research Manager, note that you are writing the brief, identifying the problem and considering the techniques required, rather than necessarily undertaking the research activity. This is important to consider in the context of your report and the standard of work you produce.

NB: Do not forget to reflect on the importance of ICT to your research process, and information selection, explaining fully its contribution overall.

- You should now be in the position to produce a rationale for your research projects, research objectives, detailed information searches, techniques for research.

- From here you will need to ensure that some research is undertaken to support your findings, so that you can make recommendations on how the two particular areas you have chosen can be improved. Your role is to show how you have used information to make decisions about the future development of two selected areas, thus illustrating your ability to analyse information for marketing decisions.

- The findings should be clearly represented perhaps graphically with underpinning explanation and justifications of their importance to the decision-making process. This particular area demonstrates your ability as a manager to solve marketing problems through research.

- Clearly you will need to exert your skills in report writing and presentation of data in order that this assignment is professionally presented. Here you will, again, truly illustrate your managerial ability, not just in collecting data, but also actually doing something concrete with it.

NB: Remember this is not an actual assignment as such, as is only partially representative of a past CIM assignment. Until the assignment is issued you will not know the content or context of it.

Unit Summary: Management Information for Marketing Decisions

You may have come to the end of the unit feeling that this is going to be hard work. Well you would be right in thinking this. But, as we suggested in the early part of this unit, it is likely to be one of the most beneficial learning processes you will embark upon, as you take your CIM qualifications.

The process of development prepares you to be a marketing professional in the future. It provides you with practical experience and an opportunity to apply the theory in a practical situation. You will demonstrate to your existing or future employer that you have the ability to learn, develop, grow, progress and contribute significantly to the marketing activity within the organisation.

You have been provided with a range of hints and tips in presentation of assignments, development of your PDP and approaches to your core and optional assignments.

Continuous assessment, like examinations, is a serious business, and you should consider the level of ongoing commitment that this process requires. The more you put in the more you are likely to get out. It will not be enough to leave all of your PDP work to the end of the course as it destroys the ethos and benefit of the assignment. Use it as a continuous development tool for the duration of the course. A structured approach to the learning process will maximise its benefits to you.

We have tried to give you some insight into how to approach the core and optional assignments that you will embark upon. However, these are only examples and do not reflect the real ones. What they do show you is the level of detail you should enter into in order to produce an effective and professional piece of work.

The CIM qualifications are professional qualifications and therefore, to be successful you must take a professional approach to your work.

BPP PUBLISHING

Part A
Management information systems

1 Management Information for Marketing Decisions

Chapter Topic List	Syllabus Reference
1 Introduction	-
2 Why does management need information for marketing decisions?	1.1, 1.5
3 Analysis, planning, implementation, control: APIC	1.0
4 Information	1.0
5 Decision making and information	5.0
6 Information systems and technology	1.2, 1.3
7 Forecasting	3.0
8 Financial analysis and tools	4.0
9 Marketing research	5.0

Learning Outcomes

Upon completion of this chapter you will have had a good general introduction to the rest of the Study Text. You will have begun to understand the importance of the various sources of information for the marketer, including:

- IT
- Forecasting
- Financial analysis
- Marketing research

Key Concepts

- Management information system
- Database
- Database marketing
- Forecast
- Marketing research
- Market research

Examples of Marketing at Work

- Vons Grocery Company
- Samsonite
- Daewoo

BPP PUBLISHING

1   INTRODUCTION

1.1   The task of marketing managers is to set plans, control operations and make decisions. To do this they need appropriate information, being provided by forecasting, financial analysis and tools, marketing research and information system technology.

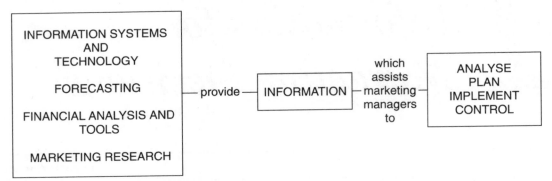

1.2   In this chapter we will be looking at the main topics in the syllabus, at information and at marketing management activities. The syllabus topics will, of course, be considered in much greater detail in the remainder of the text.

2   WHY DOES MANAGEMENT NEED INFORMATION FOR MARKETING DECISIONS?

2.1   'What use is *Management Information for Marketing Decisions* to me?' you may be thinking. 'Why do I need to know about **financial analysis**?' is a thought that might be going through your mind. 'How can I do a better job by knowing about information systems and technology? We have the **IT department** for that', might be your opinion. To quote David Soberman, marketing professor at Insead, 'Marketing has always been the art of magically combining **knowledge** about **customers and competitors** with corporate capabilities to generate **profit**'.

2.2   By the time you get to the end of this Study Text you should realise the value of management information to you as a marketer. In case you need convincing now, however, read what Laura Mazur has to say (*Accountability*, Marketing Business, February 1996).

> 'Marketing accountability is not just about speaking in a language accountants can understand. The real issue is information: does marketing have the information it needs, the tools to get it, and does it use those tools and that information effectively?

> Research carried out among 200 finance and marketing directors of blue-chip companies for the Marketing Forum suggests not. Well over half of the marketing directors surveyed replied that their companies' information systems did not provide them with the information they need to be effective.

> This is not about a lack of information. Most marketing directors are drowning in data as it is. It is about using modern technology to collect and manipulate up-to-date internal and external information both to measure the effectiveness of current marketing plans, and to examine different variables as a basis for future strategy.'

Management information systems (MIS)

Key Concept

Management information system (MIS). The combination of human and computer based resources that results in the collection, storage, retrieval, communication and use of data for the purpose of efficient management of operations and for business planning.

2.3 A marketing information system is a specific example of a management information system. It is possible to define **'management information system'** in general in a number of different ways, some of which are listed below.

> 'A system to convert data from internal and external sources into information and to communicate that information, in an appropriate form, to managers at all levels in all functions to enable them to make timely and effective decisions for planning, directing and controlling the activities for which they are responsible.'
>
> (Lucey, *Management Information Systems*)

> 'A system which may perform routine commercial processing functions, but which is designed so that such processing will also produce information that will be presented to management, including top management, to assist in decision making. The implication is that the results will be produced speedily...to enable management to ascertain the progress of the organisation in terms of satisfying its major objectives.'
>
> (*Dictionary of Computers*)

Scope of an MIS

2.4 What is common to these definitions is that information is presented to management. However, this is not the only function of an organisation's information system. A number of tasks might be performed simultaneously.

(a) **Initiating transactions** (such as automatically making a purchase order if stock levels are below a specified amount)

(b) **Recording transactions** as they occur (for example, a sale is input to the sales ledger system)

(c) **Processing data**

(d) **Producing reports** (such as summaries)

(e) **Responding to enquiries**

2.5 An MIS is good at providing regular formal information gleaned from normal commercial data. For example, an MIS relating to sales could provide managers with information relating to:

(a) **Gross profit margins** of particular products
(b) **Success in particular markets**
(c) **Credit control** information (such as payments)

It may be less efficient at presenting information which is relatively unpredictable. So, for example, an MIS could not provide information relating to the sudden emergence of a new competitor into the market.

2.6 While an MIS may not, in principle, be able to provide all the information used by management, it should be sufficiently flexible to enable management to incorporate **unpredictable, informal** or **unstructured** information into decision-making processes.

For example many decisions are made with the help of financial models (such as spreadsheets) so that the effect of new situations can be estimated easily.

Designing an MIS

2.7 A management information system should be designed with care. If an MIS is allowed to develop without any formal **planning**, it will almost certainly be inefficient. Data will be **obtained** at random and **processed** in a random and disorganised way and **communication** of information will be random. Without formal planning and design of an MIS the following might occur.

BPP PUBLISHING

(a) Some managers might prefer to keep data in their heads and not commit information to paper.

(b) Valuable information that ought to be available to management might be missing because not all necessary information is collected and processed.

(c) Information might be available but not communicated to managers.

(d) Information could be communicated late because the need to communicate it earlier is not appreciated by the data processors.

2.8 The stages of engineering a system (**system lifecycle**) are as follows (Jenkins (1969)).

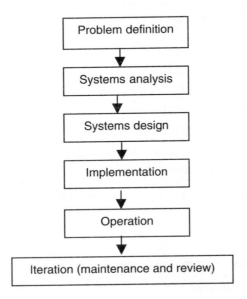

2.9 **Problem definition.** Terms of reference will include the creation of a project team which must contain the necessary expertise and experience as well as the professionals who will contribute to the design of the solution plus the representatives of those who will use the MIS.

2.10 **Systems analysis** involves the creation of a detailed description of the system under consideration. The systems boundary will be drawn, defining what elements or subsystems are regarded as being appropriate and the processes that occur will be examined and modelled using tools such as flow charts and data flow diagrams. The view of the system will depend on the purpose to which it is put and the purpose to which the user in question will wish to put the system.

2.11 **Systems design.** From the systems analysis a statement of the problem situation and an understanding of the system within which it exists should have arisen. A solution now needs to be created by the people involved using forecasting (a statement of future values and the accuracy of those values, modelling (a representation of reality), simulation (the creation of a model using a computer) and sensitivity analysis (exploration of the effect of the outcome due to changes wrought on the system).

2.12 **Implementation** - using the designed system for the first time - can involve methods such as a 'piloting' the system or parallel running it. It will involve consulting with the users of the system and those effected by it to ensure it does what it is designed and required to do. The MIS will require documentation and this will need to be prepared from the outset of this stage and the staff will need to be trained. The system will need to be tested to ensure it performs to the required standard and is acceptable to the users. An implementation strategy also needs to be drawn up to ensure a smooth transition from the old to the new system.

2.13   **Operation.** The system needs to be subjected to an initial appraisal during which points can be learned from the outcome of the above stages and performance specifications of the MIS altered where necessary and outcomes documented. The operation needs to be subjected to a process of continuous improvement in which operations and standards are regularly reviewed and improved where possible and necessary.

2.14   **Iteration.** The output of each of the above stages is fed back to each of the preceding stages to ensure a process of continuous learning to enable that the experience of the actual use of the system results in earlier work being revised and re-designed where necessary.

2.15   We will now look at the issues facing marketing management in particular.

3   ANALYSIS, PLANNING, IMPLEMENTATION, CONTROL: APIC

3.1   **APIC** is how Kotler *et al* described marketing management activities.

Analysis	Planning	Implementation	Control	= APIC

(a)   **Analysis.** 'Managing the marketing function begins with a complete analysis of the company's situation. The company must analyse its markets and marketing environment to find attractive opportunities and to avoid environmental threats. It must analyse company strengths and weaknesses, as well as current and possible marketing actions, to determine which opportunities it can best pursue. Marketing analysis feeds information and other inputs to each of the other marketing management functions.'

(b)   **Planning.** 'Through strategic planning, the company decides what it wants to do with each business unit. Marketing planning involves deciding on marketing strategies that will help the company attain its overall strategic objectives.'

(c)   **Implementation.** 'Good marketing analysis and planning are only a start toward successful company performance - the marketing plans must be carefully implemented. It is often easier to design good marketing strategies than put them into action.

People at all levels of the marketing system must work together to implement marketing strategy and plans. People in marketing must work closely with people in finance, purchasing, manufacturing and other company departments. And many outside people and organisations must help with implementation - suppliers, resellers, advertising agencies, research firms, the advertising media. All must work together effectively to implement the marketing program.'

(d)   **Control.** 'Many surprises are likely to occur as marketing plans are being implemented. The company needs control procedures to make certain that its objectives will be achieved. Companies want to make sure that they are achieving the sales, profits, and other goals set in their annual plans. This control involves measuring ongoing market performance, determining the causes of any serious gaps in performance, and deciding on the best corrective action to take to close the gaps. Corrective action may call for improving the ways in which the plan is being implemented or even changing the goals.

Companies should also stand back from time to time and look at their overall approach to the marketplace. The purpose is to make certain that the company's objectives,

BPP PUBLISHING

policies, strategies, and programs remain appropriate in the face of rapid environmental changes.'

3.2 To carry out these activities, **marketing managers need information**. They need to forecast changes in demand, to introduce, modify or delete products or services, to evaluate profitability, to set prices, to undertake promotional activity, to plan budgets and to control costs.

Action Programme 1

You should spend about 10 minutes, before you carry on reading, thinking about information you use at work and then try and classify it into the major marketing and selling activities described under ACTIVITY. The second column headed INFORMATION should describe the type of information, for example: control chart, written report, oral report, telephone call, database and so on. The third column is for you to describe what you USE the information for. You may find that you use certain types of information to do more than one marketing or sales management activity in which case you should not be afraid to list it more than once.

ACTIVITY	INFORMATION	USE
Analysing		
Planning		
Implementing		
Controlling		

4 INFORMATION 12/00

4.1 **Information is anything that is communicated.** Information is the life blood of an organisation, flowing through it and prompting actions and decisions. Without information, no one in an organisation could take a single effective action. As a simple example, giving an order to a subordinate is a flow of information: the manager or supervisor gathers information about a problem, 'processes' it to decide what needs to be done, and then communicates his or her decision as an order to the subordinate.

4.2 **Data** is the raw material for data processing. Data is collected and then processed into information. For example, '1734261' is data.

4.3 **Information** is data processed in such a way as to be of some meaning to the person who receives it. For example, 'units sold in sales area B in period 8: 1,734,261' is information.

Good information

4.4 Information must be good enough to fulfil its purpose.

(a) It should be **relevant** for its purpose.
(b) It should be **complete** for its purpose.
(c) It should be sufficiently **accurate** for its purpose.
(d) It should be **clear** to the user.
(e) The user should have **confidence** in it.
(f) It should be **communicated** to the right person.
(g) It should not be excessive - its volume should be **manageable**.
(h) It should be **timely** - that is, communicated at the most appropriate time.
(i) It should be communicated by an **appropriate channel of communication**.
(j) It should be provided at a **cost** which is less than the value of the **benefits** it provides.

Hard and soft information

4.5   Information is often said to be **hard** if it is data collected for a specific purpose in an organised way or in a scientific manner. **Soft** information is acquired by managers, often in the course of conversation with suppliers, customers and colleagues in an unstructured and unplanned manner, with no specific purpose in mind. Soft data is stored informally usually within the brain of the manager concerned and retrieved when a specific occasion triggers thought processes. Mintzberg and many management commentators stress the importance of this 'soft data' over and above 'hard data'. Soft data often contains a high degree of **qualitative information.**

4.6   For example, a sales manager on a visit to a customer may find out in the course of conversation that the customer buys from another supplier who specialises in providing a particular type of service. On returning to the office the sales manager could use this 'soft data' to investigate the possibility of supplying a similar or better type of service and thereby **competing more effectively.**

5   DECISION MAKING AND INFORMATION

5.1   The APIC activities described by Kotler *et al* culminate in marketing and selling **decisions** being taken. Because such decisions are usually made in advance of the particular time period in which marketing and selling takes place, decision making carries risks because **outcomes are uncertain.** Once provided with **good information**, the decision maker should have greater confidence about the decision he/she takes.

Information and levels of decision making

5.2   Information is required for all levels of decision making within an organisation, whether **strategic, tactical** or **operational.** The decision-making levels, and the types of marketing and selling decisions taken at these levels, are shown in the following table.

Levels of decision making	Marketing and selling decisions
Strategic	Product/market decisions Product life cycles Product development Entry into new markets Investment in new technology to provide better information Database development
Tactical	Setting short term prices Discounting Promotional campaigns Advertising Distribution Product service levels Customer service levels Packaging Planning sales territories Short-term agency agreements
Operational	Pricing, including discounting Competitor tracking Customer research Consumer research Distribution channels and logistical choices Sales and marketing budgets and sub-budgets, eg promotion/advertising Database management

BPP PUBLISHING

> ### Action Programme 2
> What types of decision making are you involved in? What information do you use to make those decisions?

6   INFORMATION SYSTEMS AND TECHNOLOGY   12/99, 12/00

Information systems

6.1   Organisations use information to make judgements, formulate plans, control activities, reach decisions and implement them. Sometimes information systems are formal, meaning that the collection of data, data analysis and interpretation is systematic; and sometimes information is obtained in a non-systematic manner.

6.2   The marketing and sales information system needs to provide management with a continuous stream of data which will be able to provide assistance with the following.

   (a)   Assessment of **current performance**

   (b)   Appropriate **performance measures** to control, decide and plan future activities

   (c)   **Comparative data** (and information) through time and across companies/industries (such as key financial ratios)

   (d)   **Resource allocation** decisions (the information including comparative cost data, activity based costing/management systems information, qualitative data and quantitative market research)

   (e)   **Trend** analysis

   (f)   **Forecasting**

   (g)   **Strategic** planning (for example, data for SWOT analysis will be required)

   (h)   Operational control and planning

   (i)   The identification of **problem areas**

   (j)   The identification of potential **opportunities**

   (k)   The identification of **further information** needs

   (l)   **Gap analysis**

   (m)   **Pricing policy**

   (n)   **Marketing mix** decisions

   (o)   **Logistics**

   (p)   **Inventory** control

   (q)   **Communication** strategies (including promotion and advertising)

   (r)   **Consumer reactions**, expectations and attitudes

   (s)   **Competitor tracking** and monitoring

6.3   The information system should provide information about organisational performance and the relative performance of competitors, and anticipate changes in the PEST environment that may impact upon performance. The information system should **guide and focus management attention**.

Marketing Information Systems (MkIS)

6.4 **Marketing Information Systems (MkIS)** can help marketing managers make better decisions. As many business environments are undergoing change at an ever increasing pace, the making of swift and well judged decisions is essential to all businesses. An efficient MkIS system will provide timely and accurate information and will also prevent managers from being overloaded with redundant information.

6.5 A marketing information system consists of four components (*Kotler*, 1988), as shown in the diagram below.

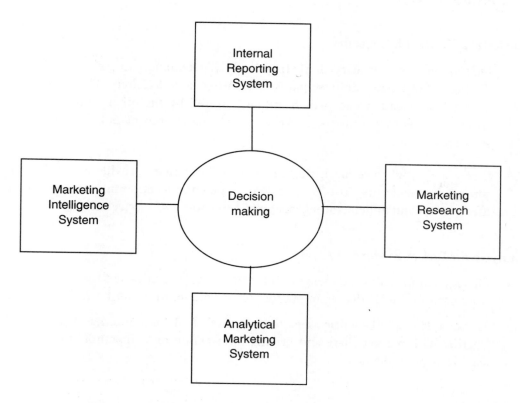

6.6 These components contain the following features.

Internal Reporting System

6.7 This part of the MkIS utilises internal records of the company. Although these records have been generated for some other purpose, they provide an invaluable insight into the current activity and performance of the company. Data such as sales records, invoices, production records and accounts are used in a system of this type. Many of these records are now stored on computerised databases and therefore storage, retrieval and analysis of such records is relatively quick and easy.

6.8 These records prove invaluable in an MkIS system as the current operations of a business can be analysed and understood. It is good marketing practice to build any strategy or plan from an understanding of 'where we are now' and this system provides that understanding.

6.9 For example, these records may be used to provide an understanding of size and growth of customer segments, buying patterns, product profitability and many other areas.

11

Marketing Intelligence System

6.10 This system collects and stores everyday information about the external environment - information such as industry reports, competitors' marketing materials and competitors' quotes. Information collected here allows a company to build a more accurate profile of the external environment.

6.11 This could allow a company to calculate market sizes and growth patterns, competitor positioning and pricing strategy, and so on. This information may help in decision making in many areas such as gap analysis, segmentation and targeting, market development and pricing strategy.

Marketing Research System

6.12 This system uses primary marketing research techniques to gather, evaluate and report findings in order to minimise guesswork in business decisions. The system is used to fill essential information gaps which are not covered by the other components of the MkIS system. In this way it provides targeted and detailed information for the decision making problem at hand.

6.13 A company might use marketing research in the past to provide detailed information on new product concepts, attitudes to marketing communication messages, testing advertising effectiveness and understanding customer perceptions of service delivery.

Analytical Market System

6.14 This system provides the tools to undertake complex analysis of the information gained in other parts of the MkIS system in order to provide solutions for business problems.

6.15 An example would be a price sensitivity analysis tool using internal data from sales records together with market share and pricing information on competitors to calculate the price sensitivity of products.

Databases

Key Concept

Database. A collection of available information on past and current customers together with future prospects, structured to allow for the implementation of effective marketing strategies.

6.16 One of the principal sources of information for marketing and sales is the **database**. Databases may be generated in two ways, by the business either building its own database or acquiring the database from an external agency. Databases are discussed in more detail in Chapter 3, but we provide an introduction here to the types of information they can store and provide.

6.17 A **mail order catalogue** company may, for example, store **customer data**: names, addresses, telephone number, when they ordered, how they ordered, how they paid, when they paid, what they bought and so on. The marketing manager can check the customer **purchasing history** to provide information for specific promotions on a certain type of product. Furthermore, by checking the database, the marketing manager could time the promotion to coincide with the customer's 'most likely to buy' period. Preferred payment methods could also be identified and used in the promotion to make it more attractive. **EPOS** systems have allowed retail chains to promote the use of **loyalty cards** for the same purposes.

6.18 Databases have always been available to managers in organisations, but it is **technology** that has transformed the way in which we view and value them. Computers have enabled managers to store vast amounts of data.

Marketing databases

6.19 A marketing database can provide an organisation with much information about its customers and target groups. **Every purchase a customer makes has two functions.**

(a) Provision of **sales revenue**

(b) Provision of **information** as to future market opportunities

6.20 A comprehensive customer database might include the following.

Element	Examples
Customer details	Names, addresses and contact (telephone, fax, e-mail) details; basic 'mailing list' data
Professional details	Company; job title; responsibilities - especially for business-to-business marketing
Personal details	Sex, age, number of people at the same address, spouse's name, children, interests, and any other relevant data known, such as newspapers read, journals subscribed to
Transaction history	What products/services are ordered, how often, how much is spent
Call/contact history	Sales or after sales service calls made, complaints/queries received, meetings at shows/exhibitions etc
Credit/payment history	Credit rating, amounts outstanding, aged debts
Credit transaction details	Items currently on order, dates, prices, delivery arrangements
Special account details	Membership number, loyalty or incentive points earned, discount awarded), where customer loyalty or incentive schemes are used

6.21 The sources of information in a customer database and the uses to which it can be put are outlined in the diagram below.

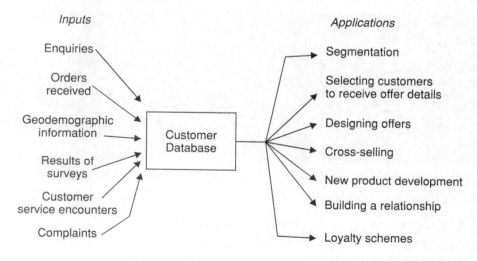

BPP PUBLISHING

(a) Customer service can be used to indicate particular concerns of customers. For example, in a DIY store, if customers have to ask service staff where items are stored, the volume of complaints might indicate poor signage and labelling.

(b) Complaints also indicate deficiencies in the product or the fact that customer expectations have been poorly communicated.

(c) Geodemographic information relates to the characteristics of people living in different areas. Even simple post-code information can contain a lot of data about the customer.

(d) Other customer information can be gleaned by orders and enquiries that they place.

Marketing at Work

The *Vons Grocery Company* of California is one of the foremost builders and users of databases in the US. Foodstore customers enter the database by filling out a cheque authorisation application, and are issued a Vons Value Plus Club Card. When swiped at checkout, this produces automatic discounts on selected items of interest *to that individual customer*. Each time the card is used, the store builds a profile of the purchases of that individual customer. As well as customising communications with individual customers (for example, sending out manufacturers' discount coupons on relevant products) the scheme is a powerful tool for building customer loyalty programs. In 1995, for example, Vons offered club members a free turkey for Thanksgiving if they purchased $300 worth of goods at Vons between September 27 and October 31: the EPOS database records total *cumulative* purchases by each customer, during that period, in each till receipt. The next generation of Value Plus Cards will contain a memory chip storing data such as the cardholder's birthday.

Samsonite Corporation, the major luggage manufacturer, maintains three customer databases. One is built on product registration cards, which include purchase details, demographic and lifestyle questions, and an incentive to send the card in. The second is built on calls to the Samsonite freecall enquiry number, which is featured on all advertising. The third is built around information request/response cards bound into magazines that carry their advertisements. Because Samsonite sells through retail outlets, it does not want to compete with its own distributors by direct marketing. However, it uses its databases to profile its customers, product by product, and to study their feedback on products so as to make design improvements. It uses answers to lifestyle questions to spot new product opportunities.   (Adapted from *Marketing Planning*, James W Taylor)

Database marketing

6.22   The old practices of market research contrast with the discipline of **database marketing**. It is very easy and relatively cheap to store vast amounts of data about individuals: indeed, the **loyalty card** schemes in British supermarkets have become data collection exercises as well as promotional tools. Database marketing holds that 'the whole point of finding out about an individual is to attach information to a name and address to which offers, product information and money-off vouchers can later be mailed'.

Key Concept

Database marketing has been defined by Shaw and Stone (1988) as "an interactive approach to marketing, which uses individually addressable marketing media and channels to extend help to a company's target audience, stimulate their demand and stay close to them by recording and keeping an electronic database memory of customer, prospect, and all communication and commercial contacts, to help them improve all future contacts and to ensure more realistic planning of all marketing."

6.23   Linton (1995) indicates the different ways that databases enable marketing managers to improve their decision-making.

(a) **Understanding customers** and their preferences

(b) Managing **customer service** (helplines, complaints)

(c) Understanding the **market** (new products, channels etc)

(d) Understanding **competitors** (market share, prices)

(e) Managing **sales operations**

(f) Managing **marketing campaigns**

(g) **Communicating** with customers

6.24 On the **quantitative** side, database marketing is becoming more popular. It is, after all, real behaviour as opposed to 'simulated' behaviour. This also makes it more attractive than **qualitative research**. A problem is that what people say in **focus groups** or to **market researchers** does not reflect their actual purchase behaviour.

6.25 In practice, the data is only as good as firms' use of it, and it can quickly go out of date. An example of how the different types of data are used is provided below.

Marketing at Work

Daewoo

The following extracts come from an article in Marketing Business (March 1997). It shows how Daewoo did not differentiate on product, rather on service.

'For the marketing director of Daewoo, customer feedback informs all of his decisions. Daewoo launched on the back of extensive research. "Before we launched, we did an enormous amount of research to develop our strategy. We used a direct response television and press campaign inviting people to tell us what they thought of the car trade. That brought an enormous response - 200,000 people contacted us. We then sent a detailed questionnaire to 30 per cent of these and to that mailing we had a 60 per cent response."

In order to deliver top service, the research never ever stops. "We are continuously doing quality tracking," says Farrell. "Every three months, we phone 200 recent buyers to ask them about their experience of our service and whether they have found any faults with the car. This is a 35-minute conversation. Then, after a year, we phone another sample."

"In the second half of each year we do 10,000 telephone interviews to people who have ordered cars but have yet to take delivery, so the experience is fresh in their minds, and then we contact them after delivery." In fact, customers are interviewed at every stage of their dealings with Daewoo - within 48 hours of having their car serviced, for instance, to find out how it went and whether the courtesy car was satisfactory.

And it is not just customers that are approached. To get a complete picture, Daewoo also interviews those who walk out of the showroom without buying. Research on this scale is a vital part of the company's strategic development but the results have a big impact on individuals as well - Daewoo staff do not work on commission but are rewarded as a result of customer feedback. Constant monitoring means that Daewoo can respond rapidly.'

Customer specific marketing

6.26 The logical extension of database marketing is referred to by Kotler as **customer specific marketing**. The company collects such data on individual customers, their past transactions, demographic and even psychographic characteristics. With such customers, the marketing task is to entice such customers into a **relationship**.

Information technology

6.27 It is the combination of **communication and computer technology** that has led to the development of information technologies as we know them. Terms like 'data superhighways' have been coined to recognise the speed at which it is possible to transmit and receive vast amounts of data globally. These information technology developments are transforming the ways in which markets, organisations and, most importantly, managers are able to operate. Traditional organisational structures and roles may be broken down in the advancement of new technologies.

BPP PUBLISHING

'Rapid growth of the Internet, bringing online information services to millions of businesses and individual computer users, is changing the way businesses communicate with their customers, suppliers and within their own organisation.'

Financial Times

6.28 As marketers we know that **customers and their needs are central** to the advancement of such technology. Organisations need to anticipate and respond to the changing needs of customers and part of the process of meeting those needs is to develop technological solutions to give satisfaction and provide service. **Retailing** has been at the forefront of many of the more familiar changes in technology. Checkouts have EPOS (Electronic Point of Sale) and EFTPOS (Electronic Funds Transfer at Point of Sale) systems. **Banking** and the **financial markets** are at the forefront of the developing technologies. **Manufacturers** and **commercial organisations** are also acquiring benefits from the innovations in information technologies.

6.29 Information systems and technology are the subjects of Chapter 3 but the following extract from the July/August 1995 edition of *Marketing Business* shows just how important they are to the marketer.

'The winners of the next decade will be those who know more about their customers and their needs than the clients know themselves. Knowledge can be one of the most valuable bases upon which relationships can be constructed.

The essence of relationship marketing is the ability to counsel customers as to what they ought to do and what products they ought to buy. Such a relationship can only be achieved if the marketing organisation is in full possession of up-to-date, comprehensive and relevant information about existing and potential customers. Remember, once a relationship has been established the need to sell is diminished because the customer is constantly ready to buy.

If your competitor has access to the same information as you, the winner is the one who is able to process such information speedily and intelligently. The technology of processing information is now available to everybody. On the other hand, the ability to convert information into valuable marketing intelligence is where the true virtuosity of the modern marketer lies. Gone are the days when a customer could be impressed by a supplier who was able to spurt out your name and address the moment he or she heard your postcode.

The problem is that in many organisations marketing people do not understand the true value of IT systems. At the same time, systems people do not always understand the marketing function. The result is that data is churned out at a gigantic rate but is not used to its full potential. As a preamble to the development or enhancement of an IT system, it is important that the IT and marketing personnel have thorough talks about what would be helpful in the pursuit of a meaningful relationship with customers. Clearly, IT staff should say what information can be assembled and at what cost but the onus of determining what the output should be and its frequency must rest with the marketers.'

7 FORECASTING

Key Concept

Forecast. A prediction of future events and their quantification for planning purposes.

7.1 Sales and marketing activities in many organisations are often taken in **reaction** to changes in the market, rather than being planned. Predictions of future changes in market size and potential tend to be rudimentary. Sales estimates are often based on the hunches of managers.

7.2 To carry out their responsibilities properly, marketing managers need **comprehensive estimates of current and future demand**. Such estimates must take account of both **market potential** (the total amount of a product customers will buy at a certain level of industry-wide marketing activity) and **sales potential** (the maximum percentage of market potential that an organisation within an industry can expect to obtain for a certain product or service). Market and sales **forecasts** must therefore be prepared. Forecasting is looked at in detail in Chapter 4.

Market forecasts

7.3 **Market forecasts** analyse the market as a whole, including external environmental factors beyond the control of the organisation which may have an impact on demand for the firm's products and services.

7.4 Market forecasts consist of three parts.

(a) The **economy**, including a review of **PEST** factors

(b) **Market research** which is designed to acquire information on specific markets and estimate total demand for a product

(c) An evaluation of **market demand** for both the firm and competitor products which are regarded as substitutes

We will be looking at how to gain information about the market in Part E of this Text.

Sales forecasts

7.5 **Sales forecasts** estimate sales for a future period and are concerned solely with the firm's **products and services**. Sales forecasts are expressed in **volume**, **value** and **profit**.

Sales forecast   = how many at a given price

          = say, 1,000 units at £10 = £10,000

7.6 The sales forecast is essential starting information required for **budgeting purposes**. The **accuracy** of such a forecast is essential since all other budgeting decisions usually hinge around the level for sales (except in non-profit making organisations where budgets may be fixed from other revenue sources such as grants). Budgeting is the topic of Chapter 11.

8 FINANCIAL ANALYSIS AND TOOLS   12/99

8.1 **Accounting systems** hold data which may provide information for marketing and sales management, which may assist with planning, control and decision making. Accounting information may help managers to:

(a) Plan and achieve **goals**

(b) Formulate **policy** (pricing, discounting, credit terms and so on)

(c) Monitor and assess **performance** (variance analysis, financial performance measures)

(d) Appreciate the **financial implications** of changes in the **external environment**

(e) Appreciate the financial implications of changes in the **internal environment** (such as changes in structure, organisation and processes)

(f) Compare and decide upon **alternative courses of action**

(g) Manage more **effectively** and **efficiently scarce resources** at their disposal

(h) **Control** day to day operations

(i) **Focus attention** on specific issues which need attention

    (j)   Solve specific **problems**

    (k)   Make **investment decisions**

This is a detailed area of the syllabus, so we will be looking at the information provided by accounting analysis and tools across Chapters 5 to 12.

8.2   **Financial statements** can provide information about the condition of a business. The analysis and interpretation of such statements can be carried out by calculating **ratios** which can be used both to identify **trends** within an individual organisation's performance and to **compare** the performance of one organisation against another.

The importance of numbers to the marketer

8.3   You may well be wondering why the numbers produced by financial analysis and tools are important to you as a **marketer**.

8.4   Imagine a large hairdressing salon has set an objective of increasing the number of clients seen by its stylists and so has decided to employ an extra part-time stylist and to advertise in the local press more regularly.

This seems reasonable. Now let's add some numbers.

8.5   The hairdressing salon, which currently has 500 appointments a month, has set an objective of increasing the number of clients seen by its stylists by 12% over a twelve-month period and so has decided to employ an extra part-time stylist on a salary of £6,000 and to advertise monthly in the local press at a cost of £220 per month.

The salon therefore expects to see an additional $500 \times 12\% \times 12 = 720$ clients each year, or 60 clients a month. This raises a number of important questions.

8.6   (a)   Is it possible for a part-time stylist to see 60 clients a month? Information would be needed on the average number of clients per stylist per hour, day, week and month as well as on the number of clients currently turned away because there is no stylist available. The information may reveal that on average, a part-time stylist could only see 40 clients a month.

    (b)   Can the additional cost of £12 per client ($\dfrac{£6,000 + (£220 \times 12)}{720}$) be justified?

           Information will be needed on the prices currently charged and the current margins made. Haircuts are likely to have a lower margin than perms, for example. An analysis of the information may reveal that the cost can only be covered if the new stylist does perms.

8.7   It should now be obvious to you that numbers are important to the marketer. By adding a sense of scale and size they provide a measure of the **viability** of plans.

9   MARKETING RESEARCH

Key Concepts

Marketing research. The objective gathering, recording and analysing of all facts about problems relating to the transfer and sales of goods and services from producer to consumer or user. Includes market research, price research etc. Marketing research involves the use of secondary data (eg government surveys) in desk research as well as field research (which the firm undertakes itself) to acquire primary data.

Market research. Sometimes used synonymously with marketing research; strictly speaking, however, it refers to the acquisition of primary data about customers and customer attitudes for example, by asking a sample of individuals to complete a questionnaire.

9.1   To give you an idea about the **scope** of marketing research, the various components are summarised below.

Research type	Application
Market research	Forecasting demand (new and existing products) Sales forecast by segment Analysis of market shares Market trends Industry trends Acquisition/diversification studies
Product research	Likely acceptance of new products Analysis of substitute products Comparison of competitors products Test marketing Product extension Brand name generation and testing Product testing of existing products Packaging design studies
Price research	Competitor prices (analysis) Cost analysis Profit analysis Market potential Sales potential Sales forecast (volume) Customer perception of price Effect of price change on demand (elasticity of demand) Discounting Credit terms
Sales promotion research	Analysing the effect of campaigns Monitoring/analysing advertising media choice Evaluation of sales force performance To decide on appropriate sales territories and make decisions as to how to cover the area Copy research Public image studies Competitor advertising studies Studies of premiums, coupons, promotions
Distribution research	Planning channel decisions Design and location of distribution centres In-house versus outsource logistics Export/international studies Channel coverage studies

9.2 The following diagram summarises the marketing research process. This process will be discussed in more detail in Part E of this Study Text.

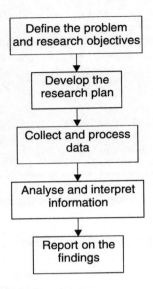

9.3 In putting together the research plan, decisions need to be made under the following headings.

Data sources	Primary data (data the organisation collects itself for the purpose)
	Secondary data (collected by someone else for another purpose which may provide useful information)
Type of data required	Continuous/ad hoc
	Quantitative (numbers)
	Qualitative (important insights)
Research methods	Observation
	Focus groups
	Survey
	Experiment
Research tools	Interviews (semi-structured, structured, unstructured; open v closed questions)
	Questionnaires
	Mechanical tools (video, audio)
Sampling plan (if required)	Sampling unit
	Sample size
	Sample procedure
Contact methods	Telephone
	Mail
	Personal

You will encounter all of these terms again in Chapters 13 to 15.

Chapter Roundup

- This chapter has hopefully given you a flavour of the topics which we will be looking at in this Study Text. Some of them you may think are more relevant to you as a marketer than others. Remember, however, that marketing and sales impact on all areas of an organisation's operations and therefore it is only right and proper that you have some awareness of the invaluable sort of information available to you as a marketer in, for example, the finance function of your organisation.

- Information is required by marketing and sales management for analysis, planning, implementation and control: APIC.

- A marketing information system is a specific example of a management information system. Management need a marketing and sales information system which will provide information to enable them to analyse, plan, make decisions, implement and control.

- Data is the raw material for data processing. Information is data processed in such a way as to be of some meaning to the person who receives it.

- Information must have a purpose otherwise it is useless. Information which fulfils its purpose is known as good information.

- Information is termed hard if it is data which has been collected for a specific purpose in an organised or scientific manner. Soft information is acquired in an unstructured and unplanned manner with no specific purpose in mind.

- Information is required for strategic, tactical and operational decisions.

- Information technology and databases, EPOS, EFTPOS and so on have transformed the ways in which markets, organisations and managers are able to operate.

- Marketing databases can provide an organisation with much information about customers and target groups. Comprehensive customer databases may contain many fields of data.

- Forecasts of future demand must take account of market potential and sales potential.

- Both the management accounting function and financial statements can provide invaluable information for marketing and sales.

- Marketing research is made up of market research, product research, price research, sales promotion research and distribution research.

- In brief, the marketing research process has the following stages.

    ○ Define the problem and research objectives
    ○ Develop the research plan
    ○ Collect and process data
    ○ Analyse and interpret information
    ○ Report on the findings

BPP PUBLISHING

Quick Quiz

1   Define a management information system (see para 2.2)
2   How does Kotler classify marketing management activities? (3.1)
3   What is the difference between data and information? (4.2, 4.3)
4   What are the qualities of good information?(4.4)
5   Distinguish between hard and soft information. (4.5)
6   At what levels can decisions be taken? (5.2)
7   To what areas can tactical decisions be applied? (5.2)
8   What may be the sources of information for a customer database? (6.21)
9   What are the three components of market forecasts? (7.4)
10 In what ways can accounting information assist managers? (8.1)
11 What is the difference between market research and marketing research? (9)
12 To what areas can price research be applied? (9.1)
13 Summarise the marketing research process. (9.2)

Action Programme Review

1   This task is useful because the examiner has said that the examining team is keen to receive scripts that relate MkIS to a specific context. You must get used to thinking and relating concepts to your own organisation, its practicalities and problems.

2 Developing a Marketing Information System

Chapter Topic List	Syllabus Reference
1 Introduction	
2 What does the organisation need to know?	1.1
3 The marketing information system	1.4
4 Marketing research for the MkIS	1.2

Learning Outcomes

When you have completed this chapter you will be able to:

- Define what is meant by the term marketing information system (MkIS)
- Understand the need for and place of a marketing information system (MkIS)
- Understand its relationship to an organisation's management information system
- Develop a suitable MkIS

Key Concepts

- Marketing information system
- Marketing intelligence system

- Decision support system

Examples of Marketing at Work

- WH Smith

- Kwikfit

1   INTRODUCTION

1.1   The marketing environment must be constantly analysed. The information produced from such an analysis is a key input to all aspects of strategy formulation.

Key Concept

The collection, organisation and analysis of marketing information is the responsibility of a **marketing information system** (MkIS) in itself is part of the hierarchy of information systems that exist within organisations. The information collected, organised and analysed by an MkIS will typically include the following.

- Details on consumers and markets
- Sales - past, current and forecast
- Production and marketing costs
- Data on the operating environment: competitors, suppliers, distributors and so on

1.2 Typically, an MkIS will have four interlinked components.

(a) **The internal database.** This includes information on costs, production schedules, orders, sales and some types of financial information relating to customers (such as credit ratings). Financial analysis and tools (which we look at in Part D) would provide much of this information.

Source: Marshall, Marketing Information Systems

(b) **The external database.** This includes all types of information collected from external sources, commonly described as **marketing intelligence.** This database may take the form of press cuttings and so forth, but can also incorporate subscriptions to external sources of competitive data. Marketing intelligence is the subject of Chapter 13.

(c) **The marketing research system.** Generally such a system involves the process of information search undertaken on an ad hoc basis to provide answers to specific questions. Marketing research is introduced in this chapter and then looked at in detail in Chapters 13-15.

(d) **The decision support system.** A DSS is a set of analytical techniques that enable marketing managers to make full use of the information provided by the other three sources. This analysis may range from simple financial ratios and projections of sales patterns to more complex statistical models, spreadsheets and other exercises in extrapolation.

1.3 The use of computers for gathering and disseminating management information is now commonplace.

2 WHAT DOES THE ORGANISATION NEED TO KNOW?

Marketing at Work

By more effective analysis of their sales information, retailers can identify changes in sales trends and change their strategy on the fly. W H Smith, for example, was able to clear its stocks of computer games while other retailers were left with stock on their hands, by accurate analysis of its point of sale information, which gave it early warning of a slowdown in games sales. But as well as defensive sales tactics, retailers can also use better information analysis to help them move proactively. *Marketing Business*, April 1996

2.1 As we explained in the introduction to this chapter, the **marketing information system** is part of the **wider management information system** and the two will link together to provide relevant data for the marketing and sales functions of an organisation. First we will look at the specifics of marketing information systems.

2.2 Marketing managers have their own **internal records** which provide the most basic form of marketing information. These include the number of brochure requests against orders taken, sales calls against order value, records of where enquiries are generated from, average order sizes and so on. Such records can be used to provide user-friendly and relevant information.

2.3 In any information system too much information is often as bad as too little. Avoiding **information overload** requires a clarification of the type of information that is needed and the rule for a successful and effective marketing information system is the same as for a good market research brief.

'Work on what we *need* to know, *not* on what it is *nice* to know.'

2.4 So what does a firm need to know? An **information specification** is suggested here.

(a) **Markets.** Who are our customers? What are they like? How are buying decisions made?

(b) **Share of the market.** What are total sales of our product? How do our sales compare with competitors' sales?

(c) **Products.** What do customers think of our product? What do they do with it? Are our products in a 'growth' or 'decline' stage of their life cycle? Should we extend our range?

(d) **Price.** How do we compare: high, average, low? Is the market price sensitive?

(e) **Distribution.** Should we distribute directly, indirectly or both? What discounts are required?

(f) **Sales force.** Do we have enough/too many salespeople? Are their territories equal to their potential? Are they contacting the right people? Should we pay commission?

(g) **Advertising.** Do we use the right media? Do we communicate the right message? Is it effective?

(h) **Customer attitudes.** What do they think of our product? firm? service? delivery?

(i) **Competitors' activities.** Who are our competitors? Are they more or less successful businesses? Why are they more or less successful?

(j) **Environmental factors** impacting on marketing planning (SLEPT factors).

2.5 Another way of viewing the marketing information needs of the organisation is to examine the marketing information needed to answer each of the **four key strategic questions** which organisations have to ask themselves.

(a) Where are we **now**?
(b) Where do we **want** to be?
(c) How might we **get there**?
(d) How can we **ensure** we get there?

The following table repeats these four questions, shows what marketing information is needed to answer each question, and suggests how the information may be obtained.

BPP PUBLISHING

Stage	Information needed	Sources of information: forms of marketing research
1 **Where are we now?** Strategic, financial and Marketing analysis	Current sales by product/ market Market share by product/market Competitor shares by product/ market Corporate image versus competitors' Company strengths and weaknesses Financial position versus competitors'	Internal accounting Market analysis/surveys Competitor intelligence Customer surveys Internal/external analyses Company accounts
2 **Where do we want to be?** Strategic direction and Strategy formulation	Market forecasts by segment Environmental changes Growth capabilities Opportunities and threats Competitor response New product/market potentials	Industry forecasts/surveys PEST analysis PIMS Competitor research Product/market research
3 **How might we get there and which way is best?** Strategic choice and Evaluation	Marketing mix evaluation Buying behaviour New product development Risk evaluation Alternative strategic options	Internal/external audits Customer research Concept testing/test marketing Feasibility studies/CVP analysis NPV analyses/competitor response modelling/focus groups/marketing mix research
4 **How can we ensure arrival?** Strategic implementation And control	Performance evaluation	Internal accounting/external auditing

2.6   This information-seeking process can be best expressed as a flow diagram.

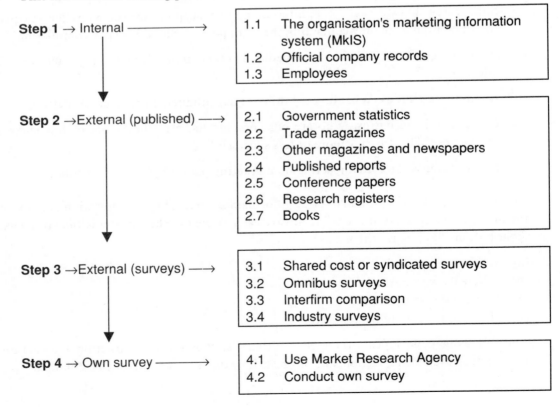

Step 1 → Internal ——————→

1.1	The organisation's marketing information system (MkIS)
1.2	Official company records
1.3	Employees

Step 2 →External (published) ——→

2.1	Government statistics
2.2	Trade magazines
2.3	Other magazines and newspapers
2.4	Published reports
2.5	Conference papers
2.6	Research registers
2.7	Books

Step 3 →External (surveys) ——→

3.1	Shared cost or syndicated surveys
3.2	Omnibus surveys
3.3	Interfirm comparison
3.4	Industry surveys

Step 4 → Own survey ————→

4.1	Use Market Research Agency
4.2	Conduct own survey

Action Programme 1

Try to find out the types of information that your organisation's marketing and sales staff use on a regular basis. Where does this information come from (in other words, what are the data sources)?

3   THE MARKETING INFORMATION SYSTEM

Exam Tip

The marketing information system is a popular topic. Imagine you are the marketing manager of a bank (which is a major provider of financial services), and you have responsibility for improving customer service levels. A question may ask you to prepare notes covering the elements of a good marketing information system and the importance of good information systems in providing customer care.

3.1   Many marketing decisions are taken on a **continuous basis** (for example, decisions are taken on various aspects of the marketing mix, such as sales, advertising and sales promotion, at least annually) and hence information is constantly required to enable management to take such decisions. A continuous source of information is also required for control purposes. A **marketing information system** (MkIS) meets these needs. A diagrammatic representation of an MkIS can be found on the next page.

3.2   It can be helpful to see the MkIS as comprising all computer and non-computer systems which can help the marketer. As a result an MkIS is often built up from several different systems which may not be directly related to marketing, and will contain the following **subsystems**.

(a)   The **internal reports (and accounts) system** (the internal database) provides:

   (i)   Results data
   (ii)   Measures of current performance
   (iii)   Sales, costs and stock information

   An improvement in the timeliness, availability and distribution of reports improves the internal report system.

(b)   The **marketing intelligence system:**

   (i)   Provides happenings data (such as what competitors are doing)
   (ii)   Provides information on developments in the environment
   (iii)   Scans and disseminates a wide range of intelligence

   (We discuss market intelligence further in Chapter 13.)

Key Concept

A **marketing intelligence system** is a set of procedures and sources used by managers to obtain everyday information about pertinent developments in the marketing environment.

(c)   The **marketing research system** studies marketing problems, opportunities and effectiveness.

(d)   The **decision support system** uses models to explain, predict and improve marketing processes. Models may be descriptive, decisional, verbal, graphical or mathematical.

The marketing information system

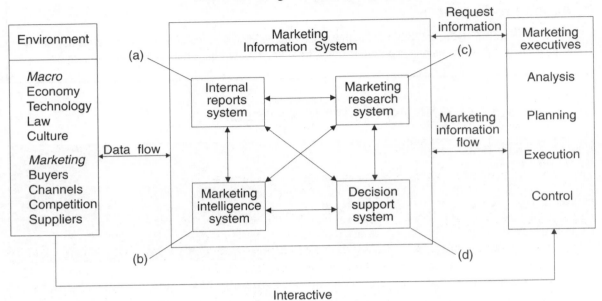

Key Concept

A **decision support system** is used by management to aid decision making on unstructured, complex, uncertain or ambiguous issues.

3.3 Data collected needs to produce coherent information.

(a) The system must allow for the easy and effective **storage and retrieval** of data and so consideration must be given to the following.

  (i) Manual or computerised
  (ii) The extent of hard copy back up
  (iii) Cross referencing of data
  (iv) Data protection legislation considerations

(b) Irrelevant data must be eliminated.

Action Programme 2

We considered the qualities of good information in Chapter 1. Can you remember what they are?

(c) **Dissemination of information** considerations include the following.

  (i) Who needs to, or who should, receive information
  (ii) The use of newsletters for standardised regular information
  (iii) How much value is added by the system?

3.4 There will be cost and **organisational implications** of an MkIS.

(a) **Training** of existing and new staff will be necessary.

(b) Staff with **specialist skills** might have to be recruited and so job descriptions and specifications might need to change.

(c) Organisational considerations might include the **reallocation of duties**.

3.5 When an MkIS is being designed the following factors should be considered.

(a) Users should **understand** the systems and be in a position to evaluate and control them.

(b) The system must be regularly **reviewed** and feedback improved.

(c) The true meaning of the information provided must be clarified.

(d) The MkIS must be **flexible**.

(e) A system is only as effective as designers and users make it.

The features of an effective MkIS

3.6 As an example of an MkIS in action, let us visualise a company which has identified **quality service** as a strategic priority. To meet this goal, the MkIS must:

(a) Provide managers with **real time** information on how customers and staff **perceive the service** being given, on the assumption that **what is not measured can't be managed**

(b) Measure quality of both service and customer care so as to provide evidence that they do matter, the implication being that **what is seen to be measured gets done**

(c) Monitor how (if at all) the **customer base is changing**

(d) Perhaps provide a basis on which bonus payments can be determined, on the grounds that **what gets paid for gets done even better**

3.7 Data and information about customer service may be gathered in many ways but overall **systems design criteria** are important.

(a) **Management's access to the information must be easy and direct**, ideally via PC or networked terminal.

(b) **The cost of data/information gathering should be minimal** so as to avoid the cost-cutter's scythe when times are hard. As Ian Ruskin Brown (1994) expresses it: 'The high-profile projects, like daisies, get cut back, but the essential MIS must be like clover, low down in the grass and the last to go'.

(c) **Data gathering should be low intensity**. In other words, it should not cause excessive inconvenience to respondents or other information sources. Preferably the data will be gathered without customers being aware of it (for example through analysis of supermarket checkout receipts which show consumer purchase patterns).

(d) **Data gathering should be regular and continuous** since a small amount of data gathered regularly can build a considerable database. Regular data gathering produces more reliable results because it reduces the likelihood of sample bias of one kind or another.

Consumer behaviour and its effect on an MkIS

3.8 An effective MkIS will be sufficiently sophisticated so as to enable marketing managers to understand that consumer behaviour is not a simple linear process in which, say, demand falls as prices increase. There is no straightforward connection between a change in one factor (price) and a consequential change in another (purchase).

BPP PUBLISHING

Non-linear consumer behaviour

3.9 As an example of what we mean by **non-linear behaviour**, we need only to look at the sales of ice-cream. Such sales are highly seasonal and begin when the sun comes out in the spring and fall off in early autumn. One somewhat surprising aspect of this process, however, is that early season good weather has a much stronger sales-boosting effect than late season sunshine. A sunny week in May, especially in northern Europe, can be worth in excess of 20 per cent in extra sales compared with a similar period in July.

3.10 Thus consumer behaviour is not irrational, because sales patterns follow what one would expect and hence there is a positive correlation between sales and sunshine. On the other hand, the response curve is non-linear: the strength of the response differs according to how far into the season it is. As Nilson (*Chaos Marketing*) points out: 'The skills required to interpret non-linear reactions are essential to marketing and are often what will differentiate the successful from the mediocre'.

Feedback loops

3.11 Marketing managers cannot operate without **feedback loops** of some description. They are only capable of being understood if there is lots of information coming into the organisation from a variety of sources such as **commissioned research**, third-party **continuous research, databases, secondary sources** of all descriptions, **sales figures**, customer surveys, environmental scanning and so forth.

3.12 Three aspects of the information-gathering system are of special significance here.

(a) **The speed of the feedback loop**. The sooner the information is collected, the more accurate it will be.

Marketing at Work

At Kwikfit, executives receive full details of the previous day's trading every morning, so that they can spot trends. This kind of virtually-instant information supply is by no means unusual. Technology is helping more companies to receive virtually 'real-time' information.

(b) **The planning horizon is becoming shorter**. It is worth emphasising that there is no value in having quicker response times in the marketing function if these are not matched by quicker response times in other parts of the organisation as well. In the retail world, for example, scanning and EPOS systems mean that retailers know very quickly if a product on the shelves is selling or not. In Nilson's words, 'technology, in addition to being nearer the ultimate customer, has meant that the retailers, as a rule, have greater awareness of emotional and tangible changes in the marketplace'.

(c) **Planning what to do is becoming less important than planning how to do it**. To be able to react quickly to change, it is important to have a clear picture of what needs to be done in various eventualities so that when any given scenario emerges, action can be initiated rapidly.

3.13 One of the consequences of an increasing reliance on widely-available computerised MkIS is that up to date information is now much more widely available to all levels of an organisation's hierarchy.

Marketing intelligence systems

3.14 A **marketing intelligence system** is a set of procedures and sources used by managers to obtain their everyday information about pertinent developments in the marketing environment, by continuous monitoring of the environment.

3.15 Managers can scan the environment in four ways.

   (a) **Undirected viewing**: having general exposure to information with no specific purpose in view

   (b) **Conditional viewing**: directed exposure

   (c) **Informal search**: an unstructured effort to obtain specific information

   (d) **Formal search**: a deliberate effort with a plan, procedure, or methodology to obtain specific information

3.16 As we saw in Chapter 1, **data** is the raw material which when processed provides information. **Information** is output but may also be considered an input for further analysis to provide **intelligence**. We may look at the definition as a 'value added' model.

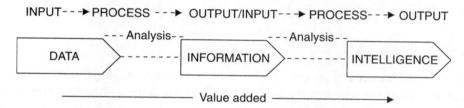

3.17 We use the term **value added** to demonstrate that information has both a cost and a benefit; providing that the **benefit is greater than the cost**, we can say that information is adding value to the activities undertaken by the organisation. For example, an organisation may gather data to examine a particular market opportunity for its products. When the data is processed it may have information about opportunities in a market segment that it may be able to exploit. The potential sales revenue that is likely to be achieved is estimated and, if it exceeds the cost of data collection and processing, data collection and processing is a value-adding activity.

The components of a computerised MkIS

3.18 A typical computerised MkIS could be described as having four components.

   (a) A **data bank** will store raw marketing data, such as data about historical sales and data from market research findings.

   (b) A **statistical bank** will store programs for carrying out computations for sales forecasts, making advertising spending projections, calculating sales force productivity and so on.

   (c) A **model bank** will store marketing models for planning and analysis.

   (d) A **display unit** (VDU screen and keyboard) will allow the marketing manager to communicate with an MkIS. Alternatively, marketing reports can be printed out in hard copy form.

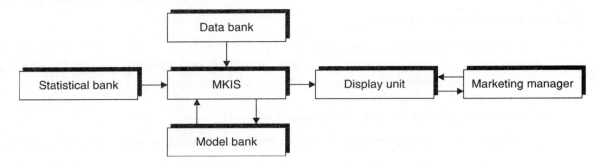

4 MARKETING RESEARCH FOR THE MKIS 12/00

4.1 Marketing research data may be collected systematically on a **continuous** basis or it may be of an occasional nature and therefore **ad hoc**. Most organisations will require both types of research to be undertaken for their information system.

4.2 As we have seen, much of the data for research will be available internally but may require organising for the specific problem the data is intended to address. For example, much of the data to answer specific aspects of pricing will be available internally in accounting and sales records.

Field research

4.3 Data collected externally or out in the field is referred to as **primary research or field research**. Consumer research tends to be of a primary nature although some is 'off the peg' or closer to secondary research because someone else has carried out the research such as a market research organisation like the British Market Research Bureau (BMRB).

4.4 Although this type of research ('off the peg') is very useful and likely to be cost effective it may not provide organisations with complete answers to the research questions they had designed.

4.5 It must be remembered that to obtain unique answers to unique questions may cost more and may or may not provide the extra benefits required. Designing **good research questions**, which can be answered giving consideration to data sources, is an essential ingredient and a definite skill for the effective marketing researcher to acquire and to practice.

Continuous research

4.6 **Continuous research** is any type of research activity planned to provide regular information from systematic data collection. For example, weekly sales by customer, by value, by quantity, by product (or product group) together with returns data and profitability analysis by customer and by product would be useful types of continuous research activity: they provide details about what customers buy, how often they buy, which products they buy, the sales values by customer/product and how profitable customers and products are.

4.7 This type of research may be designed to provide a control mechanism as well as for planning. Anticipating changes in the market and planning a response may be an important aspect of continuous research.

Inputs	Process	Action
Sales quantity and value by customer	Trend analysis	Promotion
Sales quantity and value by product	Trend analysis	Price changes
Profitability by customer	Trend analysis	Different packaging
Profitability by product	Trend analysis	Develop new channels

4.8 Databases which are relational and instantly accessible via computer technology provide a very useful data source for continuous research. There are of course secondary data sources for continuous research which are provided by commercial external marketing research organisations. For example, annual or monthly reports provided by the Central Statistical Office, the Department of Trade and Industry and organisations such as MINTEL or Key Note may form an important aspect of this continuous marketing research.

4.9 Research enables the organisation to be **proactive** rather than **reactive**; to 'make things happen' rather than merely respond to what has happened already. This external data may be used as an element in the continuous research mix to monitor a trend in the market or to monitor seasonal variation patterns.

'Ad hoc' research

4.10 **'Ad hoc' research** comprises 'one-off' research studies designed to meet a specific information need, for example when a new product/market opportunity may need to be explored. Surveys using a questionnaire (administered and self-administered) may form part of the data capture method. Alternatively semi-structured interviews or focus group interviews could be used. Usually, ad hoc research studies demand 'made-to-measure' research surveys, although some studies may be able to make use of internal data sources already in existence.

Desk research

4.11 **Desk research** is secondary data research that can usually be achieved sitting at a desk without moving into the field. The research data consists of information produced for another purpose. For example, if an organisation wanted to estimate the value of exports in a particular industry one way to achieve this research aim might be to investigate HM Customs & Excise VAT statistics. These statistics have not been collected specifically for the organisation's research aim but they will provide data required.

4.12 Detailed consideration of marketing research processes and techniques is the subject of Part E of this Study Text.

BPP PUBLISHING

Chapter Roundup

- A marketing information system comprises four elements: the internal database, the external database, the marketing research system and the decision support system.

- Organisations need to acquire and assess many types of information in order to evolve profitable marketing strategies: information about markets, products, price, distribution, sales methods, advertising, customers, competitor activities and environmental factors.

- For marketing information to be useful, it needs to be relevant, concise, appropriate (in terms of detail), cost effective and timely.

- There are four components to a computerised MkIS: a data bank, a statistical bank, a model bank and a display unit.

- Marketing intelligence is designed to describe and explain what is happening in the market as a whole, and to identify significant trends for the future.

- Marketing research data can be classified into 'continuous' or 'ad hoc'.

- Desk research can often supply valuable information without the necessity for any field study.

Quick Quiz

1   What are the four ingredients of a typical MkIS? (see para 1.2)

2   What sorts of marketing information does an organisation require if it is to construct a worthwhile marketing strategy? (2.4)

3   What are the four strategic questions which organisations have to ask (and answer)? (2.5)

4   What is the design of the flow diagram which shows the logical approach to the acquisition of data for marketing decision purposes? (2.6)

5   What are the factors to take into account when putting together a good storage and retrieval system for marketing data? (3.3)

6   What are the cost and organisational practice implications of an MkIS? (3.4)

7   What factors should be considered when an MkIS is being designed? (3.5)

8   What are some important design criteria for a MkIS? (3.7)

9   What is a marketing intelligence system? (3.14)

10   What are the distinctions between 'continuous' research versus 'ad hoc' research, and 'field research' versus 'desk research'? (4.3 - 4.11)

Action Programme Review

2   (a)   Relevance for its purpose
     (b)   Complete
     (c)   Of an appropriate level of accuracy or detail
     (d)   Cost effective
     (e)   Directed to the right person and clear to them
     (f)   Inspires confidence in the user
     (g)   Timely
     (h)   Appropriate channel of communication
     (i)   Manageable volume

Now try illustrative questions 1 and 2 at the end of the Study Text

Part B
Information and communication technology

3 *Technology Supporting Marketing Decisions*

Chapter Topic List	Syllabus Reference
1 Introduction	-
2 Information for competitive advantage	2.0, 2.2
3 Information processing	2.0
4 Transaction processing systems	2.0
5 Decision support systems	2.2, 2.3
6 Executive information systems	2.2
7 Expert systems	2.4
8 Database information	2.0, 2.1
9 Internal and external databases	2.1
10 Technological developments	2.4
11 The Internet and e-Commerce	2.1, 2.5
12 Strategies for information technology	2.0

Learning Outcomes

When you have completed this chapter, you will have a practical understanding of how information and communication technology (ICT) impacts upon marketing management decisions. Specifically, you will be able to:

- Describe decision support, executive information and expert systems
- Understand the structure and use of database systems
- Appreciate how the customer database can be used for market analysis
- Appreciate the scope of database usage
- Describe some recent technological developments
- Explain the importance of IT strategy

It should be clear after studying this chapter that ICTs are shaping the way that organisations deal with their customers and their marketing processes.

Key Concepts

- Information technology
- Transaction processing systems
- Marketing decision support system
- Executive information system
- Expert systems
- The internet

BPP PUBLISHING

Examples of Marketing at Work

- Thrift Drug
- Interactive kiosks
- HP Bulmer
- Sears Roebuck
- CACI

- Hallmark and Compaq
- Dialogue marketing
- IBM study
- Icom
- Databases

- Data gathering
- McDonalds
- Smartcards
- Thomas Cook
- Intelligent Miner

1 INTRODUCTION

1.1 Kotler (*Marketing Management*) defines a marketing information system (MkIS) as a 'continuing and interacting structure of people, equipment and procedures to gather, sort, analyse, evaluate, and distribute pertinent, timely, and accurate information for use by marketing decision makers to improve their marketing planning, implementation and control.'

1.2 This book so far has been about the creation, development and use of an effective MkIS but within this chapter we are going to look specifically at the increasing applications of **information and communication technologies** (ICTs) in the capture and analysis of information, the classification of alternatives and even (with the aid of expert systems) the making of marketing decisions. We will also briefly consider the importance of a meaningful IT strategy which can yield cost-effective results.

1.3 A recent major survey actually found that 70 per cent of users thought their IT systems were not providing a return on investment, partly because staff using IT systems are left to learn 'on the job' instead of being properly trained. Some companies have a fundamental misconception about IT: whereas some have computerised their existing manual systems rather than look for new ways of doing things, others have allowed technology to take over. This generates 'IT overkill'.

1.4 We will also see that an MkIS does not have to be expensive in order to add value. It can actually be a powerful source for competitive advantage. Already many organisations are reaping the benefits from a sophisticated MkIS.

1.5 To understand what information technology is about, you don't need to know how it works. All you need to know is what it does and what it's for - in other words, what IT delivers and why. After all, you may be able to drive a car, in which case you know what it does without necessarily knowing how it works. Likewise we will be looking at expert systems; at the end of the chapter you will appreciate what an expert system can do but you don't need to know how an expert system actually operates.

2 INFORMATION FOR COMPETITIVE ADVANTAGE

Marketing at Work

'One retailer, Thrift Drug, estimates that it had paid back its $1.3 million investment in a new information analysis system within six months. Thrift believes that the system has made profound changes to the way it goes about organising promotions, cross-selling and pricing. For example, it found that its assumptions about how to display confectionery for Valentine's Day had been quite wrong. For years it had been clearing its shelves of everything but specially-packaged products in the run-up to 14 February; by analysing its sales data, it found that it could dramatically increase its profits by displaying a mixture of ordinary and specially-packaged products.'

Marketing Business

2.1 A major impact of new technology is that firms are becoming increasingly aware of the competitive advantage that may be achieved. Information systems can affect the way the firm approaches customer service and can provide advantages over competitor approaches. Airlines, insurance companies, banks and travel companies are amongst the leading industries that have developed on-line enquiry and information systems to enhance customer service. It is, of course, only the leading firms in each of the industries that are able to achieve advantage. Customer service can only be achieved by being able to anticipate and satisfy customer needs. In order to meet this objective, information which is **up-to-date, accurate, relevant** and **timely** is essential.

2.2 The more information a firm is able to access about competitors and customers, the more it should be able to adapt its product/service offerings to meet the needs of the market place through **differentiation**. For example, mail order companies that are able to store data about customer buying habits are able to exploit such data by establishing patterns of buying behaviour, and offer products at likely buying times that are in line with the customer's profile.

2.3 Information systems may alter the way business is done and may provide organisations with **new opportunities**. For example, theatres that are able to set up a **database** of theatregoers will be able to increase awareness by establishing regular communication.

2.4 Let us take the example of a theatre which is in a tourist city and which wants to use new technology to build a **database**. The types of data it may wish to have are as follows.

(a) Analysis of theatregoers by specific **characteristics**: age, sex, home address

(b) How many **performances** each theatre customer sees in the year

(c) How many day visitors stay in the city and how they chose a day or night at the theatre

(d) **Types of production** customers like to watch

(e) **Factors** important to their decision to visit the theatre, such as price, location, play, cast, facilities

(f) Where they obtained **information** on the theatre and its productions: press, hotel, leaflets, mailings and so on

(g) **Other purchases** customers make when visiting the theatre

(h) **Other entertainment** theatregoers choose to spend their money on

This data could then be used by the theatre marketing management to build relationships with customers and to exploit sales and promotional opportunities.

2.5 Information may be viewed as a **marketing asset** since it impacts on performance as follows.

(a) It helps to increase **responsiveness** to customer demands.

(b) It helps to identify **new customer opportunities** and new product/service demands.

(c) It helps to **anticipate competitive attacks** and threats.

Marketing at Work

'Among the dinosaurs at the National History Museum or in the darkness of The London Dungeon are not obvious spots for finding out shop opening hours, getting a printout of a local map or booking theatre tickets and restaurant tables. But interactive kiosks which are due to be sited in London will provide such services, creating new marketing and advertising opportunities.

Most of the first wave of 15 or so kiosks will be in tourist attractions and hotels and will operate in six languages, providing information on sightseeing, shopping, entertainment and restaurants and bars. They are owned by City Space, which is owned by NEC, the Japanese computer company, More Group, the outdoor advertiser, and Epic Multimedia.'

The aim is for advertisers to sponsor each of the categories of information and pay to put their messages on screen, to be seen by users as they click through to find the information they want. London businesses will be able to pay to provide extra material about themselves in the appropriate listing section. Advertising space will also be sold on the back of the postcard-sized maps printed by the kiosks.

Financial Times

2.6 Marketing information technology is changing the way markets are structured and the way in which firms communicate with each other. The way in which suppliers, distributors and customers correspond and how they organise their **working relationships** is constantly shifting. Take the clothing industry as an example. It is now possible for a retail organisation in England to develop designs which may be transmitted to a remote manufacturer off-shore with production specifications and for the manufacturer to action production via an expert system, organise transportation, inform the customer, invoice the customer and despatch the goods within a matter of days rather than the weeks or months that this might have taken not so long ago. This not only opens up new market opportunities but may also present competitor threats. New technologies increase the opportunities to develop **global markets** for what once may only have been local products or services.

2.7 Information technology has created new **marketing techniques** and new **marketing channels**. **Database marketing** allows vast amounts of customer data to be stored cheaply and to be used to produce more accurate mailshots as well as other marketing tactics. This is important if a firm is able to gain an advantage over competitors by accessing and applying technologies that a competitor is unable to develop.

2.8 **Computer links to suppliers and customers** are common in some industries; a firm is able to place orders regularly via a computer link to replenish stock from a supplier; a customer is able to order from a firm directly. For example, in the motor-vehicle industry some distributing garages for particular makes are able to satisfy customer demand by entering the precise specification of the vehicle and placing the order via computer link to the factory where the vehicle will be manufactured. On placing the order the manufacturer is able to provide the distributor with a production schedule and advise a firm delivery date which can be communicated to the customer.

Marketing at Work

'It is only relatively recently that the technological tools have advanced enough so that not only are systems able to handle complex calculations, they are also far easier to use. Inexpensive PCs can now be used to run powerful analytical systems without requiring large amounts of IT expertise or investment, while advances in software mean that marketers can burrow down into vast stores of information and retrieve exactly what they want with the click of a mouse.

Such technology can be very effective. A case in point is cider maker HP Bulmer. Over the past few years, the company has undertaken an IT overhaul in order to make profit rather than volume the driver of the business. On top of a powerful database it has installed a financial management system that allows it to calculate precisely the profit contribution from different products and different customers. Under the previous system, such detailed information would have been hard, if not impossible, to determine. Now marketing staff can begin to make far more informed decisions about the product mix, which will help them streamline the portfolio and focus on higher margins.

Similarly, at snacks group Golden Wonder, marketers have software programmes that enable them to integrate sales and marketing data from both internal and external sources with a range of *ad hoc* and reporting tools. They can also analyse various scenarios by cross-referencing bits of data and asking a wide variety of "what-if" type questions. Less tangibly, but equally as important, planning and implementation of marketing activity is improving, along with greater effectiveness in promotional spend.'

Laura Mazur, Accountability, Marketing Business

3   INFORMATION PROCESSING

> ## Key Concept
>
> **Information technology** is defined by the Oxford English Reference dictionary as 'the technology involved in the recording, storage and dissemination of information, especially using computers, telecommunications etc'. Breaking it down into its key components of:
>
> - Hardware
>
> - Software
>
> - Telecommunications
>
> provides another way of understanding the term.

3.1   The emergence of IT has meant that we need to understand quite a lot about information itself. After all, if we don't know what information to collect or how to use information properly, how can we expect new technology to be put to effective use for processing information? In this section, we shall look at some of the characteristics of information and some of the features of **information processing systems**.

3.2   'Information processing is the organisation, manipulation and distribution of information. As these activities are central to almost every use of the computer, the term is in common use to mean almost the same as "computing".'   (*British Computer Society*)

3.3   Information processing can be divided into two broad categories.

(a) **Transaction processing** systems
(b) **Management information** systems

As the terms imply, transaction processing involves the routine handling of data transactions, often 'clerical' work, whereas management information involves the formulation of information for managers to use.

3.4   The division of management information into **strategic, tactical** and **operational** levels is frequently used. Given that the aim of any management information system is to provide managers with information, we have to assess how well a formal MIS can do this. The diagram below illustrates, as a simplification of course, the contrast between information at the different levels.

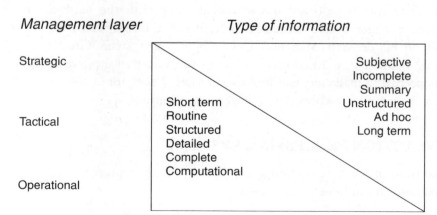

3.5   A management information system cannot realistically provide all of the information needs of management, but **computer technology** means that tools for decision support can be provided in the form of a **computer system** which is made up of the following.

(a) **Executive information systems** are (by definition) used at **strategic** level, for **unstructured** problems, or perhaps even to identify problems rather than solve them. These are described in Section 6 of this chapter.

(b) (i) **Decision support systems** are not often used by top executives, being less 'user friendly' and requiring more expertise. They are used by middle managers for routine modelling, but also to analyse unstructured problem situations for senior executives. These are described in Section 5 of this chapter.

(ii) **Expert systems** are used principally at the operational level and assist in structured problems. They are considered in Section 7.

(c) **Traditional MIS** provide structured information from transaction data for all three levels of management.

(d) **Transaction processing systems** do the essential number crunching. These are described in Section 4 of this chapter.

Action Programme 1

The mechanics of data processing are essentially the same, no matter whether it is done manually or by computer. There are differences, however, between manual and computerised data processing. Identify four differences and explain the advantages or disadvantages of the use of computers in each case.

Hardware and software

3.6 It is a good idea to get a feel for the general trends in technology, so regard the information in the next two paragraphs as background reference. With the advent of the silicon **microchip** and more recently the Intel Pentium chip, processing power is light years ahead of where it was 30 years ago. A task that would have taken a computer a year to complete in 1970 can be done on today's computers in about thirty seconds, **for the same cost**. In addition, the amount of data that can be stored has increased dramatically. Today, there is enough power available on a **personal computer** to run many applications that could previously only be carried out on **mainframes**. Database marketing, data mining and data warehousing are all made feasible by these technological changes.

3,7 The performance of **software** has increased along with the hardware improvements. A marketing manager is able to access data from a central computer and perform independent analysis on his desktop. Microsoft and its operating system Windows dominates the PC operating market. In marketing, a variety of software packages are available for functions such as preparing mailshots and forecasting sales. These are in addition to wordprocessing software, financial spreadsheets and database applications.

4   TRANSACTION PROCESSING SYSTEMS

4.1 **Transaction processing systems** could be said to represent the lowest level in an organisation's use of information systems.

Key Concept

Transaction processing systems are used for **routine tasks** in which data items or transactions must be processed so that operations can continue. Handling sales orders, purchase orders, payroll items and stock records are typical examples.

4.2 Most organisations generate a large volume of transactions which need to be processed efficiently and effectively. **Computerised transaction processing systems** have clear cost and performance advantages over manual systems for all but the most trivial applications. Small businesses are using microcomputers to provide these functions just as larger companies earlier acquired mainframe computers for these purposes.

4.3 Transaction processing systems provide the **raw material** which is often used more extensively, such as reports on cumulative sales figures to date, total amounts owed to suppliers or owed by debtors, total stock turnover to date, value of current stock-in-hand and so on, but the main purpose of transaction processing systems is operational, in other words as an integral part of day-to-day operations.

5 DECISION SUPPORT SYSTEMS

5.1 **Decision support systems** are a form of management information system. Decision support systems are used by management to assist them in making decisions on issues which are unstructured.

5.2 The term decision support systems or DSS (first coined in the late 1970s by Peter Keen, a British systems specialist) is usually taken to mean **computer systems** which are designed to produce information in such a way as to help managers to make better decisions.

5.3 Decision support systems do not make decisions. The objective is to allow the manager to consider a number of **alternatives** and **evaluate** them under a variety of potential conditions. A key element in the usefulness of these systems is their ability to function interactively.

Marketing decision support systems

Key Concept

A **marketing decision support system** is a coordinated collection of data systems, tools and techniques with supporting **software and hardware** which is used for gathering and interpreting relevant information from the business and its environment, which may be used as a basis for marketing decisions and action.

A Marketing Decision Support System

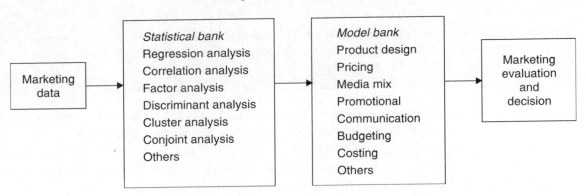

5.4 The convergence of **information** and **communication technologies** has allowed marketing and sales managers access to an array of statistical models which may be used to evaluate and support marketing and sales decisions. The technology allows **large quantities of data** to be processed quickly and to be used as inputs to the firm's own models. These may be developed to support management decisions such as those indicated in the model bank in the above diagram. **Software programs** are being developed, both commercially and in-house by larger companies, to enable **computer modelling of marketing management problems**. Examples of decision support models are listed below, to give you some idea of what they are used for in practice.

(a) **Brandaid** is a flexible marketing-mix model focused on consumer packaged goods. It contains sub-models for advertising, pricing and competition. The model allows users to use their own judgement as well as providing historical analysis, trading, field experimentation and adaptive control.

(b) **Geoline** is a model for designing sales and service territories that satisfies three criteria.

 (i) Equalised workloads
 (ii) Territories are next to each other
 (ii) Not too large

(c) **Mediac** is a model to help in planning media buying for a year. The model allows market segment delineation, sales revenue estimation, timing issues and competitor media schedules, amongst other things.

(d) **Callplan** is a model allowing sales people to plan calls which take account of travel time and selling time.

5.5 There are others, but in the main these models provide support for designing marketing research studies, segmenting markets, setting prices, analysing media, salesforce planning and promotional budgeting.

6 EXECUTIVE INFORMATION SYSTEMS

Key Concept

An **executive information system** is an 'information system which gives the executive easy access to key internal and external data'. EIS have been made possible by the increasing cheapness and sophistication of **microcomputer and network technology**. EIS are designed for use by senior managers who do not in the normal course of events interact with computers.

6.1 The minimum of technical expertise should be needed: executives do not normally have the time to become expert in a particular system. An EIS is likely to have the following features.

(a) Provision of **summary-level data**, captured from the organisation's main systems (which might involve integrating the executive's desk top micro with the organisation's mainframe)

(b) A facility which allows the executive to '**drill down**' from higher to lower levels of information for more details

(c) **Data manipulation facilities** (such as comparison with budget or prior year data, trend analysis)

(d) **Graphics**, for user-friendly presentation of data

6.2 The basic design philosophy of executive information systems is that they should:

(a) Be **easy to use** as an EIS may be consulted during a meeting, for example

(b) Make **data easy to access**, so that it describes the organisation from the executive's point of view, not just in terms of its data flows

(c) Provide **tools for analysis** (including forecasts and trends)

(d) Provide **presentational aids** so that information can be conveyed 'without bothering the executive with too many trivial choices of scale colour and layout'

7 EXPERT SYSTEMS

Key Concept

Expert systems are computer programs which allow users to benefit from expert knowledge, information and advice.

7.1 An expert system is therefore a program for which the **master/reference** file holds a large amount of **specialised data** on, for example, legal, engineering or medical information, or tax matters. The user keys in certain facts and the program uses its information on file to produce a decision about something on which an expert's input would normally be required. Expert systems and precision marketing

7.2 In theory, expert systems are essential to today's goal of **precision marketing** (the mass-customisation model in which the marketing approach is matched precisely to the needs of the individual).

Marketing at Work

In the USA, Sears-Roebuck targets those of its customers who have purchased domestic appliances without any associated maintenance cover, in a drive to sell them general maintenance contracts.

7.3 **Precision marketing is problematic** because of the difficulty of manipulating the vast quantities of data involved. Computers can easily handle the 'paperwork' involved, although they cannot take decisions without being fed sets of rules to govern every possible situation. The inadequacy of such rules helps to explain why customers sometimes receive inappropriate marketing communications, such as the potential *Readers' Digest* subscriber, living on the 10th floor of a tower block, being asked to think about how he'd feel if he opened his front door to find a brand-new car standing outside.

7.4   The expert system is the longer-term solution to this kind of dilemma. With an expert system, the computer can be taught how to make the necessary decisions using **artificial intelligence**. It may even 'learn from experience' in some circumstances.

7.5   Another immediately available option is to develop simpler ways of dealing with the data which will still allow some of the benefits to be realised. There are two main routes.

(a) **Aggregation.** Individuals (or stores) are aggregated with others who share broadly similar performance or behaviour patterns. This is the broad principle on which ACORN (A Classification of Residential Neighbourhoods) already works. The precision is limited, but at least 'individual' approaches are possible at the group level.

(b) **Simple decisions.** Instead of exactly matching the total purchasing profile of consumers, decisions can be made to relate to relatively simple factors, as in the example of the Sears Roebuck maintenance contracts. This approach can be developed incrementally, adding new decisions based upon simple combinations of factors revealed by experience.

Action Programme 2

A decision support system can be described as having the following characteristics.

Objective:	Assist management
Who makes the decision:	Manager
Orientation:	Decision making
Applications:	Functional areas
Database:	Factual

(Beaumont and Sutherland, *Information Resources Management*)

Using the same five criteria, how would you describe the features of an expert system?

---

8   DATABASE INFORMATION

8.1   A management information system or database should provide managers with a useful flow of relevant information which is easy to use and easy to access. As we said earlier, information is an important corporate resource. Managed and used effectively it can provide considerable competitive advantage and so it is a worthwhile investment.

8.2   In theory, a database is simply a coherent structure for the storage and use of data. It involves the centralised storage of information, which provides:

(a) **Common data** for all users to share

(b) Avoidance of **data duplication** in files kept by different users

(c) **Consistency** in the organisation's use of data, and in the accuracy and up-to-dateness of data accessed by different users, because all records are centrally maintained and updated

(d) **Flexibility** in the way in which shared data can be queried, analysed and formatted by individual users for specific purposes, without altering the store of data itself

8.3   Such structure could be fulfilled by a centralised file registry or library, or a self-contained data record like a master index card file. In practice, however, large scale databases are created and stored on **computer systems,** using **database application packages** such as **Microsoft Access.**

Data storage

8.4 Computer database packages allow data to be stored in a coherent structure in one place.

(a) **Data** are the raw components of information: names, dates, item descriptions, prices, colours, addresses and so on.

(b) **Fields** are the labels given to types of data. (The book *Access for Dummies* refers to them as 'places for your data to live'.) A customer database, for example, might include fields such as: title (data = Mr), first name (data = Joseph), last name (data = Bloggs), Company (data = Anon Ltd), Address, Phone Number, Fax Number, Contact Type (data = customer), interests (data = widgets) and so on.

(c) **Records** are the collection of field relevant to one entry. (*Access for Dummies* suggests 'all the homes on one block'.) So all the above data fields for a particular customer (Mr Bloggs) make up one customer record.

(d) **Tables** (or database files) are collections of records that describe similar data ('all the blocks in one neighbourhood'). All the customer records for a particular region or product may be stored in such a file.

(e) **Databases** (catalogues) are collections of all the tables (and other formats which can be created from them) relating to a particular set of information ('A community of neighbourhoods'). So your customer database may include tables for various regions, customers, product customers, customer contacts and so on, plus various reports and queries that you use to access different types of information.

8.5 There are two basic kinds of database.

(a) A **flat file system** lumps all the data into single table databases, like a phone directory where names, addresses, phone numbers and fax numbers are stored in the same file.

(b) A **relational database system** allows greater flexibility and storage efficiency by splitting the data up into a number of tables, which can nevertheless be linked and integrated together. For example, one table may contain customer names and another, customers' payment histories. A linking field such as a customer number would allow you to interrogate all three tables, generate an integrated report on a particular customer's purchases and payments, or a list of customers who had made multiple purchases with a poor payment record and so on.

8.6 **Flat systems** are easy to build and maintain, and are quite adequate for applications such as mailing lists, or membership databases. **Relational systems** integrate a wider range of business functions, for invoicing, accounting, inventory, marketing analysis and so on: they are, however, complicated to develop and use. If your organisation already operates a relational system, learn how to use it. If you are required to set up or build a relational system, get help: use a 'wizard' or template (in the database package) or ask an expert, at least the first time.

8.7 The collection of programs that are written to process data on the file in many different ways is referred to as a **database management system (DBMS). Marketing data** can be analysed using statistical techniques, in models on anything from media mix to new site locations.

8.8 Basic features of database packages allow you to:

(a) **Find particular records,** using any data item you know

(b) **Sort records alphabetically,** numerically or by date, in ascending or descending order

(c) **File records,** so that you 'pull out' and view a selection of records based on specified criteria (all addresses in a certain postcode, for example, or all purchasers of a particular product)

(d) **Interrogate records,** generating the selection of records based on a complex set of criteria, from one or more linked tables. (For example, you might specify that you want all customer records where the field 'City' equals London or Birmingham and where the field 'Product' equals Widget and where the field 'Purchase Date' is between January 2000 and January 2001. The query would generate a table consisting of customers in London and Birmingham who purchased Widgets in 2000.)

(e) **Calculate and count** data entries. (For example if you wanted to find out how many customers had purchased each product, you could run a query that asked the database to group the data by the field 'product' and then count by field 'customer ID' or 'last name': it would count the number of customer ID numbers or names linked to each product. You could also ask to 'sum' or add up all the values in a field: total number of purchases, or total purchase value.)

(f) **Format** selected data for a variety of uses, as reports, forms, mailing labels, charts and diagrams

Action Programme 3

Find out what type(s) of database your organisation (or college) uses, and for what applications. If possible, get access to the database and browse through the index, directory or switchboard to see what databases/catalogues contain what database files or tables, queries, reports and forms, with what fields. If you can't get access to a database at work, try the local library, where you may find that the 'index card' system has been computerised as a database. Or use an Internet search engine or browser to interrogate some on-line databases. This is not really something you can learn from books - have a go!

8.9 Our interest in databases is simply a user interest, because databases can provide valuable information to strategic planners and marketing management.

(a) Computer databases make it easier to collect and store more **data/information**.

(b) Computer software allows the data to be **extracted** from the file and **processed** to provide whatever information management needs.

(c) Developments in information technology allow businesses to have access to the databases of **external organisations**. Reuters, for example, provides an on-line information system about money market interest rates and foreign exchange rates to firms involved in money market and foreign exchange dealings, and to the treasury departments of a large number of companies.

(d) The growing adoption of technology at **point of sale** provides a potentially invaluable source of data to both retailer and manufacturer.

8.10 Other benefits of database systems might include:

(a) Increased **sales and/or market share** (due to enhanced lead follow-up, cross-selling, customer contact)

(b) Increased **customer retention** (through better targeting)

(c) Better use of **resources** (targeting, less duplication of information handling)

(d) Better **decision-making** (from quality management information)

Marketing at Work

CACI is a company which provides market analysis, information systems and other data products to clients. It advertises itself as 'the winning combination of marketing and technology'.

As an illustration of the information available to the marketing manager through today's technology, here is an overview of some of their products.

Paycheck	This provides income data for all 1.6 million individual post codes across the UK. This enables companies to see how mean income distribution varies from area to area.
People UK	This is a mix of geodemographics, life stage and lifestyle data. It is person rather than household specific and is designed for those companies requiring highly targeted campaigns.
InSite	This is a geographic information system (GIS). It is designed to assist with local market planning, customers and product segmentation, direct marketing and service distribution.
Acorn	This stands for A Classification of Residential Neighbourhoods, and has been used to profile residential neighbourhoods by post code since 1976. ACORN classifies people in any trading area or on any customer database into 54 types.
Lifestyles UK	This database offers over 300 lifestyle selections on 44 million consumers in the UK. It helps with cross selling and customer retention strategies.
Monica	This can help a company to identify the age of people on its database by giving the likely age profile of their first names. It uses a combination of census data and real birth registrations.

Database maintenance

8.11 If the customer database is linked to **on-line transaction processing** (for example, via EPOS), purchase data will automatically be updated with each new transaction. However, a typical contacts database will have to be regularly and systematically maintained.

(a) Contacts who become customers should be transferred to the customer database and deleted from the contacts database in order to avoid duplicated mailings.

(b) Any up-dated or altered information should be entered in the database: changes of address or customer status and so on.

(c) Additional information obtained from contacts should be added to the relevant records.

(d) New names and records should periodically be added to the database, and names which have received no response after a certain period of time or number of contacts, deleted.

(e) 'Undeliverable' items are returned to the sender, often marked with reason for non-delivery: no longer at this address, not known at this address and so on. If the mailing list has been bought or rented, any undeliverables should be returned to the owner or broker so they can update their database. If the mailing was based on an in-house list, addresses and names should be checked (common errors include misspelt names, missing lines of the address, wrong Company name and so on) and if no error can be readily identified, the record should be erased.

(f) Requests from customers or members of the public to have their details erased from the database should be honoured.

(g) New fields can be added to the database design as new types of information become available.

Identifying the most profitable customers

8.12 The Italian economist Vilfredo Pareto was the first to observe that in human affairs, 20% of the events result in 80% of the outcomes. This has become known as Pareto's law, or the 80/20 principle. It shows up quite often in marketing. For example, twenty percent of the effort you put into promotion may generate eighty percent of the sales revenue. Whatever the precise proportions, it is true that in general a small number of existing customers are 'heavy users' of a product or service and generate a high proportion of sales revenue, buying perhaps four times as much as a 'light user'.

8.13 A customer database which allows purchase frequency and value per customer to be calculated indicates to the marketer who the potential heavy users are, and therefore where the promotional budget can most profitably be spent.

Identifying buying trends

8.14 By tracking purchases per customer (or customer group) you may be able to identify:

(a) **Loyal repeat customers** (who cost less to retain than new customers cost to find and attract, and who therefore need to be retained

(b) **'Backsliding'** or lost customers, who have reduced or ceased the frequency or volume of their purchases (These may be a useful diagnostic sample for market research into declining sales or failing customer care.)

(c) **Seasonal** or local purchase patterns (heavier consumption of soup in England in winter, for example)

(d) **Demographic purchase patterns**. These may be quite unexpected. Grey Advertising carried out studies in the US in 1987 which showed that many consumers behave inconsistently to the patterns assumed for their socio-economic groups. Lower income consumers buy top-of-the-range products, which they value and save for. Prestige and luxury goods, which marketers promote largely to affluent white-collar consumers, are also purchased by students, secretaries and young families, which have been dubbed 'Ultra Consumers' because they transcend demographic clusters.

(e) Purchase patterns in response to **promotional campaigns** (Increased sales volume or frequency following promotions is an important measurement of their effectiveness.)

Identifying marketing opportunities

8.15 More detailed information (where available) on customer likes and dislikes, complaints, feedback and lifestyle values may offer useful information for:

(a) **Product** improvement

(b) **Customer care** and quality programmes

(c) New **product development,** and

(d) **Decision-making** across the marketing mix: on prices, product specifications, distribution channels, promotional messages and so on

8.16 Simple data fields such as 'contact type' will help to evaluate how contact is made with customers, of what types and in what numbers. Business leads may be generated most often by trade conferences and exhibitions, light users by promotional competitions and incentives, and loyal customers by personal contact through representatives.

8.17 Customers can be investigated using any data field included in the database: How many are on e-mail or the Internet? How many have spouses or children? Essentially, these parameters allow the marketer to **segment** the customer base for marketing purposes.

Marketing at Work

Hallmark salespeople in the US have laptop computers which allow them to analyse the mix of greeting cards sold at individual stores, in order to create a merchandising package tailored to capitalise on the strengths of each store customer.

Compaq Computers has a similar program, with sales people linked by computer to the headquarters' databases providing information on every product and every client. In the first two years of the programme, it reduced its sales force by a third - and doubled its sales volume.

Using database information

8.18 The following is a summary of the main ways in which database information can be used.

(a) **Direct mail** used to:

    (i)   Maintain customer contact between (or instead of) sales calls

    (ii)   Generate leads and 'warmed' prospects for sales calls

    (iii)   Promote and/or sell products and services direct to customers

    (iv)   Distribute product or service information

(b) **Transaction processing.** Databases can be linked to programmes which generate order confirmations, despatch notes, invoices, statements and receipts.

(c) **Marketing research and planning.** The database can be used to send out market surveys, and may itself be investigated to show purchasing patterns and trends.

(d) **Contacts planning.** The database can indicate what customers need to be contacted or given incentives to maintain their level of purchase and commitment. A separate database may similarly be used to track planned and on-going contacts at conferences and trade shows and invitation lists to marketing events.

(e) **Product development and improvement.** Product purchases can be tracked through the product life cycle, and weaknesses and opportunities identified from records of customer feedback, complaints and warranty/guarantee claims.

8.19 According to the survey *The Impact of Computerised Sales and Marketing Systems in the UK*, users consider such systems to support lead handling, telemarketing, direct mail and sales productivity particularly well, and campaign management and marketing analysis less well.

Data security and controls

8.20 Most customers, and consumers in general, are by now aware that when they supply their names and addresses, this information will be used in various ways. Most would accept that the details will be kept on file or in a mailing list, and many would expect to be sent information about goods and services by the same company. They may, however, be irritated to find that their details have been passed on to other companies, or that they are on a list for frequent or wide-ranging promotional information.

8.21 Many direct marketers now state clearly, when inviting customers or respondents to provide name and address details, the use to which the details will be put. It is also common to offer an opt-out from details being re-used or passed on.

8.22 Legislation and regulation exists to protect consumers form misuse of personal details held on computer, unsolicited mail and invasion of privacy.

(a) There are now stringent trading practices and regulations in the direct mail industry, administered by the Direct Mail Services Standards Board (DMSSB) and Mail Order Protection Scheme (for display advertisements in national newspapers that ask for money in advance).

(b) The **Mailing Preference Service** allows customers to state whether they would - and more often, would not - be willing to receive direct mail on a range of specific areas. This is the way to get taken off (or, if you are a Marketing Student, put on mailing lists!)

(c) The **Data Protection Acts 1984 and 1998** provide that data users (organisations or individuals who control the contents of files of personal data and the use of personal data) must register with the Data Protection Registrar. They must limit their use of personal data (defined as any information about an identifiable living individual) to the uses registered.

9 INTERNAL AND EXTERNAL DATABASES   Specimen paper, 6/00, 12/00

9.1 For an **internal database** to be useful to strategic planners or marketing management, it must contain certain items of data about the business itself and also about the environment of the business. We will look at both types of data in the following paragraphs.

Internal data

9.2 Internal data about the business itself can be used in the initial stages of strategic planning as follows.

(a) To carry out a **resource audit**
(b) To assess and plan **resource utilisation**
(c) To **control** the use of resources

9.3 A **resource audit** is a survey of what resources the business has in each of its functions or divisions. There are four groups of resources.

(a) **Physical** resources
(b) **Human** resources
(c) **Systems**
(d) **Intangibles** (for example, company image)

9.4 **Resource utilisation** is concerned with the **efficiency** with which resources are used, and the **effectiveness** of their use in achieving the objectives of the business. It is key information for analysing the strengths and weaknesses of the business as a whole or the effectiveness of a specific department like the marketing function.

(a) Johnson and Scholes define **efficiency** as 'how well the resources have been utilised irrespective of the purpose for which they have been employed'.

(b) They define **effectiveness** as 'whether the resources have been deployed in the best possible way'.

Efficiency and effectiveness are not the same thing. It is possible to be efficient doing things that have little or no value, and it is possible to be effective in getting a job done, but use resources inefficiently in doing so.

9.5 Once a database has been built up which recognises what resources the organisation has at its disposal and how efficiently and effectively they are being used, management can draw on information from the database for **resource control** purposes.

9.6 We first discussed **customer databases** and **database marketing** in Chapter 1. The modern organisation typically uses information technology to store customer data in a series of databases. The most valuable information in a customer-focused organisation is its knowledge of its customers. The customer database has two uses in such an organisation:

(a) **Operational support** (for example, when a telephone banking employee checks that the password given by a caller is correct before giving out details of the account)

(b) **Analytical uses** (the analysis by the same bank of the customers who receive a certain amount into their account each month and so may be targeted with personal loans or other offers)

9.7 With a good database of information, companies undertake **data mining** for information that can be used for marketing purposes. (See the example of Intelligent Miner given later in this chapter). Data mining can identify target customers for appropriate campaigns. The term **on-line analytical processing (OLAP)** is often used now to describe the analysis of huge amounts of data by **data warehouses**, creating a major source of information for marketing decisions.

Key Concepts

Data warehousing involves a centrally stored source of data that has been extracted from various organisational databases and standardised and integrated for use throughout an organisation. Data warehouses contain a wide variety of data that present a coherent picture of business conditions at a single point in time.

Data mining is a class of database applications that look for hidden patterns in a group of data. For example, data mining software can help retail companies find customers with common interests. The term is commonly misused to describe software that presents data in new ways. True data mining software does not just change the presentation, but actually discovers previously unknown relationships among the data.

Marketing at Work

Even organisations in the FMCG field, such as Nestlé, Pedigree Petfoods and Kraft General Foods, are consolidating data that they accumulate about their customers and in the USA, Sears Roebuck uses the computerised database information on its 40 million customers to promote special offers to specific target segments. MCI, the US phone company, has a database of 120 million subscribers.

9.8 The result is something called **mass customisation,** in which a large number of customers can be reached, as in the mass markets of the **industrialised economy,** and simultaneously these customers can be treated **individually,** as in the customised markets of the **pre-industrial** economy. It has been remarked how the traditional values of the 'corner shop' are returning with the resurgence of relationship marketing and customer focus.

Marketing at Work

(a) 'Dialogue marketing is the term for involving the consumer in the route from brand awareness to sale by providing information only in response to requests, and tailoring it to the individual. It is most suitable for buying decisions that are deliberate rather than impulsive – as in business-to-business marketing or large personal purchases – and is on the increase in many countries.

At one level it sounds a straightforward way of moving seamlessly from mass market advertising to clinching a sale with one customer. Along the way it includes making sure the brand is considered by the customer, through marketing that reflects the consumer's concerns, and creating a preference for the brand by providing incentives.

But dialogue marketing is possible only through the use of sophisticated technology both to create a detailed database and then to use it to respond to individual customers.

Advances such as the internet have been important in its development as they offer more varied ways to communicate with potential customers. These new methods, for example clicking on a company's web site, have the benefit of leaving consumers feeling more in control of the exchange of information than conventional forms of contact such as telemarketing, which can seem intrusive.

Allan Steinmetz, director of marketing at Arthur D Little, the consulting firm, says the core requirement for effective dialogue marketing is a good database where the information can be readily "harvested".

"If you try to do this with index cards, it is not going to work," he says. "Consumers have to feel that you are talking to them as individuals – if you're ever addressed as 'Dear customer', forget it."

Sophisticated technology is needed far more than just getting the name right in the initial communication: once someone has asked for information, any response that fails to provide an answer, or which appears mass-produced, will alienate rather than enthuse.

Mr Steinmetz says the two areas where the use of dialogue marketing is most developed are the financial services sector, particularly in promoting products such as credit cards, and the motor industry. In order to open contact, for example, Korean car maker Daewoo once asked people to reveal their worst experiences about dealing with the motor trade, providing the incentive of a car to drive for a year for those sending in the best stories.

Companies in these two sectors have access to detailed information about their customers' lives, and have become adept at using this information in communicating with them. Mr Steinmetz cites American Express, which recently launched a programme linking the rewards to the customers' own spending patterns.

Other areas in which the use of dialogue marketing is developing are healthcare – particularly in the US – and utilities, such as power and water companies. This is most notable in countries where these companies are starting to face competition and so are coming under increasing pressure to make more use of the extensive information they hold."

(b) A major photographic processing house surveys its customer base by self-completed questionnaires, responses being motivated by a free film on receipt of the questionnaire. This is done three times a year. All respondents are asked if they would like to become members of a customer panel. This panel now comprises a customer database of over 6,000 people (who regularly engage in photography) into which the company can dip when required. In addition, the company has generated feedback from some 23,000 'occasional' customers, giving data on lifestyles, customer perceptions of quality, customer requirements, and so forth. The resulting database, which given its size is statistically very powerful, has a cost of under £1 per respondent.

(c) Heinz use a magazine both to put across brand messages and to build up a database of customers.

'The vehicle for these messages about value, product range and new lines is the Heinz "At home" magazine-format mailing which is sent out quarterly to about 4m households. The database, built up from an original 1m names of consumers who had taken part in promotional offers, contains an extraordinary array of individuals' details, derived from questionnaires in "At Home". To continue receiving the magazine, recipients have to fill in the questionnaire; as an extra incentive, Heinz provides a prize draw.

Questions cover which grocery brands are bought, where the shopping is done, who does it and whether they have access to a car. Income, occupation, marital status, children's birthdays, credit card and housing details are all covered. Consumers complete details of the make and age of their car, and tick activities and interests from a list of 59 options including golf, bingo and stocks and shares.

The magazine itself contains product information, recipes .... and, very important, tear-out money-off coupons. Each coupon is personalised with a barcode and the recipient's name, enabling Heinz to tell exactly who has used their coupons for what.

Several versions of the magazine are produced, targeting, for example, families with children and "healthy eating" consumers.'

Financial Times

As well as providing invaluable information about its customers, Heinz claims that market share increases were immediately apparent after the first mailing.

(d)   There are numerous other examples.

(i)   Helena Rubenstein, the cosmetics company, has begun to build a database to promote a closer relationship with users.

(ii)   Unilever is centralising the customer data amassed by its British subsidiaries.

(iii)   Kraft (the food division of America's Philip Morris) have a database of the addresses of 30 million customers who have replied to free sample offers and other promotions.

(iv)   American Express uses its customer database to tailor offers, such as a special sale at Harrods, to small groups of cardholders according to their spending patterns.

(v)   Procter & Gamble uses its database to market Pampers disposable nappies: 'individualised' birthday cards are sent to babies and customers are sent reminder letters to move up to the next nappy size.

(e)   Charities often have extremely comprehensive and effective databases.

'Since recruitment [of donors] was the most expensive and difficult part of the equation, charities with long-term commitment and sufficient finance built databases of supporters, so they did not maintain the continuous search for new donors.

It was soon obvious that some donors gave more generously or more frequently than others. These people were therefore worth mailing more often. Thus, donor-base segmentation was conceived. Donors are split into groups depending on the "recency", "value" and "frequency" of gifts.

This is why database segmentation, relationship marketing and customer (donor) care, the buzzwords in today's direct marketing industry are old friends to many of Britain's household-name charities.'

Marketing Business

Internal databases and information overload

9.9   In most organisations, key data on performance (typically derived from order processing and invoicing) are likely to be available on the internal database. Indeed the performance figures should be available down to individual customers/clients, specific time periods, for each product and product variant, and so on.

9.10   This potentially poses the problem of there being so much information, most of it redundant, that it will effectively be useless as a management tool (**information overload**).

Marketing at Work

A recent IBM study found that in the oil and gas industry, 60% of professional time was spent on clerical activities such as locating, collecting, collating and manipulating information, rather than analysing it.

9.11   Herb Simon in 1951 propounded the characteristic of bounded **rationality** which suggested that when people have too much information to process, they will simply stop processing and go back to applying rules of thumb.

9.12   Writing in the *Financial Times*, David Soberman suggested that there are four basic steps that a company needs to take to ensure that marketing managers have information that is **sufficient, relevant** and **diagnostic** for the decisions that they need to make.

BPP
PUBLISHING

(i)   A company must **clearly define** the responsibilities of each manager in its marketing department. Total company involvement is needed to identify the key questions that must be asked.

(ii)   The marketing department must identify the **kind of information necessary** to help answer the questions. Staff in production, research and development and sales may need to get involved.

(iii)   The **cost** of getting this information must be determined. The cost must be balanced against the benefit of improved decision making.

(iv)   The **benefits** of information for making decisions needs to be evaluated. This can be difficult to quantify, but essentially the marketing department needs to verify that its expenditure on research and analysis is justified.

9.13   Recently, new **market research services** have appeared as a result of the information explosion. We have already seen examples of the products offered by CACI. This is not the only example.

Marketing at Work

Icom Information and Communications based in Canada has become on of the fastest growing database marketing companies. It collects product usage and purchase profiles from more than 20m households, and uses the information to construct a range of data products for marketers. The contents of a mailing can be targeted to the habits of each household. Han Levine, chief executive, says that the company can "create the economies of scale associated with traditional mass marketing while achieving the persuasiveness of one to one selling." Icom has also developed a program that can track brand usage among consumer segments with specific media habits.

9.14   Possible solutions to the problem of information overload include the following.

(a)   **Activity based costing (ABC) analysis.** Information is sorted in terms of, say, the volume (or value) of sales, so that customers are ranked in order of their sales, with the high-volume (and hence most important) customers at the top of the list and the many low-volume customers at the bottom. Pareto's 80:20 rule is likely to be evident and priority attention can be given to this group in a more manageable fashion. We discuss ABC in detail in Chapter 7.

(b)   **Variance analysis.** The performance of products or customers falling outside predetermined range criteria should be highlighted and action taken. The variances are only as good as the criteria, however, and setting the criteria is a major task. We present variance analysis in Chapter 11.

Environmental data

9.15   McNamee lists nine areas of environmental data that ought to be included in a database for strategic and marketing planners. These are as follows.

(a)   **Competitive data**

    (i)   The threat of new entrants

    (ii)   The threat from substitutes

    (iii)   The power of buyers

    (iv)   The power of suppliers

    (v)   The nature and intensity of competition

    (vi)   The strategies or likely strategies of competitors (for example their prices, marketing policies, product quality)

(b) **Economic data**. Details of past growth and predictions of future growth in GDP and disposable income, the pattern of interest rates, predictions of the rate of inflation, unemployment levels and tax rates, developments in international trade and so on

(c) **Political data**. The influence that the government is having on the industry

(d) **Legal data**. The likely implications of recent legislation, legislation likely to be introduced in the future and its implications

(e) **Social data**. Changing habits, attitudes, cultures and educational standards of the population as a whole, and customers in particular

(f) **Technological data**. Technological changes that have occurred or will occur, and the implications that these will have for the organisation

(g) **Geographical data**. Data about individual regions or countries, each of them potentially segments of the market with their own unique characteristics

(h) **Energy suppliers data**. Energy sources, availability and price of sources of supply generally

(i) **Data about stakeholders in the business**. Employees, management and shareholders, the influence of each group, and what each group wants from the organisation

In other words, data which covers the key elements of the general and market environment should be included in a database for strategic and marketing planners.

External databases

9.16 As well as obtaining data from its own internal database system an organisation can obtain it from an **external database** operated by another organisation.

On-line databases

9.17 Most external databases are on-line databases, which are very large computer files of information, supplied by **database providers** and managed by 'host' companies whose business revenue is generated through charges made to **users**. Access to such databases is open to anyone prepared to pay, and who is equipped with a PC plus a modem (to provide a phone link to the database) and communication software. These days there are an increasing number of companies offering free internet access. Most databases can be accessed around the clock.

9.18 Providers of **database information** include the following.

(a) Directory publishers such as Kompass

(b) Market research publishers such as Mintel, Keynote and Front & Sullivan

(c) Producers of statistical data, including the UK government and Eurostat (for EU statistics)

(d) Reuters Business Briefing

(e) FT Profile

9.19 There is an enormous breadth of data available through on-line databases. Comprehensive sources of detailed information include the *On Line Business Sourcebook* from Headland Press and two directories published by ASLIB, *On Line Business and Company Databases* by Helen Parkinson and *On Line Management and Marketing Databases* by Nick Parker. Other possible sources include the following.

BPP PUBLISHING

(a) Statistics, articles and news from the general and trade press

(b) Market research reports

(c) Key statistical data from the Central Statistical Office (for the UK), CENDATA (for the USA) and Eurostat (for the EU)

(d) Material from the foreign press and major trade journals

(e) Data from some of the providers of continuous market research such as BMRB's TGI (Target Group Index)

(f) Company information produced by organisations such as Kompass, Dunn & Bradstreet, Infocheck and Extel

Using external databases

9.20 External databases are becoming increasingly specialised.

Marketing at Work

(a) One example of using external databases is found in the motor car components supply industry. Manufacturers of motor car components supply their products to the car manufacturers, and they need to be able to spot trends in the use of components by car manufacturers throughout the world. A few years ago a number of databases became available for the component suppliers.

(i) PRS, the consultancy group built up a database which can provide a detailed breakdown of the constituent parts of motor vehicles produced worldwide, making it possible for component suppliers to identify trends in their market.

(ii) Another PRS database holds data about new car registrations in Europe for at least the last ten years. This should be of interest to component suppliers who supply replacement parts to the 'aftermarket'.

(iii) A database available from James McArdle and Associates, another consultancy firm, provides data about commercial vehicle production.

'It is possible, as just one example, to ask the database to show, over a five-year rolling period, manufacturers and their country of origin of commercial vehicles defined by the number of axles, vehicle weight, torque or power output, or cubic capacity - or a combination of these.' *Financial Times*

Such databases could be used by component suppliers to take much of the guesswork or number-crunching out of their planning, and to assess the likely future demand both for replacement parts and for original equipment.

(b) Other databases include the world's biggest on how patients react to pharmaceutical drugs, to be run by the Department of Health. Whitehall acquired the database, which covers 4.4 million British patients, after the medical company which compiled it was taken over.

(c) There is even a database of petrol stations. Due to the birth of petrol forecourts as retail outlets in their own right, information systems provider Geo-Marketing Systems Ltd (GMSL) launched a database of 15,000 petrol stations nationwide which contains data on for example, supplier brand and whether the petrol station has a shop or car wash. Users of this database include a major oil company which uses the information to create a competitor database.

9.21 Competition within the **lifestyle database industry** is reaching fever pitch. It is estimated that 60% of the population are now included on some sort of lifestyle database and so there is concern that the other 40% of the population effectively signalled their reluctance to divulge what they regard as private information. With response rates to traditional data collection methods falling, the industry needs to find new ways of reaching consumers.

Marketing at Work

(a)   Recent attempts to find more sophisticated, cost effective data gathering techniques include offering women visiting 4,000 hairdressers bags of free samples in return for filling in questionnaires, and asking one million parents of school children to fill in questionnaires by offering points towards the purchase of school equipment for each completed form.

(b)   During 1996 Bryant & May ran a promotion in which consumers buying multipack boxes of matches sent off wrappers which could be exchanged for a phonecard worth four minutes of free calls.

(c)   Other offers include being entered in free prize draws in return for filling out questionnaires.

Conclusion

9.22   The following extract provides a useful summary to this section.

> '... the attractions of database marketing are immense. Powerful, data-crunching computers known as massively parallel processors, equipped with neural-network software (which searches, like the human brain, for patterns in a mass of data), hold out a vision of marketing nirvana: instead of advertising their products indiscriminately to fuzzy segments of the population, marketers can speak directly to individuals.
>
> In a recent survey of 100 large British businesses by the Manchester Business School, more than half the respondents said that database marketing would be their main promotional tool within five years.
>
> Database tools have so far proved better at helping firms to keep existing customers, rather than winning new ones. That is not to be sniffed at: in highly competitive markets, pushing up the "lifetime value" of the customers you already have is just as useful as bringing in new ones. Building "relationships" with old customers is central to marketing's new gospel.'
>
> *The Economist*

9.23   If David Soberman (Assistant Professor of Marketing at Insead) is to be believed, continued advances should be expected in terms of the types of information products that will be available to marketers. At present, most databases are used in isolation and are rarely linked because of technical difficulties. Linking a database of frequent buyers with a database of mailing addresses would provide a big target marketing opportunity, for example.

10   TECHNOLOGICAL DEVELOPMENTS   Specimen paper, 12/99

Electronic point of sale (EPOS)

10.1   Retailing businesses have been revolutionised by **EPOS systems**. Next time you enter a supermarket or visit the high street stores observe the way in which your purchasing transactions are dealt with. Goods will usually have a barcode on them and that barcode is passed under or over a scanner by the sales assistant. The barcode holds information on stock item identification, price and store location, amongst other things. When your purchase is complete the stock account for the store will be updated, the difference between the selling price and cost price will be recorded to furnish profit on the item and if needs be the item will automatically be replenished by the EPOS system triggering a re-order.

Action Programme 4

What types of marketing and sales information can such systems provide instantly?

Marketing at Work

McDonalds, the US hamburger chain, uses its point of sale data to pinpoint where delays have been occurring, at what time of day and why.

10.2 Using EPOS and EFTPOS (Electronic Funds Transfer at Point of Sale) enables individual transactions and individual purchasers to be tracked, identified and linked. This allows retailers to build up a very detailed picture of the buying habits of individual customers.

10.3 In addition to product data, customer **loyalty cards** or membership cards can be linked to the EPOS system to provide detailed information on customer buying habits. Specific customer data captured includes the following.

(a) Number of **visits** per month
(b) Average **spend** per visit
(c) Customer **basket** analysis

How EPOS data capture can assist marketing decision making

10.4 By providing timely and accurate information, EPOS data capture can be used by management to plan and **control inventory** and **enhance levels of customer service**. It can assist in the following areas of marketing management activity.

(a) **Promotions**

Coupons can be processed electronically to facilitate statistical analysis and linked coupon initiatives (for example a customer surrendering a Coca-Cola coupon will automatically receive a coupon for own-label cola).

'Multi-buy' offers (for example buy three for the price of two) can be programmed into the system to make the appropriate deduction on the till receipt. Offers can be analysed to assess take-up and compared to other multi-buys or in-store promotions to gauge success.

Special offers and discounted prices can be accommodated and initiatives analysed to assess the increase in sales levels.

(b) **Maximising profit**

Data on margin by product, pack size, and so on can be used to make adjustments to the range of lines stocked. Certain products or pack-size options might then be deleted in order to concentrate on higher-margin products/pack sizes.

Monitoring sales of branded versus own-label products will enable managers to make decisions regarding relative shelf space allocation and stocking options so as to maximise return.

Inventory control and analysis will improve marketing decision making in this area. Lower stocking costs will lead to higher profits. Demographic data linked to data on purchases by customer type can be assembled from the use of loyalty cards. This data could be sold on to database/marketing companies to yield a financial return.

(c) **Increasing retail efficiency**

Analysis of sales by time-of-day will enable managers to use staff more efficiently. Deliveries can be timed to coincide with periods when there are fewer customers in the store so that staff are available to fill shelves. Old age pensioners can be encouraged to shop during quiet periods by offering incentives (such as 10% off on Wednesday afternoons).

The influence of store position/type of display can be measured in terms of increased or reduced sales. Analysis of data in this way can 'maximise' utilisation of floor space and give a quantitative measure of display effectiveness.

Analysis of the method of payment can assist decisions regarding number and type of tills required. For example, should a 'cash only' till be made available for processing of 12 items or less?

Reporting efficiency will be increased by the rapid generation of 'Overs and Shorts' reports, exception reports, inventory analysis reports and so on.

(d) **Building customer loyalty**

Loyalty cards, such as the Tesco Clubcard, Safeway's ABC card and Sainsbury's Reward Card, reward loyal customers by issuing money-off vouchers or cashback. The demographic data obtained can be analysed to enable decisions to be taken in respect of individual store trading strategies. Information on travel preferences and distance from store can be used by management to assess the viability of laying on special buses. Direct mailing of cardholders enables specific customers to be targeted with promotional offers.

Geographic information systems (GIS)

10.5 Geographic information systems are technology applications that store, display and manipulate geographically based information. A marketing manager can 'point and click' on a particular area and gain access to a range of information on that region. The supermarket chain Tesco uses it for examining such factors as changes in population and income when deciding on where to open new stores. It could also be used for planning distribution routes.

CD-ROM

10.6 **Compact Disc Read Only Memory** (CD-ROM) drives installed in personal computers allow pictures, sound and text to be accessed. Data compression and transmission techniques make it possible for sound, pictures and text to be transmitted around the globe using phone lines and satellite links. Converging technologies are transforming the way firms, industries, markets and individuals interact.

10.7 Some databases can be bought in CD-ROM form so that, once purchased, the database can be accessed as often as required without incurring additional costs. Databases in CD-ROM media include some of the large directory databases and other statistical sources but because initial charges are substantial, a CD-ROM version only makes sense where there is an identified need for regular and substantial use of the database.

Video conferencing

10.8 This enables managers at a number of remote locations to meet face to face to discuss important issues without the need or cost of travelling.

Action Programme 5

What are the implications of video conferencing for sales and marketing managers?

BPP
PUBLISHING

Television shopping

10.9 Television shopping is in embryonic form, but nevertheless many investors consider that TV shopping presents them with an opportunity to use the medium to sell a variety of products and services. Just as high street retailing developed from street markets, so too might the new technologies provide **convenience shopping** to future generations of customers. This presents new challenges to marketing and sales managers adapting policies, procedures, systems, communications and thinking to the new marketplace in the home. Logistics is perhaps the most important aspect of the **marketing mix** in satisfying the customer in this new environment, since availability and delivery time will be important customer considerations.

Smart cards

10.10 The smart card is a fairly simple concept. The card is unique to the individual customer and is a **substitute for money**. The card will have a credit units logged in its memory and is replenished rather like a bank account. In July 1994 a report in the Financial Times discussed the introduction of smart cards in Hong Kong for use by customers in a range of stores and on the transport systems. The customer carrying these cards would pass by a scanner on entry to the transport system and once again on exit and the charge for the journey would be made by the scanner on exit deducting the appropriate units from the card. People carrying smart cards would not even physically have to offer the card for payment but rather the scanners are able to read the card even if it is located in your pocket or in a bag.

Marketing at Work

The smartcard has been in use in France for several years and the country now boasts around 85% of all smartcards in use. There are several competing approaches to generating electronic cash.

Home banking

10.11 Several major banks have already developed **home banking services** for customers whereby access is gained to your bank 24 hours a day to execute simple transactions. These systems work in utilising communication technology via a modem, telephone link and/or a video/computer terminal link depending on which options you choose and which banking system you connect to. Bank balances, standing orders, direct debits and the issue of cheques are all possible within home banking systems.

10.12 Home banking offers increased levels of **customer service** and presents the banks with an opportunity to provide to customers (for example, insurance, mortgages, loans, brokerage, taxation). This may reduce the necessity to invest in high street retailing branches and to produce the numerous paper communications for offering services to customers. Promotional efforts could be carefully targeted using home banking systems, providing a higher return for a given promotional spend.

10.13 Telephone banking as a whole represents a triumph for those who like to challenge conventional assumptions: there were many who believed that face-to-face contact was the essential factor in bank/customer relationships.

Global technologies and communication networks

10.14 **Global technologies** mean that it is possible to exchange data across geographical areas in a matter of seconds. Speed of transmission opens up vast possibilities for firms wanting to trade globally. The speed of data exchange also poses threats in the shape of corporate fraud which could also be perpetrated in a matter of seconds. Global communication technology has no boundaries.

Multimedia

10.15 Combining telecommunications and computers has enabled the development of a new global industry, **multimedia**.

10.16 BT expects the market for multimedia to increase to £20 billion worldwide by the year 2000. Of that, £13 billion will be for network operation and £7 billion for capital equipment. Multimedia is expected to **transform consumer markets**, first by using video kiosks in major shopping centres and thoroughfares and later by entering the home. Using a combination of phone, television and personal computer, people will be able to (and in some cases can already) access directly everything from groceries to holiday bookings.

Parallel processors

10.17 **Parallel processors** are an innovative type of high-performance computer which use numerous microprocessors to process a number of pieces of information at the same time, rather than one bit at a time as in conventional computers. They are therefore ideal for sifting through massive amounts of data and identifying trends.

Neural networks

10.18 **Neural networks** are computer systems loosely modelled on the workings of the human brain and are useful to the marketer in a number of ways.

(a) They can recognise **complex patterns** within huge amounts of data, thereby allowing them to detect relationships between sales trends and factors such as pricing strategy and advertising expenditure.

(b) They can assist in **sales forecasting**. The soft drinks manufacturer Britvic predicts future sales volumes using its neural networks' analysis of the effect on demand of factors such as employment levels, advertising and the weather.

(c) They can impact upon **direct marketing** by targeting potential customers more carefully.

Marketing at Work

Thomas Cook was able to target its direct mail more carefully after using a neural network to analyse information from questionnaires which provided information about the age and hobbies of holiday makers.

BPP PUBLISHING

The internet, intranets and extranets

> ### Key Concept
>
> The **internet** is the sum of all the separate networks (or stand-alone computers) run by organisations and individuals alike. (It has been described as an **international telephone service** for computers.)
>
> > 'The internet offers efficient, fast and cost effective email, massive information search and retrieval facilities. There is a great deal of financial information available and users can also access publications and news releases issued by the Treasury and other Government departments.
> >
> > To access the internet you require a microcomputer, a modem and the services of an internet provider.
> >
> > One of the main uses of the internet is for the sending and receiving of email. This has become a popular method of communication for companies of all sizes.
> >
> > The main advantage of email is the speed of delivery; messages are delivered within a few seconds and take no longer to travel to Moscow than to Manchester. Messages can be sent to multiple addresses, they can contain images, sound and computer files in addition to the text.'
> >
> > *Certified Accountant*, August 1997

10.19 An **intranet** is a private information system, with only the company's employees or other authorised persons having access to view information. A 'firewall' prevents the rest of the world from gaining access.

> ### Key Concepts
>
> An **intranet** is a network based on TCP/IP protocols (an internet) belonging to an organisation, usually a corporation, accessible only by the organisation's members, employees, or others with authorisation. An intranet's Web sites look and act just like any other Web sites, but the firewall surrounding an intranet fends off unauthorised access. Like the Internet itself, intranets are used to share information. Secure intranets are now the fastest-growing segment of the Internet because they are much less expensive to build and manage than private networks based on proprietary protocols.
>
> This can be used to circulate information around the firm and example may be forthcoming promotions, or details of local events such as the plan for a local motor show, it can also be used to access internal databases on items such as the availability of spare parts or servicing dates and times, this can enable more staff to add value to their information services.
>
> An **extranet** is an intranet that is partially accessible to authorised outsiders. Whereas an intranet resides behind a firewall and is accessible only to people who are members of the same company or organisation, an extranet provides various levels of accessibility to outsiders. You can access an extranet only if you have a valid username and password, and your identity determines which parts of the extranet you can view. Extranets are becoming a very popular means for business partners to exchange information.
>
> This can enable dealers to, in effect, become part of the information system of the supplier. (Ford have long had electronic data interchange links with their business partners). If the dealer has customers who have fleets of cars, they too can become part of the secure web. Banks are a case in point, account holding customers can now access the relevant secure part of the banks' network with the appropriate access codes.

10.20 We look at the **internet** and **e-commerce** further in the next section of this chapter.

Exam Tip

A question on IT and the Internet was set in the June 1997 examination. Having been recently given the important responsibility of investigating marketing possibilities using IT, this question asks you to prepare a report to present to marketing staff in order to make them aware of the range of possibilities. The question also asks you to illustrate your report with appropriate examples.

The best way of approaching this question is to begin with an introduction to the subject of marketing and IT. Your answer should then, ideally, give an overview of the internet (email and the World Wide Web) and then consider the usefulness of the World Wide Web to marketing.

The effect of technological changes on marketing research

10.21 Social changes are making traditional marketing research difficult. Technological advances are also threatening the role of the 'woman with the clipboard'.

(a) Computer-assisted personal interviewing (**Capi**) is becoming more and more popular and already replaces more than 50% of face to face interviews.

(b) Computer-assisted telephone interviewing (**Cati**) is firmly established as an alternative to the written questionnaire formerly used by telephone interviewers.

10.22 Both Capi and Cati allow results to be sent direct to a computer, cutting down on data processing time and improving accuracy.

10.23 In the future, speech recognition will cut out the interviewer from some types of phone interviewing. Computers may even be able to write a report after having analysed data!

Marketing at Work

Supermarkets are increasingly at the forefront of using technology to effect marketing research. Using EPOS, they have millions of items of data at their disposal, and the data is being continuously updated. A new piece of software from IBM, called Intelligent Miner, sits on the supermarket's mainframe computer identifying associations and patterns in customer purchasing habits.

'Intelligent Miner recently discovered that during the early evening rush hour there was a surge in the sales of nappies and packs of beer.

Upon close examination, the supermarket found that it was young married men who were buying the beer and nappies. It seemed that hard-working New Man had been told to buy nappies by his wife and the thought of spending a night in with a screaming infant without a beer or two was too awful to contemplate. Needless to say, the supermarket put the beer stand closer to the nappy rack and the sale of beer increased.

'The average shopper will never see the new generation of so-called data mining software programs like Intelligent Miner', explains Derek Linney, principal consultant at IBM Retail. 'But behind the scenes the programs will be examining their spending habits and suggesting ever more ingenious merchandising schemes and promotional offers to keep customers interested and loyal.

Linney explains how data can be linked to customer loyalty schemes. If, for example, the software discovers that people tend to buy particular combinations of products or foods, information can be sent out when a special offer is planned. Whether you want yet more promotional material through your letterbox is another matter, of course, but they have the technology.' *London Evening Standard* April 1997

Technological progress: the downside

Technophobia and consumer resistance

10.24 The downside to all the excitement and opportunity presented by the new information technology revolution (much of which is still in its infancy) is the **fear and resistance** of

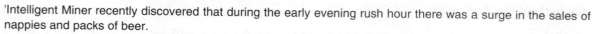

BPP PUBLISHING

technology on the part of many managers and consumers. Remember that, in spite of all this excitement about new technologies, consumers like to shop! It is a social experience; customers like to touch what they buy, they like to see the apples, the tomatoes, the clothes and other items before they purchase.

Security

10.25 This is another aspect which is of concern to many firms and consumers. Think about:

(a) The bad publicity banks attract when their automatic teller machines pay out short or record transactions on your account which belong to someone else's account

(b) Credit card fraud and computer theft

(c) An organisation's database being accessed by a competitor with all the customer tracking information that enables them to target market products and services normally supplied by that organisation

'The trade-off for being able to browse electronic malls, adopt purchaser "smart cards" and programme your own television schedule, is that somewhere someone will be tracing your every purchase and logging it into an enormous database.' *Guardian*

Other disadvantages of technological progress

10.26 The increasing reliance on technology means significant reductions in **face-to-face customer service**. It is already true that some organisations do not employ telephone operators but simply supply a series of computerised digital options.

10.27 Moreover, information technology has generated **job losses** among those whose work has been supplanted, and it has changed the activities of job categories like checkout staff in supermarkets, who now do little more than pass goods over a scanner. It is worth reminding ourselves that human beings are capable of much more!

11   THE INTERNET AND E-COMMERCE   6/00, 12/00

Growth of the Internet

11.1 It is estimated that under 60% of households in the USA will have Internet access by the year 2002. In the UK the comparable figure is 60 per cent. It thus appears likely that **by 2002** there will be at least **15 million UK Internet users**. The UK growth will be fuelled by the following factors.

(a) Many UK households have **multiple Internet access points,** for use by both parents and children.

(b) Changes in the **telecoms market** are likely to mean that Internet connection time will become much cheaper, if not free.

(c) **Digital TV** and **web-enabled mobile phones** permit the Internet to be accessed without the necessity for purchase of a personal computer. Digital TV promises to widen the market place for the Internet to encompass those in the lower socio-economic categories who are more likely to subscribe to cable or satellite TV companies.

(d) For many, the preferred Internet interface is not the PC but the **PDA** (Personal Digital Assistant).

(e) **Internet kiosks** are becoming increasingly common in shopping centres and other locations.

Exam Tip

The June 2000 exam included a question in which *either* a telephone helpline *or* an online support service was to be set up. While telephone ownership is now very widespread, you must show your awareness of the issue that only a proportion of customers are currently likely to have internet access and wish to use it.

Marketing at Work

How not to do it?

'In the same way that live television presenters have learnt to avoid working with children and animals, Britain's mobile phone companies are fast growing wary of bringing together journalist and technology in the same room. Recent demonstrations of the latest mobile phones services have led to a series of embarrassing mishaps that threaten to undermine public confidence in the industry as a whole'.

'When Vodafone, the UK's largest network, unveiled its strategy to improve the Wap experience using technology knows as GPRS (General Packet Radio Service) it chose to show a pre-recorded video of someone using one of the phones rather than risk demonstrating one live'.

Financial Times, 16 May 2001

The same article listed the 'Top of the Mobile Flops':

(1) **WAP** *(launched 1999)*: The first internet-enabled handsets using technology known as Wireless Application Protocol were launched last year but disappointed millions with slow connection rates and poor reliability.

(2) **GPRS** *(launched 2000 – 2001)*: Attempts to speed up WAP phones with a network standard known as General Packet Radio Service floundered when BT unveiled handsets that didn't work when demonstrated to journalists.

(3) **Videophones** *(developed 1999 – 2001)*: Orange tried yet another standard for its ill-fated videophone but has so far failed to launch it commercially despite two years of trials.

(4) **Third generation** *(developed 2001 – 2005)*: Hopes that next generation technology would prove more robust evaporated after Japanese, Spanish and UK operators warned of serious delays.

(5) **Transatlantic phones** *(developed 1995 – 2001)*: Many consumers would be happy with a phone that simply worked in the US and Europe, but attempts to bridge the incompatible standards remain unreliable and expensive.

11.2 A critical factor in the long-run expansion of the Internet is its **use today by children**, the adult consumers of tomorrow. By 1999, more than three million children under 17 in the UK used the Internet, and increase of 12 per cent over the previous six months - and a staggering 17 per cent of children have made on-line purchases with the aid of their parents' credit cards!

11.3 As access to the Internet accelerates, so does the **provision of websites**, which are currently being created at the rate of 6,500 **every hour**. Of course, many of these websites are not commercial, have no transaction facilities, and are not truly significant from any marketing viewpoint, yet nonetheless the scale of Internet activity continues to grow at a rate which most observers describe as impressive.

Marketing at Work

In many areas, users are proactively switching to the Internet. When Lloyds TSB first developed Internet banking facilities, they were not publicised but customers were seeking it out and joining at the rate of 380 accounts per day. At the same time, customers are not yet ready to abandon the channels they used in the past: even with Internet and telephone banking, many still visit their bank branches regularly.

11.4 At the same time, the Internet is not expanding at the same rate in every area of business. In reality its growth is very context-dependent, with the significant influencing factors being as follows.

(a) **The degree to which the customer can be persuaded to believe that using the Internet will deliver some added-value** - in terms of quickness, simplicity, price, and so on.

(b) **Whether there are 'costs' which the customer has to bear** - not exclusively 'costs' in the financial sense, but also such psychological 'costs' as the loneliness of single-person shopping.

(c) **The market segment to which the individual belongs** - since the Internet is largely the preserve of younger, more affluent, more technologically competent individuals with above-average amounts of disposable income. As Professor Sampler has written: 'Many people confused loyal customers with captive markets and as we have a choice people will begin to realise that maybe they don't have that much personal loyalty. The problem with the demographics of the Internet is that customers tend to be very well educated, with fairly high level incomes, and these are the people time is precious to. To think that they are not going to pursue potentially cheaper and time-saving alternatives is naive.'

(d) **The frequency of supplier/customer contact required.**

(e) **The availability of incentives which might stimulate Internet acceptance** - for example, interest rates on bank accounts which are higher than those available through conventional banks (egg), the absence of charges (Freeserve), the creation of penalties for over-the-counter transactions (Abbey National), and the expectations of important customers (IBM's relationships with its suppliers).

E-commerce

11.5 Many of the current tools for conducting customer research can be expensive and by their nature they are quite disjointed. Research may only be undertaken when a new store is opened, a new product launched or a crisis point reached.

11.6 **Electronic commerce** is the conducting of business 'on-line' via the Internet. It may be business-to-business, business-to-government or business-to-consumer. It provides an opportunity to listen to customers very efficiently. Online surveys, for example, have a very broad distribution and can be conducted quickly. Websites can record which pages customers look at when they are 'browsing', enabling the seller to know not only what the customer bought, but what he considered buying and what he totally ignored. This information may influence further promotions (sent directly to the customer by e-mail!)

11.7 **On-line newsgroups** serve as meeting places for consumers with similar hobbies and interests. In this way, customers are doing their own segmentation. On-line auctions take place where sellers can often realise higher prices than they would at a conventional sale, because there is such a large number of potential buyers.

11.8   We talk more about the use of the Internet for information purposes in Chapter 13 on market intelligence.

Electronic marketing

11.9   Besides its usefulness for tapping into worldwide information resources, businesses are also using the internet to **provide information** about their own products and services.

11.10   For **customers** the internet offers a **speedy and impersonal** way of getting to know about the services that a company provides. For **businesses** the advantage is that it is much cheaper to provide the information in electronic form than it would be to employ staff to man the phones on an enquiry desk, and much more effective than sending out mailshots that people would either throw away or forget about when they needed the information.

11.11   Companies will need to develop new means of promoting their wares through the medium of the internet, as opposed to shop displays or motionless graphics. Websites can provide **sound and movement** and allow **interactivity**, so that the user can, say, drill down to obtain further information or watch a video of the product in use, or get a virtual reality experience of the product or service.

11.12   For many companies this will involve a rethink of current promotional activity.

Marketing at Work

Peapod.com is an online supermarket and one of the more sophisticated recorders and users of customers' personal data and shopping behaviour. With over 100,000 customer in eight US cities, Peapod's website sells groceries that are then delivered to customer's homes, a list of previous purchases (including brand, pack size and quantity purchased) is kept on site, so the customer can make minor changes from week to week, saving time and effort.

Peapod creates a database on each shopper that includes their purchase history (what they bought), their online shopping patterns (how they bought it), questionnaires about their attitudes and opinions, and demographic data (which Peapod buys from third parties). A shopper's profile is used by the company to determine which advertisement to show and which promotions/electronic coupons to offer. Demographically identical neighbours are thus treated differently based on what Peapod has learned about their preferences and behaviours over time.

Shoppers seem to like this high-tech relationship marketing, with 94% of all sales coming from repeat customer. Manufacturers like it too, the more detailed customer information enables them to target promotions at customers who have repeatedly bought another brand, thereby not giving away promotion dollars to loyal customers.

Collecting information about customers

11.13   People who visit a site for the first time may be asked to **register**, which typically involves giving a name, physical address and post code, e-mail address and possibly other demographic data such as age, job title and income bracket.

11.14   When customers come to the site on subsequent occasions they either type their (self-chosen) user name and password or more usually now, if they are using the same computer, the website recognises then using a **cookie**, which is a small and **harmless** file containing a string of characters that uniquely identify the computer.

11.15   From the initial registration details the user record may show, say, that the user is male, aged 20 to 30 and British. The **website can respond** to this by displaying products or services likely to appeal to this segment of the market.

Clickstreams

11.16 As users visit the site more often, more is learned about them by **recording what they click on,** since this shows what they are really interested in. On a news site for instance, one user may always go to the sports pages first, while another looks at the TV listings. In a retail sense this is akin to physically following somebody about the store recording everything they do (including products they pick up and put back) and everything they look at, whether or not they buy it.

What is different about the Internet and e-commerce?

11.17 There are several features of the Internet which make it radically different from what has gone before.

(a) It **challenges traditional business models** – because, for example, it enables product/services suppliers to interact directly with their customers, instead of using intermediaries (like retail shops, travel agents, insurance brokers, and conventional banks).

(b) Although the Internet is global in its operation, its benefits are not confined to large (or global) organisations. **Small companies** can move instantly into a global marketplace, either on their own initiative or as part of what is known as a 'consumer portal'. For example, Ede and Ravenscroft is a small outfitting and tailoring business in Oxford: it could easily promote itself within a much larger 'portal' called OxfordHighStreet.com, embracing a comprehensive mixture of other Oxford retailers.

(c) It offers a **new economics of information** – because, with the Internet, much information is free. Those with Internet access can view all the world's major newspapers and periodicals without charge.

(d) It supplies an almost incredible **level of speed** – virtually instant access to organisations, plus the capacity to complete purchasing transactions within seconds. This velocity, of course, is only truly impressive if it is accompanies by equal speed so far as the delivery of tangible goods is concerned.

(e) It is created **new networks of communication** – between organisations and their customers (either individually or collectively), between customers themselves (through mutual support groups), and between organisations and their suppliers.

(f) It stimulates the appearance of **new intermediaries** and the disappearance of some existing ones. Businesses are finding that they can cut out the middle man, with electronic banking, insurance, publishing and printing as primary examples.

(g) It has led to **new business partnerships** through which small enterprises can gain access to customers on a scale which would have been viewed as impossible a few years ago. For example, a university can put its reading list on a website and students wishing to purchase any given book can click directly through to an on-line bookseller such as Amozon.com. The university gets a commission; the on-line bookseller gets increased business; the student gets a discount. Everyone benefits except the traditional bookshop.

(h) It promotes **transparent pricing** – because potential customers can readily compare prices not only from suppliers within any given country, but also from suppliers across the world.

(i) It facilitates **personalised attention** – even if such attention is actually administered through impersonal, yet highly sophisticated IT systems and customer database manipulation.

(j) It provides sophisticated **market segmentation** opportunities. Approaching such segments may be one of the few ways in which e-commerce entrepreneurs can create **competitive advantage**. As **Management Today** (March 2000) puts it:

'The starting point must be a neat niche, a funky few, a global tribe. You need to understand your particular tribe better then anyone else. The tribe is the basic unit of business ... The good news is that there are lots of tribes out there – and some are enormous. It's just a question of identifying them understanding them and meeting their needs better than anyone else.'

(k) A new phenomenon is emerging called **dynamic pricing**. Companies can rapidly change their prices to reflect the current state of demand and supply.

Some disadvantage of e-commerce   12/00

11.18 E-commerce involves an unusual mix of people – security people, web technology people, designers, marketing people – and this can be very difficult to manage. The e-business needs supervision by expensive specialists.

11.19 At present, in spite of phenomenal growth the market is still fuzzy and undefined. Many e-businesses have **yet to make a profit**, the best-known example being **Amazon.com** the Internet book-seller.

Lack of trust

11.20 Above all, however, the problem with e-commerce is one of **trust**. In most cultures, consumers grant their trust to business parties that have a close **physical presence**: buildings, facilities and people to talk to. On the Internet these familiar elements are simply not there. The seller's reputation, the size of his business, and the level of customisation in product and service also engender trust.

11.21 Internet merchants need to elicit customer trust when the level of **perceived risk** in a transaction is high. However, research has found that once consumers have build up trust in an Internet merchant such concerns are reduced.

11.22 Internet merchants need to address issues such as fear of **invasion of privacy** and abuse of customer information (about their **credit cards**, for example) because they stop people even considering the Internet as a shopping medium.

Cryptography, keys and signatures

11.23 The parties involved in e-commerce need to have confidence that any communication sent gets to its target destination **unchanged**, and **without being read by anyone else**.

11.24 One way of providing electronic signatures is to make use of what is known as **public key** (as asymmetric) **cryptography**. Public key cryptography uses **two keys – public and private**. The **private key** is only known to its owner, and is used to scramble the data contained in a file.

11.25 The 'scrambled' data is the electronic signature, and can be checked against the original file using the **public key** of the person who signed it. This confirms that it could only have been signed by someone with access to the private key. If a third party altered the message, the fact that they had done so would be easily detectable.

11.26 There is more detailed coverage of e-commerce in The BPP Study Text for Paper 5: *The Marketing/Customer Interface*.

12 STRATEGIES FOR INFORMATION TECHNOLOGY

12.1 We will begin this section by looking at the reasons why a strategy is needed for information technology in particular. Michael J Earl (in *Management Strategies for Information Technology*) lists reasons justifying the case for a strategy for information systems and information technology.

(a) IT involves **high costs**.

(b) IT is **critical to the success** of many organisations. (In the financial sector many products or services are inconceivable without IT.)

(c) IT is now used as part of **commercial strategy** as a weapon in the battle for competitive advantage. For example when the US airline system was deregulated the growth of computerised seat-reservation systems was encouraged. SABRE, when used by American Airlines, always displayed American Airlines figures preferentially.

(d) IT affects **all levels of management**.

(e) IT may mean a revolution in the way information is **created and presented**. We have already looked at executive information systems, decision support systems and expert systems.

(f) IT involves many **stakeholders**. Parties interested in an organisation's use of IT are as follows.

  (i) Other business users (for example for common standards for **electronic data interchange**)

  (ii) **Governments** (such as telecommunications regulation)

  (iii) IT manufacturers, who must often **pioneer** the development and use of the technology

  (iv) **Consumers** (for example in testing IT-based products such as teleshopping)

  (v) **Employees and internal users** (as IT affects work practices)

(g) Ignoring the **technology-based choices** in IT is rather like ignoring interest rates when you are borrowing money. A simple example from the financial services industry, which is more dependent than many on information systems, is provided by two UK building societies. A proposed merger between them was abandoned because of incompatibility between their computer systems.

(h) IT requires **effective management**.

12.2 In February 1995, *Marketing Business* included an article, supposedly written in the year 2009, about the fall and rise of marketing.

'Without doubt, the rise of techno-marketing was the touch paper to the business revolution. Information technology affected the whole scope of marketing. Multimedia and interactive systems started to replace sales staff as the optimum method of imparting detailed product information. The information super-highway enabled effective direct E-mail promotions. Most dramatic of all, the new generation of super computers enabled the development of customer information systems (CIS). So crucial have these systems become that a recent management consultant report showed that companies that had started to invest in CIS by the late nineties have significantly outperformed those which had not. The CIS enabled marketers to cut through the confusion wrought by market fragmentation and saturation by collecting detailed information on the evolving market segments. Information equity, the knowledge base that is deployed to create a sustainable competitive advantage, has become a critical corporate asset.

Using the CIS, CIMCO [the multi-billion ECU manufacturing corporation] championed the use of advanced predictive behaviour modelling using the latest artificial intelligence systems. By imitating the brain's neural structure, the new computing methodology could quickly sift through mountains of data and recognise the inherent patterns. The data from shopping scanning systems and frequent-shopper programmes, for instance, could be analysed to show trends.

Today, CIMCO knows its customer base so intimately that it can send direct mail and E-mail promotions to its customers with individually tailored offerings. For instance, customers are engaged at regular intervals after purchasing a car. Not only will the communication express thanks to Mr Smith for buying a particular car two years previously, it will also include a unique brochure for him showing only those cars in the latest range that will be of interest. It will show the right type of cars containing the right mix of standard features in the right price bracket. Whether the brochure is electronic or produced using high quality computer printers, the knowledge centre can tailor and produce an offering to exactly meet customer needs. This increases the chances of customer loyalty and repeat business. Technology and customer information systems support creativity everywhere in the CIMCO organisation. In an information economy, knowledge is money.'

12.3 **Information availability** will shape the way marketing will develop into the new millennium. Philip Kotler recently wrote down his view of some of the major developments in the evolving market place. Imagine that it is the year 2005 as he writes.

(i) Virtually all products are now available without going to a shop, thanks to e-commerce. **Business-to-business purchasing** has increased even more quickly in this medium.

(ii) Shop based retailers find traffic highly diminished. Many retailers are building entertainment into their shops.

(iii) Most companies have built proprietary customer databases including rich detail on individual preferences and requirements. They have begun 'mass customisation' and can even offer **on-line product modification**.

(iv) Companies are doing a better job of customer retention by finding new ways to **exceed expectations**. They are applying newer and more effective data mining techniques.

(v) Accounting departments now generate useful information on customer profitability, product profitability and channel profitability.

2005 is not so far away, and all of these developments are under way for a lot of companies.

BPP PUBLISHING

Chapter Roundup

- Technology and information systems can be a powerful source for competitive advantage, such as in the creation of new relationships with customers.

- Much of the information generated these days and used for marketing purposes is non-linear, which means that it does not lend itself to simplistic two-dimensional analysis.

- Data, information and intelligence are three different things.

- A management information system operates at four levels: transaction processing, traditional MIS, decision support and executive information.

- A database is a comprehensive structured collection of data (usually computerised) which can be accessed by different users for different applications.

- Databases allow for the collection and storage of data, and also for interaction with data through various forms of interrogation, calculation and report formatting.

- Customer and contact details can be sourced from a wide range of transactions, feedback mechanisms, promotional mechanisms and secondary sources. All data must be periodically reviewed for accuracy and up to dateness.

- Customer databases can be interrogated to identify profitable customers, buying patterns and trends, marketing opportunities and market segments.

- Database information can be used for a variety of sales support, direct marketing, promotion management and marketing analysis applications. However, certain constraints on data use exist to protect the individual, including the Data Protection Act and Mailing Preference Service.

- Expert systems represent another leap in information-system effectiveness, at least potentially, because of their ability to promote precision marketing.

- A good internal database will enable the organisation to carry out a resource audit, to plan resource utilisation, and to control the use of resources.

- External databases are large computer files of information, supplied by 'providers' and managed by 'host' companies.

- Future technological developments (some of which are already with us) include EPOS facilities, CD-ROM processing, videoconferencing, TV shopping, smart cards, home banking, global communications and multimedia activities.

- E-commerce is the conducting of business 'on-line' and can be a valuable source of information on customers, as well as a way of accessing them directly.

- The downsides of technological progress embrace technophobia, security and fraud fears, job losses and job deskilling.

- Organisations need to produce a coherent and explicit IT strategy which takes account of business needs, current systems and future opportunities.

Quick Quiz

1   In what ways can new information technology yield competitive advantage to an organisation? (Answer this question in relation to your own organisation or some other organisation with which you may be familiar.) (See Section 2)
2   What are the levels normally associated with a management information system? (3.4)
3   What is a transactions processing system? (4.1)
4   What does a decision support system do? (5.1- 5.3)
5   What are the basic design philosophies associated with an EIS? (6.2)
6   What are the two relatively simple ways of dealing with data which, when expert systems are not available, approach precision marketing goals? (7.5)
7   What is a 'database'? (8.2)
8   What are (a) fields, (b) records, and (c) tables in database terminology? (8.4)
9   What is a relational database system? (8.5)
10 How does the '80/20 rule' apply to marketing and how can the database be used to capitalise on it? (8.12, 8.13)
11 What are some of the main uses of database information? (8.18)
12 What are two uses for a customer database? (9.6)
13 What are some of the types of environmental data which should be included within an internal database? (9.15)
14 What is the relationship between 'users', 'providers' and 'hosts' in the operation of external databases? (9.17)
15 What is EPOS? (10.1)
16 What are smart cards? (10.10)
17 What are the advantages of home banking? (10.12)
18 What are parallel processors and neural networks? (10.17, 10.18)
19 What are the possible downsides associated with technological progress, so far as (a) customers and (b) marketers themselves, are concerned? (10.24 - 10.27)
20 How is lack of trust a problem in e-commerce? (11.20 - 11.22)
21 Why is it important for organisations to have an IT strategy? (12.1)

Action Programme Review

1   (a)   *Speed.* Computers can process data much more quickly than a human. This means that a computer has a much higher productivity and so ought to be cheaper for large volumes of data processing than doing the work manually. As computer costs have fallen, this cost advantage of the computer has become more accentuated. The ability to process data more quickly means that a computer can produce more timely information, when information is needed as soon as possible.

    (b)   *Accuracy.* Computers are generally accurate, whereas human beings are prone to error. The errors in computer data processing are normally human errors (errors in the input of data) although there can be software errors (errors in the programs) and hardware errors (faults or breakdowns in the equipment itself).

    (c)   *Volume and complexity.* As businesses grow and become more complex, the data processing requirements increase in volume and complexity too. More managers need greater amounts of information. More transactions have to be processed. The volume of DP work is often beyond the capability of even the largest clerical workforce to do manually.

    (d)   *Human judgement.* Although a computer can handle data in greater volumes, and do more complex processing, the 'manual' or 'human' method of data processing is more suitable when human judgement is involved in the work. When human judgement is involved in making a decision, computer-processed information can help the decision maker but the final part of processing (making and communicating the decision) remains a human aspect of data processing.

2   The objective of an expert system is to replace management. The decision is actually made by the computer. The orientation of an expert system is towards the transfer of experience. They are used in specific problems. The database in an expert system is procedural as well as factual.

3   Just do it!

4   Here are some ideas.

   (a)   Sales by item (stock code)
   (b)   Sales by department
   (c)   Sales by store
   (d)   Sales by in-store area location
   (e)   Fast moving stock items
   (f)   Slow moving stock items (items to delete)
   (g)   Hourly or daily sales
   (h)   Sales by customer
   (i)   Sales by staff or till location
   (j)   Overs and shorts reports
   (k)   Inventory analysis
   (l)   Analysis of exception reporting
   (m)   Profitability/contribution by item
   (n)   Transaction type: cash, credit card, switch card, cheque and so on

5   Factors to consider include the need to be more careful about body language, preferences (or otherwise) for international travel among managers, time differences, impact on levels of informal interaction, team-building and group dynamics.

Now try illustrative question 3 at the end of the Study Text

Part C
Forecasting information

4 Forecasting Information for Marketers

Chapter Topic List	Syllabus Reference
1 Introduction	-
2 Types of forecast	3.0, 3.1, 3.5
3 Sales forecasting	3.0, 3.1
4 Qualitative techniques of forecasting	3.0, 3.2, 3.3
5 Quantitative techniques of forecasting	3.0, 3.4
6 Forecasting using a demand function	3.0, 3.4
7 Sensitivity analysis and forecasting	3.0, 3.4
8 Accurate forecasts	3.0
9 The consequences of incorrect forecasting	3.0

Learning Outcomes

Upon completion of this chapter you will be able to demonstrate your understanding of the importance of forecasting information in a range of marketing contexts. You will know about the range of forecasting methods and tools that are available, such as:

- Decision trees
- Critical path analysis
- Sales forecasts

You will also begin to appreciate the importance of accuracy in forecasting.

Key Concepts

- Qualitative forecasting techniques
- Decision tree
- Network analysis
- Time series analysis

Examples of Marketing at Work

- Headlight Vision
- Tesco

BPP PUBLISHING

1 INTRODUCTION

1.1 We saw in Chapter 1 that an organisation prepares both market forecasts and sales forecasts. Market forecasts are part of marketing research, a topic which we will be looking at in Section E of this Study Text. Sales forecasts are the subject of this chapter.

1.2 We will begin by examining the three basic types of forecast: short, medium and long term. We will then move on to looking at the various techniques for forecasting sales and will end the chapter by considering the consequences of incorrect forecasting.

1.3 In Chapter 5 we will start our study of the information for marketing and sales provided by financial analysis and tools.

2 TYPES OF FORECAST   6/01

2.1 **Forecasts** are for specific time periods which may be classified as **long-term**, **medium-term** or **short-term**. In business, long-term is usually taken to mean three to five years or more; medium-term is between one and two years; short-term is monthly and quarterly. These **planning horizons** will determine the type of forecasting approach.

Long-term forecasts

2.2 Long-term forecasts help to determine the **strategic direction** of the organisation. Forecasts can be contrasted with budgets in that budgets (as we shall see in Chapter 11) provide operational detail on a department by department basis which will (hopefully) lead to the organisation's goals being achieved and activities controlled. Budgets are a **control mechanism**. Forecasts try to give a picture of the future.

2.3 Forecasts are used when putting the complete budget together. While there are no firm rules for building budgets, it is widely accepted that the driver for budget decision making will be the **sales forecast**. If there is any inaccuracy in this forecast there will be inaccuracies in all other aspects of the corporate budget. Forecasts are essential in order to plan resources.

2.4 Long-term forecasting needs to take account of and consider the effect on the organisation of macro-environmental **PEST factors**.

(a) Changes in the **political arena** (change of government or government policies)

(b) Changes in **social attitudes** towards products (for example, 'green' or 'health' attitudes)

(c) Changes in **economic structure** or spending power in certain groups owing to changes in the tax system or in employment patterns

(d) Changes in **technology** and its impact upon the organisation

This **macro-environmental** focus for long-term forecasting is important to provide a picture of what the organisation's **operating environment** is going to be like at some future time. The main focus will be to provide information about existing and new product demand, customers, suppliers, substitute products, competition, technological impacts and the workforce.

2.5 Long-term forecasts will help both short-term and long-term planning. For example, if the organisation forecasts certain changes in its markets in five years' time, such as a decline in demand for a certain product owing to legislation and consumer preference changes, then it can plan immediately by developing new products for new markets or by developing new markets for its existing products.

2.6 Long-term forecasting is a continuous process. **Communication technologies** have not only enabled firms to adapt to rapidly changing markets but have also raised expectations of customers in terms of speed. **Computer technology** has helped organisations to update their plans more frequently.

Medium-term forecasts

2.7 This is a bridge between the short and long term, for time horizons of between one and two years. **Forecast sales** are the most important determinant in the budgetary planning process for firms operating in a competitive environment, since once a figure for sales turnover is established costs and operating expenses may be realistically predicted.

Short-term forecasts

2.8 Forecasts in the short term are focused on the **micro environment**. Organisations need to predict the near future to estimate capacity needs. The **marketing department** may be able to provide forecast demand data based upon seasonal trends or current promotional activities. The **sales team** may be able to provide forecast demand data based upon actual orders obtained and the likelihood of further orders. These forecasts are essential in planning and scheduling production within a factory or staff resources to provide a service.

2.9 Short-term forecasts are also a means of **controlling the activities** of the organisation. For example, if the sales team forecast demand to be lower than that originally expected for the time of the year, they are actually providing an early warning upon which management can act. Adjustments to capacity loadings, schedules, forecast cash flows, promotional activities and tactical marketing may all result.

Rolling forecasts

6/00

2.10 A rolling forecast is one that ensures a 12 month forecast is always available by adding the lastest information from the last (say) calendar quarter, as the oldest equivalent period drops off the end of the budget frame.

2.11 The **advantage** of this is that it ensures that marketing managers are:

(i) Constantly striving to take account of the latest information

(ii) Constantly rewewing plans

(iii) Comparing performance with more realistic plans because the plans take account of timely information

2.12 The **disadvantages** of such constant reviews are as follows.

(i) The plans may assume a more short-term view due to the constantly changing information.

(ii) Short-term 'spikes' in the data frame.

(iii) Staff may be less inclined to pay so much attention to the actual results as they know the annual plans will change over that period.

Example: rolling forecast

2.13 With the advent of free internet access, companies such as BT, NTL and Freeserve changed their sales and profit forecasts to take account of the change in the consumer demand for these products after the Government put pressure on the internet companies to offer free internet access to all. These changes resulted in the companies quickly changing their pricing structure and promotional activities, yet it is unlikely that this would have been foreseeable 13 months beforehand.

3 SALES FORECASTING
Specimen Paper, 12/99

3.1 One of the main purposes of forecasting is to predict the **market demand** for particular goods and services supplied by the organisation. This assumes that one is easily able to identify a particular market for the goods or services supplied. This is not always the case, particularly in growing or newly established markets. Imagine estimating the market demand for video recorders in 1970, or for fax machines or personal computers in 1980, or for mobile telephones in 1985. The establishment, development and nature of the market demand has changed substantially.

3.2 Kotler (1994) defines market demand as follows.

> 'Market demand for a product is the total volume that would be bought by a defined customer group in a defined geographical area in a defined time period in a defined marketing environment under a defined marketing program.'

3.3 There are a number of terms which need defining before we go any further.

(a) **Market forecast** is a forecast of expected market demand.

(b) A market forecast gives the expected market demand; it does not predict the maximum market demand. Maximum market demand is a function of **market potential**.

(c) **Company (or sales) forecast** is the expected level of sales for the company based on a chosen marketing plan and an assumed marketing environment (*Kotler*, 1994). This is the share of the market demand the company expects to realise. The forecast must be based on certain assumptions about the marketing environment in which the firm will operate during the forecast time frame.

(d) **Sales budgets** are usually based on company forecasts for sales but may be adjusted to take a prudent view of the expected volume and value of sales. The sales budget is then used to budget for all costs during the period. Capital expenditure, purchasing, production and other revenue expenses may be based upon the sales budget, as will cash flow decisions.

Sales forecasts

3.4 The **sales forecast** concentrates on what the actual sales will be at a certain level of marketing effort; the **sales potential** assesses possible sales at various levels of marketing activity based on certain environmental conditions.

Who does them?

3.5 Generally sales forecasts are carried out by the marketing department and can involve the opinions of the sales force where applicable (this is a form of **qualitative** or **judgmental forecasting**). In some companies, however, sales forecasting is the responsibility of the accountants. This is ill-advised as generally all they can do is to look at the historical sales data and project any trends forward. The accountants are unlikely to have a feel for the more subtle changes in the market place, where a product is within its **life-cycle** and what **marketing activity** is planned; marketing and sales personnel should clearly be aware of these.

3.6 Sales forecasts can be for the short, medium or long term, the time chosen depending on the purpose and use of the forecast, the stability of the market and the organisations' objectives and resources.

Medium-term sales forecasts

3.7 Medium-term sales forecasts have an important role to play in helping to achieve **corporate-level financial objectives,** for example to achieve an overall profit level of 15% or to achieve a return on capital of 20%. To be able to set such objectives and to enable reasonable judgement of whether further investment is required, if a larger work force needs to be employed or whether negotiations need to be made with suppliers or customers regarding discounts, accurate sales forecasts of the company's products and services are needed.

3.8 Once the sales or marketing manager has set down medium-term forecasts in terms of quantity of each product likely to be sold, these can be translated into **targets** for the sales force and the **sales budget** for the forthcoming year (the total revenue expected from the forecast sales).

3.9 The sales budget can then be broken down into budgets for the sales/marketing department, production and administration. The sales budget therefore shows the company how much it can expect to **earn** and the other budgets show how much it will be necessary to **spend** on making those sales possible.

Short- and long-term sales forecasts

3.10 Short-term and long-term forecasts also have a role to play in helping the company achieve its corporate-level financial objectives. The former usually assist production planning and maintenance of adequate stock levels. Under-stocking can lead to customers moving to the competition, while over-stocking can have a detrimental effect on cash flow. Long-term forecasting is important when looking at capital investment plans, whether to build a new factory for example. If the wrong decision is made because of inadequate sales forecasts, the financial position of the company may be adversely affected.

Action Programme 1

List as many factors as you can which you think need to be considered when forecasting sales.

Methods of sales forecasting

3.11 Management can use a number of **forecasting methods,** often combining them to reduce the level of uncertainty by means of **corroboration** of estimates.

(a) Sales personnel can be asked to provide **estimates**.

(b) **Market research** can be used (especially if an organisation is considering introducing a new product or service).

BPP PUBLISHING

(c) **Mathematical models** can be employed. Models are programmed so that, after changing one or more factors, repetitive simulations can be run which permit managers to review the results that would be obtained in various circumstances.

(d) **Annual contracts**, under which major customers set out in advance monthly ranges of possible sales, can be reviewed.

3.12 These methods can be divided into qualitative and quantitative techniques.

4 QUALITATIVE TECHNIQUES OF FORECASTING

> ### Key Concept
>
> **Qualitative forecasting techniques**, which are also known as **subjective** or **judgmental** techniques, are used when hard data is scarce. The techniques involve the use of human judgement, flair and experience to turn qualitative information into quantitative information.

4.1 Although qualitative techniques can be used for short-, medium- and long-term forecasting, they become increasingly important as the time scale of the forecast increases, because past data becomes less and less representative of what will happen in the future.

Expert opinion

6/00

4.2 These techniques involve the selection of key knowledgeable people or industry players who are interviewed and asked to assign probabilities to possible future outcomes. The experts might include people such as dealers, distributors, suppliers, marketing consultants and trade associations. A practical application of this method would be the Delphi Method, in which each expert from a panel of experts gives an independent opinion, the teams opinions are collated and a consensus view is derived. The experts then continue to comment on the consensus until most of them agree.

Example: Expert opinion

4.3 An example of the process of using expert opinion is the Lockheed Aircraft Corporation (USA) whose executives posed as different major customers and evaluated Lockheed's offer in relation to competitors' offers. They then predicted each customer's brand choice and used this information to evaluate Lockheed's likely performance in the marketplace.

Delphi method

4.4 The Delphi method is the most refined version of expert opinion. It is a technique which can be used if there is little historical data on which to base a forecast or if results are unstable and/or uncertain. A **group of experts** are asked individually to provide their views on what will happen in the future.

(a) To begin with, each expert gives an **independent opinion**.

(b) The opinions of each expert are collated. 'Extreme' views are discarded, and a draft **'consensus'** view is formulated.

(c) The draft 'consensus' is circulated to the experts for their **further comments**, and depending on how they respond, the 'consensus' might be amended.

(d) The process will continue until a forecast for the future has been prepared which has the acceptance of all or most of the panel of experts.

(e) When there is some uncertainty among the experts, **probability weightings** might be given to different possible future 'scenarios' or events.

Executive judgement

4.5 This method of forecasting is based on the **intuition** of one or more executives. The approach is very unscientific but it has the advantages of being quick and inexpensive and it can work well if demand for the product is relatively stable and the executive in question has years of appropriate experience. Intuition is swayed heavily by recent experience, however, and so the forecast may be overly **optimistic** or **pessimistic**.

Marketing research

4.6 We will be looking at **marketing research** in detail in Section E of this Study Text. Marketing research methods include opinion surveys, analyses of market data, and questionnaires designed to gauge the reaction of the market to a product, a price and so on (all qualitative forecasting techniques). Marketing research is often very accurate in the short term but longer-term forecasts based on surveys may not be accurate because people's attitudes and opinions change.

Historical analogy

4.7 When past data is not available, data on **similar products** can be analysed to establish the life cycle and expected sales of a new product. Obviously care is needed in using analogies which relate to different products in different time periods but such techniques can be useful in forming a broad impression for the medium to long term.

Cross-impact analysis   6/00

4.8 **Key trends** are identified as those having high importance or high probability of occurring. The question is then asked 'If event A occurs, what will the impact be upon other trends?' The results are used to build sets of domino chains with one event triggering other events. In other words, cross-impacts are taken into account.

Multiple scenarios

4.9 Researchers build pictures of **alternative futures**, each one of which is internally consistent and has a certain probability of occurring. The major purpose of building alternative futures in this way is to stimulate management into thinking about and planning for **contingencies**.

Decision/hazard forecasting

4.10 Researchers identify **major events** taking place in the environment which could impact upon the organisation. Each event is rated for its convergence with several major trends taking place in society and for its appeal to major publics in society. The higher the event's convergence and appeal, the higher the probability of it taking place. The critical events identified in this way are then researched further.

Decision trees

Key Concept

Decision tree. A means of interpreting probability questions which require a logical approach to ensure that all possible choices and outcomes of a decision tree are taken into consideration. A tree diagram is drawn in which all the possible choices that can be made are shown as branches on the tree and all the possible outcomes of each choice are shown as subsidiary branches on the tree.

Exam Tip

Decision trees were examined in December 1996. Your firm has to make a choice regarding marketing research, and the question requires you to use the information given in order to draw a decision tree outlining the possible options, to calculate the possible outcomes for each option identified, and then to give a commentary on any additional factors/further information.

Use a sharp pencil and a ruler when drawing decision trees, and label each outcome point and decision point clearly. When calculating the possible outcomes, make sure that you lay out your workings neatly and conclude what you consider to be the most appropriate course of action.

4.11 **Tree structures** may help qualitative methods of forecasting by plotting decision points using a branching technique. The main value of the technique is that it attempts to consider all the possible choices and all the possible outcomes of each choice.

Constructing a decision tree

4.12 There are two stages in preparing a decision tree.

(a) **Drawing the tree** itself to show all the choices and outcomes
(b) **Putting in values** to allow quantitative forecasts

4.13 Every decision tree starts from a **decision point** with the decision choices that are currently being considered. It is conventional to draw decision trees from left to right.

(a) It helps to identify the decision point, and any subsequent decision points in the tree, with a symbol. Here, we shall use a square.

(b) There should be a branch for each choice.

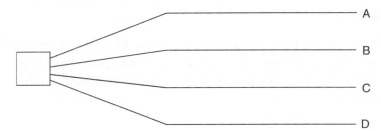

The square is the decision point, and A, B, C and D represent four **alternatives** from which a choice must be made (such as manufacture from scratch, buy in components and assemble, sub-contract production or buy in packaged product).

4.14 If the outcome from any choice is certain, the branch of the decision tree for that alternative is complete.

4.15 If, on the other hand, the outcome of a particular choice is **uncertain**, the **various possible outcomes** must be shown. We show this on a decision tree by inserting an outcome point on the branch of the tree. Each possible outcome is then shown as a **subsidiary branch**, coming out from the outcome point. We can assign probabilities to each outcome based on what we expect to happen. The total of the probabilities, expressed in decimals, will be 1.

4.16 To distinguish decision points from outcome points, a circle will be used as the symbol for an outcome point.

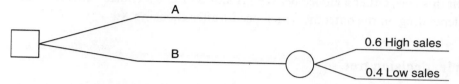

In the example above, there are two choices facing the decision-maker, A and B. The outcome if A is chosen is known with certainty, but if B is chosen, there are two possible outcomes, high sales (60% probability) or low sales (40% probability).

Example: several possible outcomes

4.17 A company can choose to launch a new product XYZ or not. If the product is launched, expected sales and expected unit costs might be as follows.

	Sales			*Unit costs*	
Units	Probability		£		Probability
10,000	80%		6		70%
15,000	20%		8		30%

The decision tree will be drawn as follows.

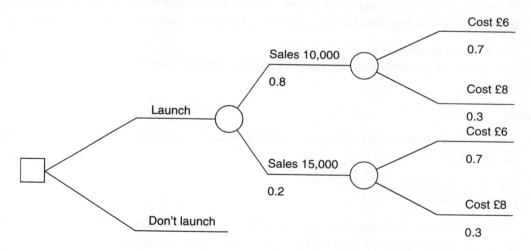

4.18 Sometimes, a decision taken now will lead to other decisions to be taken in the future. When this situation arises, the decision tree can be drawn as a two-stage tree, as follows.

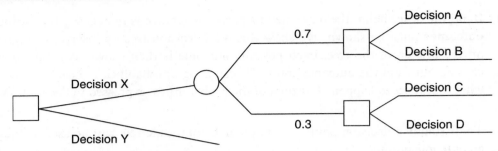

In this tree, either a choice between A and B or else a choice between C and D will be made, depending on the outcome which occurs after choosing X.

Example: decision tree

4.19 Beethoven Ltd has a new wonder product, the vylin, of which it expects great things. At the moment the company has two courses of action open to it, to test market the product or abandon it.

If the company test markets it, the cost will be £100,000 and the market response could be positive or negative with probabilities of 60% and 40%.

If the response is positive the company could either abandon the product or market it full scale.

If it markets the vylin full scale, the outcome might be low, medium or high demand, and the respective net gains would be (200), 200 or 1,000 in units of £1,000 (the result could range from a net loss of £200,000 to a gain of £1,000,000). These outcomes have probabilities of 20%, 50% and 30% respectively.

If the result of the test marketing is negative and the company goes ahead and markets the product, estimated losses would be £600,000.

If, at any point, the company abandons the product, there would be a net gain of £50,000 from the sale of scrap. All the financial values have been discounted to the present.

(a) Draw a decision tree
(b) Include figures for cost, loss or profit on the appropriate branches of the tree

Answer

4.20 The starting point for the tree is to establish what decision has to be made now. What are the options?

(a) To test market
(b) To abandon

The outcome of the 'abandon' option is known with certainty. There are two possible outcomes of the option to test market, positive response and negative response.

Depending on the outcome of the test marketing, another decision will then be made, to abandon the product or to go ahead.

4.21 This is the decision tree.

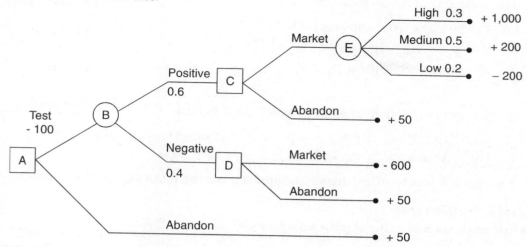

Evaluating the decision with a decision tree

4.22 The expected value of each decision option can be evaluated, using the decision tree to help by keeping the logic properly sorted out.

4.23 We start on the right hand side of the tree and work back towards the left hand side and the current decision under consideration. This is sometimes known as the 'rollback' technique.

4.24 Working from right to left, we calculate the expected value (EV) of revenue, cost, contribution or profit at each outcome point on the tree.

4.25 In the above example, the right-hand-most outcome point is point E, and the expected value is as follows (multiplying profit by the likelihood of it occurring).

	Profit £'000	*Probability*	*EV* £'000
High	1,000	0.3	300
Medium	200	0.5	100
Low	(200)	0.2	(40)
		EV	360

This is the EV of the decision to market the product if the test shows a positive response. It may help you to write the EV on the decision tree itself, at the appropriate outcome point (point E).

4.26 (a) At decision point C, the choice is as follows.

   (i)   Market, EV = + 360
   (ii) Abandon, value = + 50

   The choice would be to market the product, and so the EV at decision point C is +360.

   (b) At decision point D, the choice is as follows.

   (i)   Market, value = – 600
   (ii) Abandon, value = +50

   The choice would be to abandon, and so the EV at decision point D is +50.

The second stage decisions have therefore been made. If the original decision is to test market, the company will market the product if the test shows positive customer response, and will abandon the product if the test results are negative.

4.27 The evaluation of the decision tree is completed as follows.

    (a) Calculate the EV at outcome point B.

$$
\begin{aligned}
&0.6 \times 360 &&\text{(EV at C)} \\
+\ &0.4 \times\ \ 50 &&\text{(EV at D)} \\
=\ &216\ +\ 20 = 236.
\end{aligned}
$$

    (b) Compare the options at point A, which are as follows.

       (i)   Test: EV = EV at B minus test marketing cost = 236 – 100 = 136

       (ii)   Abandon: Value = 50

The choice would be to test market the product, because it has a higher EV of profit.

Network analysis and critical path analysis

4.28 **Network analysis** is a diagrammatic technique for planning and controlling large projects, such as the creation of a national advertising campaign.

Key Concept

The aim of **network analysis** is that the project is completed in the minimum time. It pinpoints the 'critical' parts of the project which, if delayed, would delay the completion of the project as a whole.

4.29 When a project involves carrying out a large number of different tasks, the project planner and controller has to decide three things.

    (a) What tasks must be **done first** before others can be started

    (b) What tasks could **be done at the same time**

    (c) What tasks must be **done 'now'** and completed on schedule if the completion date for the entire project isn't to slip

Drawing a network diagram

4.30 A project is **analysed into its separate tasks or activities** and the sequence of activities is presented in the form of a network diagram. The 'flow' of activities in the diagram should be from left to right.

4.31 An activity within a network is represented by an **arrowed line,** running between one 'event' and another 'event'. An event is simply the start and/or completion of an activity, which is represented on the network diagram by a **circle**.

4.32 Let us suppose that in a certain point of sale design project there are two activities A (commissioning the design) and B (rolling it out to stores). (This is obviously a gross simplification but it will help to illustrate the principles involved). Activity B cannot be started until activity A is completed. This will be represented as follows.

Event	Activity	Event	Activity	Event
(1)	A	(2)	B	(3)

Events are usually numbered, just to identify them. In this example, event 1 is the start of commissioning the designs, event 2 is the completion of the design stage and the beginning of rolling out to stores, and event 3 is the completion of the rolling out.

4.33 Let us now suppose that another marketing project includes three activities, C (listing various promotions options), D (evaluating those options) and E (undergoing market research on those options). Neither activity D nor E can start until activity C is completed, but D and E could be done simultaneously if required. This would be represented as follows.

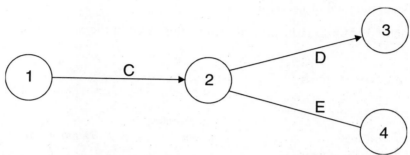

In this diagram, event 2 represents the point when activity C is completed and also the point when activities D and E can start, so the diagram clearly shows that D and E must follow C.

4.34 A third possibility is that an activity cannot start until two or more activities have been completed. If activity H cannot start until activities G and F are both complete, then we would represent the situation like this.

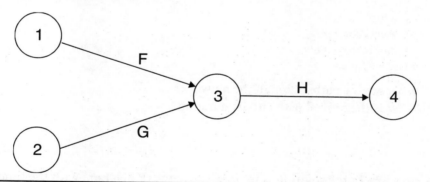

Action Programme

Draw a network diagram for the activities listed below.

Activity	Preceding activity
A	-
B, C & D	A
E & F	B
G	E
H	F
I	G & H
J	C
K	D
L	I, J & K

The critical path

4.35 Any network can be analysed into a number of different **paths** or routes. A path is simply a sequence of activities which can take you from the start to the end of the network.

4.36 The time needed to complete each individual activity in a project must be estimated. This time is shown on the network above or below the line representing the activity. The duration of the whole project will be fixed by the time taken to complete the longest path through the network. This path is called the **critical path** and activities on it are known as critical activities. The path is critical because if any of the activities on it take longer than estimated, the total project time will increase.

The method of finding the critical path is illustrated in the example below.

Example: the critical path

4.37

Activity		*Immediately preceding activity*	*Duration (weeks)*
A –	choose the store to be promoted via TV ad	-	2
B –	choose the ad agency	-	3
C –	brief the store team	A	2
D –	brief marketing director	B	1
E –	design the campaign	B	5
F –	produce TV ad	B	6
G –	produce presentation for senior management	C, D	2
H –	launch TV ad	F	1

(a) What are the paths through the network?
(b) What is the critical path and its duration?

Answer

4.38 The first step in the solution is to draw the network diagram, with the time for each activity shown.

A network should have just one start node and one completion node.

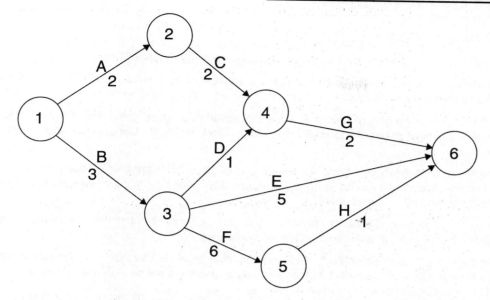

4.39 We could list the paths through the network and their overall completion times as follows.

Path	Duration (weeks)	
A C G	(2 + 2 + 2) =	6
B D G	(3 + 1 + 2) =	6
B E	(3 + 5) =	8
B F H	(3 + 6 + 1) =	10

The critical path is the longest, BFH, with a duration of 10 weeks. This is the minimum time needed to complete the project. If any of the activities on this path were to slip, the whole project would be delayed.

Sales forecast composite

4.40 The sales force is asked to produced forecasts for their territory or area for each of the products/services they sell. Clearly the sales force is close to its customers, but will not necessarily be aware of macro-economic factors which may affect overall sales or those of a particular region. There might also be problems with this method as, even though salespeople are thought to be optimists, they may err on the pessimistic side to be sure of achieving targets.

The advantages and disadvantages of qualitative techniques

4.41 The **advantages** are that many different people are involved. In some cases the sales force will be asked to produce estimates for their territories/areas, and an overall view will be built up from this. Experts from the field and from within the organisation may be brought together or alternatively approached using a questionnaire to find out their view of the future (Delphi method). As many of these people are very close to the market place, this is a good way of getting accurate, up-to-date information about customers' needs and wants. Also, involving the sales force can mean better acceptance of targets.

4.42 One of the **disadvantages** is that often these people will not be **objective**. Customers may overestimate their future requirements. Representatives may be over optimistic of their ability to sell a new product or in the situation where commission payments are linked to achievement of targets, they may put in a pessimistic view. People may also be unaware of the global picture and may not take economic factors into account.

Marketing at Work

The following extracts are from an article which appeared in the *Financial Times.*

'Forecasting tomorrow's consumer trends today is an imprecise science - all too often qualitative research is out of date before the ink is dry.

Now a joint venture between Simons Palmer, the advertising agency, and The Insight Track, the research company, is aiming to help companies spot factors likely to affect business six, nine, or even 18 months ahead.

The new venture, called Headlight Vision, will use a group of "visioneers". These opinion-formers will be drawn from around the world and will include City analysts, fashion designers, magazine editors, psychologists and even philosophers.

Each client will be offered a tailored panel of 10 or 12 visioneers. The panel members will be paid a fee and told about the subjects under discussion two weeks in advance.

During the two weeks of preparation, visioneers will be expected to use their own contacts in order to forecast factors likely to affect businesses. Interviews with panel members will be individual, rather than in a group, and the visioneers can be revisited as often as required.

Nike is the first company to sign up for Headlight Vision. Clare Dobbie, UK head of communications, says youth brands in particular are likely to benefit from the approach.

Simons Palmer believes the method would have allowed, for example, the vogue for all things Irish, or the snowboarding fad, to have been forecast earlier by marketing departments.'

5   QUANTITATIVE TECHNIQUES OF FORECASTING

5.1   **Quantitative** forecasting techniques (which are also known as **objective** techniques) are based on a **statistical analysis** of **past data** on the item to be forecast and can usually be applied using a computer. Whatever the technique used, the underlying assumption is that past data will provide some guidance as to what will happen in the future. There are circumstances, however, when there is no past data available, such as when a **new product** is launched. In such circumstances qualitative techniques are required.

5.2   Whatever the length of time covered by the data, quantitative forecasts should be treated with caution. Conditions can and do change quickly. Judgement, experience and a wide knowledge of the market place play a vital role in establishing a reliable forecast.

Time series analysis (or trend analysis)   **6/00**

Key Concept

Time series analysis uses statistical analysis on past data which has been arranged in a **time series** **(past data recorded over time)**, such as sales of product X quarter by quarter.

5.3   It is a simple technique but a number of factors should be borne in mind.

(a)   The **representativeness** of past data

(b)   The **appropriateness** of the method over the longer term when internal and external factors reduce the representativeness of past data

(c)   The **suitability** of the method in **unstable conditions**

5.4   The main idea behind time series analysis, often called **trend analysis,** is the identification of the trend (underlying long-term movement in the values of the data) and its separation from **seasonal variations** (short-term fluctuations due to different circumstances at different times of the year and so on) and random or irregular variations.

(a) **Inspection**

The trend line can be drawn by 'eye' on a graph in such a way that it appears to lie evenly between the recorded points (**a line of best fit**). Forecasts can then be read off an extrapolated trend line.

(b) **Linear regression analysis by the least squares method**

This is a statistical technique to calculate the 'line of best fit'. This method makes the assumption that the trend line, whether up or down, is a straight line with the notation $y = a + bx$. The technique is then used in combination with moving average analysis (see below) to forecast future values. The assumption that the trend line can be **extrapolated into the future**, which is not necessarily a good one, must be made.

(c) **Moving averages**

This method attempts to **remove seasonal or cyclical variations** by a process of averaging. One method of forecasting using the resulting trend line is simply to 'guess' what future movements in the trend line might be, based on movements in the past. This is a common-sense rule-of-thumb approach.

Past data should only be extrapolated if conditions are expected to be the same in the future. The further the extrapolation into the future, the less reliable the results.

Example: Trend analysis

5.5 Mixed salad sold at supermarkets sells consistently throughout the year but at summer, barbecue season sales increase and during the winter sales decrease. The salad growers will need to calculate the annual trend as well as knowing the seasonal fluctuations.

Action Programme 3

In an exam you might be given information about seasonal variations and expected to calculate the trend and work out the average growth rate. Try this example.

The sales of product P are subject to a seasonal pattern as follows.

Quarter 1	Quarter 2	Quarter 3	Quarter 4
− 10%	− 20%	+ 30%	0%

Actual sales (in £'000) for 1999 and 2000 were as follows.

	1999			2000			
Q1	Q2	Q3	Q4	Q1	Q2	Q3	Q4
200	185	325	240	220	200	350	270

Required

Calculate the trend and the average quarter-on-quarter growth rate and use this to forecast sales for 2001.

Causal techniques

5.6 Causal techniques are so-called because they seek to establish a relationship of cause and effect between variables such as economic growth, private/public investment in a particular industry and unemployment levels or the ageing population and demand for a product or service. A study of demographic changes should help a manufacturer producing products for the elderly. Projections of the future birth rate should assist suppliers of toys.

95

5.7 One causal technique is **simulation**. This uses a process of trial and error to establish a relationship between variables. There may be numerous possible outcomes and these can be taken into account by a computer.

5.8 Causal techniques can be very complex and, although not used frequently in companies, are used by forecasting specialists who advise industries and governments.

Longer-term forecasting

5.9 The techniques covered above tend to be used for short- to medium-term forecasting. Longer-term forecasting is usually less detailed and is normally concerned with forecasting the main trends on a year by year basis.

The advantages and disadvantages of quantitative techniques

5.10 One of the principal **advantages** is that computers can be used and different assumptions can therefore be made and the results viewed quickly and easily

5.11 One of the major **disadvantages** is that, due to many marketers' reluctance to get involved with numbers, accountants often produce the forecasts. The latter are probably not very close to the market place. There is also an in-built assumption that the future will look like the past and that trends will continue, which may not be the case.

5.11 Where longer-term forecasts are required, a view of factors which influence demand such as economic growth, the birth rate, interest rates, and so on must be taken into account. As the government itself revises actual figures of economic growth over a five year period, **predictions of future activity** are difficult to make accurately.

6 FORECASTING USING A DEMAND FUNCTION

6.1 A **demand function** is simply an expression which shows how sales demand for a product is dependent on several factors.

(a) **Controllable variables** or strategic variables, including the following

   (i) The product's **price** (including size of discounts, credit allowed and so on)

   (ii) The amount spent on **advertising and sales promotion**

   (iii) The amount spent on **direct selling** by a sales force

   (iv) The **design or quality** of the product

   (v) The **distribution** of the product (number and geographical extent of sales outlets and so on)

(b) **Uncontrollable variables**

   (i) **Consumer variables.** These are variables which are dependent on decisions by consumers, or the circumstances of consumers. They include the following.

      (1) Their **income**

      (2) Their **tastes,** preferences and attitudes

      (3) Their **expectations** about future price changes, which will affect their decisions about whether to buy now or later

   (ii) **Competitor variables.** These are variables which are dependent on decisions and actions by other firms, particularly competitors. They include the following.

(1) The **price** of other goods which are either substitutes or complements

(2) **Advertising** of these goods by other firms

(3) The **quality and design** of these goods

(iii) **Other variables**. These are variables which are dependent on other factors, such as decisions by other organisations (such as the government) or factors which are outside the control of anyone (such as weather conditions, or the total size of the population).

7 SENSITIVITY ANALYSIS AND FORECASTING

7.1 Any sales forecast will be dependent on a number of key variables such as price, the number of potential and existing customers in the particular target group and their disposable incomes. If any of these key variables were to change once the forecast had been completed, it would need to be revised to take account of the effect of the changes. Marketing and sales managers must anticipate the effects of such changes when preparing forecasts by asking **what if** questions.

7.2 **Sensitivity analysis** is a modelling procedure whereby changes are made to estimates of the variables in the plan so as to establish if any of them will critically affect the outcome. For example, how sensitive would a particular budget be to changes in the level of forecast sales? To answer the question you would need to analyse the costs and expenditures in the budget to see which of the costs will be affected by the change in sales volumes and estimate by how much.

8 ACCURATE FORECASTS

8.1 As forecast information improves and knowledge is gained about the probability of future events, it becomes less risky to make a decision. Forecast information is at its maximum use when the information about the future is **perfect**. In reality of course there is no such thing as **perfect information** since futures are always uncertain. The forecaster is always dealing with **imperfect information** about possible futures, so accurate forecasts are difficult.

8.2 Forecasts are rarely fully correct and it is true to say that they are frequently inadequate to predict sales revenue accurately. Some methods are more appropriate in certain circumstances. It is important to understand the limitations of forecasts and to have realistic expectations so that they are used effectively in the decision-making process.

Factors adversely affecting accuracy

8.3 Demand for the product or service is unlikely to be constant and even if the market itself is very traditional and fairly static, the economic situation will be volatile.

(a) **Political and economic changes** will create uncertainty. For example changes in interest rates, exchange rates or inflation can mean that future sales are difficult to forecast.

(b) **Environmental changes** can also cause forecasting problems. For example, the opening of the Channel Tunnel has had a considerable impact on ferry companies' markets; the effect of E-coli and BSE scares on meat product sales have been catastrophic.

(c) **Technological changes** may mean that the past is not a reliable indication of likely future events. For example, the availability of faster machinery may make it difficult to use current output levels as the basis for forecasting future production output. Without accurate output forecasts, sales are difficult to forecast.

(d) **Technological advances** can also change the nature of production. The advent of advanced manufacturing technology is changing the cost structure of many firms. Direct labour costs are reducing in significance and fixed manufacturing costs are increasing. Pricing structures may therefore vary considerably and hence sales volumes could be difficult to forecast.

(e) **Social changes** such as alterations in design, taste and fashion and changes in the social acceptability of different products can cause difficulties in forecasting future sales levels.

(f) Activity by the **competition** (promotions, pricing decisions, introduction of a new product and so on) may affect the company and are difficult to forecast.

Improving the accuracy of forecasts

8.4 The consequences of inaccurate forecasts are considered in the next section but we look here at how forecasts can be made as accurate as possible.

(a) Good, up-to-date internal **data and marketing intelligence** are needed.

(b) **Sales statistics** should be available in a suitable format.

(c) All the **factors** affecting sales should be understood by the people involved in the forecasting process. In some organisations this will be accountants but ideally sales and marketing managers and possibly sales representatives should be involved as they are closer to the market.

(d) **Appropriate methods** of forecasting should be used, whether quantitative or qualitative or a mixture of the two.

(e) Any **assumptions** made (such as the rate of inflation, exchange rates, rate of adoption of a product, increase in a competitor's promotional activity and so on) should be clearly stated so that if any of them change markedly, adjustments can easily be made.

(f) **Forecasts should be reviewed regularly** and should take into account any new information.

(g) An organisation's own **marketing strategy** must be taken into account. Increased advertising, sales promotions or a new price list must be considered when making forecasts.

(h) Research has shown that accuracy increases with the number of different methods used and it is worth **combining** quantitative methods (essentially extrapolations of past sales levels) with qualitative methods (based more on judgement and gut feeling).

9 THE CONSEQUENCES OF INCORRECT FORECASTING

9.1 It is important to remember that forecasts are only **estimates** and it is very difficult to be accurate. In being optimistic and overstating the forecasts, several problems can arise.

(a) High forecasts will form the basis for **high targets** or budgets for the sales force. This can be demoralising as salespeople like to achieve and may be relying on bonuses that are linked to that achievement.

(b) If the company is quoted on the Stock Exchange, the effect on the City of **overstating the forecast** and having to issue a profits warning may lead to a loss of confidence that could affect the share price.

(c) **Sales forecasts** feed into production budgets. Over optimistic forecasts can lead to excess stocks sitting around in the warehouse. Not only does this tie up capital, it also increases the likelihood of damage and waste.

(d) **Relationships** with suppliers of materials could be disrupted and damaged if forecast levels are not met.

9.2 However, although there are obvious problems with **overstating** the expected level of sales, **under-statement** can lead to problems as well. Actual demand will then be greater than supply.

Action Programme 4

What do you think are the consequences of understating the expected level of sales?

Marketing at Work

'Tesco will be forewarned this year if a glut of tomatoes looms after a particular hot spell.

The supermarket chain has unveiled a computer program that forecasts cropping patterns, warning the company and its growers about the prospects for a particular crop.

The program - developed in conjunction with Reading University - measures all variables affecting a crop such as weather and soil conditions. It compares this with historical information and uses it to predict the outlook for a crop six weeks ahead.

"Crop flushes can be anticipated and short-term promotions arranged to mop up surpluses without wholesale prices crashing dramatically," said Mr Andrew Grant, Tesco's produce trading manager.

"It gives us and our growers the ability to even out the rollercoaster of the market and manage supply better," he said.

Financial Times

Exam Tip

Forecasting can be examined in a number of ways, for example:

- Comparing different forecasting techniques (6/2000)

- A descriptive question about factors to take into account when forecasting (macro and micro) (6/2001)

- As part of a mini-case, where forecasting is treated as part of financial planning. In 6/2001 you had to produce a forecast profit figure (including taking revenue and costs into account).

BPP
PUBLISHING

Chapter Roundup

- Forecasts can be short, medium or long term.

- 'Market demand for a product is the total volume that would be bought by a defined customer group in a defined geographical area in a defined time period in a defined marketing environment under a defined marketing program.'

- A sales forecast is the share of the market potential an organisation expects to realise.

- Qualitative techniques of forecasting involve the use of human judgement and experience and include the following.

  - Expert opinion
  - Delphi method
  - Executive judgement
  - Marketing research
  - Historical analogy
  - Cross-impact analysis
  - Multiple scenario
  - Demand/hazard forecasting
  - Decision trees
  - Critical path analysis
  - Sales force composite

- Quantitative techniques of forecasting are based on the statistical analysis of past data and include time series analysis.

- Sensitivity analysis is a modelling procedure whereby changes are made to estimates of variables in the plan to test various outcomes.

- Forecasts should be as accurate as possible so as to avoid the consequences of overstating or understating the level of sales.

Quick Quiz

1   What macro-environmental factors should be taken into account in a long-term forecast? (see para 2.4)

2   What is the time period of medium-term forecasts? (2.7)

3   Distinguish between market forecasts, company (or sales) forecasts and sales budgets. (3.3)

4   How do medium-term sales forecasts play an important role in corporate-level financial objectives? (3.7, 3.8)

5   What is the Delphi method? (4.4)

6   What is executive judgement? (4.5)

7   How can decision trees be used in forecasting? (4.11 - 4.27)

8   What is network analysis? (4.28)

9   What are the three principal methods of identifying a trend in data and separating it from seasonal variations? (5.4)

10   What is simulation? (5.7)

11   What are the three categories of uncontrollable variables? (6.1)

12   What is perfect information? (8.1)

13   How can forecasts be made as accurate as possible? (8.4)

14   What are the consequences of overstating forecast sales? (9.1)

Action Programme Review

1 (a) Past sales patterns
   (b) The economic environment
   (c) Results of market research
   (d) Anticipated advertising during the budget period
   (e) Competition
   (f) Changing consumer tastes
   (g) New technology
   (h) Distribution and quality of sales outlets and personnel
   (i) Pricing policies and discounts offered
   (j) Legislation
   (k) Environmental factors

2

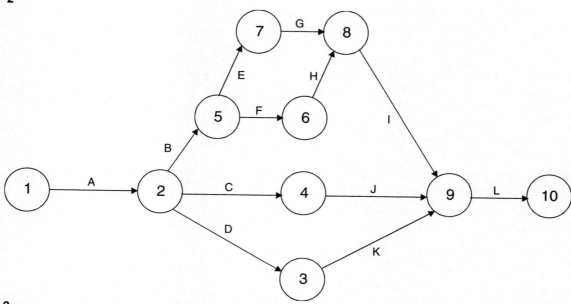

3

	1999				2000			
	Q1	Q2	Q3	Q4	Q1	Q2	Q3	Q4
Sales	200	185	325	240	220	200	350	270
S V	0.9	0.8	1.3	1	0.9	0.8	1.3	1
Trend	222	231	250	240	244	250	269	270

The trend changes from 222 to 270. The growth rate is 270/222 = 1.22 or 22%. Expressed per quarter (there are 8 quarters) this is $1.22^{1/7} = 1.029$ or 2.9% per quarter.

Sales in 2001 may be forecast as follows.

			Trend	*Sales*
Q1	270×1.029	=	277	$\times 0.9 = 250$
Q2	270×1.029^2	=	286	$\times 0.8 = 229$
Q3	270×1.029^3	=	294	$\times 1.3 = 382$
Q4	270×1.029^4	=	303	$\times 1.0 = 303$

Follow this through carefully to make sure you understand it.

4 (a) The competition benefiting from an organisation's lost sales

(b) An increase in the amount of overtime required and therefore higher salary costs

(c) An increase in bonus payments to salespeople who exceed their targets

(d) Problems with unsatisfied customers causing a long-term loss of sales

    (i) Potential (new) customers may never consider the organisation's products again

    (ii) Existing customers may go elsewhere both for the product in question and other products, both in the present and in the future.

Now try illustrative question 4 at the end of the Study Text

Part D
Financial information

5

Financial Information and Marketing

Chapter Topic List	Syllabus Reference
1 Introduction	-
2 Finance and the marketing mix	4.0
3 Financial information	4.0
4 An introduction to financial statements	4.0

Learning Outcomes

This chapter introduces you to the importance of financial information to the marketer and lays the foundation for the detail found in Chapters 6 to 12. It is important that you have a good background understanding before tackling the issues detailed in the syllabus in more depth.

Key Concepts

- Budget
- Financial accounting
- Management accounting
- Cost accounting

- Balance sheet
- Profit and loss account
- Cash flow statements

Examples of Marketing at Work

- Cat food wars

1   INTRODUCTION

1.1   We looked at information in general in Chapter 1. In this chapter we turn our attention to introducing you to financial information in particular, and its relevance to the marketing mix. The wrong financial information can damage the effectiveness of a firm's marketing strategy.

1.2   The chapter begins with a quick review of the marketing mix in a financial context and goes on to explain financial accounting information (in particular the balance sheet and profit and loss account) and cost and management accounting information.

105

1.3 This chapter forms the basis for the later detail on financial information and marketing decisions which you will find in Chapters 6 to 12. The diagram below summarises the structure of this part of the Study Text.

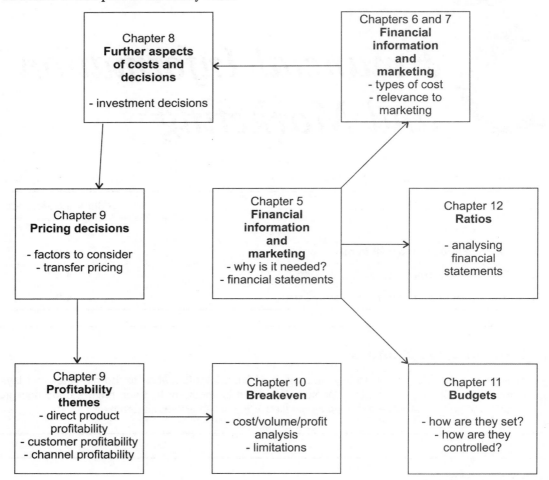

1.4 As detailed in the syllabus, you need to demonstrate an understanding of basic financial concepts and their application to marketing management decisions. This part of the Study Text begins with Chapter 5 and a general introduction to financial information and basic financial statements, and explains its use to the marketer. It then goes on in Chapters 6, 7 and 8 to look closely at cost behaviour, and techniques that are used to allocate costs and make marketing decisions. The pricing decision is given its own space in Chapter 9, alongside considerations of profitability. (Most businesses are run to make a profit!) Chapter 10 looks at 'breaking even' and the analytical techniques that can be employed. Finally, Chapters 11 and 12 discuss budget preparation and control through variance analysis, and the interpretation of financial statements using ratio analysis.

1.5 You will return to financial aspects of marketing in Paper 11 and Paper 12 at Diploma level.

2 FINANCE AND THE MARKETING MIX

2.1 You may not be too keen on the idea of studying 'numbers', but you must appreciate that the aim of marketing is, generally speaking, to **maximise profits**. As you know, there is a wide variety of possible combinations of marketing methods which management can select, and some combinations will earn a greater profit than others. This combination is the **marketing mix**.

2.2 Classical economic theory generally concentrates on **price**, assuming that the lower the price the higher the sales quantity.

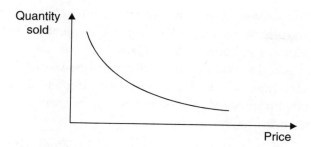

2.3 What about the other elements in the marketing mix - especially those that relate to marketing expenditure? For example:

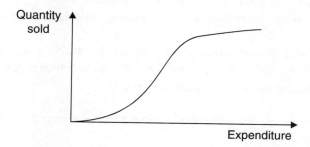

This S-shaped curve indicates that for a certain level of marketing expenditure sales grow at an increasing rate, followed by a drop in the rate of sales growth. No market is infinite.

2.4 It is likely to be the case that elements in the marketing mix act as **substitutes** for each other. For example, a firm can **raise the selling price** of its products if it also **raises product** quality or **advertising expenditure**; equally, a firm can perhaps reduce its sales promotion expenditure if it is successful in achieving larger numbers of sales outlets for its product.

2.5 If a firm has a fixed marketing budget which it can use to offer price discounts or spend on advertising, there will obviously be different combinations of expenditure-sharing which are possible. However, the point remains that the effect on sales volumes will be subject to increasing and then diminishing returns.

2.6 The stages in the formulation of a marketing mix might be as follows.

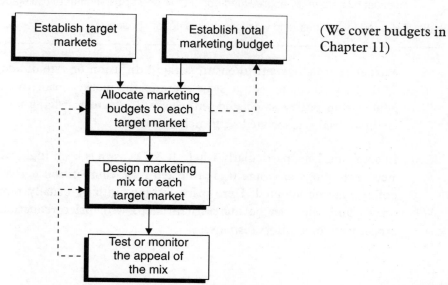

(We cover budgets in Chapter 11)

BPP PUBLISHING

2.7 The ideal marketing mix is one which holds a **proper balance** between each of these elements.

   (a) One marketing activity in the mix will not be fully effective unless proper attention is given to all the other activities. For example, if a company launches a costly promotion campaign which emphasises the superior quality of a product, the outlay on advertising, packaging and personal selling will be wasted if the quality does not live up to customer expectations. Expensive packaging and advertising will be wasted if distribution inefficiency reduces the availability of goods to the consumer, or the price is too high to attract buyers.

   (b) A company might also place too much emphasis on one aspect of the marketing mix, and much of the effort and expenditure might not be justified for the additional returns it obtains. It might for example, place too much importance on price reductions to earn higher profits, when in fact a smaller price reduction and greater spending on sales promotion or product design might have a more profitable effect.

2.8 The ideal mix for a **convenience good** (requiring a heavy emphasis on distribution and sales promotion) will be different from that for an **industrial good** (where price, design, quality and after-sales service are more important).

Marketing at Work

Cat food wars

Pedigree Petfoods owns Whiskas, for many years the UK brand leader in cat food. Spillers' brand Felix was 'a minor player in a mature market: it faced the threat of delisting (by the major supermarkets), which wanted to give greater space to the more profitable cat treat and own label sectors'.

Felix responded to this threat by advertising in 1989. Between 1989 and 1996:

	1989	1996
Brand awareness	29%	57%
Volume share	6.7%	25.4%

By some calculations, £17m of advertising generated £108m increase in sales. Four elements contributed to Felix's success.

(a) *Product.* 'Palatability' - apparently cats liked it.

(b) *Price.* Keen pricing.

(c) *Promotion.* Advertising which emphasised cats' 'rogue-ish' nature and were less 'clinical' and idealised than *Whiskas* ads. 'The rational and idealised approach of competitors' advertising didn't reflect what most cat owners really appreciated about their pets'. Spillers made a little advertising go a long way.

(d) Felix had fewer lines, and was less confusing for shoppers.

2.9 Marketers usually want to ensure a rapid diffusion or rate of adoption for a new product. This allows them to gain a large share of the market prior to competitors responding. A **penetration policy** associated with low introductory pricing and promotions designed to facilitate trial is associated with such a strategy.

2.10 In some markets, particularly where R & D cost has been high, where the product involves 'new' technology or where it is protected from competition perhaps by patent, a **skimming policy** may be adopted. Here price is high initially usually representing very high unit profits and sales can be increased in steps with price reductions, in line with available capacity or competitors responses.

3   FINANCIAL INFORMATION

3.1   Think about the type of information most commonly required by sales and marketing managers. It would probably include the following.

(a) **Sales turnover** figures, which may be totals or by product or market segment

(b) **Profitability** figures by product or market segment

(c) **Customer account** information (history of payments, outstanding debt and so on)

(d) **Cost** data

(e) **Pricing policy** and price information (such as discounts allowed and payment terms)

(f) **Budgets** (sales budgets, product profitability budgets, market segment budgets, departmental budgets)

Key Concept

Budget. A quantitative statement, for a defined period of time, which may include planned revenues, expenses, assets, liabilities and cash flows.

3.2   A large proportion of such information would come from the **cost and management accounting** function of a business.

What are the different types of accounting?

3.3   You may not have come across financial, cost and management accounting. The following descriptions should help you.

Financial accounting

3.4   (a) **Financial accounts** detail the performance of an organisation over a defined period (**profit and loss account**) and the state of affairs at the end of that period (**balance sheet**). See Section 4 of this chapter for more detail on these.

Key Concept

Financial accounting. The classification and recording of monetary transactions of an entity in accordance with established concepts, principles, accounting standards and legal requirements and their presentation by means of profit and loss accounts, balance sheets and cash flow statements, during and at the end of an accounting period.

(b) Limited companies must, by law, prepare financial accounts.

(c) The format of published financial accounts is determined by law (mainly the Companies Acts), and by Financial Reporting Standards and Statements of Standard Accounting Practice. In principle the accounts of different organisations can therefore be easily compared (which is why the interpretation of organisations' financial statements can provide invaluable information). We cover this in Chapter 12.

(d) Financial accounts concentrate on the business as a whole, aggregating revenues and costs from different operations.

(e) Financial accounts might be used by the following groups of people.

(i)   Shareholders (potential and existing)

(ii)   Employees and employee organisations (such as unions)

(iii)   Government departments (such as the Inland Revenue)

(iv)   Competition

(v)   Business analysts

(vi)   The public at large

(vii)   Other interested parties (for example creditors)

Management accounting

Key Concept

Management accounting. The process of identification, measurement, accumulation, analysis, preparation, interpretation and communication of information used by management to plan, evaluate and control within an entity and to assure appropriate use of accountability for its resources. Management accounting also comprises the preparation of financial reports for non-management groups such as shareholders, creditors, regulatory agencies and tax authorities.

3.5   (a)   The **management accounting** function provides **internally-used** accounting information for management.

(b)   Management accounts are used to help management analyse, plan and control the organisation's activities and to help the decision-making process.

(c)   The format of management accounts is entirely at management discretion. Each organisation can devise its own management accounting system and format of reports.

(d)   Management accounts incorporate non-monetary measures. Management may need to know, for example, tons of aluminium sold, or miles travelled by salesmen.

Cost accounting

3.6   **Cost accounting** is a part of management accounting. In particular, it establishes budgets, standard costs and actual costs for operations, processes, departments and products. These are then used to analyse either the cost or unprofitability of a particular product or service.

Key Concept

Cost accounting. An internal reporting system for an organisation's own management.

Sources of accounting information

The financial accounting records

3.7   These records provide a **history** of an organisation's transactions. Some of this information is of great value outside the accounts department - most obviously for our purposes for example, sales information for the marketing function.

Other internal sources of accounting information

3.8 For example, information about personnel will be linked to the payroll system. Many service businesses – such as solicitors - need to keep detailed records of the time spent on various activities, both to justify fees to clients and to assess the efficiency of operations.

External sources

3.9 Any organisation's files are also full of **invoices, letters, orders** and so on received from customers and suppliers. These are all external sources of information.

3.10 External organisations which provide information include the following.

(a) **The government**. The Department of Trade and Industry is the most obvious example in central government. The government and its various departments and agencies also publish information through The Stationery Office.

(b) **Advice or information bureaux**. These provide enquirers with information in their own particular field, in the form of advice, information leaflets and/or fact sheets. Examples include Consumer Standards Offices, Offices of Fair Trading, Law Centres, Tourist Information bureaux and so on.

(c) There are also **consultancies** of all sorts. You will have heard of general market research organisations like MORI, ICM and Gallup.

(d) **Newspaper and magazine publishers**. The quality press is a vital source of general economic information. Most industries are also served by several trade journals and magazines.

(e) There may be **specific reference works** which are used in a particular line of work.

(f) **Libraries and information services**. These may be part of the free public library system, or associated with a professional institution like the CIM.

(g) **Electronic sources** of information are becoming ever more important. Besides local and national radio and TV, and teletext services, there are also more specialised forms. Reuters offers information on the stock market. The Internet is a vast source of information, with international coverage and multi-level communication.

(h) Increasingly businesses can use each other's systems as sources of information, via **electronic data interchange** (EDI) which involves the exchange of routine business information between the computers of suppliers and their customers. Tesco, for example, has automated its systems chain to such an extent that orders, invoices and payments are triggered by shoppers passing through supermarket check-outs.

4   AN INTRODUCTION TO FINANCIAL STATEMENTS

The balance sheet

> **Key Concept**
>
> **Balance sheet**. A statement of the financial position of an entity at a given date disclosing the assets, liabilities and accumulated funds such as shareholders' contributions and reserves, prepared to give a true and fair view of the financial state of the entity at that date.

4.1 The **balance sheet** is a picture of the affairs of an organisation at a particular point in time. An example is shown below.

FALCON KITES LTD
BALANCE SHEET AT 31 DECEMBER 2001

	£	£
Fixed assets		
Tangible assets at cost	23,900	
Less accumulated depreciation	10,750	
		13,150
Intangible assets		10,000
		23,150
Current assets		
Stocks	15,400	
Debtors	26,700	
Cash at bank and in hand	-	
	42,100	
Current liabilities		
Bank overdraft	16,200	
Trade creditors	11,000	
Taxation	5,200	
Dividends	6,000	
	38,400	
Net current assets		3,700
Long-term liabilities		
Loan		750
		26,100
Capital and reserves		
Ordinary shares of £1 each		16,000
Profit and loss account		10,100
		26,100

Assets

4.2 An **asset is a possession which has a value to the business**. Examples of assets are factories, office buildings, warehouses, delivery vans, lorries, plant and machinery, computer equipment, office furniture, cash and also goods held in store awaiting sale to customers, and raw materials and components held in store by a manufacturing business for use in production.

4.3 Some assets are held and used in operations for a long time. An office building might be occupied by administrative staff for years. Other assets are held for only a short time. The owner of a newsagent shop, for example, will have to sell his newspapers on the same day that he gets them, and weekly newspapers and monthly magazines also have a short shelf life. The more quickly a business can sell the goods it has in store, the more profit it is likely to make.

4.4 Assets in the balance sheet are of two types, fixed and current.

4.5 A **fixed asset** is any asset, **tangible** (physical and can be touched) or **intangible** (has no physical existence), acquired for retention by a business for the purpose of providing a service to the business, and not held for resale. Examples of fixed assets include a salesman's car which is used by the business for three years (tangible) and a patent on a product (intangible).

4.6 Every **tangible fixed asset** has a limited life (the only exception being freehold land). As a fixed asset wears out, its value in the balance sheet must be reduced. The process by which it is reduced is known as **depreciation**. The balance sheet value of the fixed asset will be its **'net book value'** which is the value after deducting depreciation from the cost of the asset.

4.7 **Current assets** are either items owned by the business with the intention of turning them into cash within one year, or cash itself. There are three main types of current asset.

   (a) **Stocks** are the quantity of goods which are for resale. They can exist, either in their original form (for example as component parts) or as work in progress (as a part-assembled car) or as finished goods awaiting resale.

   (b) A **debtor** is a person, business or company who owes money to the business. A customer who buys goods without paying cash for them straight away is a debtor. A distinction can be made between **trade debtors** (customers who owe money for goods or services bought on credit) and **other debtors** (anyone else owing money to the business).

   Trade debtors may have to be reduced because of **bad debts**. Customers who buy goods on credit might fail to pay for them. A business might decide to give up expecting payment and to write the debt off as an expense through the profit and loss account as a 'lost cause'. When a debt is written off, the value of the debtor as a current asset in the balance sheet falls to zero.

   (c) **Cash** includes petty cash and money in the bank.

Liabilities

4.8 A **liability** is a debt which is owed to somebody else. A distinction is made between **current liabilities**, which are debts of the business that must be paid within a fairly short period of time (by convention, within one year) and **long-term liabilities**, which are debts not payable within the 'short term'.

4.9 A **creditor** is a person to whom a business owes money. A business does not always pay immediately for goods or services it buys. A **trade creditor** is a person to whom a business owes money for debts incurred in the course of trading operations.

4.10 **Taxation** may be owed to the government. A business pays tax on its profits, but there is a gap in time between when a company declares its profits (and becomes liable to pay tax) and the time when the tax bill must be paid.

4.11 **Dividends** are profits paid out to shareholders. At the end of an accounting period (when a balance sheet is prepared), a company's directors may have **proposed** a dividend payment but this will not have been paid and hence it is shown as a current liability in the balance sheet, the shareholders being creditors of the company.

Capital and reserves

4.12 The capital and reserves figures in the balance sheet represent the **shareholders' funds**. These funds consist of the original capital contributed by the shareholders with the intention of earning profit (the **share capital**) plus the profits the business has made over the years, which are accumulated in the **profit and loss account balance**.

The profit and loss account

Key Concept

Profit and loss account. An account which shows the gross profit or loss generated by an entity for a period (trading account) and after adding other income and deducting various expenses shows the profit or loss of the business (the profit and loss account).

4.13 We now turn to the profit and loss account. Once again, as an example, let us look at the accounts of Falcon Kites Ltd.

FALCON KITES LTD
PROFIT AND LOSS ACCOUNT FOR THE YEAR ENDED 31 DECEMBER 2001

	£
Sales	98,455
Cost of sales	50,728
Gross profit	47,727
Distribution and selling expenses	24,911
Administration expenses	2,176
Operating profit	20,640
Interest paid	(280)
Interest received	40
Profit before taxation	20,400
Taxation	5,200
Profit after taxation	15,200
Dividends	8,100
Retained profit for the year	7,100

4.14 The profit and loss account is a statement in which **revenues and expenditure are compared** to arrive at a figure of **profit or loss**. Many businesses try to distinguish between a **gross profit** earned on trading, and **operating profit**. They prepare a statement called a **trading, profit and loss account**: in the first part of the statement (the trading account) revenue from selling goods is compared with direct costs of acquiring or producing the goods sold to arrive at a gross profit figure; from this, deductions are made in the second half of the statement (the profit and loss account) in respect of indirect costs (overheads) to arrive at operating profit. Interest, tax and dividends are then deducted to finally arrive at the **retained profit** for the year.

4.15 The owners and managers of a business obviously want to know how much profit or loss has been made, but there is only a limited information value in the profit figure alone. In order to exercise **financial control** effectively, managers need to know how much income has been earned, what various items of costs have been, and whether the performance of sales or the control of costs appears to be satisfactory. The **management accounting function** will produce trading accounts which are much more detailed than the profit and loss account shown above.

4.16 Many of the terms included in the profit and loss account above are self explanatory but the detail of distribution and selling expenses might be useful from a marketing perspective. **Distribution and selling expenses** are expenses associated with the process of selling and delivering goods to customers and in published accounts they will include marketing expenses. They include the following items.

(i) **Salaries** of marketing and sales directors and management and sales staff

(ii) **Travelling and entertainment** expenses of sales people

(iii) **Marketing costs** (including advertising, market research costs and sales promotion expenses)

(iv) Costs of **running and maintaining** delivery vehicles

(v) **Discounts** allowed to customers for early payment of their debts

(vi) **Bad debts** written off

Cash flow statements

Key Concept

Cash flow statement. A statement produced for management showing, by broad category, cash receipts and payments in a period or forecast for future periods.

4.17 It can be argued that 'profit' as reported in the profit and loss account does not always give a meaningful picture of a company's operations. Readers of a company's financial statements might even be misled by a reported profit figure.

(a) Shareholders might believe that if a company makes a profit after tax, of say, £100,000 then this is the amount which it could afford to pay as a dividend. Unless the company has **sufficient cash** available to stay in business and also to pay a dividend, the shareholders' expectations would be wrong.

(b) Employees might believe that if a company makes profits, it can afford to pay higher wages next year. This opinion may not be correct: the ability to pay wages depends on the **availability of cash**.

(c) Creditors might consider that a profitable company can pay all its debts. If a company builds up large amounts of unsold stocks of goods, however, the cost of this stock would not be shown against profits but would be held in the balance sheet. Cash would have been used up in making them, thus weakening the company's **liquid resources**.

(d) **Survival of a business** depends not so much on profits as on its **ability to pay its debts when they fall due**. Such payments might include 'profit and loss' items such as material purchases, wages, interest and taxation and so on, but also payments for new assets and the repayment of loans.

4.18 Large companies are therefore required to produce a cash flow statement. Simply making a sale is not enough. If the sale is not for cash and the debtor does not pay quickly, stock cannot be bought and so future sales cannot be made.

Exam Tip

This chapter has given you an introduction to financial information. The financial information section of the syllabus is a big area, but should not be feared – get used to doing simple calculations right from the start and practice past questions. You need to acquire the underpinning knowledge and we give you many worked examples in the following chapters.

Action Programme 1

Classify the following as asset, liability, income or expense.

	Asset	Liability	Income	Expense
Distribution and selling				
Stocks				
Bank overdraft				
Sales				
Land and buildings				
Bank loan				

Chapter Roundup

- After reading this introductory chapter you should be able to distinguish between the various sources of financial information available to marketers. There are a number of differences between financial and management accounting but the main distinctions can be summarised as follows.

- Financial accounting systems ensure that the assets and liabilities of a business are properly accounted for, and provide information about profits and so on to shareholders and to other interested parties.

- Management accounting systems provide information specifically for the use of managers within the organisation, including marketing managers.

- Accounting information is obtainable from both internal and external sources.

- The following terminology and concepts in relation to financial statements were introduced in this chapter.

  ○ A balance sheet is a snapshot of the financial position of a business at a point in time.

  ○ A profit and loss account measures the operational performance of the company over a period of time.

  ○ Assets are things of value that a business owns or has use of. Fixed assets are assets which are acquired for use within a business with a view to facilitating the generation of revenue (and consequently profits). Current assets are assets which are owned by the business which are intended to be turned into cash within one year.

  ○ Liabilities are financial obligations to someone else.

  ○ Creditors are people to whom the business has a financial obligation.

  ○ Debtors are people who have a financial obligation to the business.

  ○ Capital is the money put into a business by the owners and it is therefore owed by the business to the owners.

  ○ Gross profit is the profit shown after the purchase or production cost of the goods sold is deducted from the value of sales.

  ○ Net profit is the gross profit, plus any other income from sources other than the sale of goods, minus other expenses of the business which are not included in the cost of goods sold.

  Cash flow statements highlight the fact that survival in business depends on the ability to generate cash.

Quick Quiz

1   What might be the stages in formulating the marketing mix? (see para 2.6)

2   What are the differences between management accounting and financial accounting? (3.4, 3.5)

3   What is cost accounting? (3.6)

4   List six external sources of financial information. (3.10)

5   What is a balance sheet? (4.1)

6   What is the difference between tangible and intangible assets? (4.5)

7   What is a liability? (4.8)

8   Write down a list of the items which appear in the profit and loss account. (4.13)

9   List four items which might be included under distribution and selling expenses. (4.16)

10   Provide two reasons why readers of an organisation's financial statements might be misled by a reported profit figure (4.17)

Action Programme Review

	Asset	Liability	Income	Expense
Distribution and selling				√
Stocks	√			
Bank overdraft		√		
Sales			√	
Land and buildings	√			
Bank loan		√		

Now try illustrative question 5 at the end of Study Text

BPP PUBLISHING

6 Introducing Cost Behaviour

Chapter Topic List	Syllabus Reference
1 Introduction	-
2 Cost behaviour	4.0
3 Direct costs and indirect costs	4.0, 4.3
4 Functional costs	4.0
5 Fixed costs and variable costs	4.0
6 Product costs and period costs	4.0
7 Controllable and uncontrollable costs	4.0
8 Benefits of a costing system for marketers	4.0, 4.3

Learning Outcomes

After studying this chapter you will begin to appreciate the importance of understanding cost information. Costs have an effect on a variety of marketing decisions, most notably pricing.

Key Concepts

- Direct cost
- Indirect cost
- Functional cost

- Fixed cost
- Variable cost

Examples of Marketing at Work

- Extract from Marketing Business

1 INTRODUCTION

1.1 This chapter will introduce you to key cost definitions and terms, to provide a foundation for the next chapters of the study text. Cost behaviour is of particular relevance to the marketer because it enables product cost to be determined.

1.2 Product cost is one of the most important issues facing marketing and sales personnel, as it is a key driver in pricing decisions and product profitability (which we will be looking at in Chapter 9).

118

2   COST BEHAVIOUR

2.1   The total cost of a product or service consists of the following elements.

(a)   The cost of **materials** consumed in making the product or providing the service.

(b)   The cost of the wages and salaries (**labour**) of employees of the organisation, who are directly or indirectly involved in producing the product or providing the service.

(c)   The cost of **other expenses**, apart from materials and labour costs. These include items such as rent and rates, electricity bills, gas bills, depreciation, interest charges, the cost of sub-contractors' services, office cleaning, telephone bills and so on.

2.2   Are the following statements true or false?

(a)   1kg of sugar costs the same now as it did in 1970.

(b)   Per kilogram, it costs the same to buy apples as it does to buy 1,000 tonnes of apples.

(c)   The wage rate of car assembly workers remains unchanged as time passes.

(d)   Gas charges have never increased.

(e)   A pocket-sized version of a product has never been introduced.

(f)   Companies never expand their operations overseas.

2.3   We hope that you believed the above statements to be false! If costs always remained unchanged and under control, and if an organisation's activities remained the same from year to year, there would be no need to understand cost behaviour.

2.4   Let's consider again why marketers need to have accurate and timely information on costs. The CIM's definition of marketing helps us focus on this:

> 'Marketing is the management process responsible for identifying, anticipating and satisfying customer requirements **profitably**.'

It is a fundamental part of marketing that the activity is undertaken so that **revenue less costs** equals a **profit**. It follows then that we need to know what the costs are, and how they behave, in order to perform the job properly.

2.5   The major influence is the level or **volume of activity**. The level of activity refers to the amount of work done, or the number of events that have occurred. Depending on circumstances, the level of activity may refer to the number of items sold, the value of items sold, the number of invoices issued, the volume of production in a period, the number of invoices received, the number of units of electricity consumed, the labour turnover and so on.

2.6   The basic principle of cost behaviour is that as the level of activity rises, costs will usually rise. It will cost more to produce 2,000 units of output than it will cost to produce 1,000 units; it will usually cost more to make five telephone calls than to make one call and so on.

2.7   This principle is common sense. The problem is to determine, for each item of cost, the way in which costs rise and by how much as the level of activity increases. For our purposes here, the level of activity for measuring cost will generally be taken to be the volume of production.

3   DIRECT COSTS AND INDIRECT COSTS

3.1   Materials, labour and other expenses can be classified as **direct** or **indirect** costs.

Direct cost

Key Concept

A **direct cost** can be identified, measured and traced in full to the product, service, or department that is being costed.

3.2 (a) Direct **material** costs are the costs of materials that are known to have been used in making and selling a product (or providing a service).

(b) Direct **labour** costs are the specific costs of the workforce used to make a product or provide a service. Direct labour costs are established by measuring the time taken for a job. Traditionally, direct labour costs have been restricted to wage-earning factory workers, but in recent years, with the development of systems for costing services, the costs of some salaried staff might also be treated as a direct labour cost.

(c) Other **direct expenses** are those that have been incurred in full as a consequence of making a product or providing a service.

Indirect cost/overhead

Key Concept

An **indirect cost** or **overhead** is incurred in the course of making a product, providing a service or running a department, but cannot be traced directly and in full to the product, service or department. Examples, respectively, might be a supervisor's wages, cleaning materials and buildings insurance.

3.3 Do the exercise below to check whether you can determine the nature of an item of expenditure.

Action Programme 1

Classify the following as either direct material costs, direct labour costs, direct expenses or overhead (production, administration, selling or distribution).

(a) Rent, rates and insurance of a factory
(b) Inspectors, analysts and testers specifically required to make a particular product
(c) Wages of packers, drivers and despatch clerks
(d) Advertising and sales promotion, market research
(e) Rent, rates and insurance of warehouses
(f) Materials specially purchased for a particular job
(g) The cost of special designs, drawings or layouts
(h) The hire of tools or equipment for a particular job
(i) Wages of general labourers
(j) Audit fees

4 FUNCTIONAL COSTS

> ### Key Concept
>
> **Functional costs** are a group of costs that were all incurred for the same basic purpose.

4.1 In the 'traditional' costing system of an organisation, costs can be broadly **classified** as follows.

(a) **Production** or manufacturing costs
(b) **Administration** costs
(c) **Marketing**, or selling and distribution costs

4.2 Classification in this way is known as classification by **function**. Other expenses that do not fall neatly into one of these classifications might be categorised as 'general overheads' or listed as a classification on their own (for example research and development costs).

4.3 Examples of cost classification are as follows:

(i) Manufacturing costs are associated with the factory.

(ii) Administration costs are associated with general office departments (such as accounting and personnel).

(iii) Selling and distribution costs are associated with the sales, marketing, warehousing and transport departments.

Action Programme 2

Within the costing system of a manufacturing company the following types of expense are incurred.

Reference number

1	Cost of oils used to lubricate production machinery
2	Motor vehicle licences for lorries
3	Depreciation of factory plant and equipment
4	Cost of chemicals used in the laboratory
5	Commission paid to sales representatives
6	Salary of the secretary to the finance director
7	Trade discount given to customers
8	Holiday pay of machine operatives
9	Salary of security guard in raw material warehouse
10	Fees to advertising agency
11	Rent of finished goods warehouse
12	Salary of scientist in laboratory
13	Insurance of the company's premises
14	Salary of supervisor working in the factory
15	Cost of typewriter ribbons in the general office
16	Protective clothing for machine operatives

Required

Place each expense within the following classifications.

(a) Production costs
(b) Selling and distribution (or marketing) costs
(c) Administration costs
(d) Research and development costs

Each type of expense should appear only once in your answer. You may use the reference numbers in your answer.

5 FIXED COSTS AND VARIABLE COSTS

5.1 A different way of analysing and classifying costs is as **fixed costs** and **variable costs**.

> ### Key Concepts
>
> **Fixed cost**. A cost which is incurred for an accounting period, and which, within certain output or turnover limits, tends to be unaffected by fluctuations in the levels of activity (output or turnover).
>
> A **variable cost** varies with the measure of activity.

5.2 The distinction between fixed and variable costs therefore lies in whether the amount of costs incurred will **rise as the volume of activity increases**, or whether the costs will remain the same. Some examples are as follows.

(a) **Sales commission** is often a fixed percentage of sales turnover, and so is a variable cost that varies with the level of sales.

(b) **Telephone call charges** are likely to increase if the volume of business expands, and so they are a variable overhead cost, varying with the volume of production and sales.

(c) The **rental cost** of business premises is a constant amount, at least within a stated time period, and so it is a fixed cost that does not vary with the level of activity conducted on the premises.

(d) **Direct material costs** will rise as more units of a product are manufactured, and so they are variable costs that vary with the volume of production.

> ### Action Programme 3
>
> Is the salary of an organisation's managing director a fixed cost or a variable cost? What about the cost of petrol used in sales representatives' cars?

5.3 At the same time as costs can be classified as direct costs or overheads, they can also be fixed or variable costs.

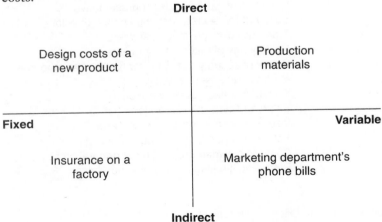

In the diagram above, the phone bill for the marketing department is an example of a variable indirect cost.

5.4 Many items of cost are fixed in nature within certain levels of activity. For example the rent on a warehouse unit may be fixed if stock remains below 1,000 units on average during the month. If stock exceeds 1,000 units, a second warehouse unit may be required, and the cost of rent, (on two units) would go up a step. This is an example of a **step cost**.

Semi-variable costs

5.5 These are cost items which are part fixed and part variable. Examples of these costs include the following.

(a) **Electricity and gas bills**. There is a standing basic charge plus a charge per unit of consumption.

(b) **Salesman's salary**. The salesman may earn a monthly basic amount of, say, £600 and then commission of 10% of the value of sales made.

(c) **Costs of running a car**. The cost is made up of a fixed cost (which includes road tax and insurance) and variable costs (of petrol, oil, repairs and so on) which depend on the number of miles travelled.

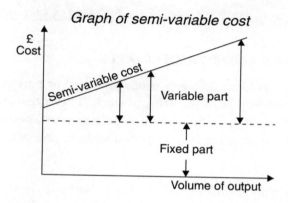

Graph of semi-variable cost

Action Programme 4

The costs of running the order processing department of an organisation are fixed at £15,000 up to a sales level of 10,000 units but thereafter vary in line with sales: an increase in sales of 1,000 units produces an increase in costs of £500.

Required

Calculate the costs of running the order processing department at the following sales levels.

(a) 17,000 units
(b) 8,000 units
(c) 23,000 units

Unit cost behaviour

5.6 We now need to look at **unit** cost behaviour.

5.7 Graph (a) below shows the **variable cost per unit** as volume of output changes. The variable cost per unit remains the same whatever the output level.

Graph (b) shows the **fixed cost per unit** as volume of output changes. The fixed cost per unit decreases as volume of output increases because the total fixed cost is spread over an increasing number of units.

Graph (c) shows the **total cost per unit** as volume of output changes. It decreases as volume increases because of the spread of fixed costs over more and more units.

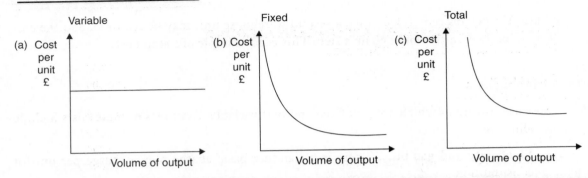

(a) Cost per unit £ — Variable — Volume of output

(b) Cost per unit £ — Fixed — Volume of output

(c) Cost per unit £ — Total — Volume of output

Exam Tip

A past question asked candidates to prepare a report which included a cost sheet showing how the costs involved in making a tracksuit which was originally budgeted for by the company, and a one-off order from an Italian company, could be analysed into fixed and variable costs.

When you are presenting solutions to numerical questions, make sure that you lay out your workings neatly and in an orderly manner.

6 PRODUCT COSTS AND PERIOD COSTS

6.1 **Product costs** are costs identified with goods produced or purchased for resale. Such costs are initially identified as part of the value of stock. They become expenses (in the form of **cost of goods sold**) only when the stock is sold. In contrast, **period costs** are costs that are deducted as expenses during the current period without ever being included in the value of stock held.

6.2 Consider a retailer who acquires goods for resale without changing their basic form. The only product cost is the purchase cost of the goods. Any goods unsold at the end of a period are held as stock, and included in the retailer's balance sheet at the end of the period. When the goods are sold in the following period, their cost becomes expenses in the form of 'cost of goods sold'. The **gross profit** is then revenue less cost of goods sold (shown in the profit and loss account). A retailer will also incur a variety of selling and administration expenses. Such costs are period costs, deducted from gross profit without ever being regarded as part of the value of stock. You are then left with the period's **net profit**.

7 CONTROLLABLE AND UNCONTROLLABLE COSTS

7.1 Costs which a business is able to **control** in the short term are generally direct costs or variable costs. Such costs may be avoided if output is lowered, pressure is put on suppliers, cheaper supplies are sought or particular activities not undertaken. Controllable costs are sometimes called **avoidable costs**.

7.2 Costs which tend to be outside the short-run control of the business are **uncontrollable costs**. Although in the longer term all costs may be avoided since all decisions taken by managers can be avoided, it is important to know which costs can be avoided in the short term, that is, the next financial period.

Example: controllable and uncontrollable costs

7.3 Supposing a business has a budgeted profit and loss account for the next financial year which in summary form looks like this.

**BUDGETED TRADING AND PROFIT & LOSS ACCOUNT
FOR THE YEAR TO 31 OCTOBER 2002**

	£'000
Sales turnover	100,000
Less variable costs:	
Materials	(50,000)
Labour	(20,000)
Variable overheads	(10,000)
Contribution or gross profit (see note (b))	20,000
Less fixed costs:	
Rent and rates	(5,000)
Administration	(2,000)
Sales and Marketing	(2,000)
Distribution	(1,000)
Finance costs	(1,500)
Net profit (see note (c))	8,500

Notes

(a) Costs are shown in brackets and are deducted from sales revenue.

(b) **Contribution** is **sales revenue** less **total variable costs**.

(c) **Net profit** is **sales revenue** less **variable costs** and **fixed costs** for the period.

7.4 In this example, managers will focus attention on sales turnover, contribution and net profit. Costs which are controllable will be those costs classified as variable (materials, labour and the variable overheads). Fixed costs, however, are not related to production levels directly (they are indirect costs), but are related to time and hence will not change for the budget period.

8 BENEFITS OF A COSTING SYSTEM FOR MARKETERS

8.1 There are a number of benefits that a costing system can provide.

(a) The identification of profitable and unprofitable products and services

(b) Assistance in setting prices

(c) The provision of accurate stock valuations

(d) The analysis of changes in costs, volume and hence profit

(e) Assistance in planning, control and decision making (budgets, pricing and so on)

8.2 You may still be wondering why, as a marketer, the costing aspects are relevant to you: after all, your main focus is the **customer**, and you might regard an inward looking concentration on costs and production processes as evidence of a **product-orientated attitude**.

8.3 Let us remember again that the essence of marketing is that **customer needs are satisfied profitably**. In the long run, profit is achieved because sales revenue from goods and services exceeds the costs.

8.4 Cost information is also important in **marketing mix decisions** because resources are always finite. To recap:

(a) **Price decisions**. A product's cost might be a constraint on the marketer's freedom to adjust the price element of the marketing mix. It is true that many supermarkets sell 'loss leader' products to entice their customers to buy higher-priced goods, but on the whole **cost is a constraint**.

(b) **Product decisions.** When deciding whether or not to launch a new product, marketers might discover that the market price is far below the cost of making a particular product or service. The marketer may then have to redesign or reposition the product to make it cheaper.

(c) **Place decisions.** Distribution expenses can affect overall profitability. Cost information can enable marketers to discover which distribution channels are the most effective use of resources.

(d) **Promotion decisions.** The marketer's budget often includes the costs of advertising, sales promotion and so on. Cost information can suggest which media might be best employed.

8.5 Kotler notes that every marketing mix strategy will lead to a certain level of profit as indicated in the equation below.

$$Z = [(P - k) - c] Q - F - M$$

where
$$
\begin{aligned}
Z &= \text{total profits} \\
P &= \text{selling price per unit} \\
k &= \text{commissions and discounts per unit} \\
c &= \text{production and distribution variable costs} \\
Q &= \text{number of units sold} \\
F &= \text{fixed costs} \\
M &= \text{discretionary marketing costs}
\end{aligned}
$$

Do not worry too much about learning this equation. We have included it to demonstrate how important costs are to the marketer and the marketing mix strategy. Hopefully by now you are starting to appreciate the relevance to you of financial information when doing your job as marketer. It isn't just a matter for the accountants!

Marketing at Work

The importance of marketers getting their heads round accounting information was emphasised in *Marketing Business*:

'From board representation through budget setting processes to effectiveness measurement, marketing and advertising come a poor second or third to other disciplines in finance directors' eyes ... Marketing directors simply must justify their activities in order to command the levels of expenditure they need.'

Chapter Roundup

- The elements of cost are materials, labour and expenses.

- A direct cost is a cost that can be traced in full to the product, service or department being costed. An indirect cost (or overhead) is a cost that is incurred in the course of making a product, providing a service or running a department, but which cannot be traced directly and in full to the product, service or department.

- Classification by function involves classifying costs as production/manufacturing costs, administration costs or marketing/selling and distribution costs.

- A different way of analysing and classifying costs is into fixed costs and variable costs. Many items of expenditure are part-fixed and part-variable and hence are termed semi-fixed or semi-variable.

- For the preparation of financial statements, costs are often classified as product costs and period costs. Product costs are costs identified with goods produced or purchased for resale. Period costs are costs deducted as expenses during the current period.

- Variable and direct costs are usually controllable and fixed costs are normally uncontrollable in the short-term. This general rule can, however, be affected by the time span under consideration.

- Costing systems *do* benefit marketers.

Quick Quiz

1   State the elements of cost. (2.1)

2   Briefly explain the following terms.

   (a)   Direct cost (3.2)

   (b)   Indirect cost (3.3)

   (c)   Variable cost (5.2)

   (d)   Fixed cost (5.2)

   (e)   Product cost (6.1)

   (f)   Period cost (6.1)

3   Is the salary of a stores supervisor a production cost or an administration cost? (4.2)

4   What is meant by controllable and uncontrollable costs? (7.1, 7.2)

5   Briefly explain the purpose and benefits of a costing system. (8.1 - 8.4)

Action Programme Review

1   (a)   Production overhead
   (b)   Direct labour
   (c)   Distribution overhead
   (d)   Selling overhead
   (e)   Distribution overhead
   (f)   Direct material
   (g)   Direct expense
   (h)   Direct expense
   (i)   Production overhead
   (j)   Administration overhead

2   The reference number for each expense can be classified as follows.

		Reference numbers
(a)	Production costs	1, 3, 8, 9, 14, 16
(b)	Selling and distribution (or marketing) costs	2, 5, 7, 10,11
(c)	Administration costs	6, 13, 15
(d)	Research and development costs	4, 12

3   The salary is a fixed cost (although any bonus element is likely to be variable) but the cost of petrol is variable, varying with miles travelled.

4   (a)   Cost = £15,000 + $(\dfrac{17,000-10,000}{1,000})$ × £500 = £18,500

         (b)   Cost = £15,000

         (c)   Cost = £15,000 + $(\dfrac{23,000-10,000}{1,000})$ × £500 = £21,500

7 Costing Techniques and their Application to Marketing

Chapter Topic List	Syllabus Reference
1 Introduction	-
2 Absorption costing	4.3
3 Activity based costing	4.4
4 Marginal costing	4.1, 4.3

Learning Outcomes

After studying this chapter you will have an understanding of:

- the effect of overheads in a marketing context and
- how they are allocated when building up a picture of costs.

We discuss:

- absorption costing
- activity based costing
- marginal costing

and their significant role in improving marketing decisions.

Key Concepts

- Absorption costing
- Apportionment
- Activity based costing

- Marginal costing
- Contribution

Examples of Marketing at Work

- Siemens
- ABC analysis

1 INTRODUCTION

1.1 In the previous chapter we considered the importance to the marketer of understanding cost behaviour and looked at a number of key terms and definitions. There are basically two types of cost to be considered – direct costs and indirect costs (or overheads).

129

1.2 Overhead costs are not directly attributable to each product made, but rather a shared cost amongst all the products that a firm makes. The marketing department needs to know how much of the overhead is attributable to each product so as to know the true cost of it.

1.3 In this chapter we are therefore going to be looking at several cost concepts and techniques which are particularly relevant to the marketer in that they enable product costs to be determined by allocating all relevant costs and overheads.

2 ABSORPTION COSTING   6/00, 6/01

2.1 The way in which this is done is by a technique known as **absorption costing**. The objective of absorption costing is to include in the total cost of a product an **appropriate share** of an organisation's total overhead. An 'appropriate share' is generally taken to mean an amount which reflects the amount of time and effort that went into producing a unit of product or service.

Key Concept

Absorption costing. A method of costing, that, in addition to direct costs, assigns all, or a proportion of, production overhead costs to cost units by means of one or a number of overhead absorption rates.

Allocation

2.2 Direct costs are **allocated** directly to **cost units**. Suppose Falcon Kites Ltd (we saw their example balance sheet and profit and loss account in Chapter 5) produces basic toy kites and competition kites. The direct material costs will be allocated to each type of kite (that is, each cost unit). Likewise the direct labour costs per unit and direct expenses per unit will be allocated to each kite.

2.3 **Indirect costs** (**overheads**) which can be completely identified with particular **cost centres** are allocated to those cost centres. The cost of the supervisor in the competition kite-making department cannot be allocated to one particular kite, and so will be allocated to the competition kite-making department cost centre.

Action Programme 1

Allocation is the process by which whole cost items are charged direct to a cost unit or cost centre. Think of three possible cost centres at Falcon Kites Ltd.

Apportionment

2.4 The overheads which cannot be completely identified with one cost centre (such as Falcon Kites Ltd's heating bill) need to be shared out among the cost centres which actually benefit from the overhead cost. The basis upon which the apportionment is made varies from cost to cost but the basis chosen should produce as fair a division as possible. The cost of heating might therefore be shared out on the basis of the floor area occupied by each cost centre.

> ## Key Concept
>
> **Apportionment**. The process of dividing overheads between cost centres.

Action Programme 2

What bases could be used for apportioning the following overheads?

(a) Rent and rates
(b) Insurance of equipment
(c) Personnel office

2.5 Suppose that the annual rental for the premises occupied by Falcon Kites is £1,750 and that the firm's four cost centres have the following floor area.

	Square metres
Toy kite producing department	75
Competition kite producing department	50
Administration department	25
Marketing department	25
	175

Each square metre of space therefore incurs a rental charge of £1,750/175 = £10.

The following overhead is therefore apportioned to each cost centre.

		Apportioned overhead
		£
Toy kite producing department	75 × £10	750
Competition kite producing department	50 × £10	500
Administration department	25 × £10	250
Marketing department	25 × £10	250
		1,750

2.6 Falcon Kites is divided into production departments and service departments such as administration and marketing, but only the production departments are directly involved in the manufacture of the kites. In order to add production overheads to unit costs, it is necessary to have **all the overheads charged** to the production departments. The next stage in absorption costing is then to **apportion** the costs of service departments to the kite production departments.

2.7 Suppose the directly allocated and apportioned overheads of the administration department total £2,000 and that the administration department does 400 hours work for the toy kite-making department and 600 hours work for the competition kite-making department. The apportionment of the overhead to the two production cost centres would be as follows.

Production cost centres	*Maintenance hours*	*Share of overhead*	
			£
Toy kites	400	400/1,000 × £2,000 =	800
Competition kites	600	600/1,000 × £2,000 =	1,200
	1,000		2,000

Absorption

2.8 All overheads associated with kite production have now been allocated or apportioned to kite production cost centres. The overheads must now be shared out (**absorbed** into) the cost units passing through each production cost centre.

2.9   The **different bases of absorption** which can be used to absorb overheads into cost units are as follows.

(a)   A percentage of direct materials cost
(b)   A percentage of direct labour cost
(c)   A percentage of prime cost
(d)   A rate per machine hour
(e)   A rate per direct labour hour
(f)   A rate per unit (effective only where units are identical).

2.10   What is required is an absorption basis which realistically reflects the characteristics of a given cost centre. For example, if overheads are incurred in proportion to the amount of labour time spent on production, then overheads should be absorbed at a rate per direct labour hour.

2.11   A machine hour rate would be used in departments where production is determined by machines. This basis is becoming more appropriate as factories become more heavily automated. Such methods are simple but depend on accurate records being maintained.

2.12   Absorption bases are derived from estimated or budgeted figures (calculated prior to the beginning of the year). Although the total actual overheads which need absorbing are not known until the end of a year, the overhead per unit needs to be set in advance so that a cost per unit can be determined. Delays in procedures such as invoicing and estimating, **price setting** and periodic stock and profit calculations could occur if a unit cost was not set until later.

2.13   Once a **basis** of absorption has been decided for each production cost centre, **overhead absorption rates** can be calculated.

(a)   The overheads likely to be incurred during the coming year are **estimated and allocated and apportioned** to production cost centres as described.

(b)   The **total hours, units or direct costs** on which the overhead absorption rates are to be based are estimated.

(c)   The **estimated overhead is divided by the budgeted activity level** to arrive at an absorption rate for each production cost centre.

2.14   Suppose that the total allocated and apportioned overhead in the toy kite-making department of Falcon Kites is budgeted to be £30,000 and that overheads are incurred in proportion to sewing machine hours, which are budgeted to be 10,000. The overhead absorption rate in the toy kite-making department would be £30,000/10,000 = £3 per machine hour. Suppose each kite takes 10 machine hours to produce. The overhead cost per kite would be £3 × 10 = £30.

Non-production overheads

Action Programme 3

The budgeted overheads allocated and apportioned to Falcon Kites' customer service department, expected to take 5,000 orders, are £12,000. Direct labour in the department is expected to work 18,000 hours at a cost of £20,000. Given that overheads are to be absorbed as a percentage of direct labour cost, calculate the customer services overhead absorbed per order.

Summary

2.15 Absorption costing can appear quite confusing at first glance. But don't panic. Remember that the aim of absorption costing is to get all **production overheads** into the production cost centres and then into the units produced. Read through Section 2 again with this aim in mind.

Exam tip

In June 2001, absorption costing was explicitly compared with activity based costing discussed below. The key difference is in the way overheads are treated. So, a good understanding of overhead absorption is necessary in order for you to identify its drawbacks and to understand how it differs from ABC.

3   ACTIVITY BASED COSTING   12/99, 6/00, 6/01

Key Concept

Activity based costing (ABC). An approach to the costing and monitoring of activities which involves tracing resource consumption and costing final outputs. Resources are assigned to activities based on consumption estimates. Identified cost drivers link costs with units of output.

The reasons for the development of ABC

3.1 The traditional cost accumulation systems which we have been looking at were developed when most organisations produced only a narrow range of products and overhead costs were only a **very small fraction** of total costs. Errors made in attributing overheads to projects were therefore not too significant.

3.2 Nowadays, however, overheads are likely to be far more important and in fact direct labour may account for as little as 5% of a product's cost. Material handling, setting up machines, scheduling production and inspection take up significant amounts of time. Moreover, **information technology** now allows more sophisticated overhead allocation methods.

3.3 It is difficult in such circumstances to justify the use of direct labour or direct material as the basis for allocating overheads or to believe that errors made in attributing overheads will not be significant. The demand for more accurate product costs has therefore increased. It was against this background that activity based costing (ABC) emerged a decade ago.

3.4 The diagram below shows the **value chain** for a typical modern firm. **Porter** has identified nine **value-adding activities**. Four of these value-adding activities are labelled **support activities,** and are typically areas where major overhead costs are incurred.

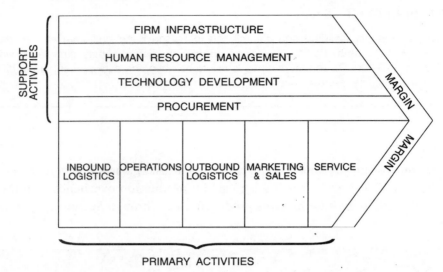

3.5 These support activities assist the efficient manufacture of a wide range of products and are not, in general, affected by changes in production volume. In traditional terms such costs would have been identified as fixed or semi-variable costs. The wider the range and the more complex the products, the more support services will be required.

3.6 The ideas behind **activity based costing** are as follows.

(a) **Activities drive costs.** Activities include ordering, materials handling, machining, assembly, production scheduling and despatching.

(b) **Producing products** creates demand for the activities.

(c) **Costs are assigned to a product** on the basis of the product's consumption of the activities.

It is therefore based upon identifying the drivers of cost and calculating the cost associated with them.

Outline of an ABC system

3.7 An ABC costing system operates as follows.

(a) *Step 1*

Identify an organisation's major activities.

(b) Step 2

Identify the factors which determine the size of the costs of an activity or drive the costs of an activity. These are known as **cost drivers.** Look at the following examples from Falcon Kites.

Activity	Cost driver
Ordering of nylon and plastic	Number of orders
Materials handling	Number of production runs
Production scheduling	Number of production runs
Despatching of kites to retail outlets	Number of despatches

For those costs that vary with production levels in the short term, ABC uses volume-related cost drivers such as labour or machine hours. The cost of oil used as a lubricant on Falcon Kites' sewing machines would be added to kite costs on the basis of the number of machine hours, since oil would have to be used for each hour the machine ran.

(c) *Step 3*

Collect the costs of each activity into what are known as **cost pools**.

(d) *Step 4*

Charge support overheads to products on the basis of their usage of the activity. A product's usage of an activity is measured by the number of the activity's cost drivers it generates.

Suppose, for example, that the cost pool for the ordering of nylon and plastic activity totalled £10,000 and that there were 1,000 orders (the cost driver). Each product would therefore be charged with £10 for each order it required. A batch of kites requiring five orders would therefore be charged with £50.

3.8 ABC uses many cost drivers as absorption bases (number of orders, number of dispatches and so on). Absorption rates under ABC should therefore be more closely linked to the causes of overhead costs and hence produce more realistic product costs, especially where support overheads are high.

ABC for marketers

3.9 The diagram below shows how cost drivers may be applied to achieve a **product cost, product and customer profitability analysis** and **market segment profitability analysis**.

Cost Driver

1	Set-up time in minutes
2	Time in minutes for total operations
3	Number of batches
4	Material value as a percentage of product cost
5	Quality control testing time
6	Number of sales orders
7	Number of sales quotes
8	Number of sales visits
9	Number of customers served
10	Marketing support time

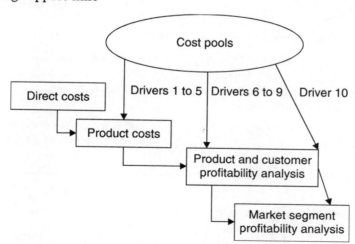

3.10 Activity based costing often confirms that some products and customers are profitable, but are **subsidising** those which make a loss. Not understanding customer and product profitability lays companies open to attack from competitors.

BPP
PUBLISHING

Marketing at Work

Siemens had a product range varying from simple toasters to complex tailor made machines. Overhead costs were allocated with little regard for these varying degrees of complexity, making some products overpriced. New entrants (especially from the Far East) were able to spot these niches and undercut Siemens. With ABC, Siemens could eventually see that some products were overpriced (thereby subsiding other products) and uncompetitive.

3.11 ABC gives marketing strategists a clear picture of where to compete and encourages them to look at customers as a portfolio. Consider the diagram below.

The appropriate action is not merely to remove non-profitable customers or products

Adapted from 'Activity Based Costing: focusing on what counts' by Michael Gering (Management Accounting, February 1999)

3.12 To focus on the diagram, it shows that customers and products that are both important and profitable must be retained. Those that are neither must be reconsidered, and possibly axed. Those that are small in size or importance, but very profitable, should be investigated and nurtured, possibly with cross-selling or other enhanced promotional techniques. Those that are big and unprofitable are typically being invested in for very little return to the company, but it may be possible to make them profitable by moving them.

Marketing at Work

Adapted from Management Accounting, February 1999:

A large German grocery wholesaler undertook ABC analysis of customer profitability and found that nearly half of its customers (retail outlets) were unprofitable. Many of them had negotiated deals that were costing the wholesaler dear. Senior management took a series of steps, including renegotiation of terms and listening to customers to find out what they valued most.

Frequency of deliveries was both a significant cost driver and keystone of customers service perceptions. The challenge was to improve the service without a proportional increase in cost. Problem solving teams were set up.

The merits of activity based costing

3.13 There is nothing difficult about ABC, once the necessary information has been obtained. This simplicity is part of its appeal. Further merits of ABC are as follows.

    (a) ABC **focuses attention** on the nature of cost behaviour and attempts to provide meaningful product costs.

(b) In a more **competitive environment**, companies must be able to assess product and customer profitability realistically. To do this, they must have a good understanding of what drives overhead costs.

(c) ABC can give **valuable insights** into product design, product mix, processing methods, administration and pricing.

'If this new product cost attribution were the end of the story, then it would just be a mildly interesting exercise. What changes this from being mildly interesting to being incredibly interesting is that you can now set about reversing the process. Because a company is able to see clearly where the majority of its indirect expenses are going, it can make changes to its processes so that these expenses can be minimised. If we can see that the costs of purchasing are directly related to the number of vendors and the lack of component commonality, then we can change the way we design products and purchase material so that purchasing costs are significantly reduced.

Pricing decisions, product mix decisions, design decisions and production decisions can all be much better understood when the background analysis and modelling from ABC is available. Many companies are selling products at a loss, subsidising their customers, because they do not understand the true cost of a product owing to the distortion of the costing system. The ABC approach gives them a better way of making that kind of assessment'. RS Kaplan, 'Relevance Regained', *Management Accounting,* September 1988

(d) ABC might be useful in contributing towards the control of **non-value-added** activities. These are activities that do not augment the customer's perception of a product's value and include the following.

(i)	Holding stocks	
(ii)	Set-up costs	
(iii)	Progress chasing	} production-related activities
(iv)	Production control	
(v)	Product development	
(vi)	Strategic planning	} support activities
(vii)	Purchasing	

(e) The review of existing costing systems and the consideration of ABC approaches helps management to identify **key business issues** which in turn leads to investigation of business processes and measures of performance. The boundaries of ABC have been extended to the setting of parameters for **benchmarking** and **strategic performance indicators**, thus working towards a concept of **activity based management**. Managers are able to focus upon, and measure, those factors critical to the success of the firm.

Action Programme 4

Summarise the benefits claimed from the introduction of ABC and from its use in practice.

Comparing ABC with traditional methods

3.14 We will now consider a full example comparing ABC and traditional overhead allocation methods. As we have seen Falcon Kites manufactures two products: basic toy kites and competition kites. The toy kites are a standard high-volume product, but the competition kites are a low-volume product. For the purposes of our example, activity levels in 2001 are well in excess of those experienced in 2000, and basic data is as follows.

	Machine hours per product	Output units	Total machine hours	Purchase orders	Materials handling
Toy kite	4	10,000	40,000	20	10
Competition kite	20	1,000	20,000	20	20
			60,000	40	30

The overheads of the business are analysed as follows.

	£
Related to volume	120,000
Related to purchasing	60,000
Related to materials handling	120,000
	300,000

Overhead allocation under ABC would be as follows.

	Volume	Purchasing	Materials handling	Total
Overheads	£120,000	£60,000	£120,000	
Cost drivers for the activity	60,000 machine hours	40 orders	30 requisitions	
Cost per unit	£2	£1,500	£4,000	
Costs charged to:				
Toy kites	40,000 × £2 = £80,000	20 × £1,500 = £30,000	10 × £4,000 = £40,000	£150,000
Competition kites	20,000 × £2 = £40,000	20 × £1,500 = £30,000	20 × £4,000 = £80,000	£150,000
				£300,000

Overhead allocated to:

Toy kites	£150,000 ÷ 10,000 units = £15 each
Competition kites	£150,000 ÷ 1,000 units = £150 each

This allocation reflects the use made of overhead activities by the two products. By contrast, traditional overhead absorption using a single **machine hour** rate on these figures would give:

Absorption rate per machine hour: £300,000 ÷ 60,000 hours = £5.00 per hour

Overhead absorbed per unit:

Toy kites	4 hrs × £5.00 = £20
Competition kites	20 hrs × £5.00 = £100

The traditional method charges more than ABC to the high-volume product (toy kites) because it is based only on machine hours. ABC uses cost drivers to relate the overheads to the use made by the product of those overhead-creating activities. The traditional method of cost allocation will lead to toy kites subsidising the competition kites and may make them uncompetitive if they are priced to reflect the extra £5 (£20 – £15) of overheads per unit.

Criticisms of ABC

3.15 It has been suggested by critics that activity based costing is flawed.

(a) It should not be introduced unless it can provide **additional information** for management to use in planning or control decisions.

(b) It is claimed by proponents of ABC that it provides more **accurate product costs**. This assumes that relevant cost drivers have been correctly identified.

(c) Any firm contemplating the introduction of ABC needs to consider the associated **systems** and **implementation cost**.

(d) The benefits of ABC may be more meaningful to the **larger enterprise** than the small firm since overhead costs will probably constitute a higher proportion of total product cost in the larger firm. Smaller firms may have fewer products to which overhead costs should be attributed and, as a result, the time and effort in implementing ABC may not provide more useful information.

3.16 In circumstances where **resources are scarce**, the use of ABC has to be compared with the marginal costing/contribution approach to dealing with **limiting factors** (a topic which we will cover later). As part of a toolkit, ABC may be useful to large firms with multi-product and multi-market operations and it may help such firms identify customer account profitability. This may lead to strategic product/market decisions. However, ABC is not an appropriate tool for making **resource allocation decisions** where product costs have to be broken down into elements of materials, labour and overheads, some or all of which may be constrained by limiting factors. Techniques employing the calculation of the **contribution per limiting factor** are more relevant.

> ### Exam Tip
>
> Activity based costing was examined for the first time in a Management Information for Marketing and Sales exam in December 1997 but has featured regularly since then. (Several managers in an organisation are to attend a meeting in order to discuss the possibility of introducing an activity based costing system. The question asked you to prepare a report for the marketing manager which explains activity based costing and describes any advantages and disadvantages of having such a system for budgeting and control.) In December 1999 and in June 2000 you had to describe ABC and its merits, similar to a question in December 1999. One of the merits of ABC is that it is **not** absorption costing, a comparison made explicitly in June 2001.

4 MARGINAL COSTING

4.1 **Marginal costing** is an alternative method of costing to absorption costing and ABC. Whereas in absorption costing and ABC an attempt is made to apportion all overhead costs to units of production, in marginal costing only those costs which **vary directly with production** are allocated to units of production.

> ### Key Concept
>
> **Marginal costing.** The system in which variable costs are charged to cost units and fixed costs of the period are written off in full against the total contribution. Its special value is in recognising cost behaviour and hence assisting in decision making.

4.2 The **marginal or incremental cost** per unit of production of an item usually consists of the following.

(a) Direct materials
(b) Direct labour
(c) Variable production overheads

4.3 The basic idea of marginal costing is that if an extra item is produced, then the total of the costs in the above paragraph will go up **slightly**. On the other hand, overheads such as rent, rates, heating and so on, will remain the same even if an extra item is produced.

4.4 In marginal costing, only variable costs are included in the calculation of the unit cost of a product. We can calculate the profit attributable to one additional unit of production by deducting from its sales value the variable cost of production. This will result in a **contribution to fixed overheads**. We can then determine how many units of production will need to be sold at a given price in order to completely cover the fixed costs of the business.

Marginal costing principles

4.5   The principles of marginal costing are set out below.

(a)   Since **period fixed costs are the same**, no matter what the volume of sales and production it follows that by selling an extra item of product, or service:

(i)   **Revenue will increase** by the sales value of the item sold

(ii)   **Costs will increase** only by the variable cost per unit

(iii)   The increase in profit will equal the **sales value minus variable costs**, defined as the amount of **contribution** earned from the item

Key Concept

The level of **contribution** made by a product or portfolio of products is defined as the total sales value less the variable costs associated with the units produced.

(b)   If the volume of sales **falls** by one item, the profit will fall by the amount of contribution earned from the item.

(c)   It is misleading to charge units of sale with a share of fixed costs. It is more appropriate to deduct fixed costs from total contribution for the period to derive a profit figure.

(d)   The **valuation of closing stocks** should be at production variable cost (direct materials, direct labour, direct expenses and variable production overhead) because these are the only costs properly attributable to the product.

4.6   Marginal costing has a major impact on the marketing manager because of its implications to both **pricing** and **decision making**, so we will look at a simple example of marginal costing.

Example: marginal costing

4.7   Falcon Kites Ltd is considering making another product, the basic training kite, which will have a variable production cost of £11 and a sales price of £30. It also expects to spend £3 per unit on marketing the product. Fixed costs for each month will be £65,000 (administration, sales and distribution).

What is the contribution to fixed costs and the profit for the month if sales are as follows.

(a)   10,000 kites
(b)   15,000 kites
(c)   20,000 kites

Answer

4.8 Firstly, we identify the variable costs and deduct them from the sales value to derive the **contribution**. We then deduct the **fixed costs** to arrive at **profit**.

	4,000 kites	*10,000 kites*	*15,000 kites*
Sales revenue	120,000	300,000	450,000
Variable costs			
Production	44,000	110,000	165,000
Marketing	12,000	30,000	45,000
Contribution	64,000	160,000	240,000
Fixed costs	65,000	65,000	65,000
(Loss)/profit	(1,000)	95,000	175,000
(Loss)/profit per unit	£(0.25)	£9.50	£11.67
Contribution per unit	£16.00	£16.00	£16.00

4.9 The conclusions which may be drawn from this example are as follows.

(a) The **profit per unit** varies at **differing levels of sales**, because the average fixed overhead cost per unit changes with the volume of output and sales.

(b) The **contribution per unit is constant** at all levels of output and sales. Total contribution increases in direct proportion to the volume of sales.

(c) The most effective way of calculating the expected profit at any level of output and sales is as follows.

   (i)   Calculate the **total contribution**.
   (ii) **Deduct fixed costs** as a period charge in order to find the profit.

(d) In our example the expected profit from the sale of 17,000 Kites would be calculated as follows.

	£
Total contribution (17,000 × £16)	27272,000
Less fixed costs	65,000
Profit	207,000

4.10 You should be able to see the following.

(a) If total contribution exceeds fixed costs, a profit is made.

(b) If total contribution exactly equals fixed costs, no profit and no loss is made. **Breakeven point** is reached. This is discussed in more detail in Chapter 10.

(c) If total contribution is less than the fixed costs, there will be a **loss**.

Marginal costing, absorption costing and decision making

4.11 For cost accounting many UK companies still use absorption costing, but this provides misleading decision information. For example, suppose that a sales manager has an item of product which he is having difficulty in selling. Its historical full cost is £80, made up of variable costs of £50 and fixed costs of £30. A customer offers £60 for it.

(a) If there is no other customer for the product, £60 would be better than nothing and the product should be sold to improve income by this amount.

(b) If the company has spare production capacity which would otherwise not be used, it would be profitable to continue making more of the same product, if customers are willing to pay £60 for each extra unit made. This is because the additional costs are only £50. Profit would be increased marginally by £10 per unit produced.

(c) If the product is not sold for £60, it will presumably be scrapped, so the choice is really between making a loss in absorption costing terms of £20, or a loss of £80 when the stock is written off.

4.12 Absorption costing information about unit profits is irrelevant in decisions in which fixed costs do not change (such as short-run tactical decisions seeking to make the best use of existing facilities). In such circumstances the decision rule is to choose the alternative which **maximises contribution**.

4.13 Costing is very relevant to your studies and in practice.

(a) You may be faced with a situation where you must decide whether in the short term to produce one of two products.

(b) You may be the brand manager for a mature product which has not increased its sales volume for the several years. How would you assess the potential benefits for the company if you increased your promotional support and reduced the price?

Example

4.14 Falcon Kites Ltd has a sister company, Kestrel Cycles Ltd. It makes one type of mountain bike in addition to a range of conventional street cycles. Unfortunately their mountain bike sales have been languishing for the past three years, and management is considering the option of spending £300,000 on extra advertising and dropping the unit selling price by £20 per bike to £150 for the coming year.

The bike has a variable product cost of £90 and current marketing costs of £5 per unit, which would continue to be spent. Sales for the coming year are expected to be 20,000 units with total fixed costs at last year's level of £250,000 (administration and distribution). The sales volume has been estimated by the marketing manager as a direct consequence of the increased advertising expenditure and reduced selling price. Sales last year were only 4,500 units.

4.15 Should management proceed? The analysis could be presented as follows.

	Last year £	*Coming year* £
Sales revenue	765,000	3,000,000
Variable costs		
Production	405,000	1,800,000
Marketing	22,500	100,000
Contribution	337,500	1,100,000
Fixed costs	250,000	550,000
Profit	87,500	550,000
Profit per unit	19.44	27.50
Contribution per unit	75.00	55.00

4.16 As can be seen from the analysis, contribution per unit has decreased by £20 because of the decreased selling price. Profit per unit has increased because the overall increased revenues have more than compensated for the increased advertising costs. On the face of it, management will want to go ahead, but they may wish to see more evidence of the achievability of the sales forecast. The fact that **break-even level** (where contribution equals fixed costs) is now $\frac{£550,000}{55.00} = 10,000$ units to be sold may give cause for concern, as this represents a sales increase of 122% on last year. (See Chapter 10 for more detail on breakeven analysis.) If sales 'only' doubled in the coming year (respectable enough in itself), then the company would make a loss on its mountain bikes, calculated as (9,000 units × £55 contribution) – £550,000 = £(55,000) loss.

Chapter Roundup

- Product costs are built up using absorption costing by a process of allocation, apportionment and absorption. In absorption costing, it is usual to add overheads into product costs by applying a predetermined overhead absorption rate.

- To work out the absorption rate, budgeted overheads are allocated to production cost centres, service department cost centres or general overhead cost centres. General overheads are then apportioned to production and service department cost centres using an appropriate basis. The service department cost centre overheads are then apportioned to production cost centres. All production overhead is thus identified with cost centres engaged directly in production. Administration overhead and selling and distribution overhead are also separately identified.

- The absorption rate is calculated by dividing the budgeted overhead by the budgeted level of activity. For production overheads, the level of activity is often budgeted direct labour hours or budgeted machine hours.

- Activity based costing (ABC) is an alternative to the more traditional absorption costing. ABC involves the identification of the factors (cost drivers) which cause the costs of an organisation's major activities. Support overheads are charged to products on the basis of their usage of an activity. When using ABC, for costs that vary with production levels in the short term, the cost driver will be volume related (labour or machine hours). Overheads that vary with some other activity (and not volume of production) should be traced to products using transaction-based cost drivers such as production runs or number of orders received.

- Marginal costing is an alternative method of costing to absorption costing. In marginal costing fixed production costs are treated as period costs and are written off as they are incurred.

- Contribution is the difference between sales value and marginal cost.

Quick Quiz

8   What is apportionment? (2.4)

9   List six possible bases of absorption. (2.9)

10   How is an overhead absorption rate calculated? (2.13)

1   What are the reasons for the development of ABC? (3.1 - 3.3)

12   What are the major ideas of activity based costing? (3.6)

13   How does an ABC system operate? (3.7)

14   What is the advantage of using cost drivers instead of traditional absorption bases? (3.8)

15   What are the merits of ABC? (3.13)

16   What does the marginal cost of a unit of production consist of? (4.2)

17   Why is marginal costing better for decision making than absorption costing? (4.11, 4.12)

Action Programme Review

1   Here are some suggestions.

   (a)   The toy kite production department, to which production overheads are charged.
   (b)   The administrative department, to which administration overheads are charged.
   (c)   The marketing department, to which marketing and overheads are charged.

2   (a)   Floor area or volume of space occupied by each cost centre
   (b)   Cost or book value of equipment in each cost centre
   (c)   Number of employees or labour hours worked in each cost centre

3   Overhead absorption rate = $\dfrac{£12,000}{£20,000} \times 100\% = 60\%$

Labour cost per order = $\dfrac{£20,000}{5,000} = £4$

Overhead absorbed per order = $60\% \times £4 = £2.40$

4   (a)   Reduction of costs
    (b)   Greater profitability
    (c)   Greater interaction between functions
    (d)   Improved cost awareness amongst departmental managers
    (e)   Improved management information
    (f)   A greater understanding of product cost
    (g)   Overhead reductions via activity analysis
    (h)   Possible changes of range of products or pricing strategy
    (i)   The identification of non value-adding activities

ABC is also thought to be likely to lead to suggestions for product innovations (like fewer component parts).

Now try illustrative question 6 at the end of the Study Text

8

Decision Making for Marketers

Learning Outcomes

Upon completion of this chapter you will have a further understanding of more financial concepts that assist in marketing decisions.

Specifically, you will have been led through investment decisions in a marketing context using

- payback
- discounted cash flow techniques.

The concept of relevant costs is key to this chapter.

Key Concepts

- Relevant cost
- Limiting factor
- Discounted cash flow

- Net present value
- Cost of capital

Examples of Marketing at Work

- Justifying marketing expenditure
- ABZ Ltd

1   INTRODUCTION

1.1   Management from all functions and at all levels within an organisation take decisions. This chapter looks at the technique required in decision-making situations, that of relevant costing, and explains how to decide which costs need taking into account when a decision is being made and which costs do not.

1.2   Section 6 of the chapter covers investment decision making and methods which management can use to assist them in making such decisions. The ways in which risk associated with long-term decisions can be assessed is also briefly considered.

1.3   In the next chapter we will look at a type of decision close to the heart of sales and marketing managers, the pricing decision.

2   TYPES OF DECISION

2.1   Marketing managers must remember that their decisions will have **financial implications**. It helps to be able to identify what the various types of decision facing a marketing manager might be.

   (a)   **Routine planning decisions,** for example budgeting. Budgeting decisions commonly analyse fixed and variable costs, together with revenues. They are also often concerned with how to make the best use of scarce resources.

   (b)   **Short-run problem decisions,** typically, unforeseen 'one-off' special decisions of a non-recurring nature, where the costs and benefits are all obtained within a relatively short period. For example, what price should be quoted in the tender for a contract?

   (c)   **Longer-range decisions,** meaning decisions made once and reviewed infrequently, but which are intended to provide a continuing solution to a continuing or recurring problem. They include decisions about selling and distribution policies. For example should goods be sold through middlemen or direct to customers? What type of customer should the sales force attempt to attract? What should the company's discount policies be? Should a new product or service be launched?

   (d)   **Control decisions,** for example: should disappointing performance be investigated, given that the benefits expected must exceed the costs from investigation and control?

2.2   **Pricing decisions** are sometimes put into a category of their own, but pricing decisions span most of the range of decision categories above: routine pricing decisions are made at periodic price reviews; 'one-off' short-run pricing decisions might be made for specific jobs or contracts or to dispose of surplus stocks; long-range decisions about price must be made for services, products or product ranges and some control decisions might have to be made about prices. (For example, are excessive discounts being allowed?) We will be looking at pricing decisions in Chapter 9.

3   RELEVANT AND NON-RELEVANT COSTS

Relevant costs

3.1   The costs which should be used for decision making are often referred to as **relevant costs**.

> ### Key Concept
>
> A **relevant cost** is a **future incremental cash flow arising as a direct consequence of a decision**.
> A decision is about the future; it cannot alter what has been done already.

3.2 The assumption used in relevant costing is that, in the end, profits earn cash. A profit that is earned will produce a net inflow of an equal amount of cash, although the timing may be different (eg giving credit will delay the receipt of cash, although the sale will be recorded). Costs which do not reflect **additional cash spending** should be ignored for the purpose of decision making.

3.3 Only costs which will **differ** under the available opportunities should be considered. Say a marketing manager has already contracted to pay £1,000 for some full page advertisements in the local newspaper to advertise a new store launch. It is the newspaper's policy that this booking is not refundable if cancelled. He now might be trying to decide whether to advertise on local radio instead. The £1,000 he is already contracted to is irrelevant to the decision, because although it is a future cash flow it will be incurred anyway whether he decides to advertise on radio or not.

3.4 Other terms used to describe relevant costs are as follows.

(a) **Avoidable costs** are the specific costs of an activity which would be avoided if that activity did not exist. One of the situations in which it is necessary to identify the avoidable costs is in deciding whether or not to discontinue a product. Costs which would be incurred whether or not the product is discontinued are known as unavoidable costs.

(b) **Opportunity cost** is the benefit which could have been earned, but which has been given up, by choosing one option instead of another. Suppose for example that there are three mutually exclusive product options, A, B and C. The net profit from each would be £80, £100 and £70 respectively. Since only one option can be selected option B would be chosen because it offers the biggest benefit.

	£
Profit from option B	100
Less opportunity cost (ie the benefit from the most profitable alternative, A)	80
Differential benefit of option B	20

The decision to choose option B would not be taken simply because it offers a profit of £100, but because it offers a differential profit of £20 in excess of the next best alternative.

Non-relevant costs

3.5 (a) **Sunk costs.** In decision making, managers require information about **future** costs and revenues which would be affected by the decision under review, and they must not be misled by events, costs and revenues in the past, about which they can do nothing. Example of sunk costs are development costs which have already been incurred. Suppose that a company has spent £250,000 in developing a new service for customers, but the marketing department's most recent findings are that the service might not gain customer acceptance. The decision whether or not to abandon the development of the new service would have to be taken, but the £250,000 spent so far should be ignored by the decision makers.

(b) **Committed costs.** A committed cost is a future cash outflow that will be incurred whatever decision is taken.

Example: identifying relevant costs

3.6 A company has been making a machine to order for a customer, but the customer has since gone into liquidation, and there is no prospect that any money will be obtained from the winding up of the company.

Costs incurred to date in manufacturing the machine are £50,000 and progress payments of £15,000 had been received from the customer prior to the liquidation.

The sales department has found another company willing to buy the machine for £34,000 once it has been completed.

To complete the work, the following costs would be incurred.

(a) Materials: these have been bought at a cost of £6,000. They have no other use, and if the machine is not finished, they would be sold for scrap for £2,000.

(b) Further labour costs would be £8,000. Labour is in short supply, and if the machine is not finished, the work force would be switched to another job, which would earn £30,000 in revenue, and incur direct costs of £12,000 and absorbed (fixed) overhead of £8,000.

(c) Consultancy fees £4,000. If the work is not completed, the consultant's contract would be cancelled at a cost of £1,500.

(d) General overheads of £8,000 would be added to the cost of the additional work.

Required

Assess whether the new customer's offer should be accepted.

Answer

3.7 (a) Costs incurred in the past, or revenue received in the past are not relevant because they cannot affect a decision about what is best for the future. Costs incurred to date of £50,000 and revenue received of £15,000 should be ignored.

(b) Similarly, the price paid in the past for the materials is irrelevant. The only **relevant cost of materials** affecting the decision is the opportunity cost of the revenue from scrap which would be forgone - £2,000.

(c) **Labour costs**

	£
Labour costs required to complete work	8,000
Opportunity costs: contribution forgone by losing	
other work £(30,000 – 12,000)	18,000
Relevant cost of labour	26,000

(d) The **incremental cost** of consultancy from completing the work is £2,500.

	£
Cost of completing work	4,000
Cost of cancelling contract	1,500
Incremental cost of completing work	2,500

(e) General overheads should be ignored because they would be incurred anyway. Actual overhead incurred (which is directly attributable to the new work) is the only overhead cost to consider.

(f)   Relevant costs may be summarised as follows.

	£	£
Revenue from completing work		34,000
Relevant costs		
Materials: opportunity cost	2,000	
Labour: basic pay	8,000	
opportunity cost	18,000	
Incremental cost of consultant	2,500	
		30,500
Extra profit to be earned by accepting the completion order		3,500

The relevant cost of scarce resources

3.8   A scarce resource is defined here as a resource (materials, labour, machine time, cash and so on) which is in short supply, so that the **total opportunities** that exist for making profitable use of the resource **exceed the amount of the resource available**.

3.9   Suppose that a customer has asked whether your company would be willing to undertake a contract for him. The work would involve the use of certain equipment for five hours and its running costs would be £2 per hour. However, your company faces heavy demand for usage of the equipment which earns a contribution of £7 per hour from this other work. If the contract is undertaken, some of this work would have to be forgone.

3.10 The contribution obtainable from putting the scarce resource to its alternative use is its **opportunity cost**. Quite simply, since the equipment can earn £7 per hour in an alternative use, the contract under consideration should also be expected to earn at least the same amount. This can be accounted for by charging the £7 per hour as an opportunity cost to the contract and the total relevant cost of five hours of equipment time would be as follows.

	£
Running costs (5 × £2)	10
Internal opportunity cost (5 × £7)	35
Relevant cost	45

It is important to notice that the variable running costs of the equipment are included in the total relevant cost. The price of the contract will need to cover the relevant cost to be worth carrying out.

Action Programme 1

Vanderbilt Ltd has been offered £21,000 by a prospective customer to make some purpose-built equipment. The extra costs of the machine would be £3,000 for materials. There would also be a requirement for 2,000 labour hours. Labour wages are £4 per hour, variable overhead is £2 per hour and fixed overhead is absorbed at the rate of £4 per hour.

Labour, however, is in limited supply, and if the job is accepted, workers would have to be diverted from other work which is expected to earn a contribution of £5 per hour towards fixed overheads and profit.

Required

Assess whether the contract should be undertaken.

---

4   LIMITING FACTOR ANALYSIS

4.1   One of the more common problems is a situation where there are not enough resources to meet the potential sales demand, and so a decision has to be made about using what resources there are as effectively as possible. The resource which limits the activity of an organisation is called a **limiting factor** or **key factor**.

> ### Key Concept
>
> **Limiting factor/key factor.** Anything which limits the activity of an entity. An entity seeks to optimise the benefit it obtains from the limiting factor.

4.2   There might be several scarce resources, with two or more of them putting an effective limit on the level of activity that can be achieved. In this chapter, however, we shall concentrate on single limiting factor problems and a technique for resolving these.

4.3   The limiting factor is often **sales demand** itself, in which case the business should produce enough goods or services to meet the demand in full, provided that sales of the goods earn a **positive contribution** towards fixed costs and profits. However, when the limiting budget factor is a **production resource**, (such as skilled labour) the business must decide which part of sales demand it should meet, and which part must be left unsatisfied.

4.4   In dealing with a **limiting factor problem,** the steps to be taken are as follows.

(a)   (i)   Calculate the **volume of resources required** to produce enough units to satisfy budgeted sales demand

(ii)   Calculate the **volume of resources available**

(iii)   Compare the two totals. If (i) exceeds (ii) there is a limiting factor

(b)   The next step is to calculate the contribution earned by each product per unit of the scarce resource. The product(s) with the **highest contribution per unit of scarce resource** should receive priority in the allocation of the resource in the budget.

Example: limiting factor problem

4.5   Jones Ltd manufactures and sells three products, X, Y and Z.

		X		Y		Z	
Budgeted sales demand		300 units		500 units		200 units	
		£	£	£	£	£	£
Unit sales price			16		18		14
Variable costs:	materials	8		6		2	
	labour	4		6		9	
			12		12		11
Contribution			4		6		3

All three products use the same direct materials and the same type of direct labour. In the next year, the available supply of materials will be restricted to £4,800, and the available supply of labour to £6,600.

Required

Determine the profit-maximising (ie contribution-maximising) budget.

Answer

4.6   (a)   Is there a limiting factor?

	Units of demand	Required materials cost	Required Labour cost
		£	£	£
X	300	2,400	1,200
Y	500	3,000	3,000
Z	200	400	1,800
Total required		5,800	6,000
Total available		4,800	6,600
(Shortfall)/Surplus		(1,000)	600

Materials are a limiting factor, but labour is not.

(b)

	X	Y	Z
	£	£	£
Unit contribution	4	6	3
Cost of materials	8	6	2
Contribution per £1 of materials	£0.50	£1.00	£1.50
Priority for manufacture	3rd	2nd	1st

Z should be manufactured up to the limit of sales demand, then Y second and X third, until the sales demand for each or the amount of materials available has been used up.

	Product	Units	Materials cost	Unit contribution	Total Contribution
			£	£	£
(i) 1st	Z	200	400	3	600
(ii) 2nd	Y	500	3,000	6	3,000
(iii) 3rd	X	175	1,400 (balance)	4	700
			4,800		4,300

The profit-maximising budget would be to make and sell 200 units of Z, 500 units of Y and 175 units of X, to earn a contribution of £4,300.

5   ACCEPTING OR REJECTING ORDERS

5.1   An order will probably be accepted if it increases contribution and profit, and rejected if it reduces profit. You may be faced with a problem relating to the acceptance or rejection of a special order.

Example: accept or reject an order

5.2   Braces Ltd makes a single product which sells for £20, and for which there is great demand. It has a variable cost of £12, made up as follows. (Unit contribution is therefore £8).

	£
Direct material	4
Direct labour (two hours)	6
Variable overhead (varies with hours worked)	2
	12

The labour force is currently working at full capacity and no extra time can be made available. A customer has approached the company with a request for the manufacture of a special order, for which he is willing to pay £5,500.

The costs of the order would be £2,000 for direct materials, and 500 labour hours will be required.

Required

Assess whether the order should be accepted.

Answer

5.3   (a)   Labour is a limiting factor. By accepting the order, work would have to be diverted away from the standard product, and associated contribution lost. The contribution from the standard product is £4 per labour hour [(£20 – £12) ÷ 2 hrs].

      (b)   Direct labour pay costs £3 per hour. Variable production overhead varies with hours worked, and must therefore be spent in addition to the wages cost of 500 hours.

		£	£
(c)	Value of order		5,500
	Cost of order		
	Direct materials	2,000	
	Direct labour (500 hours × £3)	1,500	
	Variable overhead (500 hours × £1)	500	
	Opportunity cost (500 hours × £4 contribution forgone)	2,000	
	Relevant cost of the order		6,000
	Loss incurred by accepting the order		(500)

Although accepting the order would earn a contribution of £1,500, the lost production of the standard product would reduce contribution earned elsewhere by £2,000.

6   INVESTMENT DECISIONS   6/01

Exam Tip

Although examined regularly under the old syllabus, investment appraisal only became the explicit subject of a question in June 2001. Whether this means that it will come up again – or won't – is a hard question to answer. In June 2001, you had to discuss payback and discounting – with examples – in the context of persuading managers to allocate appropriate resources to developing your marketing plans.

6.1   Businesses will need to assess proposals which will affect the long-term health of the company and which may be competing for cash resources. Managers need to assess each project to determine its suitability in terms of the corporate objectives and then to determine how, whether and when to invest the available funds.

6.2   This decision-making process will usually involve the investment in a **capital item** (an item which will add to the capacity of the business to generate revenue and profits). The capital asset investment decision would usually involve the following considerations.

      (a)   Once paid for, the asset cannot be re-sold quickly at a profit. The **capital is tied up** for several years.

      (b)   The investment will earn **profits (or returns)** over this period of several years.

      (c)   At the end of this time, the investment might have some **re-sale** or **scrap value**, but it might also be **worthless**.

Appraisal methods

6.3 There are three principal methods of evaluating a capital project. They all involve estimating future cash flows.

(a) The **accounting rate of return** method
(b) The **payback** method
(c) **Discounted cash flow** (DCF) techniques

Accounting rate of return method

6.4 A capital investment project may be assessed by calculating the **accounting rate of return** (ARR) (or **return on capital employed** (ROCE) or **return on investment** (ROI)) and comparing it with a **predetermined target** level. A formula for ARR which is common in practice is:

$$ARR = \frac{\text{Estimated average profits}}{\text{Estimated average investment}} \times 100\%$$

Example: accounting rate of return

6.5 Bee Limited is contemplating an investment decision in a new product and has two alternatives.

	Product X	Product Y
Cost	£10,000	£13,000
Estimated life	4 years	4 years
Estimated future profits:	£	£
Year 1	5,000	10,000
2	4,000	4,000
3	1,000	1,000
4	4,000	1,000
Total profits	14,000	16,000

Required

Based on the ARR method, decide which of the two products should be pursued.

Answer

6.6

	X	Y
Total profits	£14,000	£16,000
Average profits (over 4 years)	£3,500	£4,000
	X	Y
	£	£
Value of investment	10,000	13,000

The accounting rates of return are:

$$X = \frac{£3,500}{£10,000} = 35\% \qquad Y = \frac{£4,000}{£13,000} = 31\%$$

Product X would therefore be chosen.

6.7 This method of assessing an investment is a measure of **profitability** and its major advantage is that it is easily understood, but basing our decision on profits alone without considering cash flows can be extremely dangerous. For example, if we look at the profits generated by the two alternatives given above, as much emphasis is placed on the profits generated in year one as those generated in year four. If these were actually cash flows we could make an incorrect decision, particularly if the management of Bee Ltd needed a **quick return** on its cash invested. From the point of view of investment decisions it is therefore better to consider **cash flows**.

The payback method

6.8 The **payback method** is one which gives greater weight to cash flows generated in **earlier years**. The payback period is the length of time before the total cash inflows received from the project cover the original cash outlay.

6.9 In the previous example, product X pays for itself after three years and product Y in under two years. Using the payback method of investment appraisal, product Y is preferable to product X.

6.10 The payback method has disadvantages. Consider the case of two products for which the following information is available.

		Product P £	*Product Q* £
Cost		10,000	10,000
Cash inflows year	1	1,000	5,000
	2	2,000	5,000
	3	6,000	1,000
	4	7,000	500
	5	8,000	500
		24,000	12,000

Product Q pays back at the end of year two and product P not until early in year four. Using the payback method machine Q is to be preferred, but this ignores the fact that the total profitability of P (£24,000) is double that of Q.

6.11 Despite the disadvantages of the payback method it is widely used in practice, often as a supplement to more sophisticated methods. Its use will tend to **minimise risk** and **aid liquidity**. This is because greater weight is given to earlier cash flows which can probably be predicted more accurately than distant cash flows.

6.12 A more scientific method of investment appraisal is the use of discounted cash flow (DCF) techniques. Before DCF can be understood it is necessary to know something about the **time value of money**.

The time value of money

6.13 Money is spent to earn a profit. For example, if an item of machinery costs £6,000 and would earn **cash profits** (the excess of income over cash expenditure) of £2,000 per year for three years, it would not be worth buying because its total relevant cash flows (£6,000) would only just cover its cost.

6.14 We would also say that the size of cash flows or return must be sufficiently large to justify the investment. In the example above, if the machinery costing £6,000 made total cash profits of £6,300 over three years, the return on the investment would be £300, or an average of £100 per year. It would be more profitable to invest the £6,000 somewhere else (for example, on deposit at a bank).

6.15 If a capital investment is to be worthwhile, it must earn **at least a minimum profit or return** so that the size of the return will compensate the business for the length of time it must wait before the profits are made. For example, if a company could invest £6,000 now to earn a profit of £300 in seven days, that would be a very good return. If it takes three years to earn the same profits, the return would be very low.

6.16 When expenditure projects are evaluated, it is important to decide whether the investment will make enough profits to allow for the **'time value' of capital** tied up. DCF is a superior evaluation technique which takes into account the **time value of money** and also the total profitability over a project's life.

Discounting

What is discounting?

6.17 We have all seen **compound** interest rates at work. If we borrow £1,000 now at 10% interest rate and repay nothing for two years, then at the end of year one, provided interest is only calculated at the end of the year, we will owe

£1,000 plus 10% = £1,000 × 1.10 = £1,100.

If again we do not repay anything in the second year and interest is calculated at the end of the year the balance on the loan will be:

£1,100 × 1.10 = £1,210

The original borrowing has grown as follows.

£1,000 × 1.10 × 1.10 = £1,000 × $(1.10)^2$ = £1,210

This would continue forever if we left the whole balance (interest and original capital) untouched. Hence after five years we would owe:

£1,000 × $(1.10)^5$ = £1,611

6.18 **Discounting simply reverses this process.** It says that if we owed £1,611 in five years' time whilst paying interest of 10% per annum, what did we borrow today? Or more usually 'what is the **present value** of a given sum of money held in the future?' For those of you who are mathematically minded the present value calculation is:

$$P = Sn \times \frac{1}{(1+r)^n}$$

when
- Sn = sum of money in n time periods
- P = present value of that sum
- r = rate of interest or rate of return expressed as a proportion
- n = number of time periods (usually years).

Hence in our example

$$£1,000 = £1,611 \times \frac{1}{(1 + 0.1)^5}$$

Example: discounting

6.19 (a) Calculate the present value of £60,000 in year 6, if a return of 15% per annum is obtainable.

BPP PUBLISHING

(b) Calculate the present value of £100,000 in year 5, if a return of 6% per annum is obtainable.

(c) How much would a person need to invest now at 12% to earn £4,000 in year 2 and £4,000 in year 3?

Answer

6.20 (a) $PV = 60,000 \times \dfrac{1}{1.15^6}$

$= 60,000 \times 0.43$

$= £25,800$

(b) $PV = 100,000 \times \dfrac{1}{1.06^5}$

$= 100,000 \times 0.75$

$= £75,000$

(c) $PV = (4,000 \times \dfrac{1}{1.12^2}) + (4,000 \times \dfrac{1}{1.12^3})$

$= 4,000 \times (0.80 + 0.71)$

$= £6,040$

This calculation can be checked as follows.

	£
Year 0	6,040.00
Interest for the first year (12%)	724.80
	6,764.80
Interest for the second year (12%)	811.78
	7,576.58
Less withdrawal in year 2	(4,000.00)
	3,576.58
Interest for the third year (12%)	429.19
	4,005.77
Less withdrawal in year 3	(4,000.00)
Rounding	5.77

Key Concept

Discounted cash flow (DCF) involves the application of discounting arithmetic to the estimated future cash flows (receipts and expenditures) from a project in order to decide whether the project is expected to earn a satisfactory rate of return.

6.21 We will look at one appraisal method which uses DCF techniques, **the net present value (NPV)** method.

The net present value (NPV) method

6.22 The NPV method works out the present values of all items of income and expenditure related to an investment at a given rate of return, and then works out a net total. If this net total is **positive**, the investment is considered to be acceptable. If it is **negative**, the investment is considered to be unacceptable.

> **Key Concept**
>
> **Net present value (NPV)**: the difference between the sum of the projected discounted cash inflows and outflows attributable to a capital investment or other long-term project.

Example: the net present value of a project

6.23 Falcon Kites is considering whether to spend £5,000 on a car for a salesman. The cash profits resulting directly from the salesman being able to visit customers would be £3,000 in the first year and £4,000 in the second year.

The company will not invest in any project unless it offers a return in excess of 15% per annum. Assess whether the investment is worthwhile.

Answer

6.24 In this example, an outlay of £5,000 now promises a return of £3,000 during the first year and £4,000 during the second year. It is a convention in DCF, however, that cash flows are assumed to occur **at the end of the year**, so that the cash flows of the project are as follows.

	£
Year 0 (now)	(5,000)
Year 1 (at the end of the year)	3,000
Year 2 (at the end of the year)	4,000

6.25 The NPV method takes the following approach.

(a) The project offers £3,000 at year 1 and £4,000 at year 2, for an outlay of £5,000 now.

(b) The company might invest elsewhere to earn a return of 15% per annum.

(c) If the company did invest at exactly 15% per annum, how much would it need to invest now, at 15%, to earn £3,000 at the end of year 1 plus £4,000 at the end of year 2?

(d) Is it cheaper to invest £5,000 in the project, or to invest elsewhere at 15%, in order to obtain these future cash flows?

6.26 If the company did invest elsewhere at 15% per annum, the amount required to earn £3,000 in year 1 and £4,000 in year 2 would be as follows.

Year	Cash flow £	Discount factor 15%	Present value £
1	3,000	$\dfrac{1}{1.15} = 0.87$	2,610
2	4,000	$\dfrac{1}{(1.15)^2} = 0.76$	3,040
			5,650

6.27 We can invest £5,000 in the project, or £5,650 elsewhere at 15%, in order to obtain the same future cash flows. We can therefore reach the following conclusion.

(a) It is cheaper to invest in the project, by £650.

(b) The project offers a return of over 15% per annum.

6.28 The **net present value** is the difference between the present value of cash inflows from the project (£5,650) and the present value of future cash outflows (in this example, £5,000).

6.29 An NPV statement could be drawn up as follows.

Year	Cash flow £	Discount factor 15%	Present value £
0	(5,000)	1.00	(5,000)
1	3,000	$\frac{1}{1.15} = 0.87$	2,610
2	4,000	$\frac{1}{(1.15)^2} = 0.76$	3,040
		Net present value	+650

The project has a **positive net present value, so it is acceptable**.

Action Programme 2

A company is wondering whether to spend £18,000 now on an advertising campaign, in order to obtain cash profits as follows.

Year	£
1	6,000
2	8,000
3	5,000
4	1,000

The company requires a return of 10% per annum.

Required

Use the NPV method to assess whether the advertising project is acceptable.

The internal rate of return (IRR) method

6.30 The **internal rate of return** (IRR) method of evaluating investments is an alternative to the NPV method.

6.31 The NPV method determines whether an investment earns a positive or a negative NPV when discounted at a given rate of interest. If the NPV is zero (that is, the present values of costs and benefits are equal) the return from the project would be exactly the rate used for discounting. There would be nothing to choose between such a project and investing the money elsewhere at the given rate.

6.32 The IRR method of discounted cash flow determines the rate of interest (the **internal rate of return**) at which the NPV is 0. The internal rate of return is therefore the **rate of return on an investment**. If the company expects a minimum return of, say, 15%, a project would be viable if its IRR is more than 15%.

Example: internal rate of return

6.33 A promotional campaign costing £800 in year 0 is expected to earn £400 in year 1, £300 in year 2 and £200 in year 3. What is the internal rate of return?

Answer

6.34 The IRR is calculated by first of all finding the NPV at each of two interest rates. Ideally, one interest rate should give a small positive NPV and the other a small negative NPV. The IRR would then be somewhere between these two interest rates: above the rate where the NPV is positive, but below the rate where the NPV is negative.

6.35 The first interest rate you try will be a complete guess. There is no reliable way of guessing, but it does not matter a great deal what rate you choose. Our first guess is 8% (the discount factors can be calculated as before).

(a) Try 8%

Year	Cash flow	Discount factor	Present value
	£	8%	£
0	(800)	1.000	(800)
1	400	0.926	370
2	300	0.857	257
3	200	0.794	159
		NPV	(14)

The NPV is negative, therefore the project fails to earn 8% and so you now know that the IRR must be less than 8%.

(b) Try 6%

Year	Cash flow	Discount factor	Present value
	£	6%	£
0	(800)	1.000	(800)
1	400	0.943	377
2	300	0.890	267
3	200	0.840	168
		NPV	12

The NPV is positive, therefore the project earns more than 6% and less than 8%.

6.36 The IRR is now calculated by **interpolation** using the formula:

$$a + \left[\frac{A}{A-B} \times (b-a) \right]\% \text{ where}$$

a is one interest rate
b is the other interest rate
A is the NPV at rate a
B is the NPV at rate b

$$\text{IRR} = 6\% + \left[\frac{12}{(12-(-14))} \times (8-6) \right]\%$$
$$= 6\% + 0.92\%$$
$$= 6.92\% \text{ (approx)}$$

Action Programme 3

A promotional campaign costing £800 in year 0 is expected to earn £400 in year 1, £300 in year 2 and £200 in year 3.

Calculate the internal rate of return using as your first guess 15% and your second 5%.

The cost of capital

Key Concept

Cost of capital. The minimum acceptable return on an investment, generally computed as a hurdle rate for use in investment appraisal exercises.

6.37 In many cases, the return from the investment under consideration has to exceed a 'required rate of return'. The rate is a **target cost of capital** and has two aspects to it.

(a) It is the cost of funds that a company raises and uses, and the return that **investors expect** to be paid for putting funds into the company.

(b) It is therefore the **minimum return** that a company must make on its own investments, to earn the cash flows out of which investors can be paid.

6.38 The cost of capital can therefore be measured by studying the returns required by investors, and then used to derive a discount rate for DCF analysis and investment appraisal.

Marketing at Work

To illustrate what is often a divide between finance and marketing directors, one of the major sources of the gap is the fact that FDs are tuned into City expectations which are usually expressed in terms of short-term rates of return on capital tied up in a company. FDs cannot justify marketing expenditure, and the City cannot give credit for it, if the reason for that expenditure, together with some verifiable return, is not clearly set out for them.

Investment decisions in a marketing context

6.39 **Levels of marketing expenditure are often significant,** and any marketing strategy will have to be evaluated accordingly. However, according to Keith Ward, 'levels of marketing expenditure ... are often subjected to far less rigorous financial evaluations than smaller financial commitments on more tangible assets'.

6.40 Furthermore, few companies 'even apply their normal discounted cashflow procedures to major expenditures on marketing activities, and still fewer have challenged the traditional measures of accounting for such expenses'.

6.41 In other words, treating marketing expenditure as a **cost** is probably appropriate for financial reporting considerations, simply for reasons of prudence; but for decision-making purposes, there is an argument for analysing it, and controlling it, as if it were an **investment**.

6.42 Ward highlights the dilemma: 'for many marketing-led businesses, their most valuable assets are their brands ... yet ... the easiest way ... to improve profitability is to reduce expenditure on marketing or on research and development'.

6.43 Part of the strategic marketing plan should be some form of quantitative analysis of the proposed investment.

(a) For example, assume the marketing department chooses to spend £10m on re-positioning a product.

(i) How can a link between future sales and the £10m expenditure be established?

(ii) What would happen if the money was not spent? Would market share fall? Or would competitors find an opening?

(iii) Would an alternative use of £10m be more valuable?

(b) The benefits from marketing expenditure might sometimes be much less easy to quantify than, say, the cost savings on new equipment. Markets are an environment, where customers and competitors cannot be controlled. Instability and uncertainty are inherent within them.

Marketing at Work

ABZ Ltd is a privately-owned, UK-based industrial manufacturing company with an annual turnover of around £700 million and pre-tax profits of £70 million. Although primarily UK-orientated, the business has enjoyed considerable success in a large proportion of European markets and has made more limited gains further afield.

Year 1 : Reorganisation of the Marketing Function

ABZ had recently reorganised its sales and marketing functions. Previously the marketing function had a primarily tactical role, dealing with the promotional requirements of the business. Pricing strategy was handled by the finance function while new product development was dealt with by a bespoke team of personnel who did not feed directly into the marketing area. Following the reorganisation, a more extensive marketing department was developed around a series of product groups, each headed by a marketing manager with overall responsibility for marketing strategy development.

Marketing Planning Objectives : Year 1

The marketing director at ABZ was enthusiastic about market planning, believing that it would help the business capitalise on its resources to take advantage of new opportunities and to prioritise core target markets. The marketing director realised that ABZ's relative inexperience of formal marketing planning meant it would need to limit its efforts during the first year to developing a plan fort he UK market (55% of ABZ's business). The objectives of this first phase of the marketing planning were as follows:

To review the company's strengths and weaknesses.
To analyse the wider marketing environment and key environment trends for ABZ's business.
To obtain information on key customers.
To understand the sales and contribution of different customer segments and reappraise priorities.
To begin gathering competitive information.
To develop detailed marketing programmes for UK markets and broad guidelines for other European markets.

Year 2

Marketing Planning Objectives : Year 2

The basic planning objectives remained the same with the intention of broadening the analysis to include more markets in Europe and the rest of the world. A particular focus was to develop a more extensive understanding of ABZ's competitive environment. The structure of the planning programme continued as before with a combination of training days, advice sessions and regular review days for receiving feedback from the others. This was vital in planning the overall product portfolios as some products were partial substitutes for others.

Year 3

Marketing Planning Objectives : Year 3

The marketing planning was progressing well, so this year ABZ's last two remaining product teams were included in the process. Once again the analysis was combined to a limited number of customer groups and markets. For the first time it was [possible to use the sales and financial contribution analysis carried out in year 2 to identify exactly what the priorities should be.

At this stage in the marketing planning, the marketing director needed to consider the changing needs and expertise of the product teams. Although most mangers were now comfortable carrying out a range of analyses and taking strategic decisions, the recruits in the two new product teams needed some induction.

A brief refresher course was set up and arrangements were made for the new teams to each work in conjunction with another team. This allowed the more experienced managers to transfer their expertise to the others.

In order to reinforce the status of the planning programme, the original product teams were tasked with reviewing the performance of last year's plan and updating the customer, competitor and environmental analyses.

Measuring the rewards

It is difficult directly to attribute success in the market place exclusively to a programme of marketing planning. However, the marketing director at ABZ was convinced that the planning programme had measurably improved the business' financial performance. Measures of market share across the four customer groups which began the marketing planning programme had, by the end of year 3, risen by an average of 4%. A number of additional benefits, both tangible and intangible, were also being attributed to the planning programme. In all cases these benefits were either directly or indirectly aided by improved interpersonal relationships:

A new division, geared to the needs of one particular customer group, had been developed.

A total of six new products had been launched.

Greater control over the regions was possible than ever before.

More control over new product development, pricing and promotional activity was one of the most visible outcomes of the planning exercise.

A significant contribution to team building.

Long Range Planning, 30/1, Dibb, S., pp. 53-63, 1997

7 INTRODUCING RISK

7.1 Two different projects may have exactly the same capital requirement and the same present value. However, one may be extremely uncertain. For example, a retail store chain in the UK may wish to open its 100th store in the UK. At the same time it may review the possibility of opening its first store in Hong Kong. These two options may need to be assessed in a totally different light.

7.2 **Risk** is part of every management decision. The ability of management to understand the elements of risk involved and be able to act accordingly will often determine the success of any strategy. Risk in any project can be divided into three main elements.

(a) **The inherent risk of the industry or market itself**. For example, the fashion industry is a higher risk industry than the food processing industry; and to a UK firm, export markets in the Third World are likely to be higher risk markets than the UK market.

(b) **The stage in the product's life cycle**. Every product has a life cycle, and the 'classical' product life cycle consists of four stages.

Introduction	Growth	Maturity	Decline

When an investment is made in a product which is in its introductory phase, there is a high risk that it will fail to win market acceptance, and will have a very short market life. When an investment is made in a declining product, the risk of a rapid decline in sales is also high.

(c) **Proportion of fixed costs in total costs**. When an investment involves a high proportion of fixed costs (costs which are not dependent on the level of volume of production), it will need to achieve greater sales volume just to break even, and so the business risk will be higher.

Methods of analysing risk

7.3 The methods of analysing risk for capital expenditure projects include the following.

(a) **Adjusting the discount rate** to allow a premium on the cost of capital for risk
(b) Expecting projects to pay back or earn a positive NPV in a certain **time limit**
(c) **Sensitivity analysis**

Adjusting the discount rate

7.4 To allow for risk, a **premium is added to the discount rate** as a safety margin. By adding a safety margin into the discount rate, the riskiest projects are less likely to have a positive

NPV. For example, if a company's true cost of capital is 10%, all capital projects might be evaluated against a discount rate of, say 15%. Projects which would have a positive NPV at a discount rate of 10% but a negative NPV at 15% would then be considered too risky to undertake.

Payback period: applying a time limit

7.5 A method of limiting the risk on a capital project is to apply a **payback time limit**, so that a project should not be undertaken unless it pays back within, say, 4 years.

7.6 There are two ways of applying a payback time limit.

(a) A project might be expected to pay back within a certain time limit, and in addition show a positive NPV from its net cash flows.

(b) Alternatively, a project might be expected to pay back **in discounted cash flow terms** within a certain time period. For example, a project might be required to have a positive NPV on its cumulative cash flows before the end of year 4.

Sensitivity analysis

7.7 One method of applying **sensitivity tests** to a project is to re-calculate the NPV in the following circumstances.

(a) If the initial cost of the investment was, perhaps, 5% higher than expected.

(b) If running costs were, say, 10% higher, or savings/benefits were, perhaps 10% lower than estimated.

(c) If costs were, say, 5% higher and savings 5% lower.

7.8 If the NPV is negative when costs are increased by a small margin, or benefits reduced a little, the project would be rejected on the grounds that it is too sensitive to variations in one or more key items.

7.9 **Sensitivity analysis** is widely used in businesses because it is relatively easy to change a financial model to indicate the importance of one or more of the variables. It can, for example, vary the sales revenue if demand is higher than currently anticipated. Imagine how the forecast sales of an Internet bookshop such as Amazon would have looked only a few years ago, when compared to the expected explosion in e-commerce in the coming years.

Chapter Roundup

- There are a number of ways of categorising decisions. In making decisions, the only costs which are relevant are those which will be affected by the decision. Such costs will be future, incremental cash. Opportunity costs are relevant costs.

- Non-relevant costs include sunk costs, committed costs and historic costs.

- The relevant cost of a scarce resource is the *sum* of the contribution/incremental profit forgone from the *next best* opportunity for using the scarce resource and the *variable cost* of the scarce resource.

- In a limiting factor situation, contribution will be maximised by earning the biggest possible contribution per unit of scarce resource.

- There are three methods of evaluating a capital project: ARR, payback and DCF.

- DCF takes account of the time value of money. DCF methods are NPV and IRR.

- The cost of capital is a company's *cost of funds* (reflecting the return required by investors). It is thus the *minimum return* that a company must make on its own investments so as to be able to pay investors.

- The risk associated with a capital project can be analysed using an adjusted discount rate, a time-limit payback period or sensitivity analysis

Quick Quiz

1   List three categories of decision. (see para 2.1)

2   What are relevant costs? (3.1)

3   What are avoidable costs? (3.4)

4   What is an opportunity cost? (3.4)

5   Are sunk costs relevant or irrelevant? (3.5)

6   What is a scarce resource? (3.8)

7   What is a limiting factor? (4.1)

8   What are the two steps in a limiting factor problem? (4.4)

9   An order should be rejected if it increases profit. True or false? (5.1)

10   How is the ARR calculated? (6.4)

11   What is the payback method of appraising capital expenditure projects? (6.8)

12   Explain the concept of the time value of money. (6.13 - 6.16)

13   What is the NPV method of project appraisal? (6.22)

14   What are the two aspects to the cost of capital? (6.37)

15   Into what three main elements can the risk in any project be divided? (7.2)

16   What is sensitivity analysis? (7.7 - 7.9)

Action Programme Review

1   Fixed costs are ignored because there is no incremental fixed cost expenditure.

	£
Materials	3,000
Labour (2,000 hours × £4)	8,000
Variable overhead (2,000 hours × £2)	4,000
	15,000
Opportunity cost	
Contribution forgone from other work (2,000 hours × £5)	10,000
Total costs	25,000
Revenue	21,000
Net loss on contract	(4,000)

The contract should not be undertaken.

2

	Cash flow £	Discount factor 10%	Present value £
0	(18,000)	1.00	(18,000)
1	6,000	$\dfrac{1}{1.10} = 0.91$	5,460
2	8,000	$\dfrac{1}{1.10^2} = 0.83$	6,640
3	5,000	$\dfrac{1}{1.10^3} = 0.75$	3,750
4	1,000	$\dfrac{1}{1.10^4} = 0.68$	680
		Net present value	(1,470)

The NPV is negative. We can therefore draw the following conclusions.

(a)   It is cheaper to invest elsewhere at 10% than to invest in the project.

(b)   The project would earn a return of less than 10%.

3   (a)   Try 15%

Year	Cash flow £	Discount factor 15%	Present value £
0	(800)	1.000	(800)
1	400	0.870	348
2	300	0.756	227
3	200	0.658	132
			(93)

(b)   Try 5%

Year	Cash flow £	Discount factor 5%	Present value £
0	(800)	1.000	(800)
1	400	0.952	381
2	300	0.907	272
3	200	0.864	173
			26

$$\text{IRR} = 5\% + \left[\frac{26}{26 - (-93)} \times (15 - 5)\right]\%$$

$$= 7.18\%$$

As you can see, this is less accurate than our estimate using rates that gave an NPV closer to zero, but it is not far from our previous answer of 6.92%.

Now try illustrative question 7 at the end of the Study Text

9

Pricing and Profitability

Learning Outcomes

After completing this chapter you will have a sound knowledge of the financial information relevant to pricing decisions and other profitability themes. This will include:

- Setting appropriate selling prices to achieve required margins or mark-ups
- Setting appropriate transfer prices

The concepts of direct product profitability, channel profitability and customer profitability are discussed.

You will also have a good understanding of the financial implications of the pursuit of product quality.

Key Concepts

- Full cost plus pricing
- Marginal cost plus/mark up pricing
- Transfer price
- Direct product profitability
- Customer profitability analysis

Examples of Marketing at Work

- Cigarette advertising
- Petrol stations
- Ferry crossings
- Aggressive pricing
- Package holidays
- Supermarkets
- 'Everyday low prices'
- Chiroscience
- Post Office
- Siebe

---

1 INTRODUCTION

1.1 In the previous chapter we looked at some issues behind decision making. This chapter considers the pricing decision. The price of a product or service is something that is frequently decided by the marketing manager and hence it is vital that you are aware of how to take pricing decisions. All profit organisations and many non-profit organisations face the task of setting a price on their products and services. Price can go by many names: fares, tuition fees, rent, assessments and so on.

1.2 Unlike other marketing mix elements, pricing decisions affect profits through their impact on revenues rather than costs. It also has an important role as a competitive tool to differentiate a product and an organisation and thereby exploit market opportunities.

1.3 Pricing decisions are made in a variety of contexts. We discuss various approaches here. The marketing manager may want to set a price to achieve the required margins or mark ups, or the appropriate price for the transfer of goods and services within a company.

1.4 Transfer pricing is defined as 'the price at which goods or services are transferred from one process or department to another.' Do not be misled by the term 'price' here. There is not necessarily any suggestion of profit, as there usually is with an external selling price.

1.5 Prices are set in order to make a profit, and the next part of this chapter discusses the review of product performance and direct product profitability, or DPP, in particular.

1.6 Businesses derive most of their success from their most lucrative customers, so we have given some notes on trying to identify them via customer profitability analysis (or CPA). Customers expect their needs to be met, and so a consideration of basic quality issues is appropriate here, along with the related costs.

1.7 Finally, we conclude with a section on the importance of the distribution channel and the effect on profit, depending on the method chosen.

2 PRICING DECISIONS   Specimen paper

Factors to consider when making pricing decisions

2.1 The selling price of a product should exceed its average unit cost in order to make a profit, but cost is only one of the factors to bear in mind when setting a price.

(a) **The organisation's objectives**. Although we generally assume that an organisation's objective is to maximise profit, it could be that increased market share, maximisation of sales revenue, to be known as a supplier of luxury goods or to provide a service to the community is the objective.

(b) **The market in which the organisation operates**. If the organisation is operating under conditions of **perfect competition** (many buyers and many sellers all dealing in an identical product), neither producer nor user has any market power and both must accept the **prevailing market price**. If the organisation is in the position of a **monopolist** (one seller who dominates many buyers), it can use its market power to set a profit-maximising price. Most of British industry can be described as an **oligopoly** (relatively few competitive companies dominate the market). Whilst each large firm has the ability to influence market prices, the **unpredictable reaction** from the other giants makes the price difficult to determine.

(c) **Demand.** Economic theory suggests that the volume of demand for a good in the market is influenced by variables such as the price of the good, price of other goods, size and distribution of household income, tastes and fashion, expectations and obsolescence. The volume of demand for one organisation's goods rather than another's is influenced by three principal factors: **product life cycle**, **quality** and **marketing**.

  (i) **Product life cycle.** Most products pass through the phases of introduction, growth, maturity and decline. Different versions of the same product may have different life cycles, and consumers are often aware of this. For example, the prospective buyer of a new car is more likely to purchase a recently introduced Ford than a Vauxhall that has been on the market for several years, even if there is nothing to choose in terms of quality and price.

  (ii) **Quality.** One firm's product may be perceived to be better quality than another's. Other things being equal, the better quality good will be more in demand than other versions.

  (iii) **Marketing.** The 'four Ps' of the marketing mix (or 7 Ps for services) all influence demand for a firm's goods or services.

(d) **Price elasticity of demand.** The price an organisation charges will be affected by whether demand for an item is **elastic** (a small change in the price produces a large change in the quantity demanded) or **inelastic** (a small change in the price produces only a small change in the quantity demanded).

Marketing at Work

'When your biggest brand launch in three decades succeeds only on its price – especially when you have spent an estimated £20 million on advertising it – something has gone wrong.

This was the situation faced by the UK's biggest tobacco manufacturer Gallaher, which launched its mid-market cigarette brand Sovereign in an effort to claw back share from Imperial's buoyant Lambert & Butler brand.

L&B's share has been growing rapidly at the expense of more glamorous premium brands such as Gallaher's Benson & Hedges and Silk Cut, as smokers switch to cut-price cigarettes (which now account for nearly one-third of the market) in the face of relentless tax hikes and price rises.

Marketing Week

(e) **Costs.** An organisation has to decide whether a price should be based on fully absorbed cost or marginal cost.

(f) **Competition.** When competitors sell exactly the same product in the same market, price differences are likely to have a significant effect on demand. For example, the price of petrol at filling stations in a local area will be much the same. When organisations sell similar products which are not exactly identical, or where the **geographical location** of the sales point is of some significance, there is more scope for charging different prices.

(g) **Inflation.** An organisation should recognise the effects of inflation on its pricing decisions. When its costs are rising, it must try to ensure that its prices are increased to make an adequate profit or to cover its costs (in the case of non-profit-making organisations).

(h) **Legislation.** Certain organisations have their prices controlled by legislation or regulatory bodies.

(i) **Availability of substitutes.** When an organisation is making a pricing decision it must take into account products/services that customers could switch to if they were not happy with the price set.

Approaches to pricing

Full cost plus pricing

2.2 A traditional approach to pricing products is **full cost plus** pricing.

> ### Key Concept
>
> **Full cost plus pricing** is a method of determining the sales price by calculating the full cost of the product and adding a percentage mark-up for profit.

2.3 A business might have an idea of the **percentage profit margin** it would like to earn and so might decide on an average profit mark-up as a general guideline for pricing decisions. The percentage profit mark-up does not have to be fixed, but can be varied to suit the circumstances. In particular, it can be varied to suit demand conditions in the market.

2.4 This approach to pricing fails to recognise that since demand may be determined by price, there will be a **profit-maximising combination** of price and demand.

2.5 The **advantage** of full cost plus pricing is that since the size of the profit margin can be varied at management's discretion, a decision based on a price in excess of full cost should ensure that a company working at normal capacity will cover all its fixed costs and make a profit. It is also a simple and quick method.

Marginal cost plus or mark-up pricing

2.6 Instead of pricing products or services by adding a profit margin on to **full cost**, a business might add a profit margin on to **marginal cost**. This is sometimes called **mark-up pricing**.

> ### Key Concept
>
> **Marginal cost plus pricing/mark up pricing** is a method of determining the sales price by adding a profit margin on to marginal cost.

2.7 The **advantages** of a marginal cost plus approach to pricing are as follows.

(a) It can be adjusted to reflect demand conditions.

(b) It draws management attention to **contribution** and the effects of higher or lower sales volumes on profit.

(c) Mark-up pricing is convenient where there is a **readily identifiable basic variable cost.** Retail industries are the most obvious example, and it is quite common for the prices of goods in shops to be fixed by adding a mark-up (20% or 33⅓%, say) to the purchase cost. The price must of course be high enough to ensure that a profit is made after covering fixed costs.

Minimum pricing

2.8 A **minimum price** is the price that would have to be charged so that the **incremental costs** of producing and selling the item, and the **opportunity costs** of the resources consumed in making and selling the item, are just covered. A minimum price would leave the business no better or worse off than if it did not sell the item.

2.9 Two essential points about a minimum price are as follows.

(a) It is based on **relevant costs**.

(b) It is unlikely that a minimum price would be charged because it would not provide the business with any profit. However, the minimum price for an item shows the **absolute minimum below which the price should not be set** and the incremental profit that would be obtained from any price that is charged in excess of the minimum.

Limiting factor pricing

2.10 Another approach to pricing might be taken when a business is working at full capacity, and is restricted by a shortage of resources from expanding its output further. By deciding what target profit it would like to earn, it could establish a **mark-up per unit of limiting factor**.

The demand-based approach to pricing

2.11 We have now looked at a variety of cost-based approaches to pricing. **Demand-based approaches** are less common and more difficult to set.

(a) Price theory or demand theory is based on the idea that a connection can be made between price, **quantity** demanded and sold, and total **revenue**. The theory of demand cannot be applied in practice, however, unless **realistic estimates of demand at different price** levels can be made.

(b) In practice, businesses might not make estimates of demand at different price levels, but they might still make pricing decisions on the basis of **demand conditions** and **competition** in the market. When competitors sell exactly the same product in the same market, price differences are likely to have a significant effect on demand.

Marketing at Work

This is the case with oil companies and the price of petrol at filling stations: different companies sell the same product and so, within a local area, the prices charged at each station (whether BP, Shell, Esso or Texaco) will be much the same. If they were not, customers would go to the cheapest place.

2.12 When companies sell similar products which are not exactly identical, or where the geographical location of the sales point is of some significance, there is more scope for charging different prices. Even so, the prices charges by competitors cannot be ignored altogether. Price differences can be achieved in a number of ways.

(a) Through **product quality**

(b) Through **design differences** (Motor cars are an obvious example)

(c) Through **geographical location**

Marketing at Work

The prices of crossing the English Channel by ferry vary between different ports of departure. Holiday flights from different regional airports may attract varying regional supplements.

(d) Through **brand loyalty**.

2.13 An **average price strategy** and a **lowest price strategy** are two forms of price strategy based on what competitors charge.

(a) An **average price strategy** is to set prices which are average for the industry and might be adopted either if the products sold by all firms in the market are roughly the same or if the company does not wish to be an aggressor in the market, for fear of provoking a **price war** or increased competition.

(b) A **lowest price strategy** is to set the lowest prices available. A lowest price strategy might be associated with aggression in the market, in order to attract more customers or with products of a lower quality.

2.14 Generally speaking, price cuts to increase market share will be matched by competitors in some way. If a rival firm cuts its prices in the expectation of increasing its market share, a firm has the following options.

(a) **Maintain its existing prices**. This would be done if the expectation is that only a small market share would be lost, so that it is more profitable to keep prices at their existing level.

(b) **Maintain prices but responding with a non-price counter-attach**. This is a more positive response, because the firm will be securing or justifying its current prices with a product change, advertising, or better back-up services, etc.

(c) **Reduce prices**. This should protect the firm's market share so that the main beneficiary from the price reduction will be the consumer.

(d) **Raise prices and respond with a non-price counter-attack**. A price increase would be based on a campaign to emphasise the quality difference between the rival products.

Marketing at Work

During the summer of 1995 Superdrug, the fast-growing discount drugstore company, cut its branded suncare prices by 25%, in a headline-grabbing price offensive. Days after Superdrug acted Boots, Britain's largest chemists chain, announced 30% price cuts. These strategies were repeated during the summer of 1996 in the Baked Bean wars, when the price of own-brand baked beans in large retailers such as Sainsbury and Tesco fell to 9p in a bid to see off the low price strategy of Kwik-Save. Recently the supermarkets indulged in a price war over white bread, which saw loaves priced as low as 9p.

Pricing strategies

6/00

New product pricing strategies

2.15 A **new product pricing strategy** will depend on whether the product is the first of its kind on the market, in which case the company will be able to set a price at which it thinks its profits will be maximised, or if it is following a competitor's product onto the market, in which case the pricing strategy will be constrained by what the competitor is doing. There are two alternative strategies.

(a) **Market penetration pricing** is a policy of **low prices** when the product is **first launched** in order to obtain sufficient penetration into the market. A penetration policy may be appropriate in the following circumstances.

   (i) If the firm wishes to **discourage new entrants** into the market

   (ii) If the firm wishes to **shorten the initial period of the product's life cycle** in order to enter the growth and maturity stages as quickly as possible

   (iii) If there are significant **economies of scale** to be achieved from a high volume of output, so that quick penetration into the market is desirable in order to gain unit cost reductions

   (iv) If demand is **highly elastic** and so would respond well to low prices.

(b) In contrast, **market skimming** involves charging **high prices** when a product is first launched and spending heavily on **advertising and sales promotion** to obtain sales. As the product moves into the later stages of its life, progressively lower prices will be charged. The aim of market skimming is to **gain high unit profits early in the product's life**. High unit prices make it more likely that competitors will enter the market. Such a policy may be appropriate in the following circumstances.

   (i) Where the product is **new and different**, so that customers are prepared to pay high prices.

   (ii) Where the **strength of demand** and the **sensitivity of demand** to price are unknown. It is better from the point of view of marketing to start by charging high prices and then reduce them if the demand for the product turns out to be price elastic.

   (iii) Where high prices in the early stages of a product's life might generate **high initial cash flows**.

   (iv) Where the firm can identify **different market segments** for the product, each prepared to pay progressively lower prices. If **product differentiation** can be introduced, it may be possible to continue to sell at higher prices to some market segments when lower prices are charged in others.

   (v) Where products may have a **short life cycle**, and so need to recover their development costs and make a profit relatively quickly.

Product mix pricing strategies

2.16 The strategy for setting a price often has to be changed when the product is part of a **product mix**. The organisation looks for a set of prices that maximise the profit on the total mix. Various pricing strategies exist.

(a) **Product line pricing** involves developing a product line in which each successive item in the line offers more features/higher quality for a higher price. If the price difference between two successive products is small, buyers will usually buy the more advanced/better quality product. If the cost difference is smaller than the price difference, profits are increased, and the profitability of the line as a whole is maximised.

(b) **Optional product pricing** involves selling optional or accessory products along with the main product. For example a car buyer can order electric windows and a sunroof.

(c) **Captive product pricing** involves selling products that must be used along with a main product. The main products (such as razors) are priced low and the related products (such as blades) are priced high. In the case of services this strategy is called **two-part**

pricing. The price of the service is broken down into a fixed fee (entry into an amusement park) plus a variable usage rate (fees for food and rides).

(d) **By-product pricing** involves accepting any price for a low value by-product that covers more than the cost of storing and delivering it. The price of the main product can then be reduced to make it more competitive.

(e) **Product bundle pricing** involves combining several products and offering the whole bundle at a reduced price.

Marketing at Work

Hotels sell specially-priced packages which include room, meals and entertainment. Entire holidays, especially in the Caribbean, are now sold on this all-inclusive basis, covering everything from flights to jet ski hire.

Price adjustment strategies

2.17 Basic prices may need to be **adjusted** to account for customer differences and changing situations. There are a number of relevant strategies.

(a) **Discount pricing and allowances**

(i) **Cash discount** is a price reduction for buyers who pay their bills promptly.

(ii) **Quantity discount** is a price reduction for buyers who buy large volumes.

(iii) **Trade discount** (also called a **functional discount**) is a price reduction given to an intermediary for performing certain functions such as storage.

(iv) **Seasonal discount** is a price reduction for buyers who buy products or services out of season, such as cheaper hotel prices in the winter.

(v) **Allowances** include **trade in allowances and promotional allowances**.

Action Programme 1

What are the disadvantages of offering price discounts to cash customers in an attempt to increase customer numbers?

(b) **Discriminatory pricing**. Where a company can sell to two or more separate markets, it might be able to charge a different price in each market to maximise its profits. There are several ways in practice by which price discrimination can be exercised.

(i) **Negotiation with individual customers**. For example, customer A might buy a video cassette recorder from Firm X for £600 cash, whereas customer B might buy the same item and negotiate a discount for cash of, say, 10%.

(ii) **On the basis of quantities purchased**. Bulk purchase discounts are a well-established form of price discrimination, offering favourable prices to large customers.

(iii) **By product type**. This involves some form of product differentiation so that customers in one market segment will buy a product basically similar to (but differentiated from) a product sold to another market segment, but at a different price. Examples of price discrimination through product differentiation are to be found in the sale of clothing and cars (customers may pay disproportionately higher amounts for a car with a larger engine capacity or a more comfortable interior).

(iv) **By time**. Examples are services with peak time and off-peak tariffs, such as hotel accommodation in holiday resorts and charges for telephone calls.

(v) **By location**. Higher prices may be charged in some locations than in others so that a firm with several branches in various towns may set different prices in each branch. Branches in remote locations might set higher prices and in poorer areas they might set lower prices.

For price discrimination to be successful, certain **market conditions** must exist.

(i) The producer must enjoy a **dominant position** in the market, perhaps as a monopolist or as the provider of a branded product or quality product which commands a high degree of **customer loyalty**.

(ii) Where price discrimination is exercised on the basis of individual negotiation or by geographical area, there must be no opportunity for rivals to buy the product at the cheaper price and sell it at a competitive higher price to the higher priced market.

Marketing at Work

Many supermarkets and multiple retail stores sell their 'own label' products, often at a lower price than established branded products. The supermarkets or multiple retailers do this by entering into arrangements with manufacturers, to supply their goods under the 'own brand' label. This is a form of price discrimination.

(c) **Psychological pricing** considers the psychology of prices and not simply the economics. The price is used to say something about the product.

(d) **Promotional pricing** involves temporarily pricing products below list price, and sometimes below cost, to increase short-run sales.

(i) **Loss leaders** are used to attract customers in the hope that they will buy other goods at normal mark-up.

(ii) **Special event pricing** might be used in certain seasons.

(iii) **Cash rebates** are offered to consumers who buy the product from dealers within a specified time.

(iv) **Discounts** may be offered.

Marketing at Work

'Everyday low pricing strategies - the policy of scrapping promotions in favour of sharp, permanent price cuts - were pioneered by Procter & Gamble in the US where they helped the company reclaim market share from competing brands and "own label" products.

The latest company to adopt this strategy is Esso which launched its "Pricewatch" initiative offering "normally unbeatable" prices within a distance of three miles. The policy was introduced after research showed that customers valued lower prices above collections and promotions. Asda in the UK tries to differentiate itself from rivals by emphasising its "permanently low prices".

The logic of getting away from promotions is supported by research which shows that promotions are only taken up by people who were already customers.'

Financial Times

(e) **Geographical pricing strategies** cover different freight charging strategies (which depend on the location of customers).

Discount policy

2.18 The purpose of discounts is to encourage **more sales (or earlier payment)**. The cost of discounts should not exceed the benefits from extra sales or earlier payment, and the size of discounts offered should not be excessive. After all, why offer a 15% discount for a sale if the customer would still buy if he obtained a 10% discount?

2.19 Discounts help to make a firm's products more price-competitive, but the size of discount that can be offered must depend on the **variable cost/sales price ratio**. For example, a firm whose variable costs are 25% of the gross sales price will have more flexibility with discount policy than a firm whose variable costs are 80% of the gross sales price, because it has a bigger contribution margin to play with. Stepped discounts, ie bigger discounts rising in steps for bigger sales orders, must also be planned carefully, and the size of the price breaks should be sensible.

Competitive bidding and tendering

2.20 Competitive bidding calls for the preparation of cost data for the purpose of submitting a bid to a potential customer, in the hope of securing his order. There will be three factors in the customer's choice of supplier from among the tenders submitted.

(a) The **price** itself

(b) **Performance**, especially if the product is new and largely untested in the open market, reliability, service etc

(c) **Financial matters**, such as inflation (and cost escalation clauses) and foreign exchange rates (for overseas contracts), export credit insurance

2.21 Co-operation is needed between the accounting and marketing departments of a bidding company because a balance has to be drawn between putting in a bid which is too low to make an adequate profit, but keeping the bid low enough to stand a good chance of winning the contract. Consideration must be given to the following.

(a) The **contribution to profit** that would be obtained from the contract

(b) The **consequences** for the company if it failed to win the order

(c) The **probability** of winning the order, which might be assessed on the basis of past experience

(d) **Possible non-price product differentiation** in favour of the supplier eg quality of service, reliable delivery times, finance facilities offered

2.22 An article in the *Financial Times* (23 May 1996) looked at a report in the Bank of England Quarterly Bulletin (24 May 1996) on the way in which companies set prices in Britain. Although it is several years old it is a good illustration of the issues behind pricing strategy.

'The article describes the results of a survey of more than 700 companies carried out by the bank last autumn. Almost 40 per cent of the companies questioned said they set prices at the highest level they thought the market would bear. A further 25 per cent said prices were set in relation to their competitors'. In contrast, some 37 per cent said they set prices by adding a fixed or variable mark-up to their costs of production.

The survey asked the same question in a different way by asking firms to rank in order of importance a series of theories which sets out to explain why prices in the real world appear to be sticky. This suggested a greater role for cost-based pricing than the other question had, especially among small firms for which the expense of monitoring market conditions is relatively burdensome. The most popular theory was one suggesting that firms *do* change prices in

BPP PUBLISHING

response to fluctuations in market conditions, but only to a limited degree because their costs do not rise much as they increase output.

Next most popular after the cost-based theories was one based on companies' desire to avoid price wars. Under this hypothesis, businesses are reluctant to change their prices even in response to changing costs, fearing their competitors will follow suit and - in the case of a price cut - trigger a downward spiral.

One would expect policies that promoted competition to encourage market-based pricing at the expense of cost-based pricing. Competition should also reduce the size of the mark-up that companies can sustain. This is difficult to assess, but some clues emerge from a recent study of mark-ups in the manufacturing sectors of industrial countries carried out by the Organisation for Economic Co-operation and Development. This suggests that the highest mark-ups have been whittled away in most countries in recent years, perhaps because greater openness to trade has made competition tougher.

Interestingly, the pattern of mark-ups from industry to industry has changed little since the 1970s. High mark-ups remain most prevalent in industries such as tobacco products, industrial chemicals, drugs, medicines and computers, and radio, television and communications equipment. Mark-ups are relatively low for textiles, food, printing, electric machinery and motor vehicles.

Mark-ups are higher in those industries comprising relatively few competitors than in those with many. They are also higher in industries in which companies produce differentiated products rather than homogeneous ones. But this does not mean that high mark-ups are necessarily a bad thing. They may provide a reward for expensive innovation.'

Other pricing decisions

2.23 **Promotional prices** are short-term price reductions or price offers which are intended to attract an increase in sales volume. (The increase is usually short-term for the duration of the offer, which does not appear to create any substantial new customer loyalty.) Loss leaders and 'money off' coupons are a form of promotional pricing.

2.24 A **temporary price cut** may be preferable to a permanent reduction because it can be ended without unduly offending customers and can be reinstated later to give a repeated boost to sales. They may be used as sales promotions to establish new brands.

2.25 **Short-term pricing**. Marketing management should have the responsibility for estimating the relationship between price and demand for their organisation's products.

(a) The sales-revenue maximising price for a product and the profit-maximising price might not be the same.

(b) Simple **CVP analysis** can be used to estimate the breakeven point of sales, and the sales volume needed to achieve a target profit figure. We cover this in the next chapter.

(c) As we have seen in this chapter, many organisations use a **cost-plus approach** to pricing. Accounting figures are needed for cost in order to establish a floor for making a cost-plus pricing decision. The size of the profit margin will be decided by marketing management.

2.26 The marketing department's contribution to **short-run pricing decisions** is not only to assess a basic demand curve relationship between price and sales volume, and an assessment of the elasticity of demand for the firm's products, but also to consider how prices might be adjusted to allow for particular product, market or customer characteristics.

(a) **Product analysis pricing** combines the effects of cost-plus pricing and what the market will bear. An attempt is made to add up all the attributes of the product to ascertain the price that the customer will pay. The characteristics will include finish, strength and durability, and the pricing model will be built up using a sample of products with known selling prices and values for each of the characteristics. A price for other products can then be decided accordingly. It works well if the decision is fairly routine.

(b) **Quality adjusted pricing** brings in the aspect of product quality into the assessment of price.

Data for pricing decisions

2.27 Organisations need a multitude of data to make pricing decisions.

(a) **Cost data**

This can be obtained from internal cost and management accounting records and other internal secondary data sources.

(b) **Demand data**

To be able to estimate demand for products or services at different price levels an organisation may well have to commission **pricing research**. We will be looking at pricing research in detail in Part D of the Study Text. Such research will need to consider, for example, **elasticities of demand** and **customer perceptions** of price and quality.

(c) **Competitor data**

Information about competitors is vital for pricing decisions. The sources of competitor information are summarised below.

(i)   Published data sources (eg published financial statements, press releases)
(ii)   Sales force data
(iii) Trade databases
(iv) Industry experts
(v)   Trade press
(vi) Distributors
(vii) Suppliers
(viii) Customers

3   TRANSFER PRICING

Specimen paper

Key Concept

A **transfer price** is the price at which a product component or service is passed, internally, from one company division to another. There are various methods of setting a transfer price but one of the key concerns is that it reflect commercial reality.

3.1 Where there are **transfers of goods or services between divisions,** the transfers could be made 'free' to the division receiving the benefit. For example, if a garage and car showroom has two divisions, one for car repairs and servicing and the other for sales, the servicing division will be required to service cars before they are sold. The servicing division could do its work for the car sales division without making any record of the work done. However, unless the cost or value of such work is recorded, management cannot keep a check on the amount of resources (such as labour time) being used up on new car servicing. It is necessary for control purposes that some record of the inter-divisional services should be kept. Inter-divisional work can be given a cost or charge: a **transfer price**.

3.2 Since **profit centre performance** is measured according to the profit they earn, no profit centre will want to do work for another and incur costs without being paid for it. But, because the size of the transfer price will affect the costs of one profit centre and the revenues of another, profit centre managers are likely to dispute the size of transfer prices. We will talk more about **profit centres** in the context of **budgets** and **responsibility accounting** in Chapter 11.

3.3 A transfer price should be set at a level that overcomes such disputes.

    (a) The transfer price should provide an **'artificial' selling price** that enables the transferring division to earn a return for its efforts, and the receiving division to incur a cost for benefits received.

    (b) The transfer price should be set at a level that enables profit centre performance to be measured 'commercially'. This means that the transfer price should be a **fair commercial price**.

3.4 We will begin by looking at the two types of transfer price that can be used **if selling prices and costs remain constant**, whatever the quantity of products/services supplied.

    (a) Transfer prices based on **market price**
    (b) Transfer prices based on **cost**

We will then move on to consider transfer prices based on opportunity costs and, finally, how to negotiate an optimal transfer price.

Market price as the transfer price

3.5 If an external market price exists for transferred goods, profit centre managers will be aware of the price they could obtain or the price they would have to pay for their goods on the external market, and they would inevitably compare this price with the transfer price.

Example: transferring goods at market price

3.6 A company has two profit centres, A and B. Centre A sells half of its output on the open market and transfers the other half to B. Costs and external revenues in a period are as follows.

	A £	B £	Total £
External sales	8,000	24,000	32,000
Costs of production	12,000	10,000	22,000
Company profit			10,000

Required

What are the consequences of setting a transfer price at market price?

3.7 If the transfer price is at market price, A would be happy to sell the output to B for £8,000, which is what A would get by selling it externally.

	A		B		Total
	£	£	£	£	£
Market sales		8,000		24,000	32,000
Transfer sales		8,000		-	
		16,000		24,000	
Transfer costs		-	8,000		
Own costs	12,000		10,000		22,000
		12,000		18,000	
Profit		4,000		6,000	10,000

3.8 The consequences, therefore, are as follows.

(a) **A earns the same profit** on transfers as on external sales. B must pay a commercial price for transferred goods.

(b) A will be indifferent about selling externally or transferring goods to B because the profit is the same on both types of transaction. B can therefore ask for and obtain as many units as it wants from A.

Adjusted market price

3.9 Internal transfers in practice are often cheaper than external sales, with savings in selling and administration costs, bad debt risks and possibly transport/delivery costs. It would seem reasonable for the buying division to expect a **discount** on the external market price.

Cost-based approaches to transfer pricing

3.10 **Cost-based approaches to transfer pricing** are often used in practice, because there is often no external market for the product that is being transferred or because, although there is an external market, it is an imperfect one because there is only limited external demand.

Transfer prices based on full cost

3.11 Under this approach the full standard cost (including fixed overheads absorbed) that is incurred by the supplying division in making the product is charged to the receiving division. If a **full cost plus** approach is used, a profit margin is also included in this transfer price.

3.12 A company has two profit centres, A and B. Centre A can only sell half of its maximum output externally because of limited demand. It transfers the other half of its output to B which also faces limited demand. Costs and revenues in a period are as follows.

	A	B	Total
	£	£	£
External sales	8,000	24,000	32,000
Costs of production in the division	12,000	10,000	22,000
(Loss)/Profit	(4,000)	14,000	10,000

3.13 If the transfer price is at full cost, A in our example would have 'sales' to B of £6,000 (ie half of its total costs of production). This would be a cost to B, as follows.

BPP PUBLISHING

	A			B		Company as a whole
	£	£	£	£	£	£
Open market sales		8,000			24,000	32,000
Transfer sales		6,000			-	
Total sales, inc transfers		14,000			24,000	
Transfer costs				6,000		
Own costs	12,000			10,000		22,000
Total costs, inc transfers		12,000			16,000	
Profit		2,000			8,000	10,000

The transfer sales of A are self-cancelling with the transfer costs of B so that total profits are unaffected. The transfer price simply spreads the total profit of £10,000 between A and B. Division A makes no profit on its work and using this method, would prefer to sell its output on the open market if it could.

Transfer prices based on full cost plus

3.14 If the transfers are at cost plus a margin of, say, 25%, A's sales to B would be £7,500.

	A		B		Total
	£	£	£	£	£
Open market sales		8,000		24,000	32,000
Transfer sales		7,500		-	
		15,500		24,000	
Transfer costs			7,500		
Own costs	12,000		10,000		22,000
		12,000		17,500	
Profit		3,500		6,500	10,000

3.15 Compared to a transfer price at cost, A gains some profit at the expense of B. However, A makes a bigger profit on external sales in this case because the profit mark-up of 25% is less than the profit mark-up on open market sales, which is (£8,000 – 6,000)/£6,000 = 33%. The transfer price does not give A fair revenue or charge B a reasonable cost, and so their profit performance is distorted. It would seem to give A an incentive to sell more goods externally and transfer less to B. This may or may not be in the best interests of the company as a whole.

3.16 Division A's total costs of £12,000 will include an element of fixed costs. Half of division A's total costs are transferred to division B. However from the point of view of division B the cost is entirely variable.

3.17 Suppose that the cost per unit to A is £15 and that this includes a fixed element of £6, while division B's own costs are £25 per unit, including a fixed element of £10. The total variable cost is really £9 + £15 = £24, but from division B's point of view the variable cost is £15 + £15 = £30. This means that division B will be unwilling to sell the final product for less than £30, whereas any price above £24 would make a contribution.

Transfer prices based on variable cost

3.18 A variable cost approach entails charging the variable cost that has been incurred by the supplying division to the receiving division. As above, we shall suppose that A's cost per unit is £15, of which £6 is fixed and £9 variable.

	£	A £	£	B £	Company as a whole £	£
Market sales		8,000		24,000		32,000
Transfer sales at variable cost		3,600		-		
$\left(\dfrac{£9}{£15} \times 6,000\right)$						
		11,600		24,000		
Transfer costs		-		3,600		
Own variable costs	7,200		6,000		13,200	
Own fixed costs	4,800		4,000		8,800	
Total costs and transfers		12,000		13,600		22,000
(Loss)/Profit		(400)		10,400		10,000

3.19 The problem is that with a transfer price at variable cost the supplying division does not cover its fixed costs.

Transfer prices based on opportunity costs

3.20 It has been suggested that transfer prices can be set using the following rule.

> **Transfer price** per unit = **standard variable cost** in the producing division *plus* the opportunity cost to the organisation of supplying the unit internally.

3.21 The opportunity cost will be one of the following.

(a) The maximum **contribution foregone** by the supplying division in transferring internally rather than selling externally

(b) The **contribution foregone** by not using the same facilities in the producing division for their next best alternative use

3.22 (a) If there is no external market for the item being transferred, and no alternative uses for the division's facilities, the transfer price = standard variable cost of production.

(b) If there is an external market for the item being transferred and no alternative use for the facilities, the transfer price = the market price.

4 DIRECT PRODUCT PROFITABILITY   6/00, 12/00

4.1 One way of comparing the performance of individual products would be to look at levels of revenue and contribution, perhaps in one of the following ways.

(a) **Comparison of contribution level**

Product group	Sales revenue £'000	% of total	Contribution to profits £'000	% of total
B	7,500	35.7	2,500	55.6
E	2,000	9.5	1,200	26.7
C	4,500	21.4	450	10.0
A	5,000	23.8	250	5.6
D	2,000	9.5	100	2.2
	21,000	100.0	4,500	100.0

If there is an imbalance between sales and profits over various product ranges, there is a potentially dangerous situation to which planners have to address their thoughts. In the figures above, product group A accounts for 23.8% of turnover but only 5.6% of total contribution, and product group D accounts for 9.5% of turnover but only 2.2% of total contribution.

(b) An analysis of sales and profitability into **export markets** and **domestic markets**

(c) Estimated share of the market obtained by **each product group**

(d) **Sales growth and contribution growth** over the previous four years or so, for each product group

(e) **Product demand**

    (i) Growing, stable or likely to decline

    (ii) Whether new products are emerging to replace existing ones in the market

    (iii) Whether demand is price sensitive or not

    (iv) Is the market becoming fragmented, with more specialist products?

    (v) The likely total size of the market

4.2 The company might want even more detailed information so as to be able to see the profitability of each product after charging every attributable cost. This is called **direct product profitability,** or DPP, and the information is presented as a **direct product profitability statement.**

Key Concept

Direct product profitability (DPP) is a technique to analyse the profit on each **individual product line,** by calculating the value of sales less direct and suitably apportioned costs. Product marketing costs are directly related to the product.

4.3 **Supermarkets** analyse the direct profitability of every branded and non-branded product they sell. This helps them to decide on what ranges to present in-store and also provides a focus for individual marketing initiatives. The profitability of entire commodity groups is presented after taking all costs and factors into account, such as supplier discounts and wastage levels.

4.4 It is useful to analyse how DPP can be used by the marketer in practice. Let's take an example.

	Product		
	X	Y	Z
Selling price	£1.50	£1.25	£1.30
Purchase cost	£1.00	£0.80	£1.00
Contribution	£0.50	£0.45	£0.30
Contribution % of sales price	33%	36%	23%
Shelf space per unit	15 cm^2	9 cm^2	12 cm^2
Contribution per cm^2	3.3p	5p	2.5p

4.5 This analysis would imply that Y was the most profitable for the retailer: however this ignores stock turnover. Let us add sales volumes into the calculation and also estimate how much shelf space the product takes up.

	Product		
	X	Y	Z
Contribution per product	£0.50	£0.45	£0.30
Total shelf space taken up (say)	750 cm^2	600 cm^2	1,200 cm^2
Weekly sales volume	30	20	60
Contribution per cm^2 per week	$\dfrac{50p \times 30}{750} = 2p$	$\dfrac{45p \times 20}{600} = 1.5p$	$\dfrac{30p \times 60}{1,200} = 1.5p$

4.6 This analysis, based on sales volume, suggests that for the retailer X is the better bet. Why might this be so?

(a) **Stock turnover**. The manufacturer of X might offer to replenish the shelves twice a week, thereby halving the amount of space needed to support the same sales volume. This increases the contribution per unit of scarce resource.

(b) **Product size** is a reason why the unit contribution might differ. This is why packaging decisions can, from the retailer's viewpoint, affect a product's attractiveness.

4.7 **Advantages of DPP statements**

(a) The profit that is made on an individual item is calculated. This information could be used to adjust advertising expenditure, offer price discounts or promotional allowances and so on.

(b) The statement may show that a particular line makes a loss.

(c) The statement may reveal that one product is more profitable than another. Sales people might then be targeted at selling the more profitable lines, for example.

(d) The statement can focus the attention on the individual costs that make up a product. For instance, the company could analyse the costs and decide to use cheaper ingredients, transport and so on.

4.8 **Problems with DPP statements**

(a) DPP statements can be time-consuming and costly to prepare and to analyse.

(b) The allocation of costs to individual products may be artibrary.

(c) Expenditure supporting a brand can be spread over a number of different individual products, and it might not be a simple matter to allocate this expenditure properly.

(d) **Cross-subsidisation** is a feature of many product strategies. An example is provided by computer games.

(i) The hardware (eg the games console) may be priced relatively cheaply:

(1) To deter competitors (raising entry barriers)
(2) To encourage customers to buy

(ii) The software, or games which are run, will be priced relatively expensively, to recoup some of the cost. Also, barriers to entry will exist as the manufacturer will own patents, have exclusive distribution deals etc, and there will be a switching cost, of course.

(e) Organisations may waste time arguing about the allocation of costs.

> **Exam Tip**
>
> The June 2000 and December 2001 exams required an analysis of DPP, and the preparation of BPP statements based upon it.

5 PRODUCT LIFE CYCLE AND FINANCIAL INFORMATION

5.1 By this stage in your studies you will be familiar with the product life cycle and BCG analysis. Both of these models can give the marketer useful information about performance which can provide pointers for future strategy.

5.2 You might consider these to be purely marketing issues, but both the product life cycle and BCG analysis feed into **financial performance**. After all, a cash cow is so called because it generates cash, for reinvestment elsewhere.

Product life cycle

5.3 The management of a product should fit its prevailing life cycle stage. You will be familiar with the stages.

(a) **Development**. Money will be spent on market research and product development. Investment will have to be evaluated as explained in the previous chapter.

(b) **Launches** require expensive promotion campaigns.

(i) If demand is high, the firm can pursue a **price-skimming policy**, maximising the return until competitors enter the market.

(ii) It may prefer, however, to **build a market** for the products with **low prices** which will also dissuade competitors.

(iii) There is considerable uncertainty at this stage, and there is a **risk** that the launch might fail.

(iv) The risk of this stage is also influenced by the size of the launch costs: if these turn out to be greater than expected, the overall return earned by the product over its life cycle will be less.

(c) **Growth**. The market grows, as does the demand for the product.

(i) The **marketing** mix might turn out to be inappropriate for the product (eg the price is set too high).

(ii) **Competitors** will enter, thereby reducing the profits that can be earned.

(d) **Maturity**. At this stage, it is anticipated that few new competitors will enter the market.

(i) If a firm survives this far, returns perhaps are lower than before but the risk of being forced out of business for product-market reasons is reduced.

(ii) It is always possible that **technical or marketing innovation** by competitors, or the invention of **substitute products**, might change the characteristics of this supposedly mature market.

(e) **Decline**. Profits fall at this stage as demand tails off.

Control measures

5.4 Owing to the different market conditions at each stage of the life cycle, different types of suitable decision-making information will be needed.

(a) **Development and launch**

Before the launch, the firm should undertake **DCF evaluation**, treating the product as if it were an investment. This can indicate whether, despite all the costs that have been sunk so far, it is worthwhile going ahead. DCF can also give some indication of the suitability of different marketing strategies, as well as the effect of any delays on pickup of demand for the project.

(b) **Growth**. Once the product has been launched, critical success factors include relative market share, market growth and competitor activity.

(c) **Maturity**. At this stage, the business's objective should be to **maximise its earnings** from the product.

(i) Financial control measures such as **return on investment (ROI)** are now more relevant than before (see Chapter 12).

(ii) **Relative market share** is important. Marketing expenditure should be assessed on the basis of what would happen if it was not incurred: it is cheaper to keep existing customers than to win new ones.

(d) **Decline.** If exit barriers are high, firms will continue competing in a loss making industry, but short-term **cash flows** might be positive. A declining industry requires fewer assets to service it. **Opportunity costing** can be used to assess whether it is worth staying in the business at all.

5.5 It is possible to summarise the different information needs of different stages of the product life cycle below.

	Launch	Growth	Maturity	Decline
Characteristics	High business risk. Negative net cash flow. DCF evaluation for overall investment	High business risk. Neutral net cash flow	Medium business risk. Positive cash flow.	Low risk. Neutral-positive cash flow.
Critical success factors	Increasing time to launch	Market share growth. Sustaining competitive advantage	Contribution per unit of limiting factor. Customer retention.	Timely exit.
Information needs	Market research into (size and demand)	Market growth, share. Diminishing returns. Competitor marketing strategies	Comparative competitor costs. Limiting factors	Rate of decline; best time to leave; reliable sale values of assets.
Financial information	Strategic; 'milestones'. Physical evaluation. Mainly non-financial measures owing to volatility (eg rate of take up by consumers)	DCF. Market share. Marketing objectives.	ROI. Profit margin. Maintaining market share.	Free cash flow (for investment elsewhere).

Marketing at Work

Chiroscience is a UK biotechnology company. Biotechnology firms require heavy upfront development in R&D.

According to the *Financial Times* (29 April 1997):

'Chiroscience, one of the UK's largest biotechnology companies, has sharply increased spending and losses in an effort to push its most advanced products to market.

BPP
PUBLISHING

The group yesterday reported a pre-tax loss of £18.7m for the year to February, against £11.6m. Expenses were £27.1m, up 67 per cent on last year's £16.3m. There was net cash and investments of £51.4m. The spending rate was higher than analysts had expected and the shares fell 17½p to 335p.

Costs were rising because the most important drug in development, an anaesthetic levobupivacaine, had entered the final and most expensive medical tests. Mr John Padfield, chief executive, said the trials should be over in time for the drug to be submitted to European medicine regulators by the end of this year.

Financial information and the Boston Matrix

5.6   In the product life cycle model, the product is expected to grow, mature and die. The different categories of the BCG matrix might appear similar. We can simplify the BCG matrix and state the following.

(a) **Stars,** with a high share of a high growth market, still require investment, so cash flows will be neutral. Increased revenue is taken up in increased costs in building the market, raising entry barriers etc. The aim is to transform stars into cash cows.

(b) **Dogs** also have a neutral cash flow, requiring little expenditure, but enjoying only a low market share. The characteristics might be similar to the decline stage of the life cycle. Free cash flow, from sales revenue and disposals, is a useful measure.

(c) **Cash cows** are valuable because they generate cash for investment. The high market share should be maintained at minimum cost. Relevant accounting techniques might include ROI and contribution per unit of limiting factor.

(d) **Question marks** have the potential to be turned into stars or cash cows, but require more 'investment' to do so, as they have a low share of a high growth market. This investment in market share can be valued and assessed using DCF.

Action Programme 2

Product X is a product with a 5% share of a market currently worth £2m, which is expected to grow by 20% a year for the next five years, which will be stable for the five years after that, and then which will suddenly decline. Product X earns contribution of 50% of sales revenue. Fixed costs are £100,000 pa. A heavy advertising campaign, costing £200,000 in year 1 and £200,000 in year 2 would drive competitors out of the market giving the firm 10% share at the end of year 1, and 25% thereafter. However, additional advertising expenditure of £30,000 a year would have to be made thereafter. The company's cost of capital is 10% pa.

To recap from Chapter 8, how would you go about evaluating the problem? (You do not need to calculate a full answer).

6   CUSTOMER PROFITABILITY

The examiner could test pricing and profitability themes in a number of situations. Customer profitability is an obvious area, and you may be asked about the setting of appropriate selling prices for various types of customer, bringing in issues such as the giving of discounts. Remember always that you are going to be required to apply your knowledge to given contexts.

6.1 **Key customer analysis** calls for six main areas of investigation into customers. A firm might wish to identify which customers offer most profit.

(a) Key **customer identity**

(b) **Customer history**

(c) **Relationship of customer to product**

   (i)   What does the customer use the product for?

   (ii)   Do the products form part of the customer's own service/product?

(d) **Relationship of customer to potential market**

(e) **Customer attitudes and behaviour**

(f) **The financial performance of the customer**

(g) **The profitability of selling to the customer** (This is the area we will expand on below)

Such an evaluation would be a part of research into potential market opportunities. Smaller customers should not be ignored and there should be a similar analysis of the organisation's other customers, although a separate analysis for each individual customer may not be worthwhile, and customers may be grouped - ie on the basis of order sizes or another such characteristic (ie geographical basis).

Customer profitability analysis (customer account profitability)

6.2 'An immediate impact of introducing any level of strategic management accounting into virtually every organisation is to destroy totally any illusion that the same level of profit is derived from all customers.'

(Ward, *Strategic Management Accounting*)

Marketing at Work

As a basic example, take the Post Office. A uniform price is paid for a first class stamp irrespective of whether it is to be delivered to an address five miles away or five hundred (in the UK), despite the significant differences in transport costs. Of course, the advantages of a uniform price are that there are savings on the costs of administering a wide range of prices and that people are encouraged to use the postal services.

6.3 The total costs of servicing customers can vary depending on **how** customers are serviced.

(a) **Volume discounts**. A customer who places one large order is given a discount, presumably because it benefits the supplier to do so (eg savings on administrative overhead in processing the orders - as identified by an activity based costing system).

(b) **Different rates** charged by power companies to domestic as opposed to business users. This in part reflects the administrative overhead of dealing with individual customers. In practice, many domestic consumers benefit from cross-subsidy.

6.4 **Customer profitability** is the 'total sales revenue generated from a customer or customer group, less all the costs that are incurred in servicing that customer or customer group'.

Action Programme 3

Seth Ltd supplies shoes to Narayan Ltd and Kipling Ltd. Each pair of shoes has a list price of £50 each; as Kipling buys in bulk, Kipling receives a 10% trade discount for every order over 100 shoes. It costs £1,000 to deliver each order. In the year so far, Kipling has made five orders of 100 shoes each. Narayan Ltd receives a 15% discount irrespective of order size, because Narayan Ltd collects the shoes, thereby saving Seth Ltd any distribution costs. The cost of administering each order is £50. Narayan makes ten orders in the year, totalling 420 pairs of shoes. Which relationship is the most profitable for Seth?

Key Concept

Customer profitability analysis (CPA) focuses on profits generated by customers and suggests that profit does not automatically increase with sales revenue. With CPA a company:

(a) can focus its efforts on customers who promise the highest profit

(b) can rationalise its approach to those which do not.

6.5 An important area in marketing strategy is **retaining customers,** so as to generate new business from them. (Repeat business from existing customers is cheaper than fighting for new customers.)

    (a) This is especially true of the market which is declining or static, in which case retention is necessary to increase or maintain profitability.

    (b) If the business has a **high fixed cost base,** then new business from existing customers creates **additional contribution.** For example, a bookshop might sell greetings cards or compact discs. Building an image of quality helped Marks and Spencer diversify from clothing into food. A danger, of course, is that all these products must fit into the same set of customer expectations as the original, or else the brand image will be contaminated.

Identifying profitable customers/segments

6.6 But how do you identify which customers, or customer groups generate the most profit?

    (a) This is a consideration that must be brought into the design of marketing information systems.

    (b) The firm's existing customer groupings, may reflect administrative measures rather than their strategic value. We explore this in the exercise below.

Action Programme 4

Busqueros Ltd has 1,000 business customers spread fairly evenly over the UK. The sales force is organised into ten regions, each with 100 customers to be serviced. There are sales force offices at the heart of each region. Information is collected on a regional basis. The marketing director has recently carried out an analysis of the major customers by sales revenue. There are five significant customers, who between them account for 20% of the sales revenue of the firm. They do not get special treatment. What does this say about customer profitability analysis in Busqueros Ltd?

6.7 To analyse customer profitability successfully it may be necessary to structure information systems to take account of the many factors by which customers can be analysed. A relational database, whereby information can be structured in many different ways, offers a useful approach.

6.8 How do you apportion costs to customer segments? Assume you have a customer base of 15,000 people. You have just spent £20,000 on an advertising campaign in part to attract new customers, and 5,000 new customers have been found. How do you allocate the cost of the campaign?

    (a) You do not know if the advertising campaign has also encouraged **existing** customers to spend more.

(b) You do not know, on an **individual** basis, whether each new customer was attracted by the campaign, by word-of-mouth, or whatever.

6.9 To analyse **comparative** customer profitability, it is necessary to focus on the **right costs for comparison**, avoiding common costs and unavoidable overhead.

6.10 Different customer costs can arise out of the following.

(a) Order size
(b) Sales mix
(c) Order processing
(d) Transport costs
(e) Management time
(f) Cash flow problems (eg increased overdraft interest) caused by slow payers
(g) Order complexity (eg if the order has to be sent out in several stages)
(h) Stockholding costs can relate to specify customers
(i) A key customer might demand lower prices/service.

6.11 Ward suggests the following format for a **statement of customer profitability**.

	£'000
Sales revenue	X
Less direct product cost	(X)
	X
Customer-specific variable costs:	
- distribution	X
- rebates and discounts	X
- promotion etc	X
	(X)
	X
Other costs	
- sales force	X
- customer service	X
- management cost	X
	(X)
	X
Financing cost	
- credit period	X
- customer-specific inventory	X
	(X)
	X

6.12 Such a report can highlight the differences between the cost of servicing different individuals or firms which can then be applied as follows.

(a) **Directing effort to cutting customer specific costs**. Installing an electric data interchange system (EDI) can save the costs of paperwork and data input.

(b) **Identifying those customers who are expensive to service**, thereby suggesting action to increase profitability. They might have a high level of complaints because the quality of the service they receive is poor (see para 6.16 onwards for an exploration of quality issues).

(c) **Using CPA as part of a comparison with competitors' costs**. A firm which services a customer more cheaply than a competitor can use this cost advantage to offer extra benefits to the customer.

(d) Indicating cases where **profitability might be endangered,** for example by servicing customers for whom the firm's core competence is not especially relevant.

6.13 CPA might provide answers to the following questions.

(a) What **profit/contribution** is the organisation making on sales to the customer, after discounts and selling and delivery costs?

(b) What would be the **financial consequences** of losing the customer?

(c) Is the customer buying in order sizes that are **unprofitable** to supply?

(d) What is **return on investment** on plant used? (See Chapter 12 for discussion of financial ratios.)

(e) What is the level of **inventory** required specifically to supply these customers?

(f) Are there any other **specific costs** involved in supplying this customer, eg technical and test facilities, R & D facilities, special design staff?

(g) What is the ratio of net **contribution per customer** to **total investment**?

6.14 The Action Programme below explores some of these issues.

Action Programme 5

Pear Ltd supplies components to the motor trade. It currently has a small contract with a Japanese firm, Kabuki who have suggested the possibility of a long-term contract.

Taking the extra Kabuki contract would involve shedding some other customers.

	Turnover	Direct product costs
Abandon Kabuki contract	£1,100,000	£700,000
Continue Kabuki contract, but lose some business	£1,200,000	£850,000

Without Kabuki, distribution costs will be £40,000. With Kabuki, total distribution costs will only rise to £50,000.

Without Kabuki, financing costs would be £11,000; with the Kabuki contract, this will be £10,000 but there will be £1,000 of customer specific costs. In either case, sales force and customer service each amount to £60,000 pa and management costs £70,000.

Rebates, discounts and promotion are £15,000 and £100,000 without the Kabuki contract. Given the knock on effect elsewhere, if the Kabuki contract is continued, Pear will need to spend £50,000 on promotion, and £10,000 on rebates and discounts.

Is it worth going ahead with the Kabuki contract?

Quality and the customer

6.15 A **customer orientation,** seeking to satisfy the customer, is pursued in marketing by recognising that customers buy 'the sizzle, not the steak' - products are bought for the benefits they deliver: how customers can use the product to accomplish the things they want to do.

6.16 What constitutes a **'quality product or service'** must be related to what the customer wants. Indeed, quality would have no commercial value unless it delivered customer benefit, since the key reason for aiming to produce quality products is to derive **extra sales,** to establish **competitive advantage** through superiority in particular product or service features.

Marketing at Work

An article in the *Financial Times* in April 1998 described the approach taken to quality by Siebe, the British controls and engineering company.

Siebe's sales this year are expected to reach £3.5bn, 90% outside the UK. Siebe's chief executive is one of the UK industry's strongest proponents of increased quality by removing unnecessary expenses.

Senior quality or production engineers, known as 'black belts' are leading the drive for quality at the company's 300 or so factories around the world, covering all sorts of products from refrigerator controls to entire computer systems, costing from a few to millions of dollars.

Specific projects may include reducing the number of items made that fail to meet quality standards. In quality measurements, Siebe's factories on average produce 500 - 1000 defects per million parts. Japanese automotive parts companies commonly aim for defects of 10 per million or less. Siebe's goal by early next century is to get to just 3.5 defects per million.

6.17 Quality costs money, and so keeping up with customers' quality expectations will involve some kind of financial analysis covering the following issues.

Quality related costs

6.18 A **quality related cost** is the 'Cost of ensuring and assuring quality, as well as loss when quality is not achieved. Quality costs are classified as follows.

(a) **Prevention costs**: 'The cost of any action taken to investigate, prevent or reduce defects and failures'

    (i)   Quality engineering

    (ii)   Design/development of quality control equipment and inspection equipment

    (iii) Maintenance of quality control equipment and inspection equipment

    (iv) Administration of quality control

    (v)   Training in quality control

(b) **Appraisal costs**: 'The costs of assessing quality achieved'

    (i)   Acceptance testing

    (ii)   Inspection of goods inwards

    (iii) Inspection costs of in-house processing

    (iv) Performance testing

(c) **Internal failure costs**: 'Costs arising within the organisation of failure to achieve the quality specified'

    (i)   Failure analysis

    (ii)   Re-inspection costs

    (iii) Losses from failure of purchased items

    (iv) Losses due to lower selling prices for sub-quality goods

    (v)   Costs of reviewing product specifications after failures

(d) **External failure costs**: 'Costs arising outside the manufacturing organisation of failure to achieve specified quality (after transfer of ownership to the customer)'

    (i)   Administration of customer complaints section

    (ii)   Costs of customer service section

    (iii) Product liability costs

    (iv) Cost of repairing products returned from customers

    (v)   Cost of providing replacement items due to sub-standard products or marketing errors

6.19 There are other costs related to quality (or lack of it).

(a) **Opportunity cost of 'lost' orders**. In other words, poor quality may lead to failure to win orders - this would not be picked up in the accounting system, but is an important strategic consideration. Failure to generate repeat orders could obviously impact on revenues from highly profitable customers.

(b) **Opportunity cost of resources** used in rectifying quality which could be spent elsewhere. For example, a firm may spend £250,000 on rectifying defects and dealing with customer complaints. The £250,000 could have been spent on advertising or R&D. The money could have been used to generate revenue.

Continuous improvement

6.20 **Quality management** is not a one-off process, but is the continuous examination and improvement of existing processes. Continuous improvement does not only apply to the finished product, but also to the processes which give rise to it.

(a) A philosophy of continuous improvement ensures that management is not complacent.

(b) **Customers needs change,** so a philosophy of continuous improvement enables these changes to be taken into account in the normal course of events.

(c) **New technologies** or materials might be developed, enabling cost savings or design improvements.

6.21 There is a **strategic marketing role** for quality management.

(a) **Cost leadership**

(i) Attention to quality can be seen as a means of improving the **efficiency** of the total process, which will have the effect of **reducing costs.**

(ii) High quality is a way of becoming the most efficient producer. A minimum standard of quality might become a **barrier to entry** for particular industries.

(iii) **Design improvements** can reduce the cost to the buyer (eg supplying metal sheets in the size the buyer wants, so the buyer will not be purchasing waste materials).

(b) **Differentiation**

(i) **Product design quality** (ie a design that is particularly good at satisfying the needs of a particular market segment) can be used to differentiate a product.

(ii) The company is able to differentiate its offer, not so much by the design and/or conformance quality of the **end product,** but for some quality advantage in **other activities** of the value chain or in the linkages between them.

(c) In a **focus strategy**, it can be deployed in a manner similar to either (a) or (b) above, depending of course on whether a cost-focus or differentiation-focus strategy is being pursued.

(d) In competitive terms, quality is **not absolute but relative**: in other words, quality has to be as high as competitors' quality if not higher. The customer compares your quality with a competitor's quality.

7 PROFITABILITY OF DISTRIBUTION CHANNELS 12/99

7.1 Marketing involves certain basic processes.

(a) Bringing buyers and sellers into contact
(b) Offering a sufficient choice of goods to meet the needs of buyers
(c) Persuading customers to develop a favourable opinion of a particular product
(d) Distributing goods from the manufacturing point to retail outlets
(e) Maintaining an adequate level of sales
(f) Providing appropriate services (eg credit, after-sales service)
(g) Maintaining an acceptable price

7.2 The choice of **channels of distribution** will depend on how far a manufacturing company wishes to carry out these processes itself, and how far it decides to delegate them to other organisations.

7.3 An organisation often gives close scrutiny to the profitability of its products, and the profitability of its market segments, but does not have a costing system which measures the **costs of distributing the products**.

7.4 A numerical example might help to illustrate this point. Let us suppose that Biomarket Ltd sells two consumer products, X and Y, in two markets A and B. In both markets, sales are made through the following outlets.

(a) Direct sales to supermarkets
(b) Wholesalers

Sales and costs for the most recent quarter have been analysed by product and market as follows.

	Market A			Market B			Both markets		
	X	Y	Total	X	Y	Total	X	Y	Total
	£'000	£'000	£'000	£'000	£'000	£'000	£'000	£'000	£'000
Sales	900	600	1,500	1,000	2,000	3,000	1,900	2,600	4,500
Variable									
Production costs	450	450	900	500	1,500	2,000	950	1,950	2,900
	450	150	600	500	500	1,000	950	650	1,600
Variable sales costs	90	60	150	100	100	200	190	160	350
Contribution	360	90	450	400	400	800	760	490	1,250
Share of fixed costs (production, sales, distribution, administration)	170	80	250	290	170	460	460	250	710
Net profit	190	10	200	110	230	340	300	240	540

7.5 This analysis shows that both products are profitable, and both markets are profitable. But what about the channels of distribution? A further analysis of market A might show the following.

	Supermarkets	Market A wholesalers	Total
	£'000	£'000	£'000
Sales	1,125	375	1,500
Variable production costs	675	225	900
	450	150	600
Variable selling costs	105	45	150
Contribution	345	105	450
Direct distribution costs	10	80	90
	335	25	360
Share of fixed costs	120	40	160
Net profit/(loss)	215	(15)	200

7.6 This analysis shows that although sales through wholesalers make a contribution after deducting direct distribution costs, the profitability of this channel of distribution is disappointing, and some attention ought perhaps to be given to improving it. The **cost/benefit analysis** in the economic considerations of selecting channels of distribution may be summarised as follows.

(a) Intermediaries might **increase sales volumes** of a manufacturer's products and thereby increase contribution.

(b) The intermediaries might also save the manufacturer from a variety of **operating and financial costs**.

(c) Against these benefits, there is the loss of profits due to **dealer margins** (as well as the loss of control and adaptability).

The economic advantages of intermediaries

7.7 Although intermediaries take a share of the profit from a product, it might be profitable for a company to use them for the following reasons.

(a) Intermediaries might **bear the costs** of:

(i) Stockholding

(ii) Transportation

(iii) Consolidation of many small orders into fewer large ones for distribution cost savings

(iv) Providing sufficient display facilities

(b) Companies might **receive payment** more quickly from intermediaries than if they tried to sell direct to the customer.

7.8 The reasons for **direct distribution**, perhaps with a dedicated sales force, might be as follows.

(a) High intermediary profit margins affecting the final sale price to customers. These costs of intermediate stages in the distribution channel mean that direct selling in some cases will be cheaper.

(b) A **small market** with only a few target customers may make direct selling cheap (and a dealer network impracticable).

(c) As a means of retaining control over the process and maintaining good **relations with customers**, and obtaining feedback (ie market research information).

7.9 The reasons against direct distribution and in favour of using intermediaries are as follows.

(a) A **lack of financial resources** (apart from the actual costs of distribution and selling, a manufacturer will not recover his working capital until the final sale is made, or the period of credit after sale ends, which can be a much longer time than if he trades through middlemen).

(b) Financial resources may be available but can be more profitably employed elsewhere.

(c) A **wide geographical market area** makes the costs of direct selling very high.

Design of the sales force

7.10 Every organisation will have some idea about what it can afford to spend on selling. The overall size of the sales organisation is restricted by the resources available to the company and by company policy, and by the balance in the sales mix between **personal** and **non-personal** selling. Here are some hypothetical figures.

(a)   Selling expenses should not exceed, say, 10% of sales.

(b)   If a salesperson, with selling expenses and commission etc, costs, say £30,000 per annum, then turnover of £300,000 per annum would be required to support one salesperson.

(c)   If a company budgets annual turnover of, say, £6 million, then the total sales force should not exceed 20 employees.

Chapter Roundup

- Approaches to pricing include full cost plus pricing, marginal cost plus pricing, minimum pricing, limiting factor pricing and the demand based approach to pricing. An average price strategy and a lowest price strategy are two forms of price strategy based on what competitors charge.

- New product pricing strategies include market penetration pricing and market skimming.

- Other pricing strategies might involve the giving of discounts or being involved in competitive bidding.

- Transfer prices are a way of promoting divisional autonomy, ideally without prejudicing the measurement of divisional performance or discouraging overall corporate profit maximisation.

- If variable costs and market prices are constant, regardless of the volume of output, a market-based transfer price is the ideal transfer price. If there is no external market for the transferred item the optimum transfer price is likely to be one based on standard cost plus.

- It has been suggested that the transfer price per unit can be set at standard variable cost per unit in the producing division *plus* the opportunity cost to the organisation as a whole of supplying the unit internally. The opportunity cost will be one of the following.

  ○   The maximum contribution foregone by the supplying division in transferring internally rather than selling externally

  ○   The contribution foregone by not using the same facilities in the producing division for their next best alternative use

- Direct product profitability is a way of measuring the profitability of individual product lines by taking all related costs into account, including costs of marketing the product.

- The product life cycle is relevant when considering the type of financial information that may be needed.

- Customer profitability analysis attempts to identify which customers are the most profitable. Not all customers of an organisation generate the same levels of profit.

- Customer orientation implies that quality issues are important. Quality costs money.

- The choice of distribution channel may impact on profitability.

Quick Quiz

1   List the factors to consider when making pricing decisions. (see para 2.1)

2   What is the difference between full cost plus pricing and marginal cost plus pricing? (2.2, 2.6)

3   When companies can sell similar but not identical products or where the graphical location of the sales point has some significance, in what ways is it possible to charge different prices? (2.12)

4   In what circumstances might a market skimming pricing policy be appropriate? (2.15)

5   Describe five product mix pricing strategies. (2.16)

6   What is psychological pricing? (2.17)

7   What might be the purpose of a discount? (2.18)

8   What will be the factors in choosing a supplier after a competitive bidding process? (2.20)

9   Why might an adjusted market price be used as a transfer price? (3.9)

10   What is the drawback of setting a transfer price at full cost? (3.13)

11   Define the opportunity costs involved when transfer prices are based on opportunity costs. (3.21)

12   What is the purpose of DPP? (4.2)

13   What can a business achieve with customer profitability analysis? (6.13)

14   Give some examples of quality related costs. (6.19)

15   Why might a company choose direct distribution rather than using intermediaries? (7.8)

Action Programme Review

1   (a)   There is no guarantee that the discount will work to provide new customers. It may be the case that the discount simply provides a cheaper product for existing users. Indeed, existing customers may simply advance a decision whilst the production is available and then a sale is lost after the end of the promotion, causing a real loss in revenue.

   (b)   The discount promotion may only attract temporary customers and not create any brand loyalty with long-term following.

   (c)   If badly managed in any way, the scheme could create a situation where customers cannot get the goods at discounted prices and they may feel resentful, causing bad feeling against the manufacturer.

2   Basic discounted cash flow analysis was covered in the previous chapter. We offer some pointers as to how you might approach this problem.

   (a)   *Basic treatment*

      (i)   Treat the advertising campaign as an investment of £400,000 spread over two years.

      (ii)   Treat the additional advertising expenditure of £30,000 pa thereafter as an increase in fixed or committed costs - it is necessary to maintain the market share. An increase in the total contribution is thus required.

      (iii)   Draw up a schedule of the value of the market in years 1-10, and the contribution at 5% and 25%, to identify cash inflows.

      (iv)   Use the cost of capital as a discount rate.

      (v)   Find out whether the increased NPV of the contribution is worth the 'investment' in advertising

3   You can see that the profit earned by Seth in servicing Narayan is greater, despite the increased discount.

	Kipling	Narayan
Number of shoes	500	420
	£	£
Revenue (after discount)	22,500	17,850
Transport	(5,000)	-
Administration	(250)	(500)
Net profit	17,250	17,350

4   The information reflects sales force administration and convenience. However, it might obscure an analysis of customer profitability, in which case presenting information by customer size might be more important than geography.

5

	(A) Abandon Kabuki contract	(B) Continue with Kabuki contract, but lose some business	(C) Differential effect of Kabuki contract (B) − (A)
	£	£	£
Sales	1,100,000	1,200,000	100,000
Direct product costs	(700,000)	(850,000)	(150,000)
	400,000	350,000	(50,000)
Distribution	(40,000)	(50,000)	(10,000)
Rebates/discounts	(15,000)	(10,000)	5,000
Promotion	(100,000)	(50,000)	50,000
	245,000	240,000	(5,000)
Sales force	(60,000)	(60,000)	-
Customer service	(60,000)	(60,000)	-
Management	(70,000)	(70,000)	-
	55,000	50,000	(5,000)
Financing costs	(11,000)	(10,000)	1,000
Customer specific costs	-	(1,000)	(1,000)
	44,000	39,000	(5,000)

On the figures given Pear would be £5,000 pa better off if it rejected the contract. Whilst it would double its promotion spend, distribution management would be simpler, and direct product costs would be lower, more than compensating for the fall in sales revenues. Pears may need to consider the effect of a change in strategy on the sales force, customer service and management costs. These are unlikely to stay unaffected. The point of the exercise was to demonstrate the issues involved in examining all the costs associated with a customer.

However, to reject the contract is probably being unrealistic. A change in marketing strategy would certainly have implications for sales force and customer service costs. And finally, Kabuki's revenue is guaranteed.

Now try illustrative questions 8 and 9 at the end of the Study Text

10 Cost/Volume/Profit Analysis

Chapter Topic List	Syllabus Reference
1 Introduction	-
2 CVP analysis, contribution and breakeven point	4.1, 4.2
3 The margin of safety	4.1, 4.2
4 Breakeven arithmetic	4.1, 4.2
5 Breakeven charts, contribution charts and profit/volume charts	4.1, 4.2
6 Limitations of CVP analysis	4.2

Learning Outcomes

Upon completion of this chapter you will have a thorough knowledge of breakeven analysis, and will have seen cost/volume/profit decisions put into context using a variety of worked numerical examples.

Key Concepts

- Cost/volume/profit analysis
- Breakeven point
- Contribution
- Margin of safety

1 INTRODUCTION

1.1 As you are by now aware, the application of financial information is not just concerned with recording costs. It is also concerned with information provision so as to assist managers, including marketing managers, in making decisions.

1.2 One type of decision facing the marketing manager is the profit-planning decision. To be able to assess and plan future profits, marketing managers require information about future costs and revenues. One way of providing information about expected future costs and revenues for such decision making is cost/volume/profit analysis.

1.3 CVP analysis can be used to evaluate a proposed new product by estimating how many units of the product need to be sold to break even, given the price and cost structure. If management believe the breakeven price can easily be reached the product may well move into the development stage. This technique is an application of marginal costing ideas and is sometimes called breakeven analysis.

> ### Exam Tip
>
> It is important that you study the contents of this Chapter very carefully, since cost/volume/profit analysis is specifically mentioned in Section 4.2 of the syllabus at the front of this Study Text.
>
> When answering questions on this topic, as with all numerical solutions, always set out your workings neatly and in an orderly manner so that the examiner does not have to spend time in deciphering a mass of figures. If you are required to draw a breakeven or P/V chart, do make sure that you use a ruler and a sharp pencil, and that you label all of the appropriate axes, lines and regions on your graph.

2 CVP ANALYSIS, CONTRIBUTION AND BREAKEVEN POINT

12/99, 6/00, 12/00

> ### Key Concept
>
> **Cost/volume/profit** (CVP) analysis is the study of the interrelationships between costs, volume and hence profits at various levels of activity.

2.1 Large organisations spend very large sums of money on advertising, and to use the money to the best effect, it is obviously essential to produce an advertising plan which should also justify the expenditure involved. This may be done using investment evaluation technique as discussed in Chapter 8. Advertising is often intended to increase sales, but the effect of advertising on sales is not easy to measure. Why?

(i) Advertising is only one part of the marketing mix. Other factors influencing sales might be price changes, whether intermediaries have stock enough of the products to meet an increase in demand, and competitors' actions.

(ii) Advertising might succeed in maintaining a firm's existing market share, without actually increasing sales.

2.2 The difficulties of measuring the effect of an advertising campaign on **profits** are similar. **Breakeven analysis** might be used to calculate the volume of extra sales required to cover the (fixed) costs of the advertising.

2.3 As you have seen, by using **marginal costing techniques** it is possible to ascertain the contribution per unit. Any excess or deficiency of contribution over **fixed costs** represents the profit or loss for the period.

2.4 The management of an organisation usually wants to have information about not only the profit to be made if production and sales for the year are achieved, but also the **breakeven point** and the amount by which actual sales can fall below anticipated sales without a loss being incurred.

> ### Key Concept
>
> The **breakeven point** is the level of activity at which there is neither a profit nor a loss. The **contribution** is the difference between sales revenue and variable cost of sales.

2.5 The **breakeven point (BEP)** can be calculated arithmetically. The contribution is the amount 'contributed' to fixed costs. The number of units needed to be sold in order to break even will be the **total fixed costs divided by the contribution per unit.**

$$\text{Breakeven point} = \frac{\text{Total fixed costs}}{\text{Contribution per unit}}$$

$$= \textbf{Number of units of sale required to break even}$$

Example: breakeven point

2.6
Expected sales	10,000 units at £8 = £80,000
Variable cost	£5 per unit
Fixed costs (including £11,000 for a proposed advertising campaign)	£21,000

Required

Compute the breakeven point.

Answer

2.7
The contribution per unit is £(8–5)	=	£3
Contribution required to break even	=	fixed costs = £21,000
Breakeven point (BEP)	=	21,000 ÷ 3
	=	7,000 units
In revenue, BEP	=	(7,000 × £8) = £56,000

Sales above £56,000 will result in profit of £3 per unit of additional sales and sales below £56,000 will mean a loss of £3 per unit for each unit by which sales fall short of 7,000 units. In other words, profit will improve or worsen by the amount of contribution per unit.

	7,000 units £	7,001 units £
Revenue	56,000	56,008
Less variable costs	35,000	35,005
Contribution	21,000	21,003
Less fixed costs	21,000	21,000
Profit	0 (= breakeven)	3

3 THE MARGIN OF SAFETY

Key Concept

The **margin of safety** is the difference in units between the **budgeted sales volume** and the **breakeven sales volume** and it is sometimes expressed as a percentage of the budgeted sales volume.

3.1 The **margin of safety** indicates how far sales can fall short of budget before a loss is made.

Action Programme 1

Mary Ltd makes and sells a product which has a variable cost of £30 and which sells for £40. Budgeted fixed costs are £70,000 and budgeted sales are 8,000 units.

Required

Calculate the breakeven point and the margin of safety.

4 BREAKEVEN ARITHMETIC

4.1 We can use breakeven arithmetic to provide valuable management information about profits, sales volumes, selling prices and costs.

(a) **At the breakeven point, sales revenue equals total costs** and there is no profit.

$$S = V + F$$

where
$$S = \text{Sales revenue}$$
$$V = \text{Total variable costs}$$
$$F = \text{Total fixed costs}$$

(b) Subtracting V from each side of the equation, we get:

$S - V = F$, that is, **total contribution = fixed costs**.

Example: breakeven arithmetic

4.2 Butter Ltd makes a product which has a variable cost of £7 per unit.

Required

If fixed costs are £63,000 per annum, calculate the selling price per unit if the company wishes to break even with a sales volume of 12,000 units.

Answer

4.3

			£
Contribution required to break even (= Fixed costs)	=	£63,000	
Volume of sales	=	12,000 units	
Required contribution to fixed costs per unit	=	£63,000 ÷ 12,000 =	5.25
Variable cost per unit (V)	=		7.00
Required sales price per unit (S)	=		12.25

Target profits

4.4 A similar formula may be applied where a company wishes to achieve a **target profit** during a period. To achieve this profit, sales must cover all costs and leave the required profit, that is:

$$S = V + F + P, \text{ where}$$
$$P = \text{required profit}$$

Subtracting V from each side of the equation, we get:

$$S - V = F + P, \text{ so}$$
$$\textbf{Total contribution required} = \textbf{F + P}$$

Example: target profits (1)

4.5 Breeches Ltd makes and sells a single product, for which variable costs are as follows.

	£
Direct materials	10
Direct labour	8
Variable production overhead	6
	24

The sales price is £30 per unit, and fixed costs per annum are £68,000. The company wishes to make a profit of £16,000 per annum.

Required

Determine the sales required to achieve this profit.

Answer

4.6 Required contribution = fixed costs + profit

= £68,000 + £16,000 = £84,000

$$\frac{\text{Required contribution}}{\text{Contribution per unit}} = \frac{£84,000}{£(30-24)} = 14,000 \text{ units or } £420,000 \text{ in revenue}$$

Action Programme 2

Product X sells for £10.70. The variable cost per unit is £6.30. If annual fixed costs are £113,000, how many units of product X must be sold to achieve a target profit of £150,000?

Action Programme 3

Boots Ltd wishes to sell 14,000 units of its product, which has a variable cost of £15 to make and sell. Fixed costs are £47,000 and the required profit is £23,000.

Required

Calculate the sales price per unit.

Example: target profits (2)

4.7 Tripod Ltd makes and sells three products, X, Y and Z. The selling price per unit and costs are as follows.

	X	Y	Z
Selling price per unit	£80	£50	£70
Variable cost per unit	£50	£10	£20

Fixed costs per month = £160,000

The maximum sales demand per month is 2,000 units of each product and the minimum sales demand is 1,000 of each.

Required

(a) Comment on the potential profitability of the company.

(b) Suppose that there is a fixed demand for X and Y of 1,500 units per month, which will not be exceeded, but for which firm orders have been received. Determine how many units of Z would have to be sold to achieve a profit of at least £25,000 per month.

Answer

4.8 (a) When there is no indication about whether marginal or absorption costing is in use, it is simpler and more informative to assess profitability with contribution analysis and marginal costing. This is the requirement in part (a) of the problem. The obvious analysis to make is a calculation of the best possible and worst possible results.

| | | Best possible | | | Worst possible | |
	Sales units	Contrib'n per unit	Total cont'n	Sales Units	Contrib'n per unit	Total cont'n
		£	£		£	£
X	2,000	30	60,000	1,000	30	30,000
Y	2,000	40	80,000	1,000	40	40,000
Z	2,000	50	100,000	1,000	50	50,000
Total contribution			240,000			120,000
Fixed costs			160,000			160,000
Profit/(loss)			80,000			(40,000)

The company's potential profitability ranges from a profit of £80,000 to a loss of £40,000 per month.

(b) The second part of the problem is a variation of a 'target profit' calculation.

	£	£
Required (minimum) profit per month		25,000
Fixed costs per month		160,000
Required contribution per month		185,000
Contribution to be earned from:		
Product X 1,500 × £30	45,000	
Product Y 1,500 × £40	60,000	
		105,000
Contribution required from product Z		80,000
Contribution per unit of Z		£50
Minimum required sales of Z per month in units		1,600

Decisions to change sales price or costs

4.9 You may come across a problem in which you will be expected to provide information as to the effect of altering the selling price. This problem is a slight variation on basic breakeven arithmetic, and an example will be used to illustrate typical questions.

Example: change in selling price

4.10 Stomer Cakes Ltd bake and sell a single type of cake. The variable cost of production is 15p and the current sales price is 25p. Fixed costs are £2,600 per month, and the annual profit for the company at current sales volume is £36,000. The volume of sales demand is constant throughout the year.

The sales manager, Ian Eccles, wishes to raise the sales price to 29p per cake, but considers that a price rise will result in some loss of sales.

Required

Ascertain the minimum volume of sales required each month to justify a rise in price to 29p.

Answer

4.11 The minimum volume of demand which would justify a price of 29p is one which would leave total profit at least the same as before, ie £3,000 per month. Required profit should be converted into required contribution, as follows.

	£
Monthly fixed costs	2,600
Monthly profit, minimum required	3,000
Current monthly contribution	5,600
Contribution per unit (25p – 15p)	10p
Current monthly sales	56,000 cakes

The minimum volume of sales required after the price rise will be an amount which earns a contribution of £5,600 per month, no worse than at the moment. The contribution per cake at a sales price of 29p would be 14p.

$$\text{Required sales} = \frac{\text{required contribution}}{\text{contribution per unit}} = \frac{£5,600}{14p}$$

$$= 40,000 \text{ cakes per month.}$$

Sales price and sales volume

4.12 It may be clear by now that, given no change in fixed costs, **total profit is maximised when the total contribution is at its maximum**.

4.13 An **increase in the sales price will increase unit contribution, but sales volume is likely to fall**, with the reverse for a decrease in sales price. The optimum combination of sales price and sales volume is arguably the one which maximises total contribution and management obviously need information about such prices and volumes.

Example: profit maximisation

4.14 Cymbeline Ltd has developed a new product which is about to be launched on to the market. The variable cost of selling the product is £12 per unit. The marketing department has estimated that at a sales price of £20, annual demand would be 10,000 units.

However, if the sales price is set above £20, sales demand would fall by 500 units for each 50p increase above £20. Similarly, if the price is set below £20, demand would increase by 500 units for each 50p stepped reduction in price below £20.

Required

Determine the price which would maximise Cymbeline Ltd's profit in the next year.

Answer

4.15 At a price of £20 per unit, the unit contribution would be £(20 – 12) = £8. Each 50p increase (or decrease) in price would raise (or lower) the unit contribution by 50p. The total contribution is calculated at each sales price by multiplying the unit contribution by the expected sales volume.

Unit price £	Unit contribution £	Sales volume Units	Total contribution £
20.00	8.00	10,000	80,000
(a) Reduce price			
19.50	7.50	10,500	78,750
19.00	7.00	11,000	77,000
(b) Increase price			
20.50	8.50	9,500	80,750
21.00	9.00	9,000	81,000
21.50	9.50	8,500	80,750
22.00	10.00	8,000	80,000
22.50	10.50	7,500	78,750

The total contribution would be maximised, and therefore profit maximised, at a sales price of £21 per unit, and sales demand of 9,000 units.

5 BREAKEVEN CHARTS, CONTRIBUTION CHARTS AND PROFIT/VOLUME CHARTS

Breakeven charts

5.1 The breakeven point can also be determined graphically using a **breakeven chart** which shows approximate levels of profit or loss at different sales volume levels. It is prepared showing on the horizontal axis sales (in units or in value) and on the vertical axis values for sales revenue and costs. The following lines are then drawn.

(a) The **sales line**, which starts at the origin (zero sales volume = zero sales revenue) and ends at the point which signifies the expected sales.

(b) The **fixed costs** line which runs above and parallel to the horizontal axis, at a point on the vertical axis denoting the total fixed costs.

(c) The **total costs line**, which starts at the point where the fixed costs line meets the vertical axis (at zero output), and ends at the point which represents, on the horizontal axis, the anticipated sales in units, and on the vertical axis the sum of the total variable cost of those units plus the total fixed costs.

5.2 The breakeven point is the **intersection of the sales line and the total costs line**. By projecting the lines horizontally and vertically from this point to the appropriate axes, it is possible to read off the breakeven point in sales units and sales value.

5.3 The number of units represented on the chart by the distance between the breakeven point and the expected (or budgeted) sales, in units, indicates the **margin of safety**.

Example: a breakeven chart

5.4 The budgeted annual output of a factory is 120,000 units. The fixed overheads amount to £40,000 and the variable costs are 50p per unit. The sales price is £1 per unit.

Required

Construct a breakeven chart showing the current breakeven point and profit earned up to the present maximum capacity.

Answer

5.5 We begin by calculating the profit at the budgeted annual output.

	£
Sales (120,000 units)	120,000
Variable costs	60,000
Contribution	60,000
Fixed costs	40,000
Profit	20,000

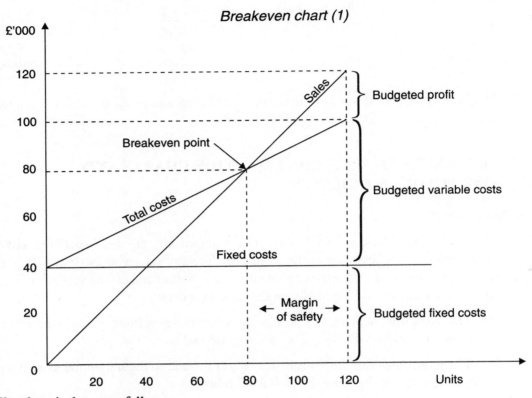

Breakeven chart (1)

The chart is drawn as follows.

(a) The vertical axis represents money and the horizontal axis represents the level of activity (production and sales).

(b) The **fixed costs** are represented by a straight line parallel to the horizontal axis (in our example, at £40,000).

(c) The **variable costs** are added 'on top of' fixed costs, to give total costs. It is assumed that fixed costs are the same in total and variable costs are the same per unit at all levels of output.

The **line of costs is therefore a straight line** and only two points need to be plotted and joined up. Perhaps the two most convenient points to plot are total costs at zero output, and total costs at the budgeted output and sales.

(i) At zero output, costs are equal to the amount of fixed costs only, £40,000, since there are no variable costs.

(ii) At the budgeted output of 120,000 units, costs are £100,000.

	£
Fixed costs	40,000
Variable costs 120,000 × 50p	60,000
Total costs	100,000

(d) The **sales line** is also drawn by plotting two points and joining them up.

(i) At zero sales, revenue is nil.

(ii) At the budgeted output and sales of 120,000 units, revenue is £120,000.

5.6 The **breakeven point is where total costs are matched exactly by total revenue**. From the chart, this can be seen to occur at output and sales of 80,000 units, when revenue and costs are both £80,000. This breakeven point can be proved mathematically as:

$$\frac{\text{Required contribution} = \text{Fixed costs}}{\text{Contribution per unit}} = \frac{£40,000}{50\text{p per unit}} = 80,000 \text{ units}$$

5.7 The **margin of safety** can be seen on the chart as the difference between the budgeted level of activity and the breakeven level.

The value of breakeven charts

5.8 Breakeven charts may be helpful to management in planning **production and marketing**. A chart gives a visual display of how much output needs to be sold to make a profit and what the likelihood would be of making a loss if actual sales fell short of the budgeted expectations.

5.9 It is important to realise that a breakeven chart is a means of demonstrating the cost/volume/profit 'arithmetic' of sales revenues, fixed costs and variable costs. In practice, management is more likely to use the arithmetical techniques of breakeven analysis without bothering to draw charts as a visual aid, unless to aid presentation to colleagues, such as the board of directors.

Action Programme 4

Streamline Ltd budgets each year to sell 5,000 units of its product at a price of £4.80 per unit. Until this year, the variable cost of sale per unit had been £2 and fixed costs £9,800 per annum. With the introduction of new electronic equipment, however, variable costs have now been reduced to £1.40 per unit, although annual fixed costs have risen to £12,000.

Required

Draw a breakeven chart to show the breakeven point and budgeted profit before and after the introduction of the new equipment.

The P/V chart

5.10 The **P/V (profit-volume) chart** is a variation of the breakeven chart which provides a simple illustration of the relationship of costs and profit to sales, by showing the effect on overall profit of changes in sales volume or value. A P/V chart is constructed as follows.

(a) Profit is on the y axis and actually comprises not only 'profit' but **contribution** to profit extending above and below the x axis with a zero point at the intersection of the two axes, and the negative section below the x axis representing fixed costs. This means that at zero production, the firm is incurring a loss equal to the fixed costs.

(b) Volume is on the x axis and comprises either **volume** of **sales** or value of sales.

(c) The profit-volume line is a straight line drawn with its starting point (at zero production) at the intercept on the y axis representing the level of fixed costs, and with a gradient of contribution/unit. The P/V line will cut the x axis at the breakeven point of sales volume. Any point on the P/V line above the x axis represents the profit to the firm for that particular level of sales.

BPP
PUBLISHING

Example: P/V Chart

5.11 Patch Ltd makes and sells a single product which has a variable cost of sale of £5. Fixed costs are £15,000 per annum. The company's management estimates that at a sales price of £8 per unit, sales per annum would be 7,000 units.

Required

Construct a P/V chart.

Answer

5.12 At sales of 7,000 units, total contribution will be $7,000 \times £(8 - 5) = £21,000$ and total profit will be £6,000.

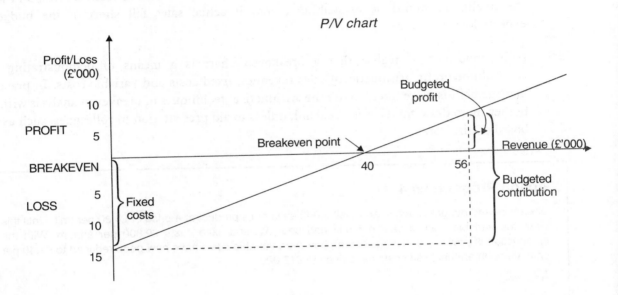

P/V chart

6 LIMITATIONS OF CVP ANALYSIS

6.1 Although CVP analysis provides valuable management information, it should be used carefully. The major limitations of such analysis are as follows.

(a) A breakeven chart can only apply to one **single product or a single mix**.

(b) It is assumed that fixed costs are the same in total and variable costs are the same per unit at all levels of output. This assumption is a **great simplification** and is only correct within a 'normal range' of output.

   (i) Fixed costs will change if output falls or increases substantially (most fixed costs are **step costs**).

   (ii) The variable cost per unit will decrease where **economies of scale** are made at higher output volumes, and the variable cost per unit will also eventually rise where diseconomies of scale begin to appear at higher volumes of output (for example the extra cost of labour in overtime working).

(c) It is assumed that **sales prices will be constant** at all levels of activity. This may not be true, especially at higher volumes of output, where the price may have to be reduced to win the extra sales.

(d) Production and sales are assumed to be the same.

6.2   In spite of limitations, however, breakeven analysis is a useful technique for managers in planning sales prices, the desired sales mix, and profitability. Managers can ask questions based on the breakeven model, such as the following.

(a)   What is the probability of achieving the desired levels of market penetration?

(b)   Do the conditions in the market lend themselves to achieving that desired penetration?

(c)   What is the state of the market?

(d)   Will the competitors allow a profitable entry?

(e)   Are the cost and quality assumptions feasible?

(f)   Are the funds available, not just to complete the development but to establish the production capacity and skilled manpower to achieve the desired penetration?

Action Programme 5

If you think that you understand the principles of CVP analysis, you may be able to work out your own solutions to the following question. Notice, by the way, that the questions deal with changes in selling prices, sales volumes, variable costs and fixed costs - hence the term 'cost/volume/profit' analysis.

(a)   If a company reduces its selling prices by 20% to 80% of their former level, but increases its sales volumes by 20% as a consequence of the price reduction, then profits will be unchanged.

   True or false?

(b)   If a company introduces automation into its work practices, so that

   (i)   unit variable costs fall, but
   (ii)   fixed costs increase substantially, so that
   (iii) profitability at current sales volumes remains unchanged,

   then the decision to automate would have been irrelevant to the future profitability of the company.

   True or false?

Chapter Roundup

- CVP analysis has a number of purposes.

   ° To provide information to management about cost behaviour for routine planning and 'one-off' decision making

   ° To determine what volume of sales is needed at any given budgeted sales price in order to break even

   ° To identify the 'risk' in the budget by measuring the margin of safety

   ° To calculate the effects on profit of changes in variable costs, C/S ratios, sales price and volume, product mix, and so on

   As such it can provide invaluable information for marketing and sales.

- Make sure that you understand how to calculate the breakeven point, the margin of safety and target profits, and can apply the principles of CVP analysis both to decisions about whether to change sales prices or costs and to problems of profit maximisation. You should also be able to construct breakeven and profit/volume charts.

- Do not forget that CVP analysis does have limitations: it is only valid within a 'relevant range' of output volumes; it measures profitability, but does not consider the volume of capital employed to achieve such profits, and so ignores return on capital employed; and it is subject to certain other limitations described earlier in this chapter.

Quick Quiz

1   What is the breakeven point? (see para 2.4)

2   What is the formula for calculating the breakeven point in terms of the number of units required to break even? (2.5)

3   What is the margin of safety? (3.1)

4   If an organisation is required to make a profit, P, and incurs fixed costs, F, what level of contribution must it earn? (4.4)

5   Total profit is maximised when total contribution is minimised. True or false? (4.12)

6   What three lines are drawn on a breakeven chart? (5.1)

7   Where is the breakeven point on a breakeven chart? (5.2)

8   What is a profit/volume chart? (5.10)

9   What does the horizontal axis of a P/V chart represent? (5.10)

10 What are the limitations of breakeven charts and CVP analysis? (6.1)

Action Programme Review

1   (a)   Breakeven point $= \dfrac{\text{Total fixed costs}}{\text{Contribution per unit}} = \dfrac{£70,000}{£(40-30)} = 7,000$ units

    (b)   Margin of safety $= 8,000 - 7,000$ units $= 1,000$ units

        which may be expressed as $\dfrac{1,000 \text{ units}}{8,000 \text{ units}} \times 100\% = 12\tfrac{1}{2}\%$ of budget

The margin of safety indicates to management that actual sales can fall short of budget by 1,000 units or 12½% before the breakeven point is reached and no profit at all is made.

2   Required contribution   = fixed costs + profit

                     = £(113,000 + 150,000)

                     = £263,000

    Number of units $= \dfrac{\text{required contribution}}{\text{contribution per unit}}$

                     $= \dfrac{£263,000}{£(10.70-6.30)} = 59,772.7$

∴ To achieve a profit of £150,000, 59,773 units must be sold.

3   Required contribution   =   fixed costs plus profit

                         =   £47,000 + £23,000

                         =   £70,000

Required sales   14,000 units

	£
Required contribution per unit sold	5
Variable cost per unit	15
Required sales price per unit	20

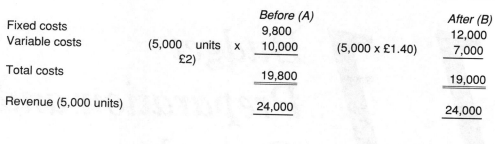

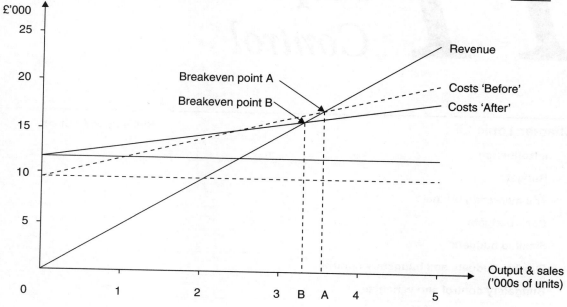

(a) Before the changeover, annual profit would be budgeted as £4,200 and the breakeven point (A) would be 3,500 units or £16,800.

(b) After the changeover, annual profit should be £5,000 and the breakeven point (B) will be 3,529 units or £16,939.

5   (a)   **False**.

The problem should be considered in terms of contribution, and it is helpful to use algebra.

Let   the current sales price be   **s**
      the variable unit cost be   **v**
      and the sales quantity be   **q**

Total contribution $= (\mathbf{q} \times \mathbf{s}) - (\mathbf{q} - \mathbf{v})$

With the reduction in sales price to 0.8s and the increase in sales volume to 1.2q, total contribution would be

$$(\mathbf{1.2q} \times \mathbf{0.8s}) - (\mathbf{1.2q} \times \mathbf{v})$$

$$= 0.96qs - 1.2qv.$$

Total contribution would be less, because sales revenue would fall (qs to 0.96qs) and total variable costs would rise (qv to 1.2qv).

If you do not follow the algebra, then put actual figures in for the factors in the question and work it through.

(b)   **False**.

Although total contribution and profits are unchanged at the current sales volume, the automation will have important consequences for any increase or fall in sales demand in the future, because the ratio of contribution to sales has increased. An increase in sales volume will now result in a faster rate of increase in profits (just as a fall in sales volume would reduce profitability at a faster rate).

Now try illustrative questions 10 and 11 at the end of the Study Text

11 Budget Preparation and Control

Learning Outcomes

Upon completing this chapter you will have made a thorough study of budget preparation and control in relation to marketing decisions.

You will also understand the concept of variances and be able to interpret them, eg between budgeted and actual sales figures.

Key Concepts

- Budget
- Principal budget factor
- Flexible budgets

- Variances and variance analysis
- Responsibility accounting

Examples of Marketing at Work

- Camelot
- The marketing and advertising budget

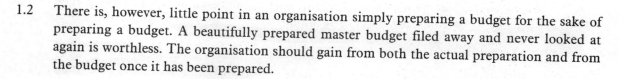

1   INTRODUCTION

1.1   Businesses must concentrate on both short-term and long-term objectives if they are to be successful. Having established a long-term corporate plan, management should develop a coordinated short-term plan which is designed to steer the business towards these long-term goals. This means that the business should use a process which concentrates management action on those areas that can be changed in the short term, so as to lead to the success of the longer-term corporate plan. This is usually done using budgeting, a process which draws together the necessary actions and coordinates the activities of management, with a master budget as an end result. We will consider both the process of budgeting and the production of a master budget at the beginning of this chapter, with a focus on the marketing budget.

1.2   There is, however, little point in an organisation simply preparing a budget for the sake of preparing a budget. A beautifully prepared master budget filed away and never looked at again is worthless. The organisation should gain from both the actual preparation and from the budget once it has been prepared.

1.3   Budgets are the concrete components of what is known as a budgetary control system. Such a system essentially ensures communication, coordination and control within an organisation and it is the control function of a budget which we will be studying in the second part of the chapter.

1.4   In the next part of the chapter we will consider variances. Variances arise when there is a difference between budgeted or expected results and actual results. We will also be looking at responsibility accounting.

2   BUDGETS
12/99, 6/00, 12/00, 6/01

Key Concept

A **budget** is a quantitative statement for a defined period of time which may include planned revenues, expenses, assets, liabilities and cash flows.

The purpose of budgetary control systems

2.1   Communication, coordination and control are general objectives of budgetary control systems: more information is provided by an inspection of specific objectives.

Exam Tip

Budgets have been examined in most sittings of the paper under the old and new syllabus since June 1995, and it is therefore essential that you have a thorough understanding of this topic. It is still a key part of the new syllabus. For example, in June 2001, 20 marks were available for estimating total costs of an event and how much you would need. In June 2000, you had to compare different ways of preparing budgets rather than identify a sum of money. This topic can be covered in a number of ways.

(a) **To ensure the achievement of the organisation's objectives**

Objectives for the organisation as a whole, and for individual departments and operations within the organisation, are set. Quantified expressions of these objectives are then drawn up as targets to be achieved.

(b) **To compel planning**

This is probably the most important feature of a budgetary planning and control system. Planning forces management to look ahead, to set out detailed plans for achieving the targets for each department, operation and each manager and to anticipate problems.

(c) **To communicate ideas and plans**

A formal system is necessary to ensure that each person affected by the plans is aware of what he or she is supposed to be doing.

(d) **To coordinate activities**

The activities of different departments of the organisation need to be coordinated. This concept of coordination implies, for example, that the production budget should be based on sales expectations. Although straightforward in concept, coordination is remarkably difficult to achieve, and there is often conflict between departmental plans in the budget.

(e) **To provide a framework for responsibility accounting**

Budgetary planning and control systems require that managers of budget centres are made responsible for the achievement of budget targets for the operations under their control.

(f) **To establish a system of control**

Control over actual performance is provided by the comparisons of actual results against the budget. Departures from budget can then be investigated and the reasons divided into controllable and uncontrollable factors.

(g) **To motivate employees to improve their performance**

The interest and commitment of employees can be retained via a system of feedback of actual results, which lets them know how well or badly they are performing.

2.2 In order to achieve these various objectives, budgets should be broken down into relevant business segments. These should naturally fit both the products and the markets in which the company operates. This will be set in the context of the **overall marketing plan**.

The budgeting process

2.3 In overall terms the budget tries to put into a **financial framework** the predicted result of all the activities that will achieve the overall corporate objectives.

Data for the budgeting process

2.4 Internal information available includes the following.

(a) **Marketing and sales information** on, for example, performance, revenues, market share and distribution channels

(b) **Production and operational information** on, for example, manufacturing capacities and capabilities and lead times

(c) **Financial information** on, for example, how much cash it has in the bank, how much it could borrow, profits, costs, cash flows and investments

(d) **Research and development information** on, for example, new products and developments

(e) **Personnel information** on, for example, labour skills, labour availability and expected wage increases

2.5 Sources of **internal information** can be divided into two groups.

(a) **Formal sources.** All output of the organisation's **management and marketing information system** including control and monitoring reports, forecasting and enquiry systems, modelling and simulation, investigative reports, budgets, job descriptions, organisation charts, correspondence and video displays.

(b) **Informal sources.** Discussions, meetings, social contact, telephone conversations, personal record keeping and correspondence.

2.6 **External information** available includes the following.

(a) **Market and competitors.** The organisation must assess its competitors. It should analyse its market (and any other markets that it is intending to enter) to identify possible **new opportunities.** This subject is covered in Part D of this Study Text.

(b) **Economic conditions.** The state of the world must be considered. Is it in recession or is it booming? The organisation should gather information on forecasts for growth, inflation, GDP and so on and the effect of developments such as the European Community single market.

(c) **Industrial structure.** The organisation should determine whether a process of rationalisation or concentration is taking place within the industry, whether there are any privatisation issues to take into consideration and whether many new firms are entering the industry.

(d) **Political factors.** Any political instability, especially in overseas markets, and any significant political decisions, should be assessed.

(e) **Technological change.** Information on any new technology of which the organisation might be able to take advantage should be collected.

(f) **Demographic trends and social factors.** The organisation should assess the effects of any changes in the population structure, the age profile of customers, family patterns, and attitudes to consumption and savings.

2.7 External information also comes from two sources.

(a) **Formal sources.** Published reports, government statistics, scientific and technical abstracts, company reports, commercial data banks, trade associations and special investigations.

(b) **Informal sources.** Discussions, social contact of all types, media coverage, conferences, business and holiday trips (at home and abroad) and correspondence.

2.8 Internal information is the most important as far as budgeting is concerned. External information should be taken into account but is usually most relevant at the long-term planning stage.

The master budget

2.9 An overall **master budget** consists of the following.

    (a) A **budgeted profit and loss account**. The total profit and loss account budget will often be sub-divided into departmental budgets (a budgeted profit and loss account for each department, division or other profit centre in the organisation).

    (b) A **cash budget**. A business needs to make sure that it will have enough cash to continue operating, or that an overdraft facility is available with a bank to cover the expected need.

    (c) An end-of-period **budgeted balance sheet**.

Identifying the principal budget factor

2.10 The initial task in the budgeting process is to identify the **principal (key) budget factor** which will drive all other costs and revenues. In most cases this will be **sales**. The interface between sales and production is fundamental since the function of the sales and marketing department is to **provide for the needs of the customer whilst maximising the benefit to the business**. This usually results in the **maximisation of sales volumes**, but it is no good believing that the business can sell 10,000 units in the year if production capacity is limited to 9,000 units.

Key Concept

The **principal budget factor** is one which will limit the activities of an undertaking and which is often the starting point in budget preparation.

2.11 There are occasions when budgeting does not begin with the sales budget, because there is a shortage of a key resource which prevents the business from selling as much as it could. For example there could be a shortage of skilled labour, of raw materials or of machine capacity. In these situations there is a **limiting budget factor**. Budgeting would start by looking at the problem of how to **maximise profits within the resource constraints**.

Preparing the sales budget

2.12 Since the sales budget is usually the budget from which cost budgets and the budgeted profit and loss account are developed, it is obviously very important that sales in the budget should be **reasonable and realistic**.

2.13 It is not easy to assess potential sales with any degree of accuracy. All that a business can do is put as much care as possible into preparing the sales budget. There are several methods that can be used to **forecast** likely sales, as we saw in Chapter 4.

2.14 An organisation might produce a large number of products or services, and sell them in a wide geographical area. In such cases, sales budgets should be prepared for each **product or product group** and for each region.

2.15 For many organisations, sales have seasonal peaks and troughs. **Seasonal variations** in sales should be recognised in the budgets.

Preparing other resource budgets

2.16 Once the sales budget has been prepared, a manufacturing organisation can go on to prepare a **production budget** and associated **resource budgets** (eg materials usage and labour). Goods may be produced for stock or sold out of stock, and so planned production and sales volumes are not necessarily the same amount. The production budget in units will be equal to the sales budget in units plus the budgeted increase in finished goods stock or minus the budgeted decrease in finished goods stock.

2.17 Budgets for **marketing and administration costs** must be prepared. Many cost items will be fixed, although there may be some variable costs (for example sales commission). Some of the marketing budget will have to be prepared in conjunction with the sales budget since the level of sales anticipated will rely on marketing support. The balance of the budget may well be determined by the activity anticipated from new products which may be launched during the year.

Action Programme 1

The actual salaries and administration expenditure of Humdinger Ltd during the 12 months to 30 June 2001 was as follows.

	£	£
Salaries		
General manager	24,000	
Supervisors (2 @ £12,500)	25,000	
Production staff (10 @ £10,000)	100,000	
Salesmen (5 @ £15,000)	75,000	
Marketing executive	18,000	
Office secretary	7,500	
		249,500
Commissions (based on sales of £4m)		
Salesmen (0.9%)	36,000	
		36,000
Travel and entertainment		
Averaging £35 per salesman per day for an annual average of 225 days per salesman		39,375
Office expenses		
Rent, utilities, suppliers and so on		25,000
Total expenditure	3	349,875

In preparing the budget for the next 12 months the following facts are anticipated.

(a) The general manager's salary will rise by £2,000. Production staff and supervisors' salaries will remain unchanged.

(b) Each salesman's base salary will remain unchanged, but the commission rate will increase to 1.0%.

(c) The office secretary's salary will be increased by £60 per month. The marketing executive's salary will be increased by £100 per month.

(d) Two additional salesmen are to be employed, on the same terms as the existing sales force.

(e) The sales quota will be £5m.

(f) Travel and entertainment expenses are likely to increase by 4% per salesman-day.

(g) A special promotional extravaganza will be undertaken at the cost of £25,000.

(h) The office expenses will rise by 10%.

Required

Prepare the 2001/2002 salaries and administration cost budget for Humdinger Ltd.

Marketing at Work

'The marketing and advertising budget is the first to be raided when a company's business targets are not being met, finds a survey of 100 finance directors from large companies, commissioned by the Institute of Practitioners in Advertising and consultants KPMG.

Those questioned placed marketing and advertising top of the list for cuts when a company is under pressure, ahead of human resources, training, research and development and information technology.

The survey indicates that marketing expenditure has not increased in line with company turnover: 79 per cent of those questioned said turnover had increased, while only 30 per cent had increased marketing budgets. It also seems that 18 per cent did not know whether marketing expenditure in their companies had grown or not.

For those marketing directors who are getting fatter budgets, the days of automatic rises appear to be over. "Zero base budgeting" - arguing from first principles each time - is now employed by half of all companies. Finance directors are also commonly involved in discussions about marketing and advertising each month.'

Here are some more interesting insights into the relationship between finance and marketing directors.

Finance directors want hard measures of advertising effectiveness, namely a figure for return on investment (ROI), rather than soft measures such as awareness, brand image or likeability.

There are cultural differences between the attitudes of the finance department in 'strong brand' companies in comparison those in 'weak brand' ones. The former rated marketers highly on financial literacy and the ability to justify spend, and allocated more resources to marketing because measurable objectives were set.

Strong brand companies, where marketing pitches for, wins, and makes good use of a larger portion of resources, are much more likely to review advertising in the Annual Report and Accounts.

---

3 THE MARKETING BUDGET

The marketing plan

3.1 The marketing **plan** is the first step and consists of several inter-related decisions.

(a) **Sales targets**: these must be set for each product and each sales division (with sub-targets also set for sales regions, sales areas and individual salesmen). Sales targets may be referred to as sales quotas.

(b) The **total marketing budget** must be set.

(c) Given an overall marketing budget, **resources (cash) must be allocated** among:

(i) **Salaries** of salespeople

(ii) **Above the line** expenditure (advertising)

(iii) **Below the line** expenditure (sales promotion items, price reduction allowances, etc)

(d) The overall sales target set by top management will incorporate sales price decisions; but there is likely to be an element of choice in the pricing decision. In other words, top management will decide on a 'rough pricing zone' and a specific price within this zone will be fixed later.

(e) Expenditure on marketing will also be allocated to **different products or services** within the organisation's range. Some products might justify additional marketing expenditure; whereas others, nearing the end of their life cycle, may lose a part of their previous allocation.

The marketing budget

3.2 There are three types of budget planning for a marketing budget, depending on how the organisation is managed.

(a) **Top-down planning** involves the setting of goals for lower management by higher management.

(b) **Bottom-up planning** exists where employees set their own goals and submit them to higher management for approval.

(c) **'Goals down - plans up'** planning is a mixture of the two styles, whereby top management sets overall goals and employees lower in the organisation hierarchy then set plans for achieving those goals. This type of planning is well suited to the formulation of sales budgets, and is similar to management by objectives.

Sales budgets

3.3 Budgeting for **sales revenue** and **selling costs** is plagued with uncertainty. The variables are so many and so difficult to estimate, even within a wide tolerance (largely because of competitive action and changing consumer habits and tastes), that both setting budgets and budgetary control on the marketing side are different from the more 'mechanical' approach which can be adopted with other budgets.

3.4 A sales and marketing budget is necessary for the following reasons.

(a) It is an element of the **overall strategic plan** of the business (the master budget) which brings together all the activities of the business.

(b) Where sales and other non-production costs are a large part of total costs, it is **financially prudent** to forecast, plan and control them.

(c) The uncertain nature of factors which influence selling makes the need for good forecasts and plans greater. If budgets are to be used for **control**, then where budget estimates are more uncertain, more budgetary control is necessary.

Matching forecast demand with estimated available capacity

3.5 One of the problems in setting budgets is matching the **forecast demand from customers** with the **estimated available capacity**.

(a) It is difficult to make an accurate forecast of demand.

(b) It is difficult to predict available capacity accurately too, given uncertainties about the following.

(i) Efficiency and productivity levels
(ii) The availability of resources
(iii) The likely down-time or time lost through industrial action

(c) There are often practical difficulties in matching demand with capacity. Demand might be seasonal, and if services or non-standard products are required, it will not be possible to build up inventories in periods of slack demand.

3.6 In order to match demand with capacity, management must be **flexible**, and be prepared to take action to achieve the following.

(a) To **suppress demand** if it exceeds capacity - eg by raising prices
(b) To **stimulate demand** if there is excess capacity - eg by advertising or price reductions
(c) To **reduce excess capacity** by selling off surplus assets
(d) To **supplement production** when there is under-capacity by sub-contracting work to other organisations, and perhaps to take steps to increase capacity (by acquiring new premises, equipment and labour, or by negotiating for more overtime from existing employees)

BPP
PUBLISHING

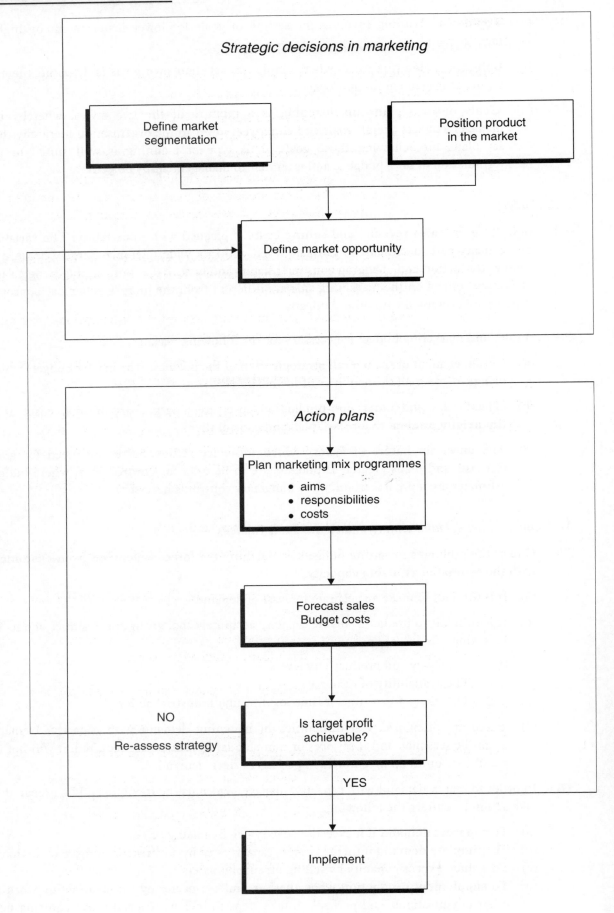

Expense budgets

3.7 There are a number of ways of setting marketing budgets.

(a) **Percentage of sales**. Research has shown that in the UK, some marketing budgets are fixed by some rule-of-thumb, non-scientific methods, such as the following.

(i) A percentage of the **previous year's sales**
(ii) A percentage of the **budgeted annual sales**
(iii) A percentage of the **previous year's profit**

There is no reason, however, why marketing costs should relate directly to either total turnover or profits. Given that large amounts of expenditure may be incurred on advertising, these arbitrary guesswork systems reveal an alarming lack of proper financial control.

(b) **Competitive parity**, ie fixing marketing expenditure in relation to the expenditure incurred by competitors. (This is unsatisfactory because it presupposes that the competitor's decision must be a good one.)

(c) **The objective and task method**. The marketing task for the organisation is set and a budget is prepared which will help to ensure that this objective is achieved.

(d) **All-you-can-afford**. Crude and unscientific, but commonly used. The firm simply takes a view on what it thinks it can afford to spend on marketing.

3.8 **Advertising** is an important feature of the marketing budget. The theory behind setting an advertising budget is the theory of **diminishing returns**, ie for every extra £1 of advertising spent, the company will earn an extra £x of profit. Further expenditure on advertising is justified until the marginal return £x diminishes until it is less than the amount spent in achieving it. Unfortunately, the marginal return from additional advertising cannot usually be measured easily in practice.

(a) Advertising is only **one aspect** of the overall marketing mix.

(b) Advertising has some **long-term effect**, which goes beyond the limits of a measurable accounting period.

(c) Where the advertising budget is fixed as a percentage of sales, **advertising costs tend to follow sales levels** and not *vice versa*.

(d) The US merchant John Wanamaker is supposed to have said: 'I know that 50 per cent of my advertising is wasted, but I don't know which 50 per cent'.

3.9 Recommended practice for fixing advertising cost budgets would include the use of the following.

(a) **Empirical testing** (eg in a mail order business or in retail operations). It may be possible to measure the effect of advertising on sales by direct observation.

(b) **Mathematical models** using data about media and consumer characteristics, desired market share, and using records of past results. Regression analysis can be conducted to find out the likely cost of advertising (through several media) to achieve a given target.

3.10 As techniques for identifying market segments becomes more sophisticated (eg through the use of **marketing databases**) advertising will become less cost-efficient compared to other types of promotion, such as direct mail.

Marketing at Work

Advertising budgets are sometimes hard to justify and easy to cut, so it helps if they can be seen to be effective.

According to an article in *Marketing Week* (May 1998), Camelot are reviewed their advertising after the appointment of a new marketing director. The 'It could be you' slogan was axed in favour of 'Maybe, just maybe', which it was thought would appear less 'selfish' Camelot has spent an estimated £100m on advertising, and in 1998 turned in sales of £5bn.

Control

3.11 Once the plan has been implemented, the task of marketing management is to control the use of resources. Aspects of control include the following.

   (a) A comparison of actual sales against the budget

   (b) A comparison of actual marketing costs against the budgeted expenditure levels and against actual sales

   (c) Analysis of the profitability of individual products, and distribution outlets

   (d) **Strategic control**, ie checking whether the company's objectives, products and resources are being directed towards the correct markets

3.12 The allocation of **direct selling costs** to products, or type of outlet and so on is fairly straightforward, but indirect costs must be allocated. This aspect of cost allocation should be carefully considered when deciding whether to eliminate an unprofitable expenditure from selling or distribution.

   (a) The cost of distributing goods to a distant area may seem unprofitable; but if, by not selling the goods in this area, there will be **unused production capacity**, the products that are produced and sold will have to bear a higher proportion of fixed costs.

   (b) The allocation of fixed selling costs to products may make a product seem unprofitable, but the product may still be making a **contribution** to those fixed costs.

3.13 Eliminating unprofitable selling and distribution expenditure is sound commercial practice, but as we have seen the concept of **avoidable and unavoidable costs** should be used in deciding what is unprofitable. If the removal of one part of selling costs relieves a company of a cost which is higher than the contribution to profit gained from it, then this part of selling activity can and should be eliminated. The unavoidable fixed costs of production as well as selling and distribution should be taken into account in any such decision.

4   CASH BUDGETS

4.1 When a budgeted profit and loss account has been prepared, a cash budget can be drawn up. The cash budget shows the expected receipts of cash and payments of cash during the forthcoming budget period, laid out in such a way as to show the cash balance of a business at defined intervals.

4.2 Receipts of cash may be from cash sales, payments by debtors, the sale of fixed assets, the issue of new shares or loans, the receipt of interest and dividends from investments outside the business and so on.

4.3   Payments of cash may be for the purchase of stocks, payment of wages or other expenses, the purchase of capital items, the payment of interest, dividends or taxation.

4.4   It is important for you to remember that **profit and cash flow during a period need not be the same amount**. The reasons for the difference between profit and cash flow might be familiar to you already. They are as follows.

(a)   There are some items in the profit and loss account which are not cash flow items. For example depreciation is a charge against profit but is not a cash flow.

(b)   There are some sources of cash income which are not fully reported, or not reported at all, in the P & L account. These include the cash earned from the sale of fixed assets.

(c)   There are some payments which are not reported fully, or at all, in the P & L account, such as the payment for new capital equipment (fixed assets) and the repayment of loans.

(d)   Increases in the volume of working capital tie up funds and reduce the cash inflow. For example an increase in debtors represents sales on credit (and so profit) without cash income yet having been received. This is normally an important element in any sales campaign which is often overlooked by marketing managers but can have a higher adverse impact on profitability since borrowing funds costs money (interest).

4.5   The purpose of the cash budget is to forewarn managers as to what the cash position of the business will be: for example whether it will run up an overdraft and if so, how large the overdraft will be. Managers will also wish to be forewarned of a cash surplus so that they can make plans to take full advantage of the excess cash resources.

5   FLEXIBLE BUDGETS

5.1   The master budget prepared before the beginning of the budget period is known as the **fixed budget**. The term 'fixed' means the following.

(a)   The budget is prepared on the basis of an **estimated volume** of production sales, but no plans are made for the event that **actual volumes** may differ from **budgeted volumes**.

(b)   When actual volumes of production and sales during a period become known, a fixed budget is not adjusted to the new levels of activity.

5.2   A **flexible budget** is designed to change to relate to the actual volumes in a period. Flexible budgets may be used in one of two ways.

Key Concept

A **flexible budget**, by recognising different cost patterns, is designed to change as volume of output or sales changes.

(a)   **At the planning stage**. For example, suppose that Falcon Kites expects to sell 10,000 kites during the next year. A fixed budget would be prepared on the basis of these expected volumes. However, if the company thinks that output and sales might be as low as 8,000 units or as high as 12,000 units, it may prepare flexible budgets, at volumes of, say 8,000, 9,000, 11,000 and 12,000 units. This enables contingency plans to be drawn up.

(b) **Retrospectively**. At the end of each month or year, flexible budgets can be used to examine actual results achieved. Flexible budgets are an essential factor in **budgetary control**.

(i) Management needs to know how good or bad actual performance has been. There must be a yardstick against which actual performance can be measured.

(ii) Business is **dynamic**, and actual volumes of output cannot be expected to conform exactly to the fixed budget.

(iii) For useful control information, it is necessary to compare actual results **at the level of activity achieved** against the results that would have been expected at this level of activity, which are shown by the flexible budget.

Action Programme 2

Explain what is meant by the terms 'fixed budget' and 'flexible budget' and state the main objective of preparing flexible budgets.

Example: flexible budgets

5.3 Suppose that Falcon Kites expects production and sales of toy kites during the next year to be 90% of the company's output capacity, that is, 9,000 units. The following historical records of cost are available.

Units of output/sales	*Cost of sales*
9,800	£44,400
7,700	£38,100

The company's management is not certain that the estimate of sales is correct, and has asked for flexible budgets to be prepared at output and sales levels of 8,000 and 10,000 units. The sales price per unit has been fixed at £10.

5.4 If we assume that within the range 8,000 to 10,000 units of sales, all costs are fixed, variable or mixed (in other words there are no stepped costs, material discounts, overtime premiums, bonus payments etc) the fixed and flexible budgets would be based on the estimate of fixed and variable cost.

		£
Total cost of 9,800 units	=	44,400
Total cost of 7,700 units	=	38,100
Variable cost of 2,100 units	=	6,300

The variable cost per unit is therefore (£6,300 ÷ 2,100) = £3

		£
Total cost of 9,800 units	=	44,400
Variable cost of 9,800 units (9,800 × £3)	=	29,400
Fixed costs (all levels of output and sales)	=	15,000

5.5 The fixed budgets and flexible budgets might now be prepared as follows.

	Flexible budget 8,000 *units* £	*Master budget* 9,000 *units* £	*Flexible budget* 10,000 *units* £
Sales (× £10)	880,000	90,000	100,000
Variable costs (× £3)	24,000	27,000	30,000
Contribution	56,000	63,000	70,000
Fixed costs	15,000	15,000	15,000
Profit	41,000	48,000	55,000

6 FLEXIBLE BUDGETS AND BUDGETARY CONTROL

Variance analysis

6.1 **Budgetary control** is the practice of establishing budgets which identify areas of responsibility for individual managers (for example brand managers) and of regularly comparing actual results against expected results. The differences between actual results and expected results are called **variances** and these are used to provide a guideline for control action. Variance analysis calculations will be covered in a later section of this chapter.

> ### Key Concepts
>
> A **variance** is the difference between a planned, budgeted or standard cost (or revenue) and the actual incurred.
>
> **Variance analysis** is the evaluation of performance by means of variances, whose timely reporting should maximise the opportunity for managerial action.

The wrong approach to budgetary control

6.2 The wrong approach to budgetary control is to compare **actual results against a fixed budget**. Consider the following example.

Alpha Limited manufactures a single product, the beta. Budgeted results and actual results for June 2000 are shown below.

	Budget	Actual results	Variances
Production and sales of the beta (units)	2,000	3,000	
	£	£	£
Sales revenue (a)	20,000	30,000	10,000 (Favourable)
Direct materials	6,000	8,500	2,500 (Adverse)
Direct labour	4,000	4,500	500 (A)
Maintenance	1,000	1,400	400 (A)
Depreciation	2,000	2,200	200 (A)
Rent and rates	1,500	1,600	100 (A)
Other costs	3,600	5,000	1,400 (A)
Total costs (b)	18,100	23,200	5,100
Profit (a) - (b)	1,900	6,800	4,900 (F)

6.3 (a) In this example, the **variances are meaningless** for purposes of control. Costs were higher than budget because the volume of output was also higher; variable costs would be expected to increase above the budgeted costs in the fixed budget. There is no information to show whether control action is needed.

(b) For control purposes, it is necessary to know the answers to questions such as the following.

(i) Were actual costs higher than they **should have been** to produce and sell 3,000 units of beta?

(ii) Was actual revenue satisfactory from the sale of 3,000 units of beta?

(iii) Did the volume of units made and sold vary from the budget favourably or adversely?

All these aspects are relevant to the decision-making process in which the marketing manager will be a key individual.

The correct approach to budgetary control

6.4   The correct approach to budgetary control is as follows.

(a)   **Identify** fixed and variable costs

(b)   **Produce a flexible budget** using marginal costing techniques

6.5   In the previous example of Alpha Ltd, let us suppose that we have the following estimates of cost behaviour.

(a)   Direct materials and maintenance costs are variable.

(b)   Direct labour is to be regarded as variable in order to measure efficiency/productivity.

(c)   Rent and rates and depreciation are fixed costs.

(d)   Other costs consist of fixed costs of £1,600 plus a variable cost of £1 per unit made and sold.

6.6   Now that the cost behaviour patterns are known, a budget cost can be shown in a flexible budget as the expected expenditure for the relevant level of activity.

(a)   Variable cost allowances   =   original budget × (3,000 units/2,000 units)
       For example, material cost allowance   =   £6,000 × 3/2 = £9,000

(b)   Fixed cost allowance   =   as original budget

(c)   Other costs allowance   =   £1,600 + (3,000 × £1) = £4,600

6.7   The budgetary control analysis should be as follows.

	Fixed budget (a)	*Flexible budget* (b)	*Actual results* (c)	*Budget variance* (b) - (c)
Production and sales (units)	2,000	3,000	3,000	
	£	£	£	£
Sales revenue	20,000	30,000	30,000	0
Variable costs				
Direct materials	6,000	9,000	8,500	500 (F)
Direct labour	4,000	6,000	4,500	1,500 (F)
Maintenance	1,000	1,500	1,400	100 (F)
Semi-variable costs				
Other costs	3,600	4,600	5,000	400 (A)
Fixed costs				
Depreciation	2,000	2,000	2,200	200 (A)
Rent and rates	1,500	1,500	1,600	100 (A)
Total costs	18,100	24,600	23,200	1,400 (F)
Profit	1,900	5,400	6,800	1,400 (F)

6.8   In selling 3,000 units the expected profit should have been £5,400. Instead, actual profit was £6,800 because, given output and sales of 3,000 units, costs were lower than expected.

6.9   Investigation of the variances, with a view to deciding whether **control action** is required, will be carried out for those variances which seem significantly large. Large favourable variances should also be checked. In our example, the sales manager may be asked to check why sales were 50% higher than budgeted.

Action Programme 3

The budgeted and actual results of Smith Ltd for September 20X1 were as follows. The company uses a marginal costing system.

Sales and production		Fixed budget 1,000 units		Actual 700 units
	£	£	£	£
Sales		20,000		14,200
Variable cost of sales				
Direct materials	8,000		5,200	
Direct labour	4,000		3,100	
Variable overhead	2,000		1,500	
		14,000		9,800
Contribution		6,000		4,400
Fixed costs		5,000		5,400
Profit/(loss)		1,000		(1,000)

Required

Prepare a budget that will be useful for management control purposes.

7 BUDGETARY CONTROL AND VARIANCES

6/00, 12/00

7.1 **Variance analysis** is an extremely important control procedure. Via an analysis of variances, seeking to explain them, possibly after discussion with different people throughout an organisation, managers are more likely to find out what is really happening.

Sales variances

7.2 All sales revenue is the product of a quantity of **sales multiplied by the unit sales price**. The actual total sales revenue can be compared with the budgeted sales revenue and the difference will indicate whether we have overachieved or underachieved the expected level of performance. But why did the variance occur? Was it due to a **price variance** (actual selling price per unit was different to budgeted selling price per unit), or to a volume variance (more or less units were sold than anticipated) or a mixture of both? In multi-product companies this can be further complicated by the **mix of products** sold.

7.3 In any budgeting process the marketing manager will be asked to estimate how many units of a product will be sold during the year and at what price. The actual performance will be different in the vast majority of cases and it is the **difference in the sales volumes and prices that determine the change in revenue**.

Sales price and sales volume variances

7.4 The **total sales variance** is the difference between budgeted sales revenue and actual sales revenue. This can be split into two sub-variances.

(a) **Sales price variances** measure the effect on profit when actual selling prices are different to budgeted selling prices. In our example of Alpha Limited in Section 5, there was no sales price variance.

Suppose, however, that the actual revenue had been £33,000. Actual selling price per unit would have been £33,000/3,000 = £11 per unit and the sales price variance would have been £(11 − 10) × 3,000 = £3,000 favourable.

(b) **Sales volume variances** measure the effect on profit when the actual volume of sales differs from that budgeted. In our example, revenue increased by £10,000 (1,000 units × £10 per unit) but variable costs also obviously increased (by 1,000 units × variable cost per unit of £6.50) and so the resulting variance and effect on profit was £(10,000 − 6,500) = £3,500 (F). When this is added to the favourable cost variance of £1,400 we get £4,900 (F). This is the difference between actual profit and the fixed budget profit.

Sales mix and sales quantity variances

7.5 A company selling two or more products is often able to control the **quantity and mix** of its sales, perhaps by adjusting expenditures on advertising, sales promotion and direct selling. Variance analysis can inform managers of the effect on profit of such changes by analysing the sales volume variance into a **sales mix variance** and a **sales quantity variance**.

7.6 The **sales mix variance** calculates whether the actual proportions of each product sold represent a more or less profitable mix than the budgeted proportions. For example if proportionately more of the most profitable products are sold then there will be a favourable sales mix variance.

7.7 The **sales quantity variance** measures the budgeted average profit gained or lost as a result of achieving a higher or lower level of sales than budgeted, regardless of the mix of sales.

Example: sales mix and quantity variances

7.8 JD Ltd makes and sells two products, coded BF and GD. The **budgeted sales and profit** are as follows.

	Sales Units	Revenue £	Costs £	Contribution £	Contribution per unit £
BF	400	8,000	6,000	2,000	5
GD	300	12,000	11,100	900	3
	700			2,900	

Actual sales were as follows.

BF   280 units
GD   630 units

The company management is able to control the sales of each product through the allocation of sales effort, advertising and sales promotion expenses. Calculate the sales volume, sales mix and sales quantity variances.

Answer

7.9 When we look at the sales figures in this example it is apparent that a bigger proportion than budgeted of the less profitable GD has been sold.

Step 1   A **sales volume variance** is calculated by comparing budgeted and actual sales and valued at the standard contribution per unit.

	BF	GD
Budgeted sales	400 units	300 units
Actual sales	280 units	630 units
Sales volume variance	120 units (A)	330 units (F)
× standard margin per unit	× £5	× £3
	£600 (A)	£990 (F)
Total sales volume variance		£390 (F)

Step 2 The method for calculating the **sales mix variance** is to compare **actual v standard** as follows.

Take the **actual total of sales** and **convert** this total into a **standard mix**, on the assumption that sales should have been in the **budgeted proportions**. In the example, total actual sales were 910 units. According to the budgeted mix, 4/7 (ie 520) of these should have been BF and 3/7 (390) GD.

The **difference** between **actual** sales and 'standard mix' sales for each individual product is then valued at the standard contribution.

	Actual mix of sales Units	Standard mix Units	Mix variance Units	Standard margin per unit £	Mix variance £
BF	280	520	240 (A)	5	1,200 (A)
GD	630	390	240 (F)	3	720 (F)
Actual total	910	910			480 (A)

The sales mix variance is £480 adverse, ie the standard profit would have been £480 higher if the 910 units sold had been in the standard mix of 4:3.

Step 3 The **sales quantity variance** compares **standard v budget**. It is the difference between the **actual** sales quantity **in the standard mix** and the **budgeted sales** quantity, valued at the standard contribution per unit.

	Standard mix Units	Budgeted sales Units	Quantity variance Units	Standard margin £	Sales margin variance £
BF	520	400	120 (F)	5	600 (F)
GD	390	300	90 (F)	3	270 (F)
	910	700			870

Summary

	£
Sales mix variance	480 (A)
Sales quantity variance	870 (F)
Sales volume variance	390 (F)

Production variances

7.10 Just as the actual sales price and the actual sales volume are likely to be different to those anticipated, so too are the resources (materials, labour, overheads) used to produce the product. This means, of course, that materials, labour and overhead variances will arise.

Direct material variances

7.11 The **direct material total variance** measures the effect on profit of the difference between what the output actually cost and what it should have cost. in terms of material) can be divided into two sub-variances.

(a) The **direct material price variance** measures the effect on profit of the difference between what the actual quantity of material purchased did cost and what it should have cost.

(b) The **direct material usage variance** measures the effect on profit of the difference between how much material should have been used and how much material was used to produce the actual output, valued at budgeted cost per unit of material.

7.12 In the example of Alpha Limited, the total direct materials cost variance was £500 (F). This could be analysed to assess whether it was due to cheaper material than budgeted being used or to material being used more efficiently than budgeted to produce the 3,000 units.

Direct labour variances

7.13 Direct labour variances are very similar to direct material variances.

The **direct labour total variance** (which measures the effect on profit of the difference between what the output should have cost and what it did cost, in terms of labour) can be divided into two sub-variances.

(a) The **direct labour rate variance** measures the effect on profit of the difference between what the labour did cost and what it should have cost to produce the actual output.

(b) The **direct labour efficiency variance** measures the effect on profit of the difference between how many hours should have been worked to produce the actual output and how many hours were worked, valued at the expected rate per hour.

7.14 In the example of Alpha Ltd the direct labour cost variance was £1,500 (F). Profit may have been increased by this amount because either the labour were not being paid as much as budgeted or because they worked more efficiently than budgeted to produce the 3,000 units.

Variable overhead variances

7.15 For the purposes of marketing it is sufficient to be aware that the variance measures the effect on profit of the cost of the overhead being different to the cost expected at the actual output level.

7.16 In our Alpha Limited example, costs should have been £1,500 but were £1,400, resulting in a favourable variance of £100.

Fixed overhead variances

7.17 As long as the actual level of output does not change dramatically from the budgeted level of output, the amount of fixed overhead should not change. The only reason for a variance is therefore if the actual cost of the fixed overhead differs from the budgeted cost.

7.18 In our Alpha Ltd example, both fixed cost variances were adverse because actual costs were greater than budgeted costs.

Interpretation of variances

7.19 We have now seen a complete family of variances which go together to complete a picture of the operating performance of a company compared to a budget. It is important that we emphasise the fact that **variance analysis is only a technique used in the control and evaluation of performance**. It is essential that the information gained from this control exercise is brought to the attention of each appropriate manager in a timely fashion: the right information must be in the right place at the right time. It is an indication of what has happened in order that appropriate explanations can be sought and decisions made, but some variances may be outside the control of any particular manager.

The reasons for cost variances

7.20 There are many possible reasons for variances arising, including efficiencies and inefficiencies of operations, errors in budgeting and changes in exchange rates. There now follows a list of a few **possible** causes of variances.

Variance	Favourable	Adverse
(a) Material price	Unforeseen discounts received Greater care taken in purchasing Change in material standard	Price increase Careless purchasing Change in material standard
(b) Material usage	Material used of higher quality than budgeted More effective use made of material Errors in allocating material to job	Defective material Excessive waste Theft Stricter quality control Errors in allocating material to job
(c) Labour rate	Use of apprentices or other workers at a rate of pay lower than budgeted	Wage rate increase
(d) Labour efficiency	Output produced more quickly than expected, because of work motivation, better quality of equipment or material Errors in allocating time to job	Lost time in excess of that Output lower than expected because of deliberate restriction, lack of training, or sub-standard material used Errors in allocating time to job
(e) Overhead	Savings in costs incurred More economical use of services	Increase in cost of services used Excessive use of services Change in type of services used

Interdependence between variances

7.21 The cause of one variance may be wholly or partly explained by the cause of another variance. Examples could be as follows.

(a) If the purchasing department buys a cheaper material which is poorer in quality than that expected, the material price variance will be favourable, but this may cause material wastage and an adverse usage variance.

(b) Similarly, if employees used to do some work are highly experienced, they may be paid a higher rate than the budgeted wage per hour, but they should do the work more efficiently than employees of 'average' skill. In other words, an adverse rate variance may be compensated for by a favourable efficiency variance.

8 OPERATING STATEMENTS

8.1 So far, we have considered how variances are calculated without considering how they combine to reconcile the difference between budgeted profit and actual profit during a period. This reconciliation is usually presented as a report to senior management at the end of each control period in the form of an **operating statement**.

8.2 An extensive example will now be introduced, both to revise the variance calculations already described, and also to show how to combine them into an operating statement.

BPP PUBLISHING

Example: variances and operating statements

8.3   Sydney Ltd manufactures one product, and the entire product is sold as soon as it is produced. The company makes an analysis of variances every month. The budgeted costs for the product, a boomerang, are as follows.

BUDGETED COSTS - BOOMERANG

		£
Direct materials	0.5 kilos at £4 per kilo	2.00
Direct wages	2 hours at £2.00 per hour	4.00
Variable overheads	2 hours at £0.30 per hour	0.60
Fixed overhead	2 hours at £3.70 per hour	7.40
Budgeted cost		14.00
Budgeted profit		6.00
Budgeted selling price		20.00

Selling and administration expenses are not included in the budgeted cost, and are deducted from profit as a period charge.

Budgeted output for the month of June 20X1 was 5,100 units. Actual results for June 20X1 were as follows.

Production of 4,850 units was sold for £95,600.
Materials consumed in production amounted to 2,300 kgs at a total cost of £9,800.
Labour hours paid for and worked amounted to 8,500 hours at a cost of £16,800.
Variable overheads amounted to £2,600.
Fixed overheads amounted to £42,300.
Selling and administration expenses amounted to £18,000.

Calculate all variances and prepare an operating statement for the month ended 30 June 20X1.

Answer

			£
8.4	(a)	2,300 kg of material should cost (× £4)	9,200
		but did cost	9,800
		Material price variance	600 (A)
	(b)	4,850 boomerangs should use (× 0.5 kgs)	2,425 kg
		but did use	2,300 kg
		Material usage variance in kgs	125 kg (F)
		× budgeted cost per kg	× £4
		Material usage variance	£500 (F)
			£
	(c)	8,500 hours of labour should cost (× £2)	17,000
		but did cost	16,800
		Labour rate variance	200 (F)
	(d)	4,850 boomerangs should take (× 2 hrs)	9,700 hrs
		but did take (active hours)	8,500 hrs
		Labour efficiency variance in hours	1,200 hrs (F)
		× budgeted cost per hour	× £2
		Labour efficiency variance	£2,400 (F)
			£
	(e)	Variable overheads should have been	
		4,850 × 2 × £0.30	2,910
		but did cost	2,600
		Variable overhead variance	310 (F)

			£
(f)	Fixed overhead should have been (4,850 units × 2 hrs × £3.70)		35,890
	but did cost		42,300
	Fixed overhead variance		6,410 (A)

			£
(g)	Revenue from 4,850 boomerangs should be (× £20)		97,000
	but was		95,600
	Selling price variance		1,400 (A)

(h)	Budgeted sales volume		5,100 units
	Actual sales volume		4,850 units
	Sales volume profit variance in units		250 units
	× budgeted profit per unit		× £6
	Sales volume profit variance		£1,500 (A)

8.5 There are several ways in which an operating statement may be presented. The most common format is one which reconciles budgeted profit to actual profit. Sales variances are reported first, and the total of the budgeted profit and the two sales variances results in a figure for 'actual sales minus the budgeted cost of sales' as follows.

	£	£
Budgeted profit, before sales and administration costs		
(5,100 units × £6 profit)		30,600
Selling price variance	1,400 (A)	
Sales volume profit variance	1,500 (A)	
		2,900 (A)
Actual sales (£95,600) less the budgeted cost of sales (4,850 × £14)		27,700

8.6 The cost variances are then reported. Sales and administration costs are then deducted to reach the actual profit for June 20X1.

SYDNEY LTD - OPERATING STATEMENT JUNE 20X1

		£	£
Budgeted profit before sales and administration costs			30,600
Sales variances: price		1,400 (A)	
Volume		1,500 (A)	
			2,900 (A)
Actual sales minus the budgeted cost of sales			27,700

Cost variances	(F)	(A)	
	£	£	
Material price		600	
Material usage	500		
Labour rate	200		
Labour efficiency	2,400		
Variable overhead	310		
Fixed overhead		6,410	
	3,410	7,010	3,600 (A)
Sales and administration costs			18,000
Actual profit, June 20X1			6,100

Check	£	£
Sales		95,600
Materials	9,800	
Labour	16,800	
Variable overhead	2,600	
Fixed overhead	42,300	
Sales and administration	18,000	
		89,500
Actual profit		6,100

Variances and the marketing manager

8.7   What is the importance to marketing of all the analysis of production and expenditure variances? The objective of most organisations is to make money. This may well be coupled with other objectives but without profitability and cash generation the company will fail in the long run. The analysis of the market place and the likely reactions to our marketing strategies are an essential part of this decision-making process.

8.8   Profitability is an essential part of the understanding of the marketing manager. Ultimately it will be of very little value if the marketing manager believes he can sell an excellent product at £10 per unit and we discover that we can only produce the product for £11 per unit. The decision-making process in this case needs to examine the options. Can the unit cost be reduced? Can we sell at a higher price by selling a different competitive advantage?

9   ACCURACY OF BUDGETS

9.1   It is important that budgets should be as **accurate as possible**. Failure to present a sufficiently accurate budget would mean that:

(a)   Plans will be made on **false assumptions** of costs and profits

(b)   Comparisons of actual results with the budget would give **meaningless control information**

9.2   There are many practical difficulties in attempting to plan accurately, some of which cannot be overcome. Unnecessary inaccuracies, however, should be avoided. Seasonal variations should be carefully allowed for and individual cost items carefully budgeted.

Zero base budgeting

9.3   One way in which many organisations ensure that inefficiencies are not concealed by the practice of 'adding on a bit' is by introducing zero-base budgeting. This is very well defined in an article in *Management Accounting* (October 1986) by Anthony R Morden.

> 'Zero-base budgeting (ZBB) is a formalised system of budgeting for the activities of an enterprise *as if each activity were being performed for the first time,* ie from a zero base. Essentially, a number of alternative levels of provision for each activity are identified, costed and evaluated in terms of the benefits to be obtained from them.
>
> ZBB is based on the belief that management should be required to justify *existing* activities in exactly the same way as new proposals. Thus, established activities will have to be compared with alternative applications of the resources that they would use during the budgetary planning period.
>
> Zero-based budgeting takes away the *implied right* of existing activities to receive a continued allocation of resources.'

9.4   Up to 50% of large companies now operate some form of ZBB and are particularly likely to require it of areas of a business where objective measures of effectiveness are not forthcoming, as is often the case with advertising expenditure.

10   RESPONSIBILITY ACCOUNTING

10.1   In **budgetary control** managers are held responsible for investigating differences between budgeted and actual results, and are then expected to take corrective action or amend the plan. Such a process is part of what is known as **responsibility accounting**.

Key Concept

Responsibility accounting is the recognition of decentralised units throughout an organisation and the tracing of costs (and revenues, assets and liabilities where pertinent) to the individual managers responsible for them.

10.2 Responsibility accounting distinguishes between **controllable** and **uncontrollable** costs.

10.3 Brand managers will be responsible for a level of expenditure which is agreed as necessary to support the sales of a product. Part of the brand manager's bonus may include an element based on sales of the brand which his budget is intended to support, even though this will depend partly on external factors over which he will have very little control.

Responsibility centres

10.4 Responsibility accounting aims to provide reports so that every manager is made aware of all the items which are within his area of authority. There are three types of responsibility centre.

Type of unit	Manager has control over	Principal performance measurement
Cost centre	Costs (only controllable cost items)	Variance analysis Efficiency measures
Profit centre	Costs (controllable costs) Sales prices (including transfer prices) Output volumes	Profit
Investment centre	Costs (controllable costs) Sales prices (including transfer prices) Output volumes Investment in fixed and current assets	Return on capital employed (ROCE)/ return on investment (ROI) Residual income (RI) Other financial ratios

Cost centres

10.5 To recap, a **cost centre** is a location or function in respect of which costs may be ascertained and related to cost units for control purposes. A brand manager may be considered a cost centre if he has responsibility for all marketing support for that brand.

Profit centres

10.6 A **profit centre** is any division of an organisation to which both revenues and costs are assigned, so that the profitability of the sub-unit may be measured.

10.7 These divisions will have their **own products** and their **own markets** and are hence self-contained businesses. **Strategic Business Units (SBU's)** come into the category. It is possible, of course, to further divide businesses so that not all the divisions have external sales but supply other parts of the same business. Here a system of **transfer pricing** will evolve in order to transfer goods and services at a price from one division to another.

Investment centres

10.8 Where a divisional manager of a company is allowed some discretion about the amount of **investment undertaken** by the division, the profit earned must be related to the amount of capital invested. Performance is measured by **return on capital employed** (ROCE), often referred to as **return on investment** (ROI), or by **residual income** (RI). We will look at these ratios in the next chapter.

Chapter Roundup

- A budget is a quantified plan of action for a forthcoming period.

- One of the problems in setting budgets is matching forecast demand from customers with the estimated available capacity.

- One method of setting the budget for marketing costs is as a percentage of sales. Some resort to 'all you can afford'.

- The objectives of budgetary control systems are as follows.

  ○ To ensure the achievement of the organisation's objectives
  ○ To compel planning
  ○ To communicate ideas and plans
  ○ To coordinate activities
  ○ To provide a framework for responsibility accounting
  ○ To establish a system of control

- The master budget comprises a budgeted profit and loss account, a cash budget and a end-of-period budgeted balance sheet.

- The principal budget factor, which should be identified at the beginning of the budgetary process, is usually sales. The budget for the principal budget factor is prepared before all the others.

- Cash budgets are important in the planning process because they give advanced warning of any cash surpluses or deficits. An organisation's reported profit for a period is usually different from the change in its cash position over the same period.

- Fixed budgets remain unchanged regardless of the level of actual activity; flexible budgets and designed to flex with the level of activity. Comparison of a fixed budget with the actual results for a different level of activity is of little use for control purposes. Flexible budgets should be used to show the cost and revenue allowances for the actual level of activity.

- The differences between the components of a flexed budget and the actual results are budget variances.

- Actual total sales revenue will differ from budgeted total sales revenue if *either* the actual sales price is different to that budgeted *or* the actual sales volume is different to the budgeted sales volume *or* both the price and volume differ. Hence the total sales revenue variance can be split into a sales price variance and a sales volume variance.

- If a company sells two or more products and is able to set the quantity and mix of its sales, the sales volume variance can be divided into a mix variance and a quantity variance.

- The direct material total variance can be subdivided into the direct material price variance and the direct material usage variance.

- The direct labour total variance can be subdivided into the direct labour rate variance and the direct labour efficiency variance.

- As long as the actual level of output does not change dramatically from the budgeted level, the amount of fixed overhead should not change. The only reason for a variance is therefore if the budgeted cost differs from the actual cost.

- Responsibility accounting is the term used to describe decentralisation of authority, with performance of the decentralised units measured in terms of accounting results. It attempts to associate costs, revenues, assets and liabilities with the managers most capable of controlling them. A disadvantage of decentralisation is dysfunctional decision making. Managers are given responsibility for the performance of responsibility centres (cost, profit and investment centres) under a system of responsibility accounting.

- Used correctly a budgetary control system can motivate but it can also produce undesirable negative reactions.

Quick Quiz

1   How can a system of budgetary control motivate employees to improve their performance? (see para 2.1)

2   List some formal sources of internal information. (2.4)

3   What is a limiting budget factor? (2.11)

4   Why is a sales and marketing budget necessary? (3.4)

5   Suggest four reasons for the difference between profit and cash flow. (4.4)

6   What does the term 'fixed' in 'fixed budget' mean? (5.1)

7   What is a variance? (6.1)

8   What is the correct approach to budgetary control? (6.4)

9   What is a budget cost allowance? (6.6)

10 Into what two sub-variances can the total sales variance be split? (7.4)

11 What does the direct labour rate variance measure? (7.13)

12 What is an operating statement? (8.1)

13 What is zero base budgeting? (9.3)

14 What is responsibility accounting? (10.1)

15 Name the three types of responsibility centre. (10.4)

Action Programme Review

1

	£	£
Salaries		
General manager £(24,000 + 2,000)	26,000	
Supervisors' (2 @ 12,500)	25,000	
Production staff (10 @ 10,000)	100,000	
Salesmen (7 @ £15,000)	105,000	
Marketing executive	19,200	
Office secretary £7,500 + (£60 × 12)	8,220	
		283,420
Commissions		
Salesmen (£5,000,000 × 1.0%)		50,000
Travel and entertainment		
(225 × £35 × 1.04 × 7)		57,330
Office expenses		
Rent, utilities etc (£25,000 × 1.10)		27,500
Promotional extravaganza		25,000
		443,250

2   Fixed budgets are based on estimated volumes of production and sales but do not include any provision for the event that actual volumes may differ from budget.

A flexible budget is designed to change so as to relate to actual volumes achieved. This has two advantages.

(a)   At the planning stage, it may be helpful to know what the effects would be if the actual outcome differs from the prediction. This would enable contingency plans to be drawn up if necessary.

(b)   At the end of each month or year, actual results may be compared with the flexible budget as a control procedure.

3   We need to prepare a flexible budget for 700 units.

	Budget 1,000 units £	Per unit £	Flexible budget 700 units £	Actual 700 units £	Variances £
Sales	20,000	20	14,000	14,200	200 (F)
Variable costs					
Direct material	8,000	8	5,600	5,200	400 (F)
Direct labour	4,000	4	2,800	3,100	300 (A)
Variable overhead	2,000	2	1,400	1,500	100 (A)
	14,000	14	9,800	9,800	
Contribution	6,000		4,200	4,400	
Fixed costs	5,000		5,000	5,400	400 (A)
Profit/(loss)	1,000		(800)	(1,000)	200 (A)

Now try illustrative questions 12, 13 and 14 at the end of the Study Text

12 *Ratio Analysis*

Chapter Topic List	Syllabus Reference
1 Introduction	-
2 Analysing financial statements	4.7
3 Profit margin, asset turnover and return on capital employed	4.7
4 Earnings per share	4.7
5 Gearing	4.7
6 Operational ratios	4.7
7 Liquidity ratios	4.7
8 Credit control	4.8

Learning Outcomes

This chapter demonstrates the application of ratio analysis in a variety of contexts.

After studying it you will be in a position to analyse and evaluate a range of quantitative data from financial statements.

Key Concepts

- Profit margin
- Mark-up
- Asset turnover
- Return on capital employed

- Gearing
- Turnover periods
- Current ratio and acid test ratio

1 INTRODUCTION

1.1 The financial statements of an organisation are sources of useful information about the condition of a business and their examination may be considered a 'health check'. The analysis and interpretation of these statements can be carried out by calculating certain ratios between one item and another, and then using the ratios for comparison between one year and the next in order to identify any trends, or significantly better or worse results than before.

1.2 Alternatively, the ratios can be used for comparison between one business and another, to establish which business has performed better, and in what ways. Such a comparison can therefore provide extremely useful information about competitors. You should be very careful when comparing two different businesses, however, to ensure that the accounts have been prepared in a similar way. If during your studies you are presented with financial data from two different companies without any additional information, it is always sensible to state your assumption that they have both been prepared on a similar and consistent basis.

1.3 Ratio analysis skills are also relevant in Paper 11 at Diploma level.

2 ANALYSING FINANCIAL STATEMENTS

2.1 In the remainder of the chapter we will be using the financial statements set out in Chapter 5 as the base data for our analysis. They are reproduced below.

FALCON KITES LTD
BALANCE SHEET AT 31 DECEMBER 1999

	£	£
Fixed assets		
Tangible assets at cost	23,900	
Less accumulated depreciation	10,750	
		13,150
Intangible assets		10,000
		23,150
Current assets		
Stocks	15,400	
Debtors	26,700	
Cash at bank and in hand	-	
	42,100	
Current liabilities		
Bank overdraft	16,200	
Trade creditors	11,000	
Taxation	5,200	
Dividends	6,000	
	38,400	
Net current assets		3,700
Long-term liabilities		
Loan		750
		26,100
Capital and reserves		
Ordinary shares of £1 each		16,000
Profit and loss account		10,100
		26,100

PROFIT AND LOSS ACCOUNT FOR THE
YEAR ENDED 31 DECEMBER 1999

	£
Sales	98,455
Cost of sales	50,728
Gross profit	47,727
Distribution and selling expenses	24,911
Administration expenses	2,176
Operating profit	20,640
Interest paid	(280)
Interest received	40
Profit before taxation	20,400
Taxation	5,200
Profit after taxation	15,200
Dividends	8,100
Retained profit for the year	7,100

2.2 When **ratio analysis** is used to assess the relative strength of a particular business, by comparing its profitability and financial ability with another business, the two businesses should be similar in size and in their line of activities, otherwise differences revealed by ratio analysis might merely arise as a consequence of the size difference, or the varying lines of business they operate in.

2.3 Suppose for example, that we compared the results of a manufacturing company with the results of a company which operates a chain of hairdressing salons and beauty parlours.

(a) The manufacturing company might specialise in undertaking large-scale contracts for major customers (such as shipbuilding). Such a company might operate so as to make a small profit percentage on a very large turnover, such as a profit of £1 million on a contract with a sales value of £20 million. In contrast, a service industry such as hairdressing and beautician service might be more likely to derive a higher profit percentage, but on a lower total sales turnover.

(b) The assets of the two companies would differ. Both might own freehold property, but the manufacturing company would have much larger amounts of both fixed assets (plant and machinery, for example) and debtors (since much shop business for the hairdresser would be paid for in cash).

2.4 Comparing the accounting ratios of the two businesses would be pointless, since the ratios would merely serve to inform us that the businesses are different, not that either business is less profitable or less financially stable than it should be.

3 PROFIT MARGIN, ASSET TURNOVER AND RETURN ON CAPITAL EMPLOYED

Specimen paper, 6/00

Exam Tip

The three principal ratios (profit margin, asset turnover and return on capital employed) are popular examination topics. You might be asked by an exam question to look at the margins on three product lines, and to prepare a report covering the following.

- Gross margins for the three products

- Calculation of new prices in order to achieve a margin of 60 per cent on each of the products

- Commentary on the profitability of each product

In order to calculate the gross margins, you must remember the formula Contribution/Sales × 100%, which makes the first part of the question relatively straightforward. The second part of the question should not provide you with too many problems, since you simply need to make sure that the variable costs need to be 40% of sales if a gross margin of 60% is to be achieved.

3.1 There are **three principal ratios** used to measure how efficiently the operations of a business have been managed.

(a) **Profit margin**
(b) **Asset turnover**
(c) **Return on capital employed** (ROCE)

Profit margin

> ### Key Concept
>
> **Profit margin is the ratio of profit to sales** For example, if a company makes a profit of £20,000 on sales of £100,000, its or profit margin is 20%. This also means that its costs are 80% of sales.

3.2   A high profit margin indicates either of the following.

(a)   **Costs are being kept well under control.** If the ratio of costs to sales goes down, the profit margin will automatically go up. For example, if the cost: sales ratio changes from 80% to 75%, the profit margin will go up from 20% to 25%.

(b)   **Sales prices are high.** For example, if a company sells goods for £100,000 and makes a profit of £16,000, costs would be £84,000 and the profit margin 16%. Now if the company can raise selling prices by 20% to £120,000 without affecting the volume of goods sold or their costs, profits would rise by the amount of revenue increase (£20,000) to £36,000 and the profit margin would also rise (from 16% to 30%).

3.3   The profit referred to above is usually the **profit before interest and tax** (PBIT), also known as the **operating profit**. In the accounts of Falcon Kites Ltd, the PBIT for 1999 is £20,640 and the profit margin is:

$$\frac{20,640}{98,455} \times 100\% = 21\%$$

You may also meet the terms **gross profit margin** (usually calculated as (contribution/sales) × 100%) and **net profit margin**.

> ### Action Programme 1
>
> What is Falcon Kites Ltd's gross margin?

3.4   During your studies you may be presented with information which compares different businesses within a group of companies and you may be given much more detail than the basic information which is contained in the published profit and loss account. In these cases you can devise your own ratios to help understand the business, provided you apply then consistently.

For example, it is not unusual to find some costs expressed as a percentage of turnover, so you may decide to investigate marketing costs and find that they are, for example 6% of turnover, while other businesses spend 10%. Similarly it may be useful to know that over time the revenue generated per person in the sales force has risen by 20% from one year to another. Be careful not to draw too many conclusions here since the price of the product may have doubled in the same period, so perhaps your sales force is now less efficient!

Mark-up

Key Concept

The **mark-up is the addition made to the cost of sales** to produce a selling price and is often expressed as a percentage. It is calculated as follows.

$$\text{Mark-up (\%)} = \frac{\text{gross profit}}{\text{cost of sales}} \times 100\%$$

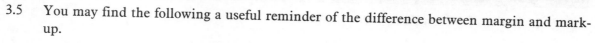

3.5 You may find the following a useful reminder of the difference between margin and mark-up.

Suppose product X costs £100 to produce and sells for £125.

	£
Cost	100
Profit	25
Selling price	125

Profit margin $= 25/125 \times 100\% = 20\%$

Mark-up $= 25/100 \times 100\% = 25\%$

Asset turnover

Key Concept

Asset turnover is the ratio of sales turnover in a year to the amount of capital employed (net assets).

3.6 For example, if a company has sales of £720,000 and assets of £360,000, the asset turnover will be:

$$\frac{\text{£720,000}}{\text{£360,000}} = 2 \text{ times}$$

This means that for every £1 of assets employed, the company can generate sales of £2 per annum. A **higher volume of sales** on the same level of assets will mean that they are being used more efficiently. This will create a higher ratio. For example, suppose that our firm with assets of £360,000 can increase its sales to £900,000 per annum. The asset turnover would **improve** to:

$$\frac{\text{£900,000}}{\text{£360,000}} = 2.5 \text{ times}$$

3.7 In the accounts of Falcon Kites Ltd, the asset turnover is: $\dfrac{98,455}{26,100} = 3.7 \text{ times}$

3.8 If a business can create more sales turnover from the same amount of assets it may make larger profits without having to increase the size of its investment. This is not always the case as increasing revenue does not necessarily lead to increased profits. However, as a generalisation it is reasonable.

Return on capital employed (ROCE)

> **Key Concept**
>
> **Return on capital employed** (ROCE) (or **return on investment** (ROI)) is the amount of profit as a percentage of capital employed. If a company makes a profit of £30,000, we do not know how good or bad the result is until we look at the amount of capital which has been invested to achieve the profit. £30,000 might be a good sized profit for a small firm, but this would not be good enough for a 'giant' firm such as Marks & Spencer. Because this is the only satisfactory ratio which judges profits in relation to the size of business, it is sometimes called the **primary ratio** in financial analysis.

3.9 The ROCE of Falcon Kites Ltd for 1999 is:

$$\frac{20,640}{26,100} = 79\%$$

3.10 You may already have realised that there is a mathematical connection between return on capital employed, profit margin and asset turnover.

$$\frac{\text{Profit}}{\text{Capital employed}} = \frac{\text{Profit}}{\text{Sales}} \times \frac{\text{Sales}}{\text{Capital employed}}$$

ROCE = **Profit margin** × **Asset turnover**

If we accept that ROCE is the single most important measure of business performance, comparing profit with the amount of capital invested, we can go on to say that business performance is dependent on two 'subsidiary' factors, each of which contributes to ROCE.

(a) **Profit margin**
(b) **Asset turnover**

The profit margin and asset turnover ratios are sometimes called the **secondary ratios**.

3.11 The implications of this relationship must be understood. Suppose that a return on capital employed of 20% is thought to be a good level of business performance in the retail trade for electrical goods.

(a) Company A might decide to sell its products at a fairly high price and make a profit margin on sales of 10%. It would then need only an asset turnover of 2.0 times to achieve a ROCE of 20%.

(b) Company B might decide to cut its prices so that its profit margin is only 2½%. Provided that it can achieve an asset turnover of 8 times a year, attracting more customers with its lower prices, it will still make a ROCE of 2½% × 8 = 20%.

3.12 Company A might be a department store and company B a discount warehouse. Each will have a different selling price policy, but each can be effective in achieving a target ROCE. In this example, suppose that both companies had capital employed of £100,000 and a target return on capital employed of 20% or £20,000.

(a) Using the equation in 3.10, we can deduce that Company A would need annual sales of £200,000 to give a profit margin of 10% and an asset turnover of 2 times, to create its 20% ROCE.

$$\frac{£20,000}{£100,000} = \frac{£20,000}{£200,000} \times 2$$

(b) Company B would need annual sales of £800,000 to give a profit margin of 2½% and an asset turnover of 8 times, to create its 20% ROCE.

$$\frac{£20,000}{£100,000} = \frac{£20,000}{£800,000} \times 8$$

The inter-relationship between profit margin and asset turnover

3.13 A higher return on capital employed can be obtained by increasing the profit margin or the asset turnover ratio. The profit margin can be increased by reducing costs or by raising selling prices. However, if selling prices are raised, it is likely that sales will fall, with the possible consequence that asset turnover will also decline, so that total return on capital employed might not improve.

Example: profit margin and asset turnover

3.14 Suppose that a company achieved the following results in 1999.

Sales	£100,000
Profit	£5,000
Capital employed	£20,000

The company's management wish to decide whether to raise its selling prices. They think that if they do so, they can raise the profit margin to 10%. By introducing extra capital of £55,000, sales turnover could be increased to £150,000. Evaluate the decision in terms of effect on ROCE, profit margin and asset turnover.

Answer

3.15 At present, ratios are:

Profit margin (5/100)	5%
Asset turnover (100/20)	5 times
ROCE (5/20)	25%

With the proposed changes, the profit would be 10% × £150,000 = £15,000, and the asset turnover would be:

$$\frac{£150,000}{£(20,000 + 55,000)} = 2 \text{ times, so that the ratios would be:}$$

Profit margin	×	Asset turnover	=	ROCE	
10%	×	2 times	=	20%	$\left(\dfrac{£15,000}{£75,000}\right)$

In spite of increasing the profit margin and raising the total volume of sales, the extra assets required (£55,000) only raise total profits by £(15,000 – 5,000) = £10,000.

The return on capital employed falls from 25% to 20% because of the sharp fall in asset turnover from 5 times to 2 times.

This does not mean that the management of the company should not raise its prices. However, the financial analysis has provided them with another piece of the decision-making jigsaw. The owners of the business, although very happy with the increased profitability, may not be happy with the reduced ROCE. The management must judge which aspect is most acceptable.

4   EARNINGS PER SHARE

4.1   A method of calculating the **return due to the ordinary shareholders** is contained in the **earnings per share calculation**. This simply divides the earnings (which is profit after tax) by the average number of ordinary shares in issue whilst the profit was generated. You will not need to calculate this figure but it is **widely used** by investors, potential investors and stock market analysts as one of the **basic measures of success**. A decline in the EPS is often frowned upon.

5   GEARING

5.1   A company is financed by different types of capital and each type expects a return in the form of **interest** or **dividend**.

> ### Key Concept
>
> **Gearing** is a method of comparing how much of the long-term capital of a business is provided by **equity** (ordinary shares and reserves) and how much is provided by investors who are entitled to interest or dividend before ordinary shareholders can have a dividend themselves. These sources of capital are **loans and preference shares**.

5.2   Gearing is usually calculated using one or other of **two basic calculations**. The first method, commonly known as the **debt: equity ratio**, is defined as:

$$\frac{\text{Long - term loans}}{\text{Equity (ordinary shares + reserves)}} \times 100\%$$

Long-term loans will normally exclude overdrafts, whilst equity will exclude any preference shares. In your studies, equity will usually equate to the total of shareholders' funds. The key is consistency since it is the level of the ratio and its movement which is important. As a guideline the figure should not exceed 100%.

5.3   The second method measures the **level of long-term debt as a percentage of all funding** raised by the company. Hence the calculation is:

$$\frac{\text{Long - term debt}}{\text{Ordinary share capital + reserves + long - term debt}} \times 100\%$$

A figure in excess of 50% is usually felt to be high.

5.4   In the case of Falcon Kites Ltd, the gearing figure is: $\dfrac{750}{16,000 + 10,100 + 750} = 2.8\%$

Why is gearing important?

5.5   Gearing is important when a company wants to raise extra capital. If its gearing is already high, it might find it difficult to raise a loan. High gearing might be considered risky because the more loan capital a business has, the bigger becomes the profit required to meet interest payments. The 'acceptable' level of gearing varies according to the country (average gearing is higher among companies in Japan than in Britain), the industry, and the size and status of the individual company within the industry. The more stable the company is, the safer gearing should be.

5.6   The **advantages** of gearing are as follows.

(a) **Debt capital is cheaper** for the following reasons.

   (i)   The reward (interest or preference dividend) is generally fixed, and therefore diminishes in real terms if there is inflation. Ordinary shareholders expect dividend growth.

   (ii)   The reward required by debtholders is usually lower than that required by equity holders, because debt capital is often secured on company assets, whereas ordinary share capital is a more risky investment.

   (iii)   Payments of interest attract **tax relief**, whereas dividends do not.

(b) Debt capital does not normally carry **voting rights**. The issue of debt capital therefore leaves pre-existing voting rights unchanged.

6 OPERATIONAL RATIOS

Specimen paper, 6/00

6.1   Having dealt with the ratios which are used to analyse the overall **strength and performance** of a business we can now turn to shorter-term operating ratios which reflect the business's **cash management**.

6.2   The ability to operate a business successfully involves the understanding of how **cash flows through the business**. It will be exchanged for stocks of raw materials, which will then be turned into a finished product. The product may then be stockpiled awaiting sale, and then sold on credit terms, creating a debtor. The business will eventually receive cash from the customer.

6.3   The business may have to pay suppliers a long time before receiving cash for the sale of goods. The ability to minimise the period from payment for goods at one end of the operating cycle to receiving cash at the other end of the cycle can be critical to performance. This **cash cycle** or **operating cycle** is represented diagrammatically below.

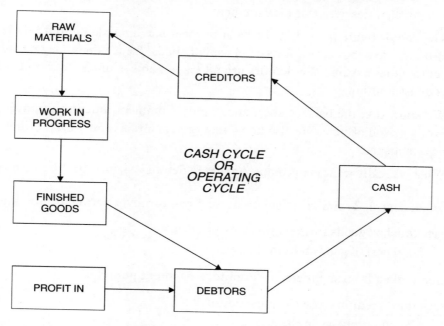

6.4   As a result the finance function will monitor the **turnover periods**.

6.5 These ratios, usually expressed in **days**, measure how long or how many times the business is **exchanging cash** during any aspect of the cash cycle.

6.6 For example, the debtor turnover period links the sale turnover to the level of debtors in the business. Hence: $\dfrac{\text{Debtors}}{\text{Sales turnover}}$

describes the level of debtors compared with the sales turnover. So the ratio for Falcon Kites Ltd is: $\dfrac{26{,}700}{98{,}455}$

This can be expressed in days. The turnover is generated over 365 days. By multiplying our ratio by 365 we recognise that the debtors average out at:

$$\frac{26{,}700}{98{,}455} \times 365 = 99 \text{ days or } \frac{26{,}700}{98{,}455} \times 12 = 3.25 \text{ months}$$

Another way of expressing this is to say that the business has the cash from 99 days' sales outstanding (ie not yet received).

6.7 There are difficulties with this measurement.

(a) The debtor figure quoted in the balance sheet may include not only trade debtors but also include debtors, say, for sale of capital goods. Hence there may be a distortion. In your studies **assume the debtors are all trade debtors** unless told otherwise and state your assumption.

(b) We know that the balance sheet shows only a point in time but turnover is generated over a period of time. We also know that ratio analysis is only useful when a trend is to be established.

(c) What we really want is to compare **average debtors** against the sales turnover.

6.8 We can, of course, do similar calculations for **stock turnover** period (or '**stockturn**'):

$$\frac{\text{Average finished goods stocks (using closing stock)}}{\text{Total cost of goods sold in the period}} \times 365 \text{ days}$$

For credit taken from suppliers, the **creditors' payment period** is:

$$\frac{\text{Average trade creditors (use closing creditors)}}{\star \text{ Total purchases in the period}} \times 365 \text{ days}$$

($\star$ Cost of sales can be substituted here as an approximation)

6.9 The calculations of these ratios for Falcon Kites Ltd are as follows.

Stock turnover period $\qquad \dfrac{15{,}400}{50{,}728} \times 365 = 111 \text{ days}$

$$\text{Creditors' payment period} \qquad \frac{11,000}{50,728} \times 365 = 79 \text{ days}$$

6.10 The importance of understanding these ratios is their impact on **cash requirements**. An increase in the stock turnover ratio or in the debtor turnover ratio means that more money is being tied up in funding working capital and this may not be desirable.

7 LIQUIDITY RATIOS

7.1 The word **liquid**, when applied to an asset, means **readily converted into cash**. A firm's liquidity is defined by its ability to convert its assets into cash to meet all the demands for payments when they fall due.

7.2 The most liquid asset, of course, is **cash** itself (or a bank balance). The next most liquid assets are **short-term investments** (stocks and shares) because these can be sold quickly for cash should this be necessary. **Debtors** are fairly liquid assets because they should be expected to pay their bills in the near future. **Stocks** are the least liquid current asset because they must first be sold (perhaps on credit) and the customers given a credit period in which to pay before they can be converted into cash.

7.3 **Current liabilities** are items which must be paid for in the near future. When payment becomes due, enough cash must be available to make the payment. The managers of a business must make sure that a regular supply of cash comes in from current assets to meet the regular flow of payments.

7.4 There are two common liquidity ratios.
   (a) The **current ratio** or **working capital** ratio
   (b) The **quick ratio** or **liquidity ratio** or **acid test ratio**

The current ratio or working capital ratio is the more commonly used and is the ratio of **current assets to current liabilities**.

> **Key Concepts**
>
> The **current ratio** is calculated as $\dfrac{\text{current assets}}{\text{current liabilities}}$
>
> The **acid test ratio** is calculated as $\dfrac{\text{current assets less stock}}{\text{current liabilities}}$
>
> The acid test ratio recognises the greater length of time it would take to convert stock into cash, and so stock is excluded from the liquidity calculation.

7.5 A 'prudent' current ratio is sometimes said to be 2:1. In other words, current assets should be twice the size of current liabilities. There are some issues to be borne in mind however.

   (a) **Bank overdrafts**. These are technically repayable on demand, and therefore must be classified as current liabilities. It would also often be relevant to know a company's overdraft limit and this may give a truer indication of liquidity than a current or quick ratio.

   (b) **Are the year-end figures are typical** of the year as a whole? This is particularly relevant in the case of seasonal businesses. Many large retail companies with an accounting year end soon after the January sales would have balance sheets showing a higher level of cash than would be usual at any other time in the year.

7.6 In practice, many businesses operate with a much lower current ratio and in these cases, the best way to judge liquidity is to look at the current ratio over a period of time. If the trend is towards a lower current ratio, we would judge that the liquidity position is getting steadily worse.

7.7 For example, the liquidity ratios of two firms A and B are as follows.

	1 Jan	1 Apr	1 July	1 Oct
Firm A	1.2 : 1	1.2 : 1	1.2 : 1	1.2 : 1
Firm B	1.3 : 1	1.2 : 1	1.1 : 1	1.0 : 1

We would say that firm A is maintaining a stable liquidity position, whereas firm B's liquidity is deteriorating. A bank may need to think carefully before granting any request from Firm B for an extended overdraft facility.

7.8 A 'prudent' acid test ratio is 1:1. In practice, many businesses have a lower acid test ratio and, as with the current ratio, the best way of judging a firm's liquidity would be to look at the trend over a period of time.

7.9 The liquidity ratios for Falcon Kites Ltd would be calculated as follows.

Current ratio $\dfrac{42,100}{38,400} = 1.1:1$

Acid test ratio $\dfrac{42,100 - 15,400}{38,400} = 0.7 : 1$

These seem healthy enough but we do not have any trend information to be able to comment further.

Action Programme 2

Calculate liquidity and working capital ratios from the following accounts of a business which provides service support (cleaning and so on) to customers worldwide.

	20X2 £m	20X1 £m
Turnover	2,176.2	2,344.8
Cost of sales	1,659.0	1,731.5
Gross profit	517.2	613.3
Current assets		
Stocks	42.7	78.0
Debtors (note 1)	378.9	431.4
Cash	205.2	145.0
	626.8	654.4
Creditors: amounts falling due within one year		
Loans and overdrafts	32.4	81.1
Corporation taxes	67.8	76.7
Dividend	11.7	17.2
Creditors (note 2)	487.2	467.2
	599.1	642.2
Net current assets	27.7	12.2
Notes		
1 Trade debtors	295.2	335.5
2 Trade creditors	190.8	188.1

8 CREDIT CONTROL

8.1 One of the most important things for a marketing professional to remember is that there is a trade off between extending credit, so as to increase sales, and the cost of carrying debtors and bad debts. However much you want to increase sales, you must remember what those sales might cost. Not all potential customers are creditworthy. Although the control of debtors is not part of the remit of a marketing professional, he or she should appreciate the impact of the marketing decisions made on the bad debt situation of the organisation.

Formulating a policy for credit control

8.2 Several factors need to be considered by management when a **policy** for credit control is formulated.

(a) The **administrative costs** of debt collection. They should not exceed the benefits incurred. Debt collecting procedures would be expected to reduce bad debt losses and speed up cash collection.

(b) The **procedures** for controlling credit to individual customers. New customers should be investigated for creditworthiness and credit limits fixed at appropriate levels.

(c) The ways in which credit policy can be implemented, such as the following.

(i) Credit can be eased by giving debtors a longer period in which to settle their account. The **cost of credit** would be the finance cost of the resulting increase in debtors.

(ii) A **discount** can be offered for early payment. The cost of the credit policy would then be the cost of the discounts.

(d) The effect of easing credit might be to encourage a higher proportion of bad debts or to increase sales. Provided that the extra contribution from the increase in sales exceeds the increase in fixed cost expenses, bad debts, discounts and the finance cost of an increase in working capital, a policy to relax credit terms would be profitable.

8.3 To determine whether it would be profitable to **extend the level of total credit**, it is necessary to assess the following.

(i) The **additional sales volume**
(ii) The **profitability** of the extra sales
(iii) The extra length of the average **debt collection period**
(iv) The **required rate of return** on the investment in additional debtors

8.4 In summary, the marketing professional must consider the **impact of credit control** on the marketing strategy he or she is implementing. For example, if a new customer is granted instant credit to secure a sale, the risk of that customer not paying may be high and could result in a loss to the company. By waiting a few days for a credit application to be processed, the sale may be lost. This kind of risk may be quantified by estimating the risk of non-payment, but in general it is not considered good practice to give instant credit.

Chapter Roundup

- The interpretation of financial data is the key to the understanding of any business, either in a practical application or during your studies. Companies as large as GEC have been effectively managed for many years simply by ensuring that the ratios relevant to their businesses were kept within acceptable limits.

- Ratios are a useful measure when in comparison with something else: either the company's history, or a competitor or an industry norm.

- Consistency in calculation and in the base data is important otherwise we could end up comparing apples and oranges.

- Return on capital employed is the product of two other ratios: ROCE = profit margin × asset turnover.

- Gearing is a measure of how funds have been generated to buy assets. Remember if those funds have been entirely generated from operations then the money has been effectively raised by the shareholders.

- There are two main measures for gearing. Neither is more correct than the other but both are widely used. Be consistent in your approach.

- Proper control of cash is vital to the continued financial strength of any company. Marketing managers should be aware of the debtor collection periods (also known as the debtor turnover or day sales outstanding) which is measured as:

$$\frac{\text{Average debtors}}{\text{Annual turnover}} \times 365 \text{ days}$$

- Two important tests of a business liquidity are:

  ○ the current ratio $= \dfrac{\text{current assets}}{\text{current liabilities}}$

  ○ the quick or acid test ratio $= \dfrac{\text{current assets (excluding stocks)}}{\text{current liabilities}}$

- Organisations should operate an effective credit control policy.

Quick Quiz

1. What might a high profit margin indicate? (3.2)
2. Explain the difference between margin and mark-up. (3.5)
3. Write down the formula which shows the ROCE broken down into the secondary ratios.(3.10)
4. Explain two ways a business may change its overall ROCE. (3.11, 3.12)
5. What is EPS? (4.1)
6. How is gearing calculated using the two common methods? (5.2, 5.3)
7. Why is gearing important? (5.5)
8. What does a debtors' turnover period indicate? (6.4)
9. How is stock turnover period calculated? (6.8)
10. What ratios would you use to determine whether a business could pay its liabilities as they fall due? (7.4)
11. How is the quick ratio calculated? (7.4)
12. List some factors that need to be considered by management when a policy for credit control is formulated. (8.2)

Action Programme Review

1    $\dfrac{£47,727}{£98,455} \times 100\% = 48\%$

2

	20X2	20X1
Current ratio	$\dfrac{626.8}{599.1} = 1.05$	$\dfrac{654.4}{642.2} = 1.02$
Acid test ratio	$\dfrac{584.1}{599.1} = 0.97$	$\dfrac{576.4}{642.2} = 0.90$
Debtors' payment period	$\dfrac{295.2}{2,176.2} \times 385 = 49.5$ days	$\dfrac{335.5}{2,344.8} \times 365 = 52.2$ days
Stock turnover period	$\dfrac{42.7}{1,659.0} \times 365 = 9.4$ days	$\dfrac{78.0}{1,731.5} \times 365 = 16.4$ days
Creditors' turnover period	$\dfrac{190.8}{1,659.0} \times 365 = 42.0$ days	$\dfrac{188.1}{1,731.5} \times 365 = 40.0$ days

Now try illustrative question 15 at the end of the Study Text

BPP PUBLISHING

Part E
Marketing research information

13 *Market Intelligence*

Chapter Topic List	Syllabus Reference
1 Introduction	-
2 Customer intelligence	5.0, 5.4, 5.5
3 Competitor intelligence	5.0
4 Secondary data	5.0
5 Internal secondary data	5.0
6 External secondary data	5.0

Learning Outcomes

Upon completion of this chapter you will have a thorough knowledge of the sources of information for customer and competitor intelligence, as the basis of marketing research information for marketing decisions.

Key Concepts

- Secondary data

Examples of Marketing at Work

- British Airways
- Customer loyalty
- Ford

1 INTRODUCTION

1.1 In its early days, marketing research was seen simply as a data collection service. Clients stated what data they wanted, market researchers collected the data, and the client took away tables of results. When a company was one of only a few using the results of marketing research, any data on customers might enable it to exploit market opportunities.

1.2 Nowadays, virtually all organisations have access to sophisticated data on customers, markets, products and services. Being customer orientated is no longer adequate. Organisations must be outward facing in other ways. A constant review of what is

257

happening in the marketplace, what may happen in the marketplace, what actual and potential competitors are up to and whether environmental changes are likely to present significant opportunities or threats is a necessity.

1.3 Market intelligence, sometimes called market analysis, addresses this necessity. In this chapter, we will be looking at two divisions of market intelligence, customer and competitor, and at secondary data, the collection and analysis of which is vital for effective customer and competitor intelligence.

Links with other papers

1.4 Clearly, this section overlaps with the *Marketing/Customer Interface* paper. The difference is that the marketing/customer interface paper is particularly concerned with customer dynamics and, to a degree with the **content** on the information obtained. Here, the focus, perhaps, is on using that information for management decision making.

2 CUSTOMER INTELLIGENCE

Customer intelligence - why is it so important?

2.1 For years the rhetoric of marketing has been that of warfare: targets, campaigns, offensives. The approach has been one of trying to beat the 'enemy' into submission and 'win' new customers. Many organisations have begun to realise that there is more to be gained from alternative strategies.

(a) Investing in activities which seek to **retain existing customers,** based on the argument that it costs more to attract new customers

(b) Encouraging existing customers to **spend more**

2.2 Retaining customers is the basis of such relationship marketing techniques as the Tesco ClubCard and loyalty discounts like the Barclaycard Profiles Scheme. These organisations see customers not only in terms of what they are buying today, but also in terms of their **potential for future purchases**.

2.3 Most authorities and marketing practitioners say that **added services** and **quality of service** are the key to retaining customers.

Marketing at Work

BA's 'Putting People First' programme of improved service was aimed at retentions; so are all frequent flier and Air Miles schemes.

2.4 The implications for marketing research are clear. To be effective at **retention marketing,** the organisation has to have a good database about present and past customers, with details of the nature of the relationship; it has to know about their attitudes, their perceptions of the organisation's products and service, and their expectations. Just as importantly, the organisation must know, from systematically-acquired **customer feedback**, precisely what it is doing wrong.

What do customers want?

2.5 Most customers are easy to please. They simply want companies to do what they say they are going to do when they say they are going to do it. More detail behind this can be found in the 'four fundamentals of customer satisfaction' reported by Milind Lele and Jagdish Sheth.

(a) **Product-related variables.** The product - its functionality and design quality - is a key determinant of customer satisfaction. Product design, in particular, can enhance or restrict the company's ability to keep the customer happy during and after the sales. Bad design places constraints on promotional messages and also on channel choices. It can also add considerably to the cost and difficulty of providing customers with adequate after-sales support.

(b) **Sales and promotion-related variables.** Three key variables affect customer satisfaction in this area.

   (i) **Messages** which help to shape customers' ideas about the product's benefits before they have experienced it in use.

   (ii) **Attitudes** of everyone in the organisation who comes into contact with customers: salespeople, service staff, telephone operators, and so forth.

   (iii) The use of **intermediaries** to sell on behalf of the organisation: similar selection, training and performance criteria should be applied to intermediaries as are applied to an organisation's own staff.

(c) **After-sales variables.** There are two aspects of after-sales which are especially significant for organisations.

   (i) **Support services.** Covering traditional after-sales activities like warranties, parts and service, and user training.

   (ii) **Feedback and restitution.** The way the organisation handles complaints and the level of priority attached by management to such activities.

(d) **Culture-related variables.** The crucial question here is whether the corporate culture is built around maximising customer satisfaction, or whether management merely pays lip service to it. Would it be acceptable for an employee to postpone a meeting with the managing director in order to meet a customer, for example?

Marketing at Work

'Rude and unhelpful staff are the biggest single hurdle to developing customer loyalty, according to an Air Miles UK survey exclusive to *Marketing Week*. The survey found that 54 per cent of the 1,000 people interviewed were most likely to become disloyal because of rude and unhelpful staff. Young people in the 18-to-24 age bracket are the group most affected by rude staff – 60 per cent cited it as a reason for "disloyalty" to a retailer or service provider. Judith Thorne, Air Miles UK marketing director, says: "This shows that customer service and the way companies interact with customers is an integral part of building customer loyalty."

According to Thorne, advertising which over-hypes the offer can seriously damage loyalty. She says: "Advertising is fantastic for putting a thought into the consumer's mind, but people will be very disappointed if the promise isn't delivered."

One in five of the survey's respondents said poor value for money would challenge their loyalty and one in ten would turn their backs on suppliers who "do not seem to listen". Complaints are most likely to come from extremely loyal customers while those claiming to "feel no loyalty" will simply switch retailer without explaining why. Combining fair prices with good service is the surest way to win loyalty, say 54 per cent of respondents.'

Marketing Week, 5 March 1998

Problems with measuring customer satisfaction

2.6 Measuring whether customers have got what they wanted can be extremely problematic for a number of reasons.

(a) **Weak anecdotal evidence**, often based on single incidents, is given too much weight, especially if such evidence reinforces what people in an organisation want to hear (wishful thinking).

(b) **Single-incident disasters** may be used by one part of the organisation to attack another, rather than as an opportunity for improving performance.

(c) The views of those customers who complain, which may be **a typical**, are not counter-balanced by the views of those who do not.

(d) Many badly-served customers will not complain, but will simply take their business elsewhere if they can.

Marketing at Work

The Ford Motor Company found that customers satisfied with their cars told (on average) eight other people, dissatisfied customers told 22 (who in turn told 22 more, with the story becoming more elaborate and embellished with each repetition).

(e) The opinions of small numbers of **highly articulate** customers, especially if of high status and personally known to top management, or expressed through the public media, will be given excessive emphasis.

(f) **Preconceptions** within the organisation about its customer-service standing and performance may be out-of-date or mistaken, especially if insufficient attention is paid to what the competition is doing.

Customer segmentation

2.7 So far we have treated customers as if they were all alike, all wanting much the same things, all applying similar criteria when judging the product, the service, or the organisation as a whole. In practice, this is bound to be misleading, especially for organisations with a large customer base, a wide range of products, a global market, and several discrete product/brand names. Customer A may want reliability of delivery on an hourly basis; Customer B may want an unusual range of financial options; Customer C may want the highest possible standards of after-sales support; Customer D is only interested in one product; and so on.

2.8 Research shows that there are differences in customers' expectations which can be exploited by offering levels of service which match the needs of particular sectors, possibly withdrawing from some or increasing prices/charges to an economically-justified level.

Obtaining customer intelligence

Customer research survey method

2.9 One way in which customer intelligence can be gathered is via a customer (or consumer) **survey** using a questionnaire. The key steps in planning and implementing such a survey are:

Step 1 **Carry out analysis** of the organisation's customers, to decide whether they already fall into categories with differing service expectations.

Step 2 Decide whether to cover all customers or a **sample**. If the organisation only has a small group of customers, semi-structured interviews may be preferable to written questionnaires.

Step 3   **Pilot-test the questionnaire** to ensure that the questions make sense and that all potential customer concerns are being covered.

Step 4   Decide whether to conduct the survey **in person,** by **telephone** or via the **post**. Postal distribution may be unavoidable, though it will drastically reduce the response rate and may introduce bias into the sample (unless incentives are offered).

Step 5   If the survey has been well designed and administered, **analyse the results** to reveal gaps in customer-service performance.

2.10   Other methods of obtaining customer intelligence via surveys include diary panels, interviews (often known as mall intercept surveys), instore surveys and hall tests. These are all discussed in Chapter 16.

The complaints system as a research tool

2.11   It is surprising how few organisations positively encourage **complaints**, despite the fact that complaints are an essential form of feedback if properly organised. Complaints represent only a small proportion of dissatisfied customers, however: organisations never know the precise number of customers who do not complain but who simply take their business elsewhere. The number of such customers must, of course, be reduced.

Action Programme 1

In what ways could you obtain complaints feedback?

---

3   COMPETITOR INTELLIGENCE

3.1   Organisations must understand competitors and having a **competitive intelligence system** is one way to achieve this objective. Organisations need answers to the following type of questions.

   (a)   Who are our competitors?
   (b)   What strategies are they pursuing?
   (c)   How effective are those strategies?
   (d)   What objectives do they have?
   (e)   What are their strengths and weaknesses?
   (f)   How do they react to competitive behaviour?

Identifying the competition

3.2   On the face of it this seems a relatively easy task. For example, Pepsi Cola may identify Coca Cola as its major competitor; Du Pont may identify Rhone Poulenc as a major fibre competitor; Unilever may identify Procter and Gamble and so on. However, an organisation's actual and potential competition may be much greater. For example, Coca Cola and Pepsi are major players in a global market for soft fizzy drinks in which there are many operators. The range of competition is much greater than earlier identified. The range may differ in each geographical market segment. The competition may come from other producers of Cola-like drinks including supermarkets but may include substitute products such as fruit drinks, lemonade, Seven-up, Sprite, carbonated water and light beers.

3.3   Competition may take place based on the degree of product substitution. This will depend upon:

(a) **Brand** competition, say Coca Cola v Pepsi;

(b) **Industry** competition, for example all soft carbonated drinks

(c) **Form** competition, for example Pepsi v all drinks

(d) **Generic** competition, for example Pepsi v chocolate bars, ice creams and so on

Action Programme 2

Provide an example of brand competition, industry competition, form competition and generic competition for Thomas Cook package holidays to Greece.

Strengths and weaknesses of competitors

3.4 This is the essence that any competitive information system needs to address. Competitive strategies will be developed from the information and intelligence gathered by the organisation. Competitor information is required under the following headings.

(a) Sales

(b) Market share

(c) Costs

(d) Profit levels

(e) Returns on capital invested

(f) Cash flow

(g) Profitability by segment

(h) Production processes and technologies employed

(i) Capacity levels and utilisation

(j) Product quality

(k) Range of products and any new developments

(l) Size and structure of the customer base

(m) Suppliers

(n) Culture of the organisation

(o) Level of brand loyalty

(p) Dealer networks and distribution channels

(q) Core capabilities and competence

(r) Marketing and selling capability

(s) Operations and logistics

(t) Financial structure and capability

(u) Management capability and attitudes to risk

(v) Ownership and owner expectations

(w) Human resource capability

(x) Response patterns

3.5 The major sources of competitor information are listed below.

Recorded data

(a) Market research

(b) Secondary data, eg Mintel, Keynote

(c) Business Press

(d) Trade Press

(e) Technical journals

(f) BRAD (British Rate And Data)

(g) Government publications and statistics

(h) Stockbroker and analyst reports

(i)   Credit reports

(j)   Annual reports

(k)   Public documents

Observable data

(a)   Competitor prices

(b)   Promotions

(c)   Patent applications

(d)   Competitor advertising

(e)   Planning applications

(f)   Salesforce feedback

(g)   Buying competitor products with a view to analysing the cost and processes of manufacture

Opportunistic data

(a)   Material suppliers

(b)   Equipment suppliers

(c)   Trade exhibitions

(d)   Customers

(e)   Packaging suppliers

(f)   Distributors

(g)   Sub-contractors

(h)   Newsletters

(i)   Disgruntled employees

(j)   Head hunting competitors' managers

(k)   Conferences

Competitive behaviour models

3.6   Competitors react in a variety of ways and Kotler has identified four common response profiles.

(a)   The **laid back competitor** does not respond quickly or strongly to competitor moves.

(b)   The **selective competitor** only responds to some moves and not those which it does not perceive to be any major threat.

(c)   The **tiger competitor** acts swiftly to any threats posed. For example, Procter and Gamble always react to the introduction of new soap powders. It is signalling that it will always defend its position and attack competitors, who should avoid any attacks unless competitors are prepared to go the full distance.

(d)   **Stochastic competitors** are unpredictable in nature. They may or may not respond and there is no predictable pattern of behaviour.

Competitor information systems

3.7   A competitor information system (CIS) is an essential ingredient of strategy. A CIS needs to follow six steps.

Step 1   Decide what information is required

Step 2   Design appropriate data capture systems and collect the data

Step 3   Analyse and evaluate the data

Step 4   Communicate the resulting information

Step 5   Incorporate the information and conclusions reached into strategy

Step 6   Feedback results so that the information system may be refined

Market signals

3.8   Market signals might come from the following sources.

(a) **A competitor making an announcement of what he intends to do,** but before he has done it. Prior announcements are publicity measures intended to achieve the following.

   (i)   Warn off competitors from trying to do the same, because the organisation making the announcement intends to get in first

   (ii) Test competitors' reactions

   (iii) Win support for the move from the investing public, on which it will rely for financial support

   (iv) Create a threat of retaliatory action against something another competitor has already done

(b) **A competitor making an announcement of what he has done,** after the event, for example, signing a major contract with a supplier or customer, or making a takeover bid for another organisation.

(c) **Competitors adopting a particular course of action** when they would have been expected to do something else. What does their unexpected action signal?

(d) **An aggressive marketing action by a competitor.** When a competitor takes an aggressive marketing action directed specifically against the organisation, it might be a signal that the competitor thinks the organisation is gaining too much market share, and the aggressive action might be the first stage in an intensification of competition.

4   SECONDARY DATA

Key Concept

In marketing research, **secondary data** is data neither collected directly by the user nor specifically for the user, often under conditions not known to the user. Examples include government reports.

4.1   As consumers ourselves we are continually using secondary data for our own purchasing decisions. Secondary data is data neither collected by, nor specifically for, the user, and is often collected under conditions not known by the user. If you plan a trip to the theatre you will read the reviews or talk to friends who have seen the production. We make use of such secondary data sources on a daily basis. However, these sources cannot replace the experience itself, nor the more energetic enquiries we might decide to make ourselves.

The use of secondary data

As a backdrop to primary research

4.2   In unfamiliar territory, it is natural that the marketer will carry out some basic research in the area, using journals, existing market reports, the press and any contacts with relevant knowledge. Such investigations will aid the marketer by providing guidance on a number of areas.

(a)   Possible data sources

(b)   Data collection

(c)   Methods of collection (relevant populations, sampling methods and so on)

(d)   The general state of the market (demand, competition and the like)

As a substitute for field research

4.3   The (often substantial) cost of primary research might be avoided should existing secondary data be sufficient. This data would not be perfect for the needs of the business; and to judge whether it **is** enough, or whether primary research ought to be undertaken, a cost-benefit analysis should be implemented.

As a technique in itself

4.4   Some types of information can only be acquired through secondary data, in particular trends over time. The historical data published on, say, trends in the behaviour of a market over time, cannot realistically be replaced by a one-off study.

4.5   **Advantages of secondary data**

(a)   Secondary data may solve the problem without the need for any primary research: **time and money** is thereby saved.

(b)   Secondary data, while not necessarily fulfilling all the needs of the business, can be of great use by:

   (i)   Setting the parameters, defining a hypothesis, highlighting variables, in other words, helping to **focus on the central problem**

   (ii)   **Providing guidance**, by showing past methods of research and so on, for primary data collection

   (iii)   Helping to assimilate the primary research with past research, **highlighting trends** and the like

   (iv)   Defining **sampling** parameters, (target populations, variables and so on)

4.6   **Disadvantages of secondary data**

(a)   **Relevance**. The data may not be relevant to the research objectives in terms of the data content itself, classifications used or units of measurement.

(b)   **Cost**. Although secondary data is usually cheaper than primary data, some specialist reports can cost large amounts of money. A cost-benefit analysis will determine whether such secondary data should be used or whether primary research would be more economical.

(c)   **Availability**. Secondary data may not exist in the specific product or market area.

(d)   **Bias**. The secondary data may be biased, depending on who originally carried it out and for what purpose. Attempts should be made to obtain the most original source of the data, to assess it for such bias.

(e)   **Accuracy**. The accuracy of the data should be questioned. Weiers (1988) suggests the following checklist.

   (i)   Was the sample representative?

(ii) Was the questionnaire or other measurement instrument(s) properly constructed?

(iii) Were possible biases in response or in non-response corrected and accounted for?

(iv) Was the data properly analysed using appropriate statistical techniques?

(v) Was a sufficiently large sample used?

(vi) Does the report include the raw data?

(vii) To what degree were the field-workers supervised?

In addition, was any raw data omitted from the final report, and why?

(f) **Sufficiency.** Even after fulfilling all the above criteria, the secondary data may be insufficient and primary research would therefore be necessary.

Action Programme 3

How can secondary data help when a firm is considering an international advertising campaign?

---

5 INTERNAL SECONDARY DATA

12/99

5.1 **Internal secondary data** are records inside the organisation, gathered by another department or section for the research task in hand.

Examples

(a) **Production data** about quantities produced, materials and labour resources used and so on

(b) Data about **stock**

(c) Data about **sales volumes**, analysed by sales area, sales person, quantity, price, profitability, distribution outlet, customer and the like

(d) Data about marketing itself, such as **promotion and brand** data

(e) **Financial management data**

5.2 Internal secondary data can be extremely useful for sales and marketing, as the following examples show.

(a) **Order/sales statistics (by customer).** An understanding of who the customers are allows marketing activity to be directed appropriately (promotions, invitation to sponsored events and so on). Having a correct view of the types of existing customers and where they live allows consumer product companies to use geodemographic databases to target other like-minded people susceptible to buying the product.

Sales representatives need to understand who their most important customers are to be able to manager their time effectively. Very important customers may be categorised as needing contact once a month, medium-sized customers as needing to be seen every quarter and so on.

(b) **Sales statistics (by product).** These allow product managers to monitor the popularity of products to help decide where to direct the marketing activity and which products to withdraw so that the most appropriate ones are available. Having an appropriate mix of products is required to maintain good customer relationships.

(c) **Delivery details.** Where these are different from customer/order details, these help the representatives identify new contacts and new sites/establishments.

(d) **Profitability (by product/by customer).** It is important that the sales force put their energy into spending time with their most profitable customers and building relations with them accordingly.

(e) **Complaints.** Having an understanding of the nature of complaints can help sales and marketing people communicate with customers more effectively. It may be a question of explaining the functioning of the product differently or changing the customers' expectation and perceptions.

(f) **Stock levels.** Knowing that there is stock that needs to be shifted quickly or that a particular item will need two weeks' notice can help the sales staff seem more professional and interested in their customers.

(g) **Debtor information.** A representative could have spent a lot of time building up a good relationship only to have the time wasted by a letter going out from the accounts department threatening to withdraw credit facilities.

6 EXTERNAL SECONDARY DATA 12/99

6.1 It is with external data that the problems of volume and multiplicity of sources becomes a problem. The best approach, particularly in completely unknown areas, is to start with general information and then 'telescope' on to more specific data on industries and then individual companies or markets.

6.2 Tull and Hawkins (1988) use the following categories of **external secondary data**.

(a) Business directories
(b) Computerised databases
(c) Associations
(d) Government agencies
(e) Syndicated services
(f) Other published sources
(g) External experts

Business directories

6.3 **Examples**

(a) Kompass Register (Kompass)
(b) Who owns Whom (Dun and Bradstreet)
(c) Key British Enterprises (Dun and Bradstreet)

As mentioned above, these directories can make a good starting point. The information provided is usually on industries and markets, manufacturers (size, location), products, sales and profits.

Computerised databases

6.4 These include the following.

(a) ACORN (consumption indices by class of neighbourhood)
(b) PRESTEL (British Telecom)
(c) TEXTLINE (abstracts and articles from approximately 80 newspapers)
(d) Marketing Surveys Index (CIM)

(e)   MRS Yearbook (Market Research Agencies and their specialisms)

(f)   TGI and other syndicated omnibus surveys

6.5   Webb (1992) also lists European databases.

(a)   European Kompass Online
(b)   Financial Times Company Information
(c)   Hoppenstedt Austria/Germany/Netherlands
(d)   Jordanwatch
(e)   PTS Prompt
(f)   Reuters Textline

6.6   With computer databases, it is usual for the researcher's computer to be connected to the database computer by modem. These databases are not cheap to use, but it is usually much less expensive than collecting the information oneself. A trained operator should be used to begin with, to avoid expensive waste of the resources.

The Internet

6.7   As we saw in the chapter on information technology, the **Internet** is the name given to the technology that allows any computer with a telecommunications link to send and receive information from any other suitably equipped computer.

6.8   Most people use the Net on personal computers through interface programs called **browsers** that make it more user-friendly and accessible. These guide users to destinations throughout the world: the user simply types in a word or phrase like 'beer' to find a list of thousands of websites that contain something connected with beer. New wireless application protocol (**WAP**) products allow specially adapted versions of websites to be accessed from mobile devices such as telephones.

6.9   Companies like Yahoo! make money by selling advertising space. For instance if you type in 'beer' as a search term, an advertisement for Miller Genuine Draft may appear, as well as your list of beer-related sites. If you click on the advertisement you are taken to the advertiser's website, perhaps just to be told more about the product, perhaps to be favourably influenced by the entertainment provided by the site, or perhaps even to buy some of the product. The advertiser may get you to register your interest in the product so that you can be directly targeted in future. Thus the Web is increasingly being used for marketing research purposes. At the very least, advertisers know exactly how many people have viewed their message and how many were interested enough in it to click on it to find out more.

Commercial use of the Internet   Specimen paper

6.10 Besides its usefulness for tapping into worldwide information resources, businesses are also using the Internet to provide information about their own products and services. Customers are often reluctant to phone a company or ask to see a sales person to ask basic questions because they do not know whom they should speak to, they are not quite sure what they want to know, and they are conscious of appearing to waste the provider's time.

6.11 The Internet offers a speedy and impersonal way of getting to know the basics (or even the details) of the services that a company provides. For businesses the advantage is that it is much cheaper to provide the information in electronic form than it would be to employ staff to man the phones on an enquiry desk, and much more effective than sending out mailshots that people would either throw away or forget about when they needed the information.

Associations

6.12 There are associations in almost every field of business and leisure activity. All these bodies collect and publish data for their members which can be of great interest to other users. Examples of such bodies include the Road Haulage Association (RHA), the British Association of Ski Instructors and the Institute of Chartered Accountants in England and Wales.

Government agencies

6.13 The government is a major source of economic information and information about industry and population trends. Examples of government publications are as follows.

(a) The Annual Abstract of Statistics and its monthly equivalent, the Monthly Digest of Statistics, which contain data about manufacturing output, housing, population and so on

(b) The Digest of UK Energy Statistics (published annually)

(c) Housing and Construction Statistics (published quarterly)

(d) Financial Statistics (monthly)

(e) Economic Trends (monthly)

(f) Census of Production (annual) has been described as 'one of the most important sources of desk research for industrial marketers', providing data about production by firms in each industry in the UK

(g) Department of Employment Gazette (monthly) giving details of employment in the UK

(h) British Business, published weekly by the Department of Trade and Industry, giving data on industrial and commercial trends at home and overseas

(i) Business Monitors, giving detailed information about various industries

Note. Similar information will be published for other countries and can provide a useful starting point for assessing overseas market opportunities.

Syndicated services

6.14 If the expense of conducting their own surveys is too great, companies and organisations can obtain general surveys that they can buy into on a shared basis, for example the Nielsen Retail Audit. A particular form of shared cost research is the omnibus survey, a variety of which are advertised in the Market Research Society Newsletters and range from general weekly surveys done by telephone (such as phonebus) to special sector surveys (for example, Omnicar - motoring, Carrick James - children and youth, small businesses and so on).

6.15 The advantage is that for a few hundred as opposed to a few thousand pounds, a company can ask a few questions of a reasonably representative sample and have a report sent within two or three weeks.

6.16 Companies can also link up with others in an industry through their federations so as to conduct shared-cost marketing research surveys.

6.17   In the following paragraphs we will look at some examples of syndicated services.

The Nielsen Retail Index

6.18   Nielsen was the first market research organisation to establish continuous retail tracking operations in the UK. The Nielsen Index is not an index in the statistical sense (the ratio of a current value to a past value expressed as a percentage), but refers instead to a range of continuous sales and distribution measurements, embracing ten separate product fields.

(a)   Grocery
(b)   Health and beauty
(c)   Confectionery
(d)   Home improvements
(e)   Cash and carry outlets
(f)   Sportswear
(g)   Liquor
(h)   Toys
(i)   Tobacco
(j)   Electrical

6.19   These indexes together measure a large number of sales and distribution variables for over 600 different product categories and over 120,000 brands and associated brand variants.

6.20   Data are collected from the major multiples (like Tesco and Sainsbury) through their EPOS systems. For other types of shop where EPOS data are not available, a monthly audit of stocks is undertaken and, using data from deliveries, the level of what sales must have been since the last audit is determined. It is essential to take account of non-EPOS retail units otherwise the survey would generate misleading data.

6.21   Increasingly, Nielsen clients receive their data electronically on databases, Nielsen having developed a range of data management and analysis software. A Nielsen service called Inf★Act Workstation offers a powerful yet flexible personal, computer-based decision support system.

AGB's Superpanel

6.22   AGB's Superpanel consists of 8,500 households, covering the purchases of some 28,000 individuals aged between 5 and 79, who are resident in domestic households across Great Britain which are equipped with telephones.

6.23   Data collection is through personal data terminals equipped with a laser light pen. The terminal is designed to resemble a digital phone and is kept in a modem linked to the domestic power supply and the telephone socket. Data capture is via overnight polling (which means that AGB's central computer dials each panel number in turn and accesses the data stored in the modem).

6.24   All that is required from informants is that when they unpack their shopping, they pass the laser light pen over the barcode for each item, and also enter standardised data about the date, shop(s) visited, prices paid and so on. The process incorporates procedures for entering details of products either without barcodes or which have a bar-code that is difficult to read.

6.25   Recruitment to the AGB Superpanel uses a multi-stage procedure. A large sample of households are screened to identify those in each sampling point eligible for the service and with known demographics. For this purpose, AGB uses personal home interviews, some 200,000 annually, within 270 parliamentary constituencies (about half the total number).

6.26 The households with the relevant target demographics are then selected and the 'housewife' (who may be male or female) for each household is contacted by phone. If the initial contact proves positive, the household as a whole is briefed and the equipment installed.

Taylor Nelson's Omnimas

6.27 Taylor Nelson claims Omnimas to be one of the largest single random omnibus surveys in the world, with some 2,100 adults being interviewed face-to-face every week.

6.28 A random sampling approach is employed, using the electoral registers from 233 parliamentary constituencies selected in proportion to size within each of the ten standard regions of the UK.

6.29 Each interviewer has a minimum of 13 interviews to do a week. Because the only quota set is that the interviewer should obtain either six men and seven women, or vice versa, there is a control on sex, but everything else depends on the randomness of the sample.

6.30 The Omnimas questionnaire is divided into three sections.

(a) A continuous section, including questions asked on every survey and inserted on behalf of a particular client

(b) An ad-hoc section of questions included on a one-off basis

(c) A classification section that includes all the demographic questions

6.31 Given an average completion time of 25 minutes per respondent and the 20-30 seconds needed to administer an average question, the total number of Omnimas questions will not be more than about 60-70. Most questions are fixed-choice, with a predetermined number of possible responses, but some clients require open-ended questions and the Omnimas approach allows for a few of these to be included.

BMRB's Target Group Index (TGI)

6.32 TGI's purpose is to increase the efficiency of marketing operations by identifying and describing target groups of consumers and their exposure to the media (newspapers, magazines, television and radio) and the extent to which they see or hear other media.

6.33 In design, the TGI is a regular interval survey and is also 'single source', in that it covers both product usage data and media exposure data.

6.34 Respondents are questioned on a number of areas; purchase behaviour and media use are cross-tabulated to enable more accurate media audience targeting.

(a) Their use of 400 different products covering 3,500 brands
(b) Their readership of over 170 magazines and newspapers
(c) Cinema attendance
(d) ITV television watching
(e) Listening patterns for commercial radio stations
(f) Their lifestyles, based on nearly 200 attitude questions

6.35 The major product fields covered are foods, household goods, medicaments, toiletries and cosmetics, drink, confectionery, tobacco, motoring, clothing, leisure, holidays, financial services and consumer durables. It is worth noting that respondents are only asked about the use, ownership and consumption of the products identified, not about purchases made or prices paid.

6.36 The lifestyle questions are in the form of Likert-type attitude statements with which people are asked to agree or disagree on a five-point scale from 'definitely agree' to 'definitely disagree'. These attitude statements cover the main areas of food, drink, shopping, diet/health, personal appearance, DIY, holidays, finance, travel, media, motivation/self-perception, plus questions on some specific products and attitudes to sponsorship.

6.37 Each questionnaire runs to more than 90 pages and can take four hours to complete. However, the document is totally pre-coded and adapted for optical mark reading, with respondents being able to indicate their replies by pencil strokes. There are three versions of the questionnaire, for men, for housewives, and for other women.

6.38 TGI results supply enormous amounts of information, both within categories and cross-tabulated against other relevant categories. There are about 25,000 responses per annum.

(a) Total numbers of product users for each demographic category

(b) Percentages of product users in each demographic category

(c) Information on heavy/medium/light and non-users for each product or product category

(d) For brands and product fields with more than one million claimed users, consumption can be cross-tabulated against a range of demographic variables including sex, age, social class, area, number of children, and media usage

(e) Brand usage tables, listing the following.

(i) **Solus users** - users of the product group who use the brand exclusively
(ii) **Most-often users** - those who prefer it, but use another brand as well
(iii) **Minor users** - whose who do not discriminate between brands

6.39 TGI appears in 34 volumes, published annually in July and August, but subscribers have on-line access to datasets for which they have subscribed, and they can analyse the data on their own PCs.

Other published sources

6.40 This group includes all other publications, including the following.

(a) Some digests and pocket books

(i) Lifestyle Pocket Book (annual by the Advertising Association)
(ii) Retail Pocket Book (annual by Nielsen)
(iii) A to Z of UK Marketing Data (Euromonitor)
(iv) UK in figures (annual, free from Office for National Statistics)

(b) Some important periodicals (often available in the public libraries)

(i) Economist (general)
(ii) Campaign (advertising)
(iii) ADMAP (advertising)
(iv) Mintel (consumer market reports)
(v) Retail Business (consumer market reports)
(vi) BRAD (all media selling advertising space in the UK including TV, radio, newspapers and magazines)

6.41 Since this heading can include all newspapers, journals and so on, it would be wise to use an expert librarian as a guide to the 'way in' to this information. Webb (1992) also suggests hard copy directories of abstracts including the following.

(a) Business Periodicals Index
(b) ANBAR Management Abstracts
(c) Research Index
(d) ABI/Inform

6.42 Non-government sources of information include the following.

(a) The national press (Financial Times and so on) and financial and professional magazines and journals

(b) Companies and other organisations specialising in the provision of economic and financial data (for example the Financial Times Business Information Service, the Data Research Institute, Reuters and the Extel Group)

(c) Directories and yearbooks

(d) Professional institutions (for example Chartered Institute of Marketing, Industrial Marketing Research Association, Institute of Management, Institute of Practitioners in Advertising)

(e) Specialist libraries, such as the City Business Library in London, which collect published information from a wide variety of sources

(f) Companies' websites on the Internet and unofficial chatrooms devoted to particular products

Exam Tip

The contents of this Chapter have been fairly heavily tested in the past examinations. For example, as part of a marketing team undertaking market research on the European market for a possible new product launch you may be asked to explain the meaning of the terms 'primary and secondary data' in the context of market research, and how secondary data may be used, and any advantages that it may have over primary data.

Chapter Roundup

- Customer and competitor intelligence are vital tools in any organisation's marketing strategy.

- Customer intelligence depends on understanding customer priorities, segmenting customers into differing expectation groups, and designing appropriate methods for the systematic acquisition of customer feedback.

- Relying on customer complaints as a source of evidence for measuring customer satisfaction is extremely dangerous.

- Securing information about actual and potential competitors can be achieved through diligent attention to secondary data.

- A competitor information system may use data acquired from various sources, plus market signals transmitted by competitors themselves.

- Secondary data can be immensely cost-effective, but have to be used with care.

- There are several well-known sources of secondary data supplying market intelligence on a continuous basis.

- Remember the growing importance of information technology (eg the Internet and databases) in this area.

Quick Quiz

1   Why is customer intelligence so important? (see paras 2.1 - 2.4)

2   What are the four fundamentals of customer satisfaction? (2.5)

3   Why is measuring customer satisfaction such a problem? (2.6)

4   How can differences in customers' expectations be exploited? (2.8)

5   How should a customer intelligence survey be planned and implemented? (2.9)

6   Under what headings is competitor information required? (3.4)

7   What are the steps involved in setting up a competitor information system? (3.7)

8   What are the origins of 'market signals'? (3.8)

9   Secondary data can perform three roles: what are they? (4.2 - 4.4)

10 What are the disadvantages of secondary data? (4.6)

11 What are the principal sources of internal secondary data for an organisation? (5.1)

12 Provide five examples of computerised databases. (6.4)

13 What are the commercial information uses of the Internet? (6.10, 6.11)

14 What are the principal sources of government information in the field of secondary data? (6.13)

Action Programme Review

1   (a)   Make it easy for people to complain, using complaint forms, 0800 (free) phone numbers and a Freepost address.

    (b)   Ask for complaints by seeking out customers at random (as Rank Xerox does) and asking them for their views.

    (c)   When customers are purchasing high-value consumer durables like a new car, it makes sense to phone them after several days to seek reactions and suggestions for improvement.

2   Do people want to go somewhere in particular or do they want a particular type of holiday?

    Brand competition   - Thomson package holidays to Greece

    Industry competition   - all holidays to Greece (*or* all package holidays?)

    Form competition   - all holidays (eg cruises etc)

    Generic competition   - other leisure pursuits

3   Secondary data sources can be used to investigate the advertising regulations in different countries. In certain countries there may be restrictions on advertising directed at children, on advertising tobacco or alcohol. Some countries may insist on pre-broadcast screening and so on. The secondary data could also provide information on the advertising authorities in each country (if any).

Now try illustrative questions 16 and 17 at the end of the Study Text

14

The Marketing Research Process

Learning Outcomes

After studying this chapter you will have an understanding of the appropriate marketing research process to generate information for a range of research objectives.

This may include the use of both internal and external resources.

Key Concepts

- Primary data
- Sampling
- Sampling frame

- Random sample
- Quota sampling

Examples of Marketing at Work

- Organic produce

1 INTRODUCTION

1.1 Although some aspects of this chapter are not specifically mentioned in the syllabus, an awareness of them, both by researchers and project (marketing) managers, nonetheless ensures an adequate understanding of what is involved in the professional design and implementation of a marketing research project. Marketing research is essential to the development of a proactive marketing strategy, but research is worse than useless if not properly constructed and executed, and meaningful data systematically collected, analysed and presented.

1.2 Alternative definitions of marketing research you may already be familiar with include the following.

(a) 'The objective gathering, recording and analysing of all facts about problems relating to the transfer and sales of goods and services from producer to consumer or user'

(Chartered Institute of Marketing)

(b) 'Systematic problem analysis, model-building and fact-finding for the purposes of improved decision making and control in the marketing of goods and services'

(Kotler)

1.3 The basic rationale for marketing research is the **widening communications gap** between an organisation and its customers in a modern economy and the need to provide an informed basis for strategic decisions. There are other reasons, too.

(a) **Increasing competition** necessitates a detailed knowledge of competitors' activities.
(b) Rapid changes in **technology** must be taken into account.
(c) Growing affluence creates changes in **tastes** and purchasing **habits**.
(d) **Marketing costs** (largely labour costs) are increasing faster than production costs.

1.4 Marketing research also extends into other areas, such as the following.

(a) The study of corporate responsibility (for example towards the environment)
(b) Economic forecasting
(c) International and export studies
(d) Long-term business forecasting

1.5 By focusing on the specific information needed for an identified decision to be made, marketing research helps managers to make the correct decision, reducing the chance of 'getting it wrong'. But the quantity and quality of information provided by marketing research have an associated cost and the trade-off between cost and accuracy is important.

1.6 Raymond Kent (*Marketing Research in Action*) advances several reasons why marketing research can sometimes be a waste of effort and resources.

(a) The research undertaken may be designed without reference to the decisions that will depend on, or be strongly influenced by, the results of the research.

(b) The research results may be ignored, misused, misunderstood, or misinterpreted. Sometimes this happens accidentally; more often it is deliberate because the results do not fit in with some senior person's prejudices or established beliefs.

(c) The research is poorly designed or carried out.

(d) The results of the research are themselves inconclusive, giving rise to different opinions about what the research signifies.

1.7 Bear in mind that marketing research, however well organised, is no substitute for decision making. It can help to reduce the risks in business decision making, but it will not make the decision. Professional marketing depends partially on sound judgement and reliable information, but it also needs flair and creativity, the ability to see the wood from the trees.

2   THE MARKETING RESEARCH PROCESS

2.1   Webb suggests a 10-step marketing research process.

Step 1: Set the objectives of the research

2.2   Webb suggests that 'marketing research should reduce the need for a company to have to react, by making the organisation proactive, ie by sensitising management to oncoming threats and opportunities in a timely way, such that steps can be taken to avoid those threats or to take maximum advantage of the opportunities'.

Action Programme 1

Your company manufactures cruelty-free beauty products (bubble bath, talcum powder and so on) for a number of supermarket chains. You have been given responsibility for finding out about the market for a new line of cruelty-free cosmetics (lipsticks, eyeshadow and so on).

Required

List the likely research objectives.

2.3   Research objectives need to be SMART.

Research objectives	Discover re Action Programme above:
Specific	Size of market for *cruelty-free* cosmetics not cosmetics in general
Measurable	Respective market share in percentage terms of leading players
Actionable	Price range within which consumers will buy
Reasonable	A defined number of preferred colours
Timescaled	Information within 3 months so product can be marketed for Christmas

Step 2: Define the research problem

2.4   This vital step in the process establishes the area of research and the type(s) of data required. An accurate assessment of the environment in which the problem/opportunity exists must be made. This may necessitate building a model of the situation so as to allow researchers to put forward possible ways in which the research question may be answered.

Step 3: Assess the value of the research

2.5   This step involves carrying out a **cost/benefit exercise** on the desired information. The cost of a research project should always be less than the value of the information provided. DCF and payback techniques may be required in this step.

Step 4: Construct the research proposal

2.6   If the results of marketing research are to prove useful they must provide 'a true, life-like representation of the situation and not a distorted cartoon-like image' (Webb). Both client and researcher must agree on the exact constituents of the research proposal.

2.7   The category of research (exploratory, descriptive or causal) must be decided upon.

BPP PUBLISHING

(a) **Exploratory research** is the least formal and most flexible, looking at the variables which impact on a situation.

(b) **Descriptive research** describes the variables.

(c) **Causal research** (the most formal and inflexible) looks at the relationships between the variables.

Step 5: Specify data collection methods

2.8 Data can be collected from either primary or secondary data sources. Secondary data, which we looked at in detail in Chapter 13, is 'data neither collected directly by the user nor specifically for the user, often under conditions that are not well known to the user' (American Marketing Association). Primary data is information collected specifically for the study under consideration.

Step 6: Specify the techniques of measurement

2.9 Measurement is the process of turning the factors under investigation into quantitative data. The scale will depend on both the data collection methods being used and the type of data required.

Step 7: Select the sample

2.10 Time and money will preclude the researcher from conducting a census of each member of the population in which he/she has an interest unless the population is very small. The researcher must therefore examine a sample.

Step 8: Data collection

2.11 This is when the researcher actually goes out and gets the data.

Step 9: Analysis of results

2.12 The data collected in Step 8 will not answer the research problem defined in Step 2. The data will have to be processed into information. Note that certain types or levels of analysis are only possible if the data has been collected in a certain way and has been measured using certain instruments and scales of measurement. The researcher, prior to steps 6, 7 and 8 should therefore have decided upon the way in which the data should be analysed.

Step 10: Presentation of final report

2.13 We will be looking at this aspect of the marketing research process in Section 7.

The research brief

2.14 The key to good research information, whether collected by an in house section or an external agency lies in the quality of the research brief. You need to be familiar with the content of a brief as you may be called upon to produce one in the examination.

2.15 The structure of a research brief will normally cover the following.

(a) **Background.** This covers relevant information about the company product, market place and the factors which have led to the current need for market information.

(b) **The problem.** This may be undertaken in conjunction with the researcher, but defining the problem carefully and agreeing objectives for the research is an essential first step in the research process and is central to the brief.

2.16 The brief should also contain any **constraining factors** relevant to the process. These can involve time scale, budget or the degree of secrecy necessary.

Exam Tip

You might be asked the following type of question. The marketing director of your company wants to find out how customers view the firm and its level of service as compared to its major competitors. He is convinced that the only way to do this is to use an external agency to carry out field research, even though your firm actually has the resources in-house to conduct such studies. The question asks you to write a report for the director which outlines the following.

- The alternatives available

- The appropriateness of these alternatives

- Steps to be taken if an external agency is commissioned to conduct the research

Begin with a brief description of the alternatives available, and continue with an analysis of the advantages and disadvantages of each (in order to consider how appropriate each one is). The final part of your solution should include the ten-step marketing process as suggested by Webb, with some notes on the steps that make up the research brief, the research proposal, and the programme in action.

3 PRIMARY DATA COLLECTION 6/01

Key Concept

Primary data is data collected by or specifically for the user (as opposed to secondary data).

Field research

3.1 **Research in the field** is concerned with the generation and collection of original research data.

Off the peg research

3.2 **'Off the peg'** research may consist of **syndicated research or omnibus research**.

(a) **Syndicated research** is collected by a research organisation on behalf of a number of organisations requiring the research. Syndicated research is usually too expensive for any individual organisation to collect. The research data is sold on to all the firms who have a use for it and hence the cost of data generation and collection is shared.

(b) **Omnibus research** is where regular surveys of defined populations are undertaken. The research agency doing the work may make the service available as an 'omnibus' for other organisations to climb aboard. Each organisation climbing aboard the omnibus may be allowed to ask a few specific questions.

Made to measure research

3.3 **'Made to measure' research** is the most **expensive** type of research to undertake. The organisation requiring information decides what it is that it exactly wants to know. The organisation then has two choices.

(a) To carry out the research itself
(b) To buy in the services of a research agency

3.4 Although it is the most expensive type of research to undertake, it is also the most useful type of research since it is **'customised'**.

Experimentation

3.5 In a **controlled experiment,** a controlled research environment is established and selected stimuli are then introduced. To the extent that 'outside' factors can be eliminated from the environment the observed effects can be measured and related to each stimulus. Controlled experiments have been used to find the best advertising campaign, the best price level, the best incentive scheme, the best sales training method and so on.

3.6 When experiments are conducted in more realistic market settings, results are less reliable because of the researcher's inability to control outside factors. Nevertheless, the local market reaction to a new product, for example, is often a prerequisite to a national launch. This is known as a **test market**.

Survey (census or sample)

3.7 The **survey** approach involves asking questions of the target market or population. In marketing research for consumer goods, it will be impossible to obtain data from every consumer in the market. To obtain data, it is therefore usually necessary to obtain a **sample** to provide an estimate of the characteristics of the entire 'population'. The accuracy of the sample will depend on the following.

(a) **How** the sample is taken
(b) The amount of **variability** in the population
(c) The **size** of the sample

The larger the sample, the greater the likelihood that the sample will provide an accurate reflection of the population as a whole. Questions can be limited and highly structured, in the form of questionnaires delivered by post, telephone or in person.

3.8 On the other hand, questions can be asked in great depth of a relatively small sample. This is **qualitative or motivational research** and provides information on behaviour and attitudes.

Observation

3.9 **Observation** is frequently used when managers want to evaluate the impact of a new store layout or the response to a proposed new pack design.

Qualitative or quantitative research

3.10 **Quantitative research** provides measurable results from a sample of a population which can be taken to be respresentative of the whole. Qualitative research does not aspire to statistical accuracy. It main purpose is to understand consumer behaviour and perceptions, not to measure them.

3.11 **Examples of qualitative research**

Unstructured interviews	Whereas a questionnaire by its nature restricts the possibility of varying responses, an unstructured approach allows the respondent to bring his or her perspectives to bear on the interpretation.
Depth interviews	Motivational research uses the psychoanalytic method of depth interviews, probing beneath the surface.
Projective techniques	Attitudes are drawn out through various stimuli,
Focus groups	A group of people hold a discussion on a particular matter, under the watchful eye of a moderator.

3.12 Value and uses of qualitative research

Although qualitative research cannot produce statistically meaningful results, it is still often used.

(a) **To suggest areas for later quantitative research**

Quantitative research implies that people know what sort of question to ask – however this is putting the cart before the horse. Qualitative research provides underlying background

(b) **To explore nuances in data that cannot be quantified.**

(c) **To explore the underlying motivation mix of target consumers.**

(d) **Where it is impossible to obtain a meaningful sample.**

4 OBTAINING A REPRESENTATIVE SAMPLE

12/99

4.1 Conducting a survey by sampling is one of the most important subjects in marketing research. In most practical situations a population will be too large to carry out a complete survey and only a sample will be examined. The results from the sample are used to estimate the perceptions of the whole population.

Key Concept

Sampling involves taking a limited number of a large population so that by studying the part something may be learnt about the whole. The population is all those people who have the characteristics in which the researcher is interested.

4.2 Occasionally a population is small enough that all of it can be examined: for example, the examination results of one class of students. When all of the population is examined, the survey is called a **census**. This type of survey is quite rare, however.

Action Programme 2

What do you see as the advantages of sampling over complete coverage?

Selecting a representative sample

4.3 We need to be sure of the following.

(a) Our sample is not **unrepresentative or biased**. If the characteristics of the sample are different from those of the population, then the inferences we draw about the population from studying the sample will be unreliable.

(b) The **cost and time** involved in selecting the sample produces the required benefits of **usefulness and accuracy**.

Sampling frames

> ### Key Concept
>
> A **sampling frame** is the list, index, map or any other population record from which the sample can be selected.

4.4 Every factor of the survey design is influenced by the sampling frame - the population coverage, the stratifications that are used, the method of sample selection and so on.

(a) Does it adequately cover the population to be surveyed?
(b) Is it complete? Are all members of the population on it? Is it accurate and up-to-date?
(c) No items should appear more than once.
(d) Is it arranged in a convenient way for sampling? is it readily accessible?

No frame is likely to completely satisfy all the above criteria.

Types of sampling frame

4.5 These can be broadly classified as follows.

(a) **Lists of individuals.** Such lists, either of the whole population or of the groups within it can be used. Examples include the electoral register, the lists of members of professional bodies and lists of company employees.

(b) **Complete census returns.** Unfortunately the manner in which the data is collected and processed tends to prevent its use as a frame.

(c) **Returns from an earlier survey.** How useful previous surveys are depends on the questions asked in the original survey and if the data is up to date.

(d) **Lists of dwellings.** Council tax lists are useful as a sampling frame for dwellings.

(e) **Large scale maps.** Ordnance Survey maps have a grid system which enables areas to be broken down into suitably sized blocks. Sometimes a problem is the availability of up-to-date large scale maps, given recent town and city re-development.

4.6 The two frames most generally available are council tax or valuation lists and electoral registers. These can be stratified along ACORN geodemographic lines to assist accurate stratified random sampling.

Action Programme 3

What are the problems associated with using a telephone directory for a certain area as a sampling frame of the people who live in that area?

Practical points regarding sample sizes

4.7 Although it is possible to calculate an ideal sample size from a **statistical** point of view, administrative and practical factors have to be taken into account.

(a) The amount of **money and time** available
(b) The **aims** of the survey
(c) The **degree of precision** required
(d) The number of **sub-samples** required

A sample need only be **large enough to be reasonably representative** of the population.

Random versus quota (non random) sampling

4.8 The aim of sampling is to get accurate and usable data at a reasonable cost within a reasonable timescale. The two main sampling methods are **random** (probability) sampling and **quota** (non-probability) sampling.

Random sampling

> **Key Concept**
>
> A **simple random sample** is a sample selected in such a way that every item of the population has an equal and known chance of being selected.

4.9 Random samples are not perfect because they may be highly unrepresentative. It is important to appreciate that random selection does not guarantee that the sample will be free from bias - only that the method of selection is free from bias.

4.10 Random selection methods are, however, an essential part of the protection against selection error. 'Random' is not equivalent to 'haphazard'; random sampling is a careful, systematic procedure which generates statistically valid data suitable for further statistical analysis.

Stratified random sampling

4.11 In theory, **stratification** uses knowledge of the population to increase the representativeness and precision of the sample. For example, a random sample of Europeans could result in the sample all being Germans. We would therefore select from each country in proportion to its population. Populations can be stratified in many ways (eg sex, age groups, regions etc).

Multi-stage random sampling

4.12 To reduce the distance a researcher would have to travel which would probably result from simple random sampling, **multi-stage sampling** can be used. The procedure is simple. The country is divided into areas, say counties, and three or four of these are selected at random. These large areas are divided and sub-divided until a sample of small areas is obtained and number of householders can be selected at random in each small area.

4.13 **Area sampling** is basically a form of random sampling in which maps are used in place of lists. This is common in the USA where cities are often laid out in regular patterns and roads dividing blocks make convenient area boundaries. An alternative is to place a grid over a map, number the squares and take a random sample of them.

BPP PUBLISHING

Quota sampling

Key Concept

Quota sampling is used to avoid the time and expense necessary to search for individuals chosen by a random sample. This method of sampling differs fundamentally from random methods in that once the general breakdown is decided (such as how many men and women, how many people in each age group and social class are to be included) the interviewers are left to select the persons to fit this framework.

4.14 Opinion on the validity of quota sampling is divided. Statisticians tend to criticise the method for its theoretical weakness, but market and opinion researchers defend it for its cheapness and administrative convenience.

4.15 The quotas given to the interviewers need to be arranged in such a way that for the whole country and maybe even for each region, the sexes, age groups, and social classes are represented in the correct proportions on the basis of available data. **Age** and **sex** present few problems but **social class** has always been one of the most dubious areas of marketing research investigation. 'Class' is a highly personal and subjective phenomenon, to the extent that some people are 'class conscious' or class aware and have a sense of belonging to a particular group. JICNAR's social grade definitions (A-E), are often used in quota setting.

JICNAR Social grades	Social status	Characteristics of occupation (of head of household)
A	Upper middle class	Higher managerial/professional eg lawyers, directors
B	Middle class	Intermediate managerial/administrative/ professional eg teachers, managers, computer operators, sales managers
C_1	Lower middle class	Supervisory, clerical, junior managerial/ administrative/professional eg foremen, shop assistants
C_2	Skilled working class	Skilled manual labour eg electricians, mechanics
D	Working class	Semi-skilled manual labour eg machine operators
		Unskilled manual labour eg cleaning, waiting tables, assembly
E	Lowest level of subsistence	State pensioners, widows (no other earner), casual workers

From 2001 UK Office for National Statistics used a new categorisation system, reflecting recent changes in the UK population.

New social class	Occupations	Example
1	Higher managerial and professional occupations	
1.1	Employers and managers in larger organisations	Bank managers, company directors
1.2	Higher professional	Doctors, lawyers
2	Lower managerial and professional occupations	Police officers
3	Intermediate occupations	Secretaries/PAs, clerical workers
4	Small employers and own-account workers	
5	Lower supervisory, craft and related occupations	Electricians
6	Semi-routine occupations	Drivers, hairdressers, bricklayers
7	Routine occupations	Car park attendants, cleaners

5 MARKETING RESEARCH CONSULTANTS

5.1 Marketing research has been a growing source of organisation expenditure in recent years. Very few organisations can shoulder the cost of a large full-time staff of marketing research workers, especially a 'field force' of researchers spread around the country. In addition to market research agencies, there are market research departments in many of the large UK advertising agencies.

Choosing and using consultants

5.2 Choosing the right agency or consultant to work with is a key element in a successful working relationship. The external expert must become a trusted part of the team.

5.3 It is equally important that the market researcher has the specialist knowledge and research service capabilities needed by the organisation. In the UK you would expect a research organisation to be associated to the professional body, the Market Research Society, and for those working on the account to have relevant qualifications.

5.4 It helps if the agency has some knowledge of the market or business in which the company operates. Therefore, it is worthwhile developing a long-standing relationship with the research organisation. As the understanding of the company's business and the marketplace develops over time, there is a real dividend from the two operations working together.

External agencies versus in-house programmes

5.5 There are a number of advantages and disadvantages to each alternative.

  (a) **Using an external agency**

   (i) **Advantages**

    (1) External agencies **specialising** in research will have the necessary expertise in marketing research techniques. This should allow them to develop a cost-effective research programme to a **tighter timescale**.

    (2) Skills in **monitoring and interpreting data** will allow the programme to be reviewed and modified as required.

    (3) There will be **minimal disruption** to the working of the marketing department which might result from releasing internal staff from existing duties.

    (4) An external agency can provide an **objective input** without the bias which often results from a dependence on internal resources.

    (5) **Costs** can be determined from the outset, allowing better **budgetary control**.

    (6) Such an approach might be advantageous when conducting **confidential research** into sensitive area, there being less risk of information being 'leaked' to competitors.

   (ii) **Disadvantage**

    Agency knowledge of the industry will be limited: a serious drawback if the agency needs a disproportionate amount of time to familiarise itself with the sector.

  (b) **In-house programme**

   (i) **Advantages**

    (1) **Costs can be absorbed** into existing departmental overheads.

    (2) It offers an opportunity to **broaden the experience** and skill levels of existing staff.

           (3)   It might be useful in promoting a **team spirit** and encouraging a 'results-oriented' approach.

     (ii)   **Disadvantages**

           (1)   There is a danger of **overstretching current resources** and adversely affecting other projects.

           (2)   There is a risk of developing an **inappropriate programme**, yielding insufficient or poor quality data with inadequate analysis and control.

           (3)   If additional **training or recruitment** is required this could prove expensive and time consuming.

           (4)   **Bias** could result from using staff with pre-conceived views.

           (5)   **Company politics** may influence the results.

           (6)   Considerable **computing resources** with appropriate software packages would be required to analyse the data.

           (7)   There may be a lack of **appropriate facilities**. For example, focus group research would normally be conducted off premises during an evening or weekend.

5.6   In view of the shortcomings of a purely in-house or external agency approach, a **combination** of the two might be more appropriate. For example, it might be deemed preferable to design the programme in-house but contract out certain aspects.

6   MANAGEMENT ASPECTS OF MARKETING RESEARCH

6.1   Management issues when undertaking research projects can be summarised with the mnemonic **CATS**.

> **C**ost
> **A**ccuracy
> **T**iming
> **S**ecurity

6.2   AS well as the **cost/accuracy trade-off,** managers must also compare the costs with the **benefits** of additional information, before briefing research projects. What is the risk involved in making the wrong decision? What is the extra information 'worth'?

6.3   A good market research plan will often embrace more than one method of **data collection**. It is quite common for research to start with qualitative interviews with a small sample, designed to establish key issues, concerns and language used and to follow this up with a quantitative survey targeted at a more significant sample taken from the same target group.

6.4   It can take a **considerable time** to conduct research. Managers must not use research as an excuse for not making decisions when they need to be made. Opportunities should not be missed or threats ignored for the sake of waiting for more information.

6.5   The final management consideration is **security**. Research can sometimes give competitors an insight into a company's proposed strategy and so allow them to react. This is most obvious in the circumstances of a test market. On many occasions test markets have reduced the impact of an innovative new product launch.

The presentation of research findings

6.6   Once the research process has been completed, the researcher will present the findings in a face-to-face session, giving managers the opportunity to ask questions about the results. It takes time and skill to convert the findings into a well-structured oral presentation.

6.7 It is very likely that the research must be organised in report form as well. It is a mistake simply to prepare the oral presentation from the written report, since the conventions of report writing are quite different from the criteria that govern effective presentations.

7 APPROACHES TO THE ASSESSMENT OF THE VALUE AND VALIDITY OF DATA

7.1 Whilst the CIM does not expect you to be a statistician, competent marketing managers should be able to assess the value and the validity of data upon which they are basing important decisions.

7.2 Some approaches to this assessment are outlined below.

(a) **Common sense**. Clearly data which is dated, which emanates from dubious sources or which is based on unrepresentative samples should be treated with extreme caution, if not totally disregarded.

(b) **Statistical approaches**. There are a variety of sampling methods for survey data as already described, which are appropriate to different situations. All of them involve some degree of risk (some probability of error). The degree of risk of statistical error can, however, be computed as we have seen.

(c) **Expert judgement**. 'There are lies, damned lies and statistics.' The same data can be interpreted differently by different people - you have only to look at differences between economists or between politicians of different parties on the latest figures to see ample evidence of this. The following array - 98.7, 98.6, 98.6, 98.4, 98.1, 98.1 - might be regarded by a statistician as a declining trend but to a marketing manager the figures may represent a very steady state, especially if they were percentages of actual sales against budgeted sales for the last six years. In using this approach, therefore, the marketing manager might be wise to consult more than one expert before making a decision.

(d) **The intuitive approach**. Some people have a better feel for figures than others and seem able to judge the value and validity of data intuitively. For example, it is said that Rank Xerox ignored survey findings that there was no market for a dry copier and in doing so went on to become a world leader in this field. This approach, whilst perhaps successful for a chosen few, is not, however, recommended.

(e) **The questioning approach**. Always question the origin and the basis of the data. Ask for further information. An actual spend of 180% of budget is not important if the amount concerned is only £10. A much smaller variance on a much large amount could, however, be quite serious. Recognise that human errors occur when manipulating data, that bias can occur in questionnaire design: ask to see the questionnaire, check the figures.

8 THE LIMITATIONS OF MARKETING RESEARCH

8.1 You should be aware that research cannot supply marketers with perfect and comprehensive answers to all the questions. This may be because the research itself is badly designed (the sample populations inappropriate, the questions misleading and so on) but it can also happen because systematic research, by definition, can only ask the questions which exist in marketers' mind and elicit responses within the framework of respondents' imaginations.

8.2 The most important point in building marketing strategy is not logical analysis or investigative excellence, but creative action (Nishikawa, *Journal of Long Range Planning*). Only proactive creativity, generating products and services *in anticipation of* customer needs

BPP PUBLISHING

and expectations, can create marketing advantage; organisations which are customer driven (as opposed to being customer focused) are invariably *reactive*. Responding to declared customer needs is acting too late for successful marketing: in order to forecast the future, organisations require creativity rather than responsiveness, challenge rather than passivity.

8.3   Nishikawa claimed that marketing research linked to new products and services is especially defective, because of certain features in customer psychology.

(a) **Indifference**. Customers often provide negative responses to ideas for new products/services simply because they are indifferent to something they have not thought about or tried before.

(b) **Absence of responsibility**. People will say more or less anything when responding to research surveys, often out of a desire to please the researcher.

(c) **Conservative attitudes**. Most customers choose conventional and familiar products/services. Only about 3% of customers are Early Adopters.

(d) **Vanity**. Customers will try to put on a good appearance about their motives and will seldom want to admit that cheapness, say, was the major reason for a purchase.

(e) **Insufficient information**. Researchers often approach customers with information and ideas seen from the seller's rather than from the customer's point of view.

(f) Customers are sincere when **spending rather than talking**.

Marketing at Work

Many growers and retailers, had been misled by surveys suggesting that 70 per cent of consumers would purchase organic vegetables and fruit. In the event only 11 per cent are doing so, the remainder have demonstrated by their actions that *behaviour* and *attitudes* are not necessarily synonymous. Perhaps they had not seriously considered the possibility that organic produce would cost more or that it would look less attractive; quite possibly they gave 'ethically correct' responses when completing a questionnaire, but had no real intention of acting differently.

Chapter Roundup

Webb has suggested a ten-step marketing research process.

1:	Set the objectives of the research	6:	Specify techniques of measurement
2:	Define the research problem	7:	Select the sample
3:	Assess the value of the research	8:	Collect data
4:	Construct the research proposal	9:	Analyse the results
5:	Specify data collection methods	10:	Present the final report

- The research brief is a critical part of the execution of effective research.

- Primary data may be secured principally through experimentation, surveys and observation.

- Various techniques for sampling include random sampling, stratified sampling, multi-stage sampling, quota sampling, systematic sampling and cluster sampling.

- There are various types of non-response encountered when carrying out marketing research.

- When undertaking research, management should consider cost, accuracy, timing and security.

- Marketing managers need to be able to assess the value and validity of research data.

- Marketing research is of limited value when organisations are seeking to develop new products or services.

Quick Quiz

1   What are the ten principal steps in the research process? (2.1 - 2.13)

2   What two areas does a research brief cover? (2.15)

3   What are the differences between 'syndicated research' and 'omnibus research'? (3.2)

4   What is a controlled experiment? (3.5)

5   What is a sampling frame? (4.4)

6   What are the merits and disadvantages of random sampling? (4.9, 4.10)

7   What are the merits and drawbacks of quota sampling? (4.14, 4.15)

8   What should be borne in mind when selecting a market research consultant? (5.2 - 5.4)

9   What does the mnemonic 'CATS' mean? To what does it refer? (6.1 - 6.5)

10 What five approaches can you use to assess the value and validity of the marketing research data? (7.2)

11 Why is marketing research linked to new products and services likely to be defective? (8.3)

Action Programme Review

1   Useable information for a marketing plan to be drawn up and implemented.

   (a)   The size of market, value, number of items sold, number of customers
   (b)   The leading companies and their respective market share
   (c)   The breakdown of market by type of cosmetic (lipstick, eyeshadow etc)
   (d)   Current consumer trends in buying cruelty-free cosmetics (price, colour and so on)
   (e)   Consumer preferences in terms of packaging/presentation
   (f)   The importance of having a choice of colours within the range
   (g)   The influence of advertising and promotion

2   (a)   Sampling saves money.
   (b)   Sampling saves labour.
   (c)   Sampling saves time.
   (d)   More elaborate and detailed information can be collected.

3   Some people are ex-directory and so are not listed. Others don't have a telephone and so are not listed either. Moreover, there will usually be only one telephone number and one person listed per residence whereas, in most cases, more than one person will be living in each residence.

Now try illustrative question 18 at the end of the Study Text

15 *Marketing Research Applications*

Chapter Topic List	Syllabus Reference
1 Introduction	-
2 The scope of marketing research	5.0
3 Market research	5.3, 5.9
4 Product research	5.2, 5.7
5 Price research	5.8
6 Distribution research	5.6
7 Advertising and communications research	5.1

Learning Outcomes

After studying this chapter you will understand the application of marketing research to a variety of marketing decisions:

- product development
- category management
- choice of distribution channels
- pricing and sales decisions
- advertising and communications

Key Concepts

- Marketing research and market research
- Product research
- Category management
- Product testing

Examples of Marketing at Work

- Bell Telephones
- Supermarkets
- Advertisement recognition

1 INTRODUCTION

1.1 Marketing research is about finding out about the market and its structure, competitors, consumer behaviour and the needs and wants of customers. All organisations require marketing research and there are many different marketing research techniques to assist in this quest for information.

1.2 By far the biggest users of marketing research have been large **fast-moving consumer goods (FMCG)** companies, such as soap powder manufacturers, or major retail organisations like Sainsbury, Tesco, Asda and Littlewoods. These days, however, more and more smaller and medium-sized companies need to know more about their competitive environments and their customers.

1.3 Privatisation of many public services previously provided by central and local government has meant that even many non-traditional, non-profit making organisations need to find out about the needs of people who require their services.

1.4 Marketing research can help with resource allocation decisions. Accurate, relevant and timely data is an essential input to this decision-making process.

1.5 There are three initial questions which any researcher must address.

(a) What is the purpose of the research (research aims)?
(b) What type of research data is available?
(c) How can the organisation best acquire the research it needs? (In-house, or buy in?)

2 THE SCOPE OF MARKETING RESEARCH

2.1 Marketing research is a term often used to refer to both **market research and marketing research**.

Key Concept

Marketing research is 'the systematic gathering, recording and analysing of data about problems relating to the marketing of goods and services' (American Marketing Association). It is a broadly-based concept which includes market research, product research, price, place (distribution) and promotion. Marketing research provides information for managers to make decisions about all aspects of the marketing mix. **Market research**, on the other hand, is that part of marketing research which provides information about the market for a particular product or service.

Action Programme 1

List the six subdivisions of marketing research and the applications of each subdivision.

3 MARKET RESEARCH   Specimen paper, 12/00

3.1 **Market research** is one aspect of marketing research. The two concepts are different, even though their names are similar. Market research is concerned with quantifying information to provide a forecast of sales and to assess potential sales. Market research is therefore based on the use of **mathematical and statistical techniques** to reduce uncertainty.

Market forecasts and sales forecasts

3.2 Market forecasts and sales forecasts complement each other. They should not be undertaken separately and the market forecast should be carried out first of all and should cover a longer period of time.

    (a) **Market forecast.** This is a forecast for the market as a whole. It is mainly involved in the assessment of environmental factors, outside the organisation's control, which will affect the demand for its products/services. Often it consists of three components.

        (i) **The economic review** (national economy, government policy, covering forecasts on investment, population, gross national product, and so on)

        (ii) **Specific market research** (to obtain data about specific markets and forecasts concerning total market demand)

        (iii) **Evaluation of total market demand for the firm's and similar products** (covering profitability, market potential and so on)

    (b) **Sales forecasts.** These are estimates of sales of a product in a future period at a given price and using a stated method(s) of sales promotion which will cost a given amount of money.

        Unlike the market forecast, a sales forecast concerns the firm's activity directly. It takes into account such aspects as sales to certain categories of customer, sales promotion activities, the extent of competition, product life cycle, performance of major products. Sales forecasts are expressed in volume, value and profit.

Research into potential sales

3.3 **Sales potential** is an estimate of the part of the market which is within the possible reach of a product. The potential will vary according to the price of the product and the amount of money spent on sales promotion, and market research should attempt to quantify these variations. Sales potential also depends on:

    (a) How essential the product is to consumers
    (b) Whether it is a durable commodity whose purchase is postponable
    (c) The overall size of the possible market
    (d) Competition

3.4 Whether sales potential is worth exploiting will depend on the cost of sales promotion and selling which must be incurred to realise the potential. Consider a company which has done market research which has led it to the opinion that the sales potential of product X is as follows.

	Sales value	*Contribution earned before selling costs deducted*	*Cost of selling*
either	£100,000	£40,000	£10,000
or	£110,000	£44,000	£15,000

In this example, it would not be worth spending an extra £5,000 on selling in order to realise an extra sales potential of £10,000, because the net effect would be a loss of £(5,000 – 4,000) = £1,000.

3.5 Sales potential will influence the decisions by a company on how much of each product to make. The market situation is dynamic, and market research should reveal changing situations. A company might decide that maximum profits will be earned by concentrating all its production and sales promotion efforts on one segment of a market. Action by competitors might then adversely affect sales and market research might reveal that another market segment has become relatively more profitable. The company might therefore decide to divert some production capacity and sales promotion spending to the new segment in order to revive its profits.

Other aspects of market research

3.6 Market research, to be comprehensive, must show an awareness of the various environmental influences which may affect supply and demand for a product.

3.7 Market research also involves investigation of the following.

(a) The expansion or decline of demand within a particular market segment
(b) The expansion or decline of demand within a particular geographical area
(c) The timing of demand (Is there a cyclical or seasonal pattern of demand?)

Concentration ratios

3.8 One way of expressing concentration ratios is to assess the percentage of the market that is held by the top firms. For example, an industry might have the following concentration ratios.

	% of market
Top three firms	60
Top five firms	68
Top ten firms	85

4   PRODUCT RESEARCH

Key Concept

Product research is concerned with the product itself, whether new, improved or already on the market, and customer reactions to it.

4.1 This aspect of marketing research attempts to make product **research and development** customer orientated.

4.2 New product ideas may come from anywhere - from research and development personnel, marketing and sales personnel, competitors, customers, outside scientific or technological discoveries, individual employees or executives and so on. Research and development is carried out by company scientists, engineers or designers; much wasted effort can be saved for them, however, if new ideas are first tested in the market, in other words if product research is carried out.

The process of product research

4.3 New ideas are first screened by a range of specialists (market researchers, designers, research and development staff and so on) and are rejected if they have any of the following characteristics.

(a) They have a low profit potential or insufficient market potential.
(b) They have a high cost and involve high risk.
(c) They do not conform to company objectives.
(d) They cannot be produced and distributed with the available resources.

4.4 Ideas which survive the screening process should be product tested and possibly test marketed. Test marketing in selected areas will give a better indication of how well the product will sell if produced for a wider market, but it also gives competitors an early warning of what is happening.

4.5 Product research also includes the need to keep the product range of a company's goods under review for the following reasons.

(a) **Variety reduction** may be desirable to reduce production costs, or when there are insufficient sales of certain items in the product range to justify continued production. In practice, there is often strong resistance, both from within a company and from customers, to the elimination of products from the market.

(b) **Product diversification** increases a product range by introducing new items, and a wide range of products can often improve a company's market image.

(c) **Segmentation** is a policy which aims at securing a new class of customers for an existing range of products, perhaps by making some adjustments to the products to appeal to the new segments.

4.6 Product research also involves finding **new uses for existing products**, and this could be considered a means of extending a product range. The uses for plastics and nylon, for example, have been extended rapidly in the past as a result of effective research.

Product life cycle research

The product life cycle

4.7 The profitability and sales of a product can be expected to change over time. The **product life cycle** (PLC) is an attempt to recognise distinct stages in a product's sales history. Although you will have encountered the PLC before, a brief recap is provided below.

4.8 Marketing managers distinguish between the following.

(a) **Product class**: this is a broad category of product, such as cars, washing machines, newspapers, also referred to as the generic product.

(b) **Product form**: within a product class there are different forms that the product can take, for example five-door hatchback cars or two-seater sports cars; twin tub or front loading automatic washing machines; national daily newspapers or weekly local papers and so on.

(c) The particular **brand or make** of the product form (for example Ford Escort, Vauxhall Astra; Financial Times, Daily Mail and Sun).

4.9 The product life cycle applies in differing degrees to each of the three cases. A product-class may have a long maturity stage, and a particular make or brand might have an erratic life cycle. Product forms however tend to conform to the 'classic' life cycle pattern, commonly described by a curve as follows. You will be familiar with each of the stages.

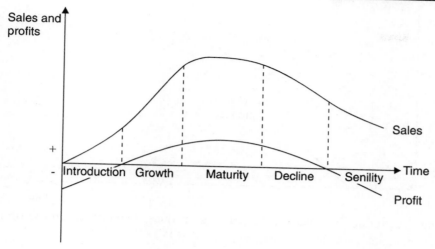

The relevance of the product life cycle to planning and control

4.10 A company selling a range of products must try to look into the longer term, beyond the immediate budget period, and estimate how much each of its products is likely to contribute towards sales revenue and profitability. It is therefore necessary to make an assessment of the following.

(a) The stage of its life cycle that any product has reached

(b) Allowing for price changes, other marketing strategies, cost control and product modifications, for how much longer the product will be able to contribute significantly to profits and sales

4.11 Another aspect of product life cycle analysis is new product development, and strategic planners must consider the following.

(a) How urgent is the need to innovate, and how much will have to be spent on R & D to develop new products in time?

(b) New products cost money to introduce. Not only are there R & D costs, but there is also capital expenditure on plant and equipment, and probably heavy expenditure on advertising and sales promotion. A new product will use up substantial amounts of cash in its early life, and it will not be until its growth phase is well under way, or even the maturity phase reached, that a product will pay back the initial outlays of capital and marketing expenditure.

4.12 It is essential that firms plan their portfolio of products to ensure that new products are generating positive cash flow before existing 'earners' enter the decline stage.

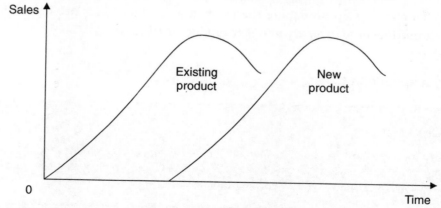

In this situation the company is likely to experience cash flow problems.

BPP
PUBLISHING

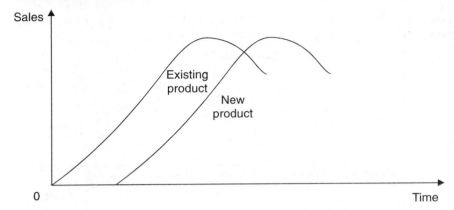

By considering the product life cycle of the existing product, when planning the timing for launch of a new product, cash flow problems can be avoided.

4.13 It is perhaps easy enough to accept that products have a life cycle, but it is not so easy to sort out how far through its life a product is, and what its expected future life might be. Information about the stage a product has reached in its life cycle may be an important indication of how long its market will continue and how soon new product developments must be introduced to replace it.

(a) There ought to be a **regular review** of existing products, as a part of marketing management responsibilities.

(b) Information should be obtained about the likely future of each product and sources of such information might be as follows.

(i) An analysis of past sales and profit trends
(ii) The history of other products
(iii) Market research
(iv) If possible, an analysis of competitors

The future of each product should be estimated in terms of both sales revenue and profits.

4.14 Once the assessments have been made, decisions must be taken about what to do with each product. The choices are as follows.

(a) To **continue selling** the product, with no foreseeable intention yet of stopping production

(b) To initiate action to **prolong a product's life**, perhaps by product modification, advertising more, by trying to cut costs or raise prices, by improving distribution, or packaging or sales promotion methods, or by putting in more direct selling effort

(c) To plan to **stop producing the product** and either to replace it with new ones in the same line or to diversify into new product-market areas

Category management

Key Concept

Category management has been defined as 'the distributor/supplier process of managing categories as strategic business units, producing enhanced business results by focusing on delivering consumer value' (Joint Industry Project on Efficient Consumer Response).

4.15 Category management is a comparatively new theme in retailing and emphasises decision making based upon analysis of consumer data, EPOS data and market research data. The aim of the new discipline is to reduce costs and inventories while improving the consumer's choice.

4.16 A category is defined as 'a distinct, manageable group of products or services that customers perceive to be related and/or substitutable in meeting a consumer need'. Thus tinned vegetables (tomatoes, baked beans, sweetcorn) might form a category, or frozen desserts or household paper products. The retailer manages each category as a **strategic business unit**.

4.17 Each category is managed according to its own particular strategy. Typical strategies might include traffic building (increasing the number of customers passing through the category shelfspace), profit contribution or cash penetration. Category management is therefore intensely data-driven, and needs accurate data at store level. For example, a store might want to rank profit or volume sales of a particular product and compare that with national or regional figures. The scanned data from the store can be combined with market sales data and consumer information to identify where, for example, sales are below what would be expected. The category or product may become the focus for enhanced promotion to boost sales, or re-pricing to improve its contribution margin.

Product testing

> ### Key Concept
>
> **Product testing** is 'the evaluation and development of the products themselves from a marketing point of view'.

4.18 It necessitates 'a physical product to which a representative sample of target consumers may be exposed under controlled conditions; which they can use under realistic circumstances; and about which they can express their opinion in a structured way' (Kent).

4.19 The following circumstances should be taken into account when establishing the most appropriate product test design.

(a) **Management information required**. For example, is information required on the best shape/colour mix, or on whether it is worth investing more time and money in the product, or which is the best of a group of similar products and so on.

(b) **The market in which the product will be sold**. If the market consists of children, for example, their inability to perform certain tasks must be taken into account. Industrial and consumer markets obviously differ and a highly-branded market means that the product will need to be well branded.

(c) **The type of product being tested**. The following product characteristics are likely to affect the design of product tests.

   (i) How new the product is to users (a new product cannot be compared to another)

   (ii) How easily the product can be assessed by users

   (iii) How much information consumers gather before selecting a product

(d) **The availability of time and finance**.

(e) **The need for standardisation of the procedures across a wide range of products.** Standardised tests mean that researchers gain more experience of the procedures, the procedure can be refined and results of different tests are more likely to be comparable.

4.20 The essential differences between product tests centre around the following.

(a) **Sample size** (cost and data reliability must be weighed up)

(b) **The type of people used as testers** (current users of the brand, current users in the product field, users in the product field plus potential users or a general cross section of the population?)

(c) **The type of test given to the testers**

    (i) **Monadic.** Each person is given just one product (either a new product or a line extension) to evaluate.

    (ii) **Comparative.** Each person is given two or more products to compare on the same occasion. Such tests are typically used for new product formulation.

    (iii) **Sequential.** Each person tries one product, waits a specific time period, tries a second and then gives an opinion.

    (iv) **Conjoint.** Such tests focus on product features rather than identifying the best product.

Kent lists other choices facing the researcher in terms of what testers are asked to do.

    (i) Whether the products should be branded or blind
    (ii) Whether competitors' brands should be included among the products tested
    (iii) Which order the products should be presented in comparative tests
    (iv) Whether the test should be on the spot or in use (at home)
    (v) Which attributes are to be tested
    (vi) The time given to testers

(d) **The analysis techniques used on the collected data**

Attitude measurement

Key Concept

An **attitude** is a predisposition to act in a particular way. A knowledge of attitudes may therefore enable **predictions** about likely behaviour patterns. A significant proportion of marketing research is aimed at finding out about consumer attitudes.

4.21 A favourable pre-disposition towards a product may lead to a purchase. However, such causal relationships are very seldom this direct.

4.22 There are three components to 'attitude'.

(a) A **cognitive component** which is what the individual knows or believes about an object or act

(b) An **affective component** which is what the individual feels emotionally about an object or act

(c) A **conative component** which is how the individual is disposed to behave towards an object or act

4.23 Attitude is multi-dimensional and any attempt to measure attitudes needs to recognise this. For example, a number of different attitudes could affect a particular buying decision. 'I like the coat, it's red' but 'red reminds me of blood and danger' and 'it's not a bad price, I can afford it' but 'my parents would never have spent so much on a coat' and yet 'it does feel good on' and 'the shop assistant said it looks good on' but 'it has a real fur collar and an animal has been killed to make this coat' and yet 'animal skins have been a source of clothing for thousands of years' but 'I'm a vegetarian' and so on. Eventually, a decision to buy or not to buy may be made on the basis of the buyer's various attitudes and which attitudes are the most powerful, but these attitudes may also be balanced by social pressures.

4.24 It is therefore important that attitudes are incorporated into marketing research. Two scaling techniques which attempt to measure attitude are **Likert scales** and **semantic differential scales**. These are covered in the BPP Study Text for Paper 5: *The Marketing/Customer Interface*.

Buyer motivation

4.25 It is in an organisation's interests to know the **reasons or motives** behind people's behaviour. The reasons why people seek a product or product category, and how they go about obtaining it, are of vital importance to the marketer.

4.26 **Patronage motives** (price, service, location, honesty, product variety and so on) influence where a person purchases products on a regular basis.

4.27 To analyse the major motives that influence consumers to buy or not buy their products, markets conduct motivation research using **in-depth interviews**, **focus groups** and **projective techniques** (see the BPP Study Text for Paper 5).

5 PRICE RESEARCH

6/00

Reasons for conducting price research

5.1 Reasons for conducting price research are as follows.

(i) Where a firm is aware of competitive pricing and offers, it can use the data as a reference point for its own pricing.

(ii) Once the firm has established the market prices, it can, through market research, calculate the price elasticity of demand and hence derive anticipated sales volume based on proposed price levels.

(iii) Given the market price, the firm can benchmark its level of product / service quality

(iv) Pricing research can help identify more profitable customers and market segments as well as compare costs with a view to maximising profitability.

Exam Tip

The June 1996 examination under the previous syllabus included a question in which candidates were required to write a short report to the sales and marketing manager of a firm that is contemplating the introduction of a new Cola drink.

A good answer would list the key stages in the research which should be carried out, and then each stage looked at in more detail (giving explanations and justifications).

Many candidates who chose this question had difficulty in relating the pricing research to the context given. Do make sure that you are able to apply your knowledge to different situations which may be given to you in examination questions.

Price sensitivity

5.2 **Price sensitivity** will vary amongst purchasers. Those who can pass on the cost of purchases will be least sensitive and will respond more to other elements of the marketing mix.

(a) Provided that it fits the corporate budget, the business traveller will be more concerned about the level of service and quality of food when looking for an hotel than price. In contrast, a family on holiday are likely to be very price sensitive when choosing an overnight stay.

(b) In industrial marketing the purchasing manager is likely to be more price sensitive than the engineer who might be the actual user of new equipment that is being sourced. The engineer and purchasing manager are using different criteria in making the choice. The engineer places product characteristics as first priority, the purchasing manager is more price oriented.

5.3 Price decisions are often seen as highly sensitive and as such may involve top management more clearly than other marketing decisions. Price has a very obvious and direct relationship with profit. Ethical consideration, such as whether or not to exploit short-term shortages through higher prices are a further factor. Illustrative of this dilemma is the outcry surrounding the series of petrol price rises following the outbreak of the Gulf Crisis in 1990.

Finding out about price sensitivity

5.4 **Research on price sensitivity** of customers has demonstrated the following.

(a) Customers have a concept of a **'just price'** - a feel for what is about the right price to pay for a commodity.

(b) Unless a regular purchase is involved, customers search for price information before buying, becoming price aware when wanting to buy but forgetting soon afterwards.

(c) Customers will buy at what they consider to be a bargain price without full regard for need and actual price.

Marketing at Work

Bell Telephones in the US were concerned about the lack of sales of extension telephones. When, as part of a market research survey, customers were asked to name the actual price of an extension telephone, most overestimated it. By keeping the existing price but running an advertising campaign featuring it, Bell were able to increase sales as customers became aware of the lower than anticipated price.

Finding out about price perception

5.5 **Price perception** is important as it determines ways customers react to prices. The economist's downward sloping demand curve may not in fact hold, at least in the short term. For example, customers may react to a price increase by buying for one or more of a number of reasons.

(a) They expect further price increases to follow. (They are 'stocking up'.)
(b) They assume the quality has increased.
(c) The brand takes on a 'snob appeal' because of the high price.

Factors affecting pricing decisions

5.6   Several factors complicate the pricing decisions which an organisation has to make.

Intermediaries' objectives

5.7   If an organisation distributes products or services to the market through independent intermediaries, the objectives of these intermediaries have an effect on the pricing decision. Thus conflict over price can arise between suppliers and intermediaries which may be difficult to resolve.

Competitors' actions and reactions

5.8   An organisation, in setting prices, sends out signals to **rivals**. These rivals are likely to react in some way. In some industries (such as petrol retailing) pricing moves in unison; in others, price changes by one supplier may initiate a price war, with each supplier undercutting the others.

Suppliers

5.9   If an organisation's **suppliers** notice that the prices for an organisation's products are rising, they may seek a rise in the price for their supplies to the organisation.

Inflation

5.10   In periods of inflation the organisation's prices may need to change in order to reflect increases in the prices of supplies, labour, rent and so on. Such changes may be needed to keep relative (real) prices unchanged (this is the process of prices being adjusted for the rate of inflation).

Quality connotations

5.11   In the absence of other information, customers tend to judge quality by price. Thus a price change may send signals to customers concerning the quality of the product. A rise may be taken to indicate improvements, a reduction may signal reduced quality.

New product pricing

5.12   Most pricing decisions for existing products relate to price changes. Such changes have a reference point from which to move (the existing price). But when a new product is introduced for the first time there may be no such reference points; pricing decisions are most difficult to make in such circumstances. It may be possible to seek alternative reference points, such as the price in another market where the new product has already been launched, or the price set by a competitor.

Income effects

5.13   In times of rising incomes, price may become a less important marketing variable than, for instance, product quality or convenience of access. When income levels are falling and/or unemployment levels rising, price will become a much more important marketing variable.

BPP PUBLISHING

Marketing at Work

In the recession of the early 1990s, the major grocery multiples such as Tesco, Sainsbury, Safeway and Waitrose, who steadily moved up-market in the 1980s with great success leaving the 'pile it high, sell it cheap' philosophy behind, suddenly found bargain stores such as Foodgiant, Aldi, Kwik Save and Netto a more serious threat. They responded by cutting prices on 'staples' (such as baked beans) to draw consumers into their stores. This was backed up by continued product development, customer service pledges and loyalty cards.

Multiple products

5.14 Most organisations market not just one product but a range of products. These products are commonly interrelated, perhaps being **complements** or **substitutes**. Take, for example, the use of **loss leaders**: a very low price for one product is intended to make consumers buy other products in the range which carry higher profit margins: razors are sold at very low prices whilst blades for them are sold at a higher profit margin. Loss leaders also attract customers into retail stores where they will usually buy normally priced products as well as the loss leaders. This is the rationale behind the leading supermarkets' own-label and price-conscious ranges.

5.15 Remember that we looked at pricing decisions in Chapter 9.

6 DISTRIBUTION RESEARCH

6.1 **Place** as an element in the marketing mix is largely concerned with the selection of distribution channels and with the physical distribution of goods.

6.2 In selecting an **appropriate marketing channel** for a product, a firm has the following options.

(a) **Selling direct to the customer.** Consumer goods can be sold direct with mail order catalogues, telephone selling, door-to-door selling of consumer goods, or selling 'off the page' with magazine advertisements. Industrial goods are commonly sold direct by sales representatives, visiting industrial buyers.

(b) **Selling through agents or recognised distributors**, who specialise in the firm's products. For example, a chain of garden centres might act as specialist stockists and distributors for the products of just one garden shed manufacturer.

(c) **Selling through wholesalers** or to retailers who stock and sell the goods and brands of several rival manufacturers.

6.3 Some organisations might use channels of distribution for their goods which are unprofitable to use, and which should either be abandoned in favour of more profitable channels, or made profitable by giving some attention to cutting costs or increasing minimum order sizes.

6.4 As well as **cost and profitability analyses,** distribution research can embrace the following.

(a) To what extent is the distribution channel **actually working**? In other words, how effective is the distributor at delivering products to customers?

(b) To what extent is the distributor favouring its own brand or competitors' products over your own, in terms of shelf space and positioning and in-store promotions.

6.5 This latter point is important as own-brand products are becoming increasingly competitive with branded goods. Supermarket chains promote their own brand extensively.

6.6 Normal **market research techniques** can be used to assess the effectiveness of distribution channels. Questions in market research questionnaires can ask how easy it is for customers to obtain products and information, and where they are obtained. An example might be a newspaper readership questionnaire, which will ask where the customer acquires the newspaper (eg delivered at home, or bought on way to work).

7 ADVERTISING AND COMMUNICATIONS RESEARCH

7.1 Advertising may be judged to have been effective if it has met the objectives or tasks previously set for it. The following table gives some examples.

Advertising task/objectives	Example of measure of effect
Support increase in sales For example a local plumber's advert in a regional newspaper	Orders; levels of enquiries
Inform consumers For example an Amnesty International advert about political prisoners	Donations Number of new members clipping appeal coupon
Remind For example a Yellow Pages television commercial	Awareness levels
Create/re-inforce image For example the Halifax plc's 'people' commercials	Awareness levels Image created
Change attitude For example British Nuclear Fuel Ltd's Sellafield open door poster campaign	Attitude

7.2 Although there may well be a number of short-term effects resulting fairly soon after an advertising campaign has appeared, a brand will probably reap positive long-term effects from advertising effort stretching over a number of years. All advertising, whatever the objectives for any individual campaign, will contribute to the overall perception of that brand by the consumer.

Creative development research

7.3 This is research carried out early in the advertising process, using **qualitative techniques** to guide and help develop the advertising for a product or service. It can be used to help feed into initial creative ideas or, alternatively, to check whether a rough idea is understood by consumers. Storyboards, outline scripts or rough layouts of mocked up adverts may be shown to groups of consumers to monitor their response.

Pre-testing

7.4 Advertising pre-testing is research for **predictive** and evaluative purposes. Advertisements are tested quantitatively, at a much more highly finished stage than in creative development research, against set criteria. Recently, quantitative pre testing has seen a resurgence in popularity. As advertising budgets are made to work harder, advertisers have felt the need to build in more checks to ensure that their advertising is on target.

7.5 Quantitative testing can be administered via **hall or studio tests**. Specialist research agencies can cater for all kinds of media executions. Respondents are shown clusters of TV commercials either on their own or within television programmes; print executions are shown in folders amongst other adverts; poster executions may be shown in a simulated road drive scene via 35mm slides.

7.6 Adverts are measured against specific criteria such as those listed below.

(a) **Impact**. Does the advert stand out against others?

(b) **Persuasion**. Does the advert create favourable predisposition towards the brand?

(c) **Message delivery**. Does the advert deliver the message in terms of understanding and credibility?

(d) **Liking**. This attribute is deemed to mean not only that the advert is enjoyable and interesting, but also covers the notion of an advert being personally meaningful to the consumer, relevant and believable. Thus, an RSPCA advert depicting a maltreated animal might not be likeable in the conventional sense, but may be rated highly by a respondent on this attribute because it draws attention to an important issue that is relevant to the consumer.

7.7 The specialist research agencies that carry out this form of research have developed a set of normal values or scores, which act as **benchmarks** against which to measure quantitative results.

Tracking studies

7.8 Advertising effects may be measured over time via tracking studies which monitor **pre- and post-advertising variables**. Clients will normally buy into a series of **omnibus surveys** to monitor criteria such as:

(a) Brand/product awareness (unprompted *versus* prompted recall)
(b) Attitudinal change
(c) Imagery associations

7.9 **Panel research** is another form of tracking study. For instance, Taylor Nelson's Superpanel monitors changes in grocery shopping behaviour of 8,500 households. The research company have placed portable bar code scanners in homes and families undertake to use the device to record purchases made. The data is collated every week and gives diagnostic information. For instance, if the panel buy less of a particular brand, it is possible to identify what brand they have switched to instead.

7.10 With tracking studies, it is important to try to examine **all possible reasons** for any changes in audience behaviour. An increase in level of sales as tracked over time by panel-based research may be ascribed in part to the effect of the advertising. However, sales increases are equally likely to have come about due to changes in price levels, seasonality, competitive activity or a change in product quality levels.

Marketing at Work

'RSL showed 300 adults, aged between 18 and 60 years old, pictures of ten posters, with brands removed, and asked which they recognised and which they liked.

Benetton emerges as a clear winner in the poll. Fifty four per cent of adults said they had seen this poster before, rising to more than three quarters of 18 to 24 year olds, the campaigns main target market.

Forty seven per cent of the interviewees had noticed Lee Jean's "Stiletto" poster; only slightly fewer – four out of ten - recognised Kit Kat, the Teletubbies and The Times, Virgin Direct Pension and PEPs ads, Superkings and The Independent tie for sixth place, being remembered by just over a third. L'Oreal and Cable & Wireless were recognised by about a quarter.

Liking is high in this Posterwatch, with seven campaigns scoring sixty per cent or more. Kit Kat is the clear winner with sixty nine per cent approval. Four posters – The Independent, The Times, L'Oreal and Benetton tie for second place, all of them liked by about two thirds of respondents.

Lee Jeans and the Teletubbies were only just behind, scoring six out of ten. Forty four per cent liked Virgin Direct, and slightly fewer Superkings and Cable & Wireless.

The posters appealed particularly to the strongest sector of the market: 18 to 24 year olds. Liking for all the posters was highest in this age group, with the exception of Virgin Direct, whose subject matter – complex financial products – probably accounts for its focus of appeal to over 45 year olds.

The Times, The Independent and Benetton achieved particularly high scores among the under 25s, each one achieving 80 per cent approval.

Kit Kat's overall leadership in the liking rating is based on its strong appeal to a more general market, performing well across the age spectrum.'

Communications research

7.11   Advertising research as described above is but one aspect of communications research. As a marketing manager you will be concerned with the following aspects of your decision making.

(a)   **Economy** - The need to minimise the cost of inputs

(b)   **Efficiency** - The process of maximising the productivity of inputs

(c)   **Effectiveness** - The extent to which the output generated meets the objectives set for the organisation

7.12   You will therefore be continuously assessing the effectiveness as well as the relative costs of each element of the promotional mix using research methods.

(a)   **Sales research**

(i)   What are the selling costs for different customers?

(ii)   How can we improve sales presentations so as to obtain more orders?

(iii)   Should we have fewer personal visits and more telephone calls?

(iv)   Is personal selling more effective than direct marketing?

(b)   **Sales promotion research**

(i)   What extra sales resulted from the extra costs for these promotions?

(ii)   What level of retention of extra sales was there post promotion?

(iii)   What proportion of the budget should go on consumer incentives as opposed to dealer incentives or salesforce incentives?

(c)   **PR/publicity research**

(i)   How effective is PR relative to other forms of promotion?

(ii)   How can changes in image and attitudes be measured?

(iii)   How much notice do potential customers take of editorials?

Chapter Roundup

- Marketing research typically embraces six major areas: market research; product research; sales research; price research; distribution research; and advertising/communications research.

- Market research tries to quantify information to provide sales forecasts and assess potential sales.

- Product research seeks to achieve a marketing orientation to the organisation's research-and-development focus.

- The product life cycle is a useful model for marketing planning and control, although there are difficulties in predicting the precise shape of the PLC curve for any given product/service.

- Effective category management requires analysis of accurate data from consumers, EPOS and market research.

- Price sensitivity is influenced by five major factors, including the extent to which customers use the 'just price' concept, the nature of the purchase involved, and perceptions of price versus 'value'.

- Distribution research addresses such issues as timeliness of distribution channels, the distribution options available (and whether traditions can be challenged) and the profitability of various distribution methods.

- Advertising is normally measured against four specific criteria: impact, persuasion, message delivery and liking.

Quick Quiz

1   What is the difference between marketing research and market research? (see para 2.1)

2   What are three common components of a market forecast? (3.2)

3   What is meant by the term 'concentration ratio'? (3.8)

4   Why might a new product idea be rejected? (4.3)

5   Why does product research include the need to keep the product range of a company's goods under review? (4.5)

6   What is category management? (4.15)

7   What circumstances should be taken into account when establishing the most appropriate product test design? (4.19)

8   What is meant by the term 'attitude'? (4.21, 4.22)

9   Why conduct price research? (5.1)

10   List some factors which affect pricing decisions. (5.7 - 5.13)

11   What are the distribution options normally available to organisations? (6.2)

12   List five possible objectives or aims associated with advertising. (7.1)

13   What are the four criteria used to assess the effectiveness of advertising? (7.6)

14   What is 'communications research' about? (7.11)

Action Programme Review

1   *Type*

    Market research

                                  Application

Market research	Forecasting demand (new and existing products)
	Sales forecast by segment
	Analysis of market shares
	Market trends
	Industry trends
	Acquisition/diversification studies
Product research	Likely acceptance of new products
	Analysis of substitute products
	Comparison of competition products
	Test marketing
	Product extension
	Brand name generation and testing
	Product testing of existing products
	Packaging design studies
Price research	Competitor prices (analysis)
	Cost analysis
	Profit analysis
	Market potential
	Sales potential
	Sales forecast (volume)
	Customer perception of price
	Effect of price change on demand (elasticity of demand)
	Discounting
	Credit terms
Sales research	Analysing the effect of campaigns
	Monitoring/analysing advertising media choice
	Evaluation of sales force performance

To decide as appropriate sales territories and make decisions on how to cover the area

Copy research
Public image studies
Competitor advertising studies
Studies of premiums, coupons, promotions

Distribution research	Planning channel decisions
	Design and location of distribution centres
	In-house versus outsource logistics
	Export/international studies
	Channel coverage studies
Advertising and communications research	Brand preferences
	Brand attitude
	Product satisfaction
	Brand awareness studies
	Segmentation studies
	Buying intentions
	Monitor and evaluate buyer behaviour
	Buying habit/pattern studies

Now try illustrative question 19 at the end of the Study Text

Illustrative questions and suggested answers

1 MARKETING INFORMATION SYSTEM (MKIS)

Consider an organisation of your choice wanting to introduce a comprehensive marketing information system to achieve the following objectives.

(a) To improve customer service levels
(b) To provide marketing and sales managers with more accurate information

Required

You have been asked in your role as project manager to prepare a preliminary statement that outlines:

(a) The key elements of such a marketing information system   **(5 marks)**
(b) What technology can support the system   **(5 marks)**
(c) An outline plan of how you propose to investigate and design such a system **(10 marks)**
                                                                                (20 marks)

2 FEATURES OF THE MKIS

List and describe the features that you would expect to find in any organisation's marketing information system (MkIS). Explain the importance of each feature identified in providing key information giving specific examples from your own organisation or any organisation of your choice.   **(20 marks)**

3 INTEGRATING INTERNAL DATA SOURCES

Either for your own organisation or an organisation of your choice assume you have just taken on a new role in the marketing department and your first task is to produce a feasibility report on integrating internal data sources to begin the process of developing a company wide marketing information system. Prepare a brief report that covers:

(a) Internal data sources and their possible application in the new system.   **(10 marks)**
(b) An outline of the hardware required and how it will be used.   **(5 marks)**
(c) An outline of any specific software that you will use to achieve your objectives. **(5 marks)**
                                                                                (20 marks)

4 SALES FORECASTING

Why do companies forecast sales? Explain briefly *three* methods of sales forecasting in use.

(20 marks)

5 PROFIT VS CASH

(a) Explain why a company's reported profit for a particular financial period is different from the change in its cash position over the same period.

(b) Why is this difference significant to marketing or sales managers?   **(20 marks)**

6 ACTIVITY BASED COSTING

Your Marketing Manager has been asked to attend a meeting with several other managers and the Finance Director to discuss the possible introduction of Activity Based Costing. Since he knows very little about this subject he has asked you to prepare a brief report covering the following points.

(a) An explanation of Activity Based Costing   **(6 marks)**

(b) Any advantages and disadvantages of using such a system for budgeting and control, illustrating your answer with specific examples drawn from a marketing or sales perspective   **(14 marks)**
                                                                                (20 marks)

7 PAYBACK AND NET PRESENT VALUE

You are a member of a new product development team evaluating the introduction of new products. Using payback and Net Present Value with a discount rate at 10% per period consider an investment decision in a new product that has expected cash flows as follows.

Start of year 1	outflow	−£100,000
End of year 1	inflow	+£20,000
End of year 2	inflow	+£50,000
End of year 3	inflow	+£50,000

You are asked to provide a short report covering the following points.

(a) Your recommendation to proceed or hold back from investing in this particular new product together with supporting calculations showing the payback and NPV outcome   (10 marks)

(b) List of the main factors that influence your recommendation, commenting specifically on uncertainty and risk   (10 marks)
       (20 marks)

8   PRICING POLICIES

A producer of high quality executive motor cars has developed a new model which it knows to be very advanced both technically and in style by comparison with the competition in its market segment.

The company's reputation for high quality is well established and its servicing network in its major markets is excellent. However, its record in timely delivery has not been so good in previous years, though this has been improving considerably.

In the past few years it has introduced annual variations and improvements in its major models. When it launched a major new vehicle some six years ago the recommended retail price was so low in relation to the excellent specification of the car that a tremendous demand built up quickly and a two-year queue for the car developed within six months. Within three months a secondhand model had been sold at an auction for nearly 50% more than the list price and even after a year of production a sizeable premium above the list price was being obtained.

The company considers that, in relation to the competition, the proposed new model will be as attractive as was its predecessor six years ago. Control of costs is very good so that accurate cost data for the new model are to hand. For the previous model, the company assessed the long-term targeted annual production level and calculated its price on that basis. In the first year, production was 30% of that total.

For the present model the company expects that the relationship between the first year's production and longer-term annual production will also be about 30%, though the absolute levels in both cases are expected to be higher than previously.

The senior management committee, of which you are a member, has been asked to recommend the pricing approach that the company should adopt for the new model.

Required

List the major pricing approaches available in this situation and discuss in some detail the relative merits and disadvantages to the company of each approach in the context of the new model.

       (20 marks)

9   TRANSFER PRICING

Your organisation is currently trying to develop an internal transfer price that truly reflects all costs involved and acts as a motivator to the internal supplier as well as being attractive to the internal purchaser. Internal purchasers are being encouraged to seek outside tenders to compete with internal suppliers. You have been asked to write a brief report to the marketing director that explains clearly:

(a) The principle behind transfer prices   (5 marks)

(b) The *two* most common methods of setting a transfer price   (5 marks)

(c) An evaluation of the relative merits for each method you have described (You should illustrate your answer with examples drawn from your own organisation or an organisation of your choice.)   (10 marks)
       (20 marks)

10 BREAKEVEN

A business breaks even when the contribution from the sales activity is equal to all the fixed expenses.

This is frequently expressed in graphical or computational form. In computational form:

$$\text{Sales} - \text{Variable Costs} - \text{Fixed Costs} = 0 \quad or$$
$$S - V - F = 0$$

Required

(a) Use your understanding of this concept to produce a formula that could be used to establish the level of sales required to produce a profit of £40,000 from a production company which makes two products Q and R in the fixed proportion 9:17. Assume that 26X (9 + 17) units are produced in total, 9X being product Q and 17X being product R.

(b) Calculate the turnover figure needed if the fixed costs are £45,000 and the contribution is 15% from Q and 20% from R. The selling price of Q is £30 and the selling price of R is £40.

11 PROMOTIONAL CAMPAIGN APPRAISAL

The existing retail price for a particular carbonated drink brand is £0.50 and the product is sold in cased packs of 12 cans. The average retail margin is 20 pence a can, which means that the manufacturers achieve a gross selling price of 30 pence per can or £3.60 per pack. It has been suggested that a reduction of 10 pence per can in retail price will increase overall sales. Promotion costs are to be absorbed by the manufacturer and the retailer's margin will be maintained at 20% per can.

Cost structure-manufacturer

	£
Selling price per cased pack	3.60
Direct costs	1.00
Contribution per case	2.60

Sales forecast   *'000 cases*

Week	1	2	3	4	5	6
With promotion	10	10	12	12	14	12
Without promotion	10	10	10	10	10	10
Gain/(loss)	0	0	2	2	4	2

The promotion is forecast to result in an additional 20,000 cases of the product being sold.

Required

As a marketing manager responsible for evaluating the possible effect of the promotion, write a brief report to the sales and marketing director which evaluates and explains the possible financial gains and losses and your recommendation as to whether or not the promotion should go ahead, with supporting reasons and appropriate calculations. You are specifically asked to comment upon the sensitivity of the promotion to a 10% variation in sales forecasts. **(20 marks)**

12 FLEXIBLE BUDGETS

Your company has a particular product which it sells at a premium price to a small number of major customers. The product is very profitable achieving 50% gross margin. The product selling price is £200 per unit sold and the company forecast for this year is to sell 5000 units. The company's other products achieve an average gross margin of 30% and total forecast sales for these products this year are £2 million. Fixed overheads are budgeted at £1,000,000 for the company for the year.

(a) Prepare a flexible budget which shows what the profitability of the premium product and other products would be if forecasts overall are only 70% of the expected sales level forecast. (8 marks)

(b) Discuss the importance of having accurate sales forecasts in the context of the flexed budgets you have prepared. (8 marks)

(c) Sales of the premium product only take place twice a year and in equal volume in June and December. The major customers who buy this product take 6 months' credit. Your company's current cost of capital is estimated to be 10% per annum. Briefly explain the effect of allowing extended credit to these customers upon (i) cash flow and (ii) profitability. (4 marks)
(20 marks)

13   DEPARTMENTAL BUDGET

You have been asked to work with the Finance Department in your organisation to prepare the sales and marketing departmental budget.

Write a report that covers the following points.

(a)   An explanation outlining the ways in which such a budget might be prepared   (10 marks)

(b)   An explanation of the key objectives that such a budget should achieve   (10 marks)

(20 marks)

14   THE BIG EVENT MARKETING GROUP

You have joined the Big Event Marketing (BEM) Group from the Marketing Department of a national newspaper where you have been involved with promotional and marketing activities similar to those that the BEM Group organise. The group are currently bidding to secure a number of major contracts for 1999 and 2000. You have been asked to lead one of the teams bidding for the contract to run four high profile seminars with the title 'Managing in the New Millennium'. There are a number of aspects to the organisation of the tender for the contract that the client has specifically requested in their brief:

(a)   It is important that an Internet Website is established to publicise and inform prospective delegates about the event.

(b)   The whole event must make a profit and this had been set at a minimum of 25%.

You have already done some preliminary market research and established the following facts:

(a)   Demand is likely to be high for such seminars providing you are able to attract high quality speakers. You hope to attract 150 delegates to each event. In this context it is likely that the daily cost for a small number of speakers of reasonable repute will be in the region of £20,000. In addition it will be necessary to attract other speakers with a small expense budget who may be prepared to come to publicise their own organisation (eg management consultancy firms, high technology providers and the like).

(b)   In order to keep costs down and to maximise profitability you have already decided to hold a series of four one day events with optional overnight accommodation. You have negotiated a special rate with a five star hotel group at £60 per person per night. The normal rate is more than double this. It is your intention to achieve the required rate of profit that still offers the room at a discount to the delegate. However, you will have to offer speakers their rooms free on the night before the event. It is expected that you will need to keep six rooms for use by speakers at each daily seminar and two rooms for your own BEM Group staff.

(c)   Other costs include: cost per delegate per day rate £100; conference proceedings and delegate bags £10 per head; incidental costs allowed for at £5 per delegate; your preliminary preparation costs amounting to £3,000 will need to be recovered against the event; you will also need to budget for staffing the event at £2,500 per event; you have allowed a budget of £2,000 for development and maintenance of the Internet site.

You now need to prepare a short report for an internal briefing of senior managers that covers the following points.

(a)   A budget that clearly shows the expected income and expenditure for the four planned events

(16 marks)

(b)   The price you will need to set for the event given that you need to achieve a 25% profit margin as a minimum   (8 marks)

(c)   An explanation of how your price and profit margins could be affected if you achieve only 80% of the planned number of delegates at the event   (8 marks)

(d)   Suggestions on how the internet website will be used by both your own company in establishing the event and by the delegates before, during and after the event   (8 marks)

(40 marks)

15   FINANCIAL PERFORMANCE INDICATORS

The company you work for has the following performance indicators for the last financial year.

(a)   Stock turnover four times per annum

(b)   Return on investment 6% per annum

(c)   Gross margin 50%

(d)   Net margin 10%

(e)   Debtor turnover three times per annum

Your current marketing manager has asked you to prepare a memorandum to explain to team members what each of the performance measures means and why they are important indicators of performance.

(20 marks)

16 SOURCES OF INFORMATION

What sources of information are available to marketing and sales managers wanting to gather market intelligence on competitors? Explain how each of the sources you have identified might be used in practice.

(20 marks)

17 DATA SOURCES FOR ASSESSING MARKET ENTRY VIABILITY

For an organisation of your choice describe the most useful sources of data for assessing the viability of an existing product in a new market. State clearly how the data you have suggested would be used in evaluating market entry viability.

(20 marks)

18 MARKETING RESEARCH PROCESS

Your organisation is concerned to improve customer service through better distribution of its product lines to retail stores. Currently the computer ordering system is linked directly to major retail customers who represent more than 70% of your total business through Electronic Data Interchange. Using this technology your firm is able to supply 90% of its product lines in less than three working days and 50% within 24 hours. You have been given the responsibility of conducting specific marketing research with the aim of identifying areas of possible improvement in the distribution and logistics function. You are asked to provide a report to your Marketing Manager that clearly outlines:

(a) The key stages necessary in conducting such research

(10 marks)

(b) What the specific objectives of the marketing research should be and how you propose to conduct the research

(10 marks)

(20 marks)

19 RESEARCH FOR PRODUCT LAUNCH

You are newly appointed as a marketing manager in a publishing company and have been given specific responsibility for a new product launch. Your organisation wants to introduce a new magazine aimed at the teenage female market as identified as part of last year's strategic review. In this respect you have been given a budget of £30,000 to conduct further market research prior to the launch. Explain how you would plan and conduct this research. You are required to give the specific stages in your research plan and evaluate and justify each of your chosen options.

(20 marks)

20 RESEARCH TECHNIQUES

There are a number of specific marketing research techniques that may be employed to research consumer behaviour. An airline you are advising on marketing research is concerned to find out why customers:

(a) Choose their airline, and
(b) The services that customer value highly and are prepared to pay a premium price for

Required

Write a brief report on the three specific research techniques that are listed below and explain the appropriateness of the techniques listed to achieve the stated research objectives. You should provide a brief but clear explanation of each technique and discuss how it may be used in this context.

(a) Shopping mall tests
(b) Focus groups
(c) Postal questionnaires

(20 marks)

1   **MARKETING INFORMATION SYSTEM (MKIS)**

(a)   A Marketing Information System (MkIS) is a system designed to supply relevant information into the marketing management's decision making process. A well designed MkIS will allow easy access to information on the market and business environment. The system is usually part of the company's Management Information System and is often computerised.

The key elements of the Marketing Information System (MkIS) are outlined below. The diagram shows the linkages between these elements.

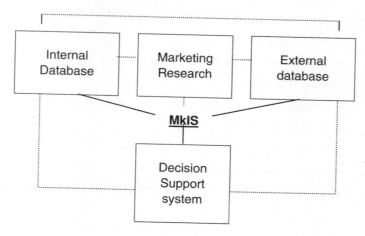

Hines '97

Internal Database

This part of the system contains data that are readily available within the organisation, for example data on sales, stocks, purchases, accounts, customer records, costs, complaints and any other relevant records which are generated and used for other purposes.

External Database

This database is populated from externally available sources of information such as Government reports, Trade reports, DTI databases, Mintel and so on.

Marketing Research

This is systematically collected data relating to the marketing of the organisation's products and services. This can be research specially commissioned by the company or can be syndicated research or general research by an external agency or organisation.

Decision Support Systems

These are internal systems that have been devised to help with decision making. These systems allow the data from the databases to be manipulated to produce forecasts and to examine different scenarios. In this way they assist in the decision making process by indicating likely solutions.

(b)   The most suitable technology for such a system is computer based. The information will need to be held in a database or series of databases (eg MS Access databases) which can be accessed, to produce the management information required. The most effective solution is to network the information so that it can be accessible in a number of different locations around the organisation. Historically the choice would be either a WAN or LAN, however now there is the added possibility of hosting such a system on an Intranet. The choice of which route is likely to be dictated by budget and availability of hardware and software.

Software and programming would be required to manipulate and to display the required data in a useable format. This can be 'off-the-shelf' software or can be written to your own specifications and requirements. The latter may be marginally more expensive, but this type of solution produces a system which is tailored to the organisation's needs as opposed to the compromise usually offered by off-the-shelf software.

Whichever system is chosen, consideration must be given to how both internal and external information will be incorporated into the system, as it is important to ensure that the systems are fully compatible.

(c) **Plan**

The introduction a system of this type is fraught with potential problems and therefore correct planning into the investigation of requirements and system design is essential. I propose that the planning process consists of the following elements.

(i) **Setting of objectives**

Objectives should be SMART and should state what the system is needed for what it is intended to do.

(ii) **Information should be identified for each element of the system**

(1) **Internal Databases**

Eg Sales records, stock information and costs

(2) **External Databases**

Eg Inflation forecasts, DTI records, Trade and Industry Databases

(3) **Marketing Research**

Eg Syndicated and general industry research

(4) **Decision Support System**

How data will be taken from the above databases, amalgamated and manipulated.

2 FEATURES OF THE MKIS

Applied Marketing Information System (MkIS)

Marketing Information Systems (MkIS) are used to help marketing managers make better decisions. As many business environments are undergoing change at an ever increasing pace, the making of swift and well judged decisions is essential to all businesses. An efficient MkIS system will provide timely and accurate information and will also prevent managers from being overloaded with redundant information.

A Marketing Information System consists of four major components (Kotler, 1988).

Internal Reporting System

This part of the MkIS utilises internal records of the company. Although these records have been generated for some other purpose, they provide an invaluable insight into the current activity and performance of the company. Data such as sales records, invoices, production records, accounts and so on are used in a system of this type. Many of these records are now stored on computerised databases and therefore storage, retrieval and analysis of such records is relatively quick and easy.

These records prove invaluable in an MkIS system as the current operations of a business can be analysed and understood. It is good marketing practice to build any strategy or plan from an understanding of 'where we are now' and this system provides that understanding.

In our organisation, for example, these records have been used to provide an understanding of size and growth of customer segments, buying patterns, product profitability's and many other areas.

Marketing Intelligence System

This system collects and stores everyday information about the external environment. Information such as industry reports, competitors marketing materials and competitors quotes. Information collected here allows a company to build a more accurate profile of the external environment.

Taking our company as an example, it allows us to calculate market sizes and growth patterns, competitor positioning and pricing strategy etc. This information has assisted us in decision making in many areas such as gap analysis, segmentation and targeting, market development and pricing strategy.

Marketing Research System

This system uses primary marketing research techniques to gather, evaluate and report findings in order to minimise guesswork in business decisions. The system is used to fill essential information gaps which are not covered by the other components of the MkIS system. In this way it provides targeted and detailed information for the decision making problem at hand.

We have used marketing research in the past to provide detailed information on new product concepts, attitudes to marketing communication messages, testing advertising effectiveness and understanding our customer perceptions of our service delivery.

Analytical Market System

This system provides the tools to undertake complex analysis of the information gained in other parts of the MkIS system in order to provide solutions for business problems.

In our organisation the analytical marketing system is still under development. However, we have developed a price sensitivity analysis tool which provides a good example of this type of system. This computerised tool uses internal data from our sales records, together with market share and pricing information on competitors from our intelligence system to calculate the price sensitivity on our best selling products.

Each of the components of the MkIS system is important in providing key information for business decision making. By using information of this type, decisions can be based on more detailed and accurate information and therefore the risk associated with decision making is minimised.

3   **INTEGRATING INTERNAL DATA SOURCES**

To: Managing Director
From: Marketing Manager
Subject: Integrating internal data sources
Date: 8 December 20XX

The following report examines the feasibility of integrating internal sources of data to begin the process of developing a company wide marketing information system.

Within our industry, the licence trade, availability of information has grown rapidly since the introduction of IT into our pubs and bars. Information availability has bee further enhanced by the computerisation of our head office with its centrally located functional departments.

As almost all sales, stock, ordering and invoicing systems are now computerised the possibilities for storing, retrieving and analysing information has been made easier and quicker.

(a)   Internal **data sources** and possible system applications

A comprehensive marketing information system (MkIS) comprises the four components of an internal reporting system, a market intelligence system, a marketing research system and an analytical marketing system. Being multi-faceted, MkIS systems are complex and therefore time consuming and difficult to establish. As we already have a wealth of computerised internal information, it is appropriate for us to begin the process of MkIS development with an internal reporting system. Information to be used in this system would be as follows.

(i)   **From bars and pubs**

Overall and by product sales, stocking and ordering information from the individual outlets.

(ii)   **From head office**

Outlet accounting information such as variable and fixed costs, product profitability, personnel and staffing records.

This information could be analysed in order to assist decision making in different areas such as product and outlet life cycle analysis, price sensitivity analysis, product promotions effectiveness, supplier performance analysis and even non marketing related area such as management incentive schemes and staff appraisal.

(b)   **Hardware** requirement

Most of the hardware requirement for setting up an internal records system is already in place. At the outlets we already use EPOS (Electronic point of sales) technology to gather sales information. Information gathered by the system is very comprehensive and currently we do not use it to its fullest extent. As each operator has to swipe their personal swipe card to enter the tills, we gather information on product sales, price, time sold and staff member serving. All this information is stored on site on a PC and is used to run the stocking and ordering systems for the outlet.

In order to take full advantage of the information we must collect and analyse it centrally at Head Office. To do this we must incorporate communications technology within the outlet PCs. By

BPP
PUBLISHING

placing a modem on each of these machines, we could send the information to a PC at Head Office.

(c) Specific **software**

Major software to be used on such a system would be database, spreadsheet and communications software. Even though we are dealing with large amounts of data it would be possible to use Windows based packages such as MS Access database, Excel spreadsheets and FTP software (File Transfer Protocol) to transfer information via phone lines between the PCs.

Currently the EPOS systems are storing data on a bespoke software package designed specifically for stocking and ordering purposes. I am informed by IT however, that the information can be easily transferred to a proprietary database such as Access. Having it in this format is recommended, as this package is far more flexible in manipulating and analysing the data. The data can also easily be transferred to a spreadsheet for time series analysis and graphing purposes.

4 SALES FORECASTING

For a company to plan adequately for the future it must make some assessment regarding future sales. Factory contraction or expansion will depend on forecasts of future demand for the products. As well as having objectives, companies have resources such as plants, employees and money. For objectives to be met, resources must be allocated, and the basis of this planning is sales forecasting.

Forecasts are, of course, only as good as the assumptions on which they are based. They have to take account of both the controllable and the uncontrollable factors which surround the business environment. **Controllable elements** include the marketing mix variables of product, price, place and promotion. **Uncontrollable elements** are not within the company's control and include legal and political changes, consumer tastes and competitors' actions.

From these forecasts, decisions must be made as to the strategy of the firm. Within a company, sales forecasting is used to determine the actions of a number of departments.

In the **marketing department** sales forecasts are used to plan the marketing mix requirements.

Production will require sales forecasts to determine future product types and specifications. It can therefore produce the products in an efficient manner and keep stocks at appropriate levels.

Personnel departments need to assess the future staffing needs of the company.

The **finance department** will want to have sales forecasts on which to base forecasts of future profit.

Three methods of sales forecasting will now be discussed.

(a) **Time series models**

Time series models take historical data and project trends in to the future. The basic reasoning behind this is that what has happened in the past is indicative of what will happen in the future. This, of course, will be more likely in the short term than in the long term when changing customer tastes or technological innovation will change sales dramatically. For this reason it is suitable as a method of forecasting short-term sales so that an accurate assessment of production needs can be made. It also requires that there is an adequate amount of historical data available to base predictions on. It is therefore not very appropriate to use in the early stages of the product's life.

The first task of the forecaster is to plot the data and look at the shape of the trend in sales, often taking moving averages to view the sales.

If there is not much fluctuation and the data plotted is more or less horizontal this usually indicates the product is in the maturity stage of the product life cycle and is relatively well established.

If the data shows short-term fluctuations this is often due to *seasonal aspects*. Seasonal data can indicate climatic changes in demand, or changes due to seasonal celebrations such as Christmas or Easter. This can allow management to plan production and staffing levels that take into account fluctuating seasonal demand.

Cyclical fluctuations are similar to seasonal changes but last longer. Data that shows a trend of growth or decline can often be related to these stages in the PLC.

Inflation needs to be taken into account when analysing time series data, as otherwise sales value figures are distorted upwards. It is also worth noting that data can show seasonality at the same time as the business cycle is affecting the data, although if needed some of the trends can be 'smoothed' so the important data can be analysed.

(b) **Causal models**

Causal models, like time series, use quantitative data. Equations relating the dependent variable (future sales) to a number of independent variables are calculated. For example, sales could be said to be a function of relative price, complementary goods sales and advertising. Each of the independent variables are weighted to take account of their importance. Variables can also be lagged, so last year's sales figures can be incorporated. This method also uses historical data and therefore enough of this type of data is necessary to make an accurate forecast.

As this method looks for causal relationships, statistical measures and tests can be applied to the results and regression analysis applied.

Causal models are longer term than time series and therefore can be used to predict the future needs of plant size and/or workforce. However, although these models are easier to formulate with the increased use of computers, they are still expensive and difficult to construct and analyse. They are very useful, though, because they analyse what the determinants of sales are and the impact of changes to these variables can be measured. They are only as good as the variables that have been incorporated, however, and if a major variable has been omitted then this can ruin the analysis.

(c) **Qualitative models**

If there is little quantitative data on which to base sales forecasts then qualitative methods can be used. Lack of historical data can be caused because the product is new on the market or because of a major social or technological change that makes past data obsolete.

Qualitative models are usually used for long-term forecasts, and they have the advantages of being relatively cheap and easy to understand. However, they are not very accurate because of the uncertainty associated with long-term forecasts. Examples of the type of forecasts that can be made using this method are forecasts of technological and social changes. These type of forecasts rely on expert opinions to predict the future. There are two main types of technique available.

The first is **explorative**, which starts at the present date with current knowledge and then tries to predict the future from this.

The second is **normative**, which looks at an innovation at a future date (such as a commercially viable electric car) and investigates the stages that are required to fulfil this change.

As can be seen from the descriptions of some of the available techniques outlined above, the 'best' technique will depend entirely on what needs to be forecast.

5   PROFIT VS CASH

(a) The measurement of profitability is governed by two basic concepts of accounting, those of prudence and matching. Where these two concepts conflict, then the prudence aspect will generally be pre-eminent. Added to this is the premise that accountants will attempt to reflect the activity basis of any action or transaction within the accounts.

These fundamental concepts will regularly result in differences in timing between an activity and the result or benefit of that activity. For example, it is common business practice to sell goods on credit. The accountant will recognise a sale well before the cash has been collected. If we sell goods on very long periods of credit or even on a sale and return bases the activity of the sale will be recognised well before the cash has been received.

Similarly, the accountant will wish to rely on the prudence concept in trying to provide for or measure the extent to which a fixed asset of the business is being used up. This is known as depreciation, and it reflects the extent to which, say, a machine used in the manufacture of a product has been utilised in making that product. It is not a cash-based activity but a way of identifying a need to replace assets which will lose value over time. This permanent reduction in the asset value is charged to profit but no cash will have been spent.

Finally, cash can be generated and used up in a number of ways which are not a part of the trading activities of the business. These sources and utilisations of funds would include cash movements caused by way of issuing shares or by way of loan, by the buying and selling of fixed assets such as machinery, cars or offices and by the payment of items such as company tax and dividends which are usually identified in the last year's profit statement.

The net result is that profit is not synonymous with cash and the need to monitor and manage both aspects is critical to business performance.

(b)   Most of a marketing manager's effort is channelled into the activity of order filling. For an existing product or service this may mean that the marketing manager will wish to spend cash now in order to generate a future benefit. The most obvious example of this is the use of current expenditure on media support, the benefit of which in term of sales activity may not be felt for some time.

The accountant will rely in this case on the concept of prudence. There may be an argument to suggest that the cost of the marketing activity (in this example advertising) should be deferred and notched against the future benefit (the sales revenue). However, because this revenue shown in the future is not absolutely certain the accountant will charge the cost immediately and only account for the sales activity when it occurs.

Similarly, a sale may be considered complete when the goods are transferred from seller to buyer. Indeed this will be reflected in the accounts of a company; but the cash may not have been collected. The inability of the company to collect that cash will result in a bad debt being incurred and this is considered a business expense which will again be reflected in the profit statement. So two transactions have been reflected in the profit statement, a sale and a bad debt, but no cash has changed hands.

One area where specific attention to the difference between cash and profit is most evident in the development of a new product. Here the marketing manager will be involved in market research, product design, product testing, product launching, asset purchasing (to perhaps expand existing production facilities) and finally product portfolio management. Many of these activities will need to be funded by a scarce resource: cash. But the benefits will only accrue at some time in the future. Some of his activity will not affect the profit statement immediately (such as buying the production assets, although they will depreciate over time as they are used). Certainly the majority of these activities will affect both cash and the current year's profits but in different measures. The benefits will be shown in the profit statement of a future period.

The marketing manager must be aware of the need for cash to fund his projects and the understanding that being profitable today does not mean the business has surplus funds. He must identify his needs within the overall corporate framework.

6   ACTIVITY BASED COSTING

To: Marketing Manager
From: John Kemp
Date: 12 June 20XX
Subject: **Activity Based Costing - Advantages and Disadvantages for Budgetary Control**

(a)   **An explanation of Activity Based Costing**

Traditionally, overheads were allocated to products, activities or departments on a simple basis, such as in proportion to the direct labour or direct materials that they consumed. Errors made in attributing overheads in this way were not too significant because organisations had narrow ranges of products and the overheads were likely to form only a small proportion of total costs.

As firms have become more efficient overheads have made up an increasing proportion of total costs.

Support activities may make up a high proportion of these overheads. Traditional costing systems assume that all products consume all resources in proportion to their production volumes. They therefore tend to allocate too great a proportion to high volume products, and too little too low volume products (which cause great diversity and therefore use more support services).

It is important, therefore, to allocate overheads more accurately and modern sophisticated computer systems can enable organisations to do this.

Activity based costing (ABC) attempts to overcome the shortcomings of traditional methods. It recognises the following.

(i)   Activities cause costs. Activities may include ordering, materials handling, machining, assembly, production scheduling and dispatching.

(ii)   Producing product creates demand for the activities.

(iii)   Costs are assigned to a product on the basis of the product's consumption of the activities.

To summarise

In both traditional costing and ABC, costs are grouped together (into cost centres in traditional systems, and cost pools in ABC). Whereas costs are usually absorbed on the basis of labour hours or machine hours using traditional methods, ABC absorbs them using many **cost drivers** such as number of orders, number of deliveries, etc. Thus ABC should produce more realistic product costs.

(b) **Advantages and disadvantages of using Activity Based Costing from a marketing perspective**

Advantages

(i) ABC recognises that traditional costing methods often place great emphasis on labour or machine costs, and allocates overheads on a more realistic basis. This assists in making sensible production, pricing and marketing decisions.

(ii) ABC recognises that the complexity of manufacturing has increased with wide product ranges, short product life cycles, short product runs, etc. ABC recognises this with the use of multiple cost drivers.

(iii) ABC takes costing beyond its traditional factory floor boundaries. It recognises the importance of many non-factory floor activities such as product design, quality control, production planning, customer service, sales administration, etc.

(iv) More meaningful product costs are calculated. Therefore correct decisions can be taken when deciding, for example, whether to continue production of a product or discontinue production.

(v) ABC can give valuable insights into product design, product mix, processing methods, administration and pricing. It can help highlight non-value-added activities such as stock holding, set-up costs, etc and help identify the drivers that produce these costs. These can then be controlled which should allow a more competitive price to be established. This in turn should increase sales volumes, although greater efficiency should mean that levels of profitability are maintained.

(vi) The review of existing costing systems and the consideration of ABC approaches help management (including sales and marketing) direct attention on key business issues and investigate business processes and measures of performance. ABC has been extended to the setting of benchmarking parameters and strategic performance indicators, thus working towards a concept of activity based management.

Disadvantages

(i) ABC should only be introduced if managers will gain something from it. If it is to be used to determine the best product mix, or to control non-value added activities, it may be worthwhile. If not, it is easier to stick to a simple traditional absorption costing system.

(ii) If it is to be useful, cost drivers (such as number of sales orders), need to be identified correctly. If this is not the case, the system will produce inaccurate product costings.

(iii) ABC systems are likely to be costly, in terms of the initial computer hardware and software, and in terms of administration time needed to work the system.

(iv) ABC is more useful where overheads constitute a high proportion of costs. If this is not the case it is better to use a simpler and cheaper system.

(v) If an ABC system is to be adopted the change needs to be managed. For instance there may be resistance to the new system from marketing and operations managers who are used to a traditional absorption costing system.

7   PAYBACK AND NET PRESENT VALUE

REPORT ON NEW PRODUCT X

(a) **Recommendation on whether or not to invest**

On the basis of the payback period and NPV calculations set out below, I recommend that we do not invest in new product X. Although the investment is paid back within three years, the payback method of investment appraisal does not take account of the time value of money and hence is inferior to the net present value method of investment appraisal, which shows that the overall net present value of the investment will be negative. The investment should therefore not go ahead.

(i) **Payback method**

Year	Cash flow £	Cumulative cash flow £
0	(100,000)	(100,000)
1	20,000	(80,000)
2	50,000	(30,000)
3	50,000	20,000

The investment is therefore paid back during year 3 (after 2 years and 31.2 weeks to be exact).

(ii) **NPV method**

Year	Cash flow £	Discount factor 10%	Present value £
0	(100,000)	1.000	(100,000)
1	20,000	0.909	18,180
2	50,000	0.826	41,300
3	50,000	0.751	37,550
NPV			(2,970)

(b) **Other factors to consider**

(i) Quantitative methods of investment appraisal (such as the NPV method and the payback method) ignore qualitative and other business reasons that may exist for proceeding with or holding back from an investment. They also ignore the cost of 'doing nothing'. Taking no action often has a cost which is frequently overlooked.

(ii) The calculations in (a) above are based on **estimates** of future cash flows and discount rates and hence what **actually** occurs may turn out to be entirely different to the scenario painted using the estimates. Some attempt should therefore be made to account for the risk and uncertainty surrounding the future.

(1) Cash flows and discount rates representing the best possible and worst possible scenarios could be used in payback and NPV calculations in order to ascertain what might happen under the most favourable and the most unfavourable conditions.

(2) Sensitivity analysis could be performed whereby key variables such as the various cash inflows or the discount rate could be varied in order to determine at what point the NPV becomes positive and the investment worthwhile.

It should be noted that the longer the period covered by the forecast or estimated figures, the greater the risk and uncertainty surrounding the decision.

(iv) The selection of an appropriate discount rate can be difficult. Both internal and external factors play a part.

(v) There may be other business or strategic reasons why the investment should proceed, despite the indication of the payback and NPV calculations. Product X may be the first in a product range to be released and is to be a loss leader, for example.

8 PRICING POLICIES

The major pricing approaches available to the company are as follows.

(a) **A high price policy**

The company could charge prices which are higher than those of their competitors with the result that profit margins would be high but sales volumes would probably be lower than with a low price policy.

(b) **A low price policy**

Prices could be the lowest in the market which would probably lead to high sales volumes but low profit margins.

(c) **An average price policy**

An average price policy would involve setting prices at the average level for the market and the effects would probably be between those of a high price policy and a low price policy.

One other option that might be available is to operate a policy of price discrimination. This would mean charging different prices to different groups of customers. It is unlikely that the company would be able to keep markets separate in this way and therefore this option has not been analysed further.

The merits and disadvantages of each approach are as follows.

(a) **A high price policy**

Merits

The company has a reputation for high quality and an excellent servicing network; a high price would be in keeping with this quality image.

A high price would enable the company to pursue a skimming strategy of creaming off the high profits available from the new model before competitors enter the market with comparable products.

The new model is advanced both technically and in style compared with competitors and a high price would take full advantage of these differentiating factors.

The executive car market may not be price sensitive and could have a low price elasticity of demand. Sales volumes might not therefore be too adversely affected by a high price. In fact a high price might encourage more executives to purchase because of the prestige attached to driving an expensive car.

A high price will enable the company to recoup research and development costs more quickly.

A high price might enable the company to avoid losses in the early years, especially in view of the fact that the first year's production is expected to be only 30% of the longer-term annual production.

The company will have more room to adjust prices if they begin with a high price. It is generally easier to decrease prices than it is to increase them. In addition they will be able to reduce prices in the future as competitors launch products which begin to erode the advantage of the new model's differentiating factors.

Disadvantages

High prices may lead to lower sales volumes than might otherwise be achieved. The company will lose the opportunity to build market share at the expense of their competitors.

The experience of customer queues six years ago may mean that customers do not view the company favourably and will not be willing to pay a high price.

Lower sales volumes are likely to result in higher unit costs than with a policy of lower prices.

There is no evidence that any research has been carried out to see whether customers would actually be prepared to pay a higher price for the new model's differentiating factors.

(b) **A low price policy**

Merits

Charging lower prices means that the company will be pursuing a market penetration policy and attempting to build up market share. Research has shown that market share is a major factor in determining a company's long-term profitability. Japanese companies in particular have achieved success through a policy of target costing which involves identifying the price necessary to achieve a required market share and then using cost reduction techniques to bring costs down below this target price.

The company's control of costs is very good and therefore there may be scope for a cost reduction campaign to bring costs into line with the low target price.

Sales volumes are likely to be higher with a low price and the company will be able to benefit from the spreading of fixed costs and from any potential learning curve savings.

Disadvantages

The experience of the company six years ago suggests that a low price policy was not the correct one. Assuming that the executive car market has not changed substantially in this time then a low price policy should not be pursued.

A low price may have an adverse effect on the perceived quality of the car.

It may be difficult to increase prices in the future once the company has established a low price.

Losses are likely in the early years.

There is a risk that low prices will cause competitors to cut their prices and a price war could reduce the overall profitability of all competitors in the market.

(c) **An average price policy**

Merits

The risk of a price war is reduced if the company charges a price which is in line with competitor's prices.

There is a low risk of any of the problems which might arise with a very high price or a very low price.

The company has the ability to reduce prices in the future.

Disadvantages

There is a risk that demand will exceed supply, although the excess demand is not likely to be as great as with a low price policy.

If the company pursues an average price policy it will not be able to reap any of the advantages to be gained from a more extreme pricing strategy.

9 TRANSFER PRICING

Report to: The Marketing Director
From: Steve M Jones
Subject: Transfer Pricing
Date: 9 December 20XX

(a) A transfer price is the price at which goods or services are transferred from one process or department of a company to another. Transfer prices are often necessary where there is not a market price for the product. For instance, they can be used where internal departments of an organisation are transferring products or services to other departments. This is necessary so that the organisation can set the correct price, based on true costs, to the end customer. Prices have to be set which are fair and administratively simple.

For instance, **Department A** may produce a product which it passes on to **Department B**. The costs of **Department A** need to be incorporated into the product, which is eventually sold by **Department B** to the organisation's end customer.

If a transfer price was not set, **Department B** would have no real way of knowing the costs of **Department A**. If that were the case, **Department B** might sell the product to the end customer at an unrealistic price. Transfer prices can be seen as a way of promoting divisional autonomy, but without discouraging corporate profit maximisation.

(b) (i) **At cost**

The transfer price can be set at cost. In this case, the costing system in **Department A** would merely record all the costs which are involved in the product or service before it is passed on to **Department B**. When a transfer is made, **Department A** would show revenue and **Department B** would show a cost.

(ii) **Cost plus a mark-up**

Another common method of setting a transfer price is at cost plus a mark-up. So, **Department A** records the costs which go into the product or service and then adds a mark-up so that the department can sell on to **Department B** at a profit.

(c) (i) **At cost**

The merits are as follows.

(1) The system is simple to set up and administer. There is no need to establish a mark-up. However, the transferring division makes no profit.

(2) There is no conflict between departments over the mark-up on the product or service. Mark-up can certainly lead to arguments between departments. Head office mediation is often required.

(3) If a mark-up is set on internal products, there is a danger that the organisation can price itself out of the market, ie each department establishes a mark-up before passing the product or service on, and the end price to the customer is inflated. If products are charged on a cost however, there is no danger of this happening.

(4) The organisation can focus on the cost of producing its goods or services. If the costs of the goods or services are inflated by a mark-up, it can be difficult for managers within the organisation to determine the real costs of production and therefore it can be more difficult for them to make cost savings.

(ii) **Cost plus a mark-up**

The merits are as follows.

(1) If a mark-up is added, the department which is passing the product or service on can make a profit. This can mean that the staff are motivated to do their job more efficiently and effectively. The problem is establishing a transfer price at which both profit centres will maximise their profits.

(2) Managers within a department are made responsible for producing a profit and targeted accordingly. This can encourage innovation and entrepreneurship.

(3) This method can make it easier for senior managers to benchmark their organisation against other organisations. For instance, they can compare the costs of an internally produced product or service with the cost of products or services which are produced outside of the organisation. This can make it easier for them to decide whether to continue to produce in-house or subcontract outside.

10   BREAKEVEN

(a) There are several methods of approaching the break even calculation but it matters not how it is arrived at, the result will be the same. The breakeven level of activity for any business is the level at which the business revenue is exactly equal to all the expenses. This is expressed as a formula in the question. The formula can be adjusted to determine other levels of turnover needed to meet other targets. This can be done by adding the new requirements to the fixed cost. In this question, to meet management requirements the sum of the required profits and the fixed costs can be treated as notional 'fixed costs' and the formula used as follows.

Sales − Variable Costs − (Fixed Costs + Profit)　　　= 0

This is abbreviated for convenience: $S − V − (F + P) = 0$

In this particular case, we also need to note that the contribution is derived from two products made in the constant ratio 9:17. Let us say that the number of units to be produced will be $(9 + 17) X = 26X$ ∴$9X$ units of Q will be produced and $17X$ units of R.

This gives us:

$$((30 \times 9X)+(40 \times 17X)) − ((9X \times 25.50^*) + (17X \times 32.00^{**})) − (45,000+40,000) = \quad 0$$
$$950X − (229.5X + 544X) − 85,000 = \quad 0$$
$$176.5X = \quad 85,000$$
$$X = \quad 482$$
$$(481.5864)$$

* $£30 \times (100 − 15)\%$
** $£40 \times (100 − 20)\%$

	Q	R
(b) The required sales are therefore		
In units $(482 \times 9)/(482 \times 17)$	4,338	8,194
In value $(4,338 \times £30)/(8,194 \times £40)$	£130,140	£327,760

Proof

	£
Sales of Q = $482 \times 9 \times 30$	130,140
R = $482 \times 17 \times 40$	327,760
	457,900
Variable Costs	
Q = $482 \times 9 \times 25.5$	110,619
R = $482 \times 17 \times 32$	262,208
	372,827
Gross profit	85,073
Fixed expenses	45,000
Budgeted net profit	40,073*

*Difference due to rounding

11   PROMOTIONAL CAMPAIGN APPRAISAL

FORECASTS FOR DRINKS PROMOTION - APPENDIX I

The costs can be reviewed as follows.

	Values per pack	
	Original	*With promotion*
	£	£
Retail selling price (12 × £0.50)/(12 × £0.40)	6.00	4.80
Retailer's margin (12 × £0.20)	2.40	2.40
Therefore maximum manufacturer's selling price	3.60	2.40
Since the manufacturer's direct costs are	1.00	1.00
The *contribution* will be	2.60	1.40

Projected total contribution	60,000 cases		£156,000	
	80,000 cases			£112,000

The matter is further complicated by the fact that only 10,000 in the increased sales are budgeted for the **immediate** future and there is no information about the projected sales **without** the promotion during the period that the second 10,000 increased sales are generated.

Sensitivity

If the sales forecasts are subject to a 10% variation the figures to be considered are as follows.

| | *Original* | *With promotion* |
	£	£
Forecast understated by 10%		
Contribution from 66,000 cases	171,600	
Contribution from 88,000 cases		123,200
Forecast overstated by 10%		
Contribution from 54,000 cases	140,400	
Contribution from 72,000 cases		100,800

REPORT

To: Sales and Marketing Director
From: Marketing Manager
Date: 11 June 20XX
Subject: Fizzy Drinks Promotion

As requested I have carried out a review of the proposed promotion of the Fizzy Drink. I have attached a separate computational appendix (Appendix I) which I will refer to in this report.

You will see from these computations that in the short term there can be no justification for this campaign.

The revised contribution from this product line will result in a loss of contribution of some £44,000 [ie £156,000 − £112,000] over the short term, assuming sales change from 60,000 cases to 80,000 cases. It is not clear, however, whether a further contribution could be anticipated from sales under the original budget during the period of the extra 10,000 sales not detailed in the brief.

The question of **sensitivity** has been reviewed. It is clear that there can be no financial case for this promotion. Even if the forecasts for the original budget are revised down by 10% and the promotional figures revised up by 10% there is still a shortfall of contribution for 34,000 [88,000 − 54,000] units of more than £17,000 [£140,400 − £123,200 = £17,200]. You can see the consequences of changing the budgeted sales in Appendix I.

There are additional problems. The sales pattern for the short term suggests that there will be no changes in sales in the first two weeks of the campaign but we will have to produce more to **create stock** for sale in week three. This may have some effect on **cash flow**. Also, with increased sales we will have **increased debtors** that will have to be funded at a time when our contribution is being reduced.

This campaign could only be justified if it could be demonstrated that the additional sales could be retained in the **long term** when we revert to the original price. There is no such evidence to hand at the present time and therefore I strongly recommend that this campaign is abandoned.

12 FLEXIBLE BUDGETS

(a)

	Premium Activity Level 100% £	Activity level 70% £	Others Activity level 100% £	Activity level 70% £	Total Activity level 100% £	Activity level 70% £
Sales	1,000,000	700,000	2,000,000	1,400,000	3,000,000	2,100,000
Gross Margin	500,000	350,000	600,000	420,000	1,100,000	770,000
Fixed o/hds					1,000,000	1,000,000
Profit/(loss)					100,000	(230,000)

The above flexed budget shows the profit position if the sales forecast is achieved at 100% activity level and the position if the activity level is only 70% of the forecast sales.

(b) It is very important to have accurate sales forecasts when preparing financial plans and, in particular, budgets for specific periods. This is because the sales level is the principal factor in determining all other cost and expense figures. For this reason it is important to be as realistic as possible when forecasting sales. An optimistic view will overstate costs and expenses in the budget and managers in the organisation will plan their departmental or sectional budgets based upon this. This could lead to overspending in certain areas if the sales forecast has been too optimistic. Conversely, if the sales forecasts turned out to be pessimistic, unless flexible budgeting is in operation and is fully understood by budget holders and those responsible for controlling them, it may mean working to a fixed budget which restricts costs and expense budgets to the understated sales activity level.

In our example above, if the sales forecast turned out to be only 70% of the original forecast, it would result in an overall loss for the firm of £230,000 (even after taking account of flexible budgeting and allowing for costs that vary in proportion to the sales activity). It would appear that the company may be carrying too many fixed costs in proportion to sales turnover and that the gross margins being achieved are too tight to support them. This is evident if we look at the 100% activity level. The firm will only achieve a net profit equivalent to 3.3% of sales. £100,000 net profit is low on the turnover achieved compared with a gross margin equivalent to 36.66% of sales. Fixed costs appear to be at the heart of this problem.

(c) Cash flow would be adversely affected and operating costs would increase if extended credit were allowed to customers either by agreement or through weak financial controls. The effect could be to cause a cash flow problem and this may force the firm to take on or increase an overdraft facility to fund the customer's credit. Even if the firm was able and willing to fund extended credit out of its own cash resources this would involve the firm in cost. We are informed that the company's cost of capital is 10% per annum. If the firm decides to extend credit or customers take extended credit it has a cost implication of 10% per annum; the firm could have reduced its cost in other areas by using the cash from sales rather than buying in cash from external funding sources. Furthermore, even if a cost of capital had not been mentioned, it is important to recognise that the firm would incur an opportunity cost. For example, supposing the firm could invest cash and earn a return of 10%; this opportunity would be foregone if it had to use funds to support customer credit.

From a profitability point of view, assuming sales from the original forecast are £500,000 in June and £500,000 in December, the payment for June would be received in December and the one for December in the following June. Funding credit for six months would mean incurring a cost of £500,000 × 10% × 6/12 = £25,000.

Thus, if the cost of capital is 10% per annum, it would be costing £25,000 to fund extended credit over six months. Over a year this would involve the company incurring £50,000 in additional finance costs on the credit sale. This, in effect, would reduce profitability on the sales by £50,000 at the 100% sales activity level or £35,000 at the 70% level of sales activity.

13   DEPARTMENTAL BUDGET

REPORT

TO: Managing Director & Members of the Management Team
FROM: Andrew Jackson, Marketing Manager
SUBJECT: Sales and Marketing Departmental Budget
DATE: 21 July 20XX

(a)   **How the budget will be prepared**

In order to prepare the Sales & Marketing Departmental Budget, it is necessary to work closely with the finance department.

Firstly, I need to carry out an information gathering exercise. Internal information will be available from sources such as control and monitoring reports, and informal sources such as discussions and meetings. The information may include the following.

(i)   Marketing and sales information, eg revenue performance

(ii)   Production and operational information, eg production capacity

(iii)   Research and development information, eg new product launches

(iv)   Personnel information, eg anticipated salary increases for departmental staff

External information will also be available from formal sources, such as trade associations, and then from informal sources such as discussions and meetings. The information may include:

(i)   Market and competitors, eg level of competitor promotional activity.

(ii)   Economic conditions, eg level of inflation.

(iii)   Demographic trends and social factors, eg changes in the age profile of customers, which may affect promotional activity.

Although I shall be concerned mainly with producing a budgeted profit and loss account for the department, I shall also provide information to the Finance Department, so that they can input to their budgeted cash flow statement and balance sheet.

I intend to start with the budgeted sales. The sales figure is fundamental to the preparation of a sensible budget and I shall place great emphasis on being as accurate as possible.

Other headings which I shall need to budget for will be promotional spend, advertising, gifts, donations, wages, light and heat, motor and travelling expenses, subsistence, postage, printing and stationery, telephone, subscriptions, publications, sundry expenses, subcontracted work and apportionment of fixed overheads. There may well be additional headings to these and some of the above categories will be further analysed to give a greater level of detail.

The budget headings need to be discussed with appropriate personnel. For example, I shall discuss the wages budget with the Personnel Department and my fellow managers within the department, and I shall discuss apportionment of fixed overheads with the Finance Department. We shall take account of what happened in the last financial year and also take account of any changes which are planned. When we have prepared the total budget, we shall break it down into periods.

(b)   **An Explanation of the key objectives that such a budget should achieve**

The following are some of the reasons that budgets are prepared.

(i)   **To establish a system of control**

Control over actual performance is provided by the comparison of actual results against the budget plan. Departures from budget can then be investigated and action can be taken to improve performance.

(ii)   **To motivate employees to improve their performance**

The budget sets targets that employees can try to achieve.

(iii)   To provide a framework for responsibility accounting

Budgetary planning and control systems require that managers of budget centres are made responsible for the achievement of budget targets for the operations under their personal control.

(iv) **To co-ordinate activities**

The activities of different departments or sub-units of the organisation need to be co-ordinated to ensure maximum integration of efforts towards common goals. This means that each department is working towards the same ends, rather than working for different objectives.

(v) **To communicate ideas and plans**

A formal system is necessary to ensure that each person affected by the plans is aware of what he or she is supposed to be doing.

(vi) **To compel planning**

Planning is extremely important for an organisation. The budget helps to force management to look ahead and to set out detailed plans for achieving the targets for each department, operation and each manager.

(vii) **To estimate cash requirements**

A budget for each department enables the Finance Department to co-ordinate the cash requirements for the whole organisation. The Finance Department needs to have an estimate of the amount of expenditure that the department will incur on any major items, eg computer equipment.

14   **THE BIG EVENT MARKETING GROUP**

TO: Senior Managers
FROM: Marketing Manager
SUBJECT: Managing for the New Millennium
DATE: 25 July 20XX

(a)

		Event Budget (150 delegates) £	Event Budget (120 delegates) £	
Speakers		20,000	20,000	
Speakers & staff - Hotel room	(8 × £60)	480	480	
Delegate cost	(150 × £100)	15,000	12,000	(120 × £100)
Conference proceedings & delegate packs	(150 × £10)	1,500	1,200	(120 × £10)
Incidental costs	(150 × £5)	750	600	(120 × £5)
Preliminary preparation costs	(£3,000 ÷ 4)	750	750	
Staffing costs		2,500	2,500	
Internet site	(£2,000 ÷ 4)	500	500	
		41,480	38,030	
Number of events:		4	4	
Total Expenditure:		165,920	152,120	
Profit margin required: (Expenditure × 100/75)		221,227	202,827	
Price per delegate:	(£221,227 ÷ 600)	369	423	(£202,827 ÷ 480)

The budget above shows that the total expenditure for all four events, (given that 150 delegates attend each one), is envisaged to be £165,920.

(b)   The price which will be set for each delegate will be £369 - (see workings above).

(c)   The table above shows that if only 80% of the planned number of delegates pay for the events, the price would have to be £423 to achieve the same level of profit. Alternatively, the price could be maintained at £369 per delegate, but less profit margin would be made on the events.

An examination of the table shows that if delegate numbers decrease, less profit is achieved because less delegates are covering the fixed costs. Looking at this in another way, there are less delegates to pay for the fixed costs such as staffing or preliminary preparation costs. Therefore, as the number of delegates goes down, the cost per delegate goes up.

(d)   An Internet web site could be established before the event so that the event can be advertised. The web site could provide details of the dates and price of the event and also provide details of the speakers who are being invited. The web site could also provide information about previous successful seminars which have been run by the company.

There are many ways in which the web site can be used by delegates before, during and after the event. Before the event, delegates will be able to see details of the event and will be able to book and pay for it. This would be by way of a computerised booking form. They could also send by e-mail, suggestions of what they would like to see included in the event.

During the event, they will be able to access the web site to get up-to-date information about some of the topics which are being discussed. They will also be able to make bookings for future similar events. They might also be able to leave information on the web site for other delegates to contact them, should they have similar interests.

After the event, delegates could send in suggestions as to how to improve the event. They could also send in questions which could be forwarded to the speakers, so that the delegates may receive a reply. In addition, they could use the web site to book future events.

15   FINANCIAL PERFORMANCE INDICATORS

MEMORANDUM

TO: Marketing Manager & Members of Team
FROM: Tricia Radford
SUBJECT: Performance Indicators
DATE: 16 April 20XX

(i)   Stock turnover

In the last financial year, the stock turned over four times. The ratios were arrived at by estimating our average stockholding at any one time during the year. We then calculated that we managed to sell this amount of stock four times in the year.

Another way of looking at it is to say that at any one time, we are holding stock of thirteen weeks on average, ie if we continued to trade at our normal rate without buying in further stock, we would run out in thirteen weeks time.

In general, it is better to have a high stock turnover ratio rather than a low stock turnover ratio. This is because one wants as little money tied up in stock as possible. If money is not tied up in stock, it can be used for other things. If the stock turnover rate is too high however, it can be dangerous because our organisation might run out of some lines of stock.

(ii)   Return on investment

This was 6% in the last financial year. This means that for every pound invested in the company, we achieved a return of six pence.

This is a fundamental ratio for those who are already investing in our business, or contemplating investing in our business. Investors can compare the rate of return from our business with the rate of return that they might get from other investments, eg other companies or building societies.

(iii) Gross margin

In the last financial year, this was 50%. This means that for each pound of sales, after taking out the direct costs we were left with fifty pence gross profit.

This gross profit is then used to pay off expenses and should leave us with a profit. This is an important indicator because it can show whether our prices are set at the right level, or whether our direct costs are at the right level.

Generally, one would want to see a gross margin that is rising, ie one would want to be making more for each pound of sales that one makes. Too high a gross margin can be dangerous however, as it can mean that one prices oneself out of the market.

(iv)   Net margin

In the last financial year, this was 10%. This means that for every pound of sales, we were left with ten pence profit after taking out all direct and indirect costs.

It is important because one can see whether we are managing to make a profit and whether we can continue to exist as a business in the long term.

One would want to see a net margin that is increasing, ie one would want to make higher levels of net margin out of each pound of sales. If net margins are rising, it should indicate that our sales prices are rising or that our costs are falling.

A net margin that is too high can mean that there are problems however. For instance, it could be that the business is pricing itself out of the market or costs could have fallen to such a level that quality is impaired.

(v)   **Debtor turnover**

In the last financial year, the debtor turnover was three times per annum.

One calculates this by firstly arriving at the average level of debtors at any one point during the year. One can then calculate how many times during the year this average level of debt is received in from customers.

In our case, it means that in the last financial year, we received in our average level of debt three times during the year. Looking at this in another way, one can say that we have a level of debt, at any one point, of just over seventeen weeks, ie we have debts owing to us at any one point of just over seventeen weeks of average trade.

This is important because it indicates how much money we have tied up in debtors. It is preferable not to have much money tied up in debtors because then we can make use of the cash ourselves. For instance, we can buy stock with it or we could invest in capital equipment.

16   SOURCES OF INFORMATION

There are a number of possible sources of information which include the following.

Identification of competitors

(a)   Advertisements placed by competitors
(b)   Customers of the competitor
(c)   Suppliers
(d)   Trade associations
(e)   Yellow pages and other directories
(f)   Chamber of Commerce
(g)   Observation in the street (retail competitors)
(h)   Trade fairs
(i)   Exhibitions

Gathering intelligence

(a)   Send for catalogues and promotional material

(b)   Visit competitors

(c)   Send for published reports about the company or its products and services

(d)   Obtain press cuttings

(e)   Review company reports

(f)   Study market research reports

(g)   Look at ICC tables

(h)   Examine products

(i)   Ask customers and suppliers

(j)   Be vigilant

(k)   Use sales visits if a competitor is also a customer or if a customer come into contact with your competitor

Sales contacts in the field are often in a good position to gather qualitative intelligence about competitors. Sales personnel will know customers and other sales people in other organisations who may either know the competitor being tracked or may actually work for the competitor.

Promotional literature can often be a good source of information which, when pieced with other snippets of information, leads to intelligence about a competitor. This type of literature is designed to impress customers so it is going to provide a lot of information about product/service benefits and some details about the company itself.

Published annual reports containing the financial statements often provide a great deal of background on the companies and their products, together with details of their top management teams and their qualifications and experience. Directors' remuneration is detailed within this report. This may give some indication of how profitable or successful the firm is. Five-year financial summaries can provide information on sales growth and profitability.

Trade exhibitions, displays and conventions may provide an opportunity to gather intelligence about a number of competitors. Such intelligence is usually gleaned through open discussion and tends to be qualitative in nature. Sometimes it is possible to see promotional videos or demonstrations involving competitors' products.

An investigation of the product itself can produce much valuable information. Often a firm will purchase competitor products and take them apart and analyse them to gather important information that can be added to the databank about competitors.

It is important to be aware of the possible sources which may be used to gather intelligence. It is also important to recognise that to analyse competitors, data must be gathered systematically and stored so to be accessible as and when required by those forming a view of competition. A marketing intelligence system is a set of procedures and sources used by managers to obtain their everyday information about pertinent developments in the marketing environment. Intelligence consists of scanning the full marketing environment in a number of ways: undirected viewing (which simply involves exposure to the environment), directed exposure, informal searches and formal searches (to find out specific information).

Marketing managers may carry out marketing intelligence in a number of ways, but usually on their own, reading or talking to customers, suppliers, distributors and others. Much intelligence is qualitative in nature and may be regarded as 'soft'. This means it may not consist of hard facts but impression and opinion.

17   DATA SOURCES FOR ASSESSING MARKET ENTRY VIABILITY

It has been identified that a major growth strategy of the company is to take our existing Health Market software product and to develop a new market for it within Further Education Colleges within the UK.

It must be recognised that market development of this type is a medium risk growth strategy. As the strategy focuses on market expansion utilising an existing product, the high costs associated with product development are avoided. However, even without these costs, market development can be an expensive exercise and it is therefore important to reduce risk by basing decisions on good information.

To determine the viability of the new Further Education market, information should be sought in the following areas.

- Market size
- Market trends
- Market structure and characteristics
- Competitor information
- Customer information
- Segmentation studies

Background information on the education market is available through a number of secondary sources such as Government reports and market reports produced by companies such as Mintel, Keynote and Euromonitor. These reports will supply information on market size, projected trends, market structure and so on.

Competitor information can also be gained from secondary sources such as industry reports and also from other published data sources such as newspapers and trade journals. Product and pricing information can be gained from competitors communications materials such as brochures, pricelists and web pages. Primary sources can also be useful in this area such as distributors and customers for example.

Customer information will usually be gained from a primary research projects. This source can be used to gain either quantitative or qualitative information on such areas as usage and attitudes towards competitive products, pricing issues and distributors used.

A final source of information in this area could be the use of syndicated research or omnibus surveys. It is believed that a syndicated service is not available in the Education market, but appropriate omnibus surveys should be considered as they carry a cost advantage over other primary research methods.

The information collected from the above sources can be used in a wide range of strategic and tactical decision making. The main areas are as follows.

(a) **To gauge market attractiveness**

The information gained would allow forecasts to be produced gauging sales, profits and costs of the market development. Although we are not considering any other markets at this stage, it may also allow future attractiveness comparisons with other market segments.

(b) **To assist the development of a marketing strategy**

By understanding and quantifying the market background, structure, characteristics, competitiveness and so on, we will be basing our segmentation, targeting and positioning strategy on known information.

(c) **To assist with marketing mix decisions**

Although we have an existing product, information gained from this exercise could help decision making in the other marketing mix areas, as follows.

(i) **Pricing** – To assist with pricing strategy and pricing tactics decisions.

(ii) **Promotion** – To produce promotional activities to appeal to the target audience. This could also include highlighting appropriate media choices and communication messages.

(iii) **Distribution** – To identify the most appropriate channels.

As discussed, gaining better market information will allow us to minimise the risk of market development. Using the many sources that are available, we will be able to build a clear picture of the market and this knowledge will be useful in a range of strategic and tactical marketing decisions that we will need to take.

18 MARKETING RESEARCH PROCESS

REPORT

To: Marketing Manager
From: Jill Riley Date: 21 January 20XX
Subject: Identifying areas of improvement in the distribution and logistics function

This report outlines the marketing research process, giving the key stages in undertaking research and the specific research objectives and methodology to be followed.

(a) **Marketing research process - key stages**

(i)   Set the objectives of the research
(ii)   Define the research problem
(iii)   Assess the value of the research
(iv)   Construct the research proposal
(v)   Specify data collection method(s)
(vi)   Specify technique(s) of measurement
(vii)   Select the sample
(viii) Collect the data
(ix)   Analyse the result
(x)   Present the final report

The following points relating to each key stage should be borne in mind.

(i)   Research objectives need to be SMART - Specific, Measurable, Actionable, Reasonable and Timescaled.

(ii)   Some exploratory research may be necessary to clarify problem areas and further understand customer requirements.

(iii)   A cost benefit exercise will need to be carried out to ensure that undertaking the research is cost-effective.

(iv)   Proposals need to be submitted for the category of research to be undertaken and must be agreed by all parties.

(v)   Data can be primary (field research) or secondary (desk research). Collection methods will vary according to the type of research.

(vi)   At the measurement stage, all the factors under investigation will need to be converted into quantitative data to allow for analysis.

(vii)   Sample size will be dependent on time and resources but must be sufficient to be statistically significant.

(viii) Decisions as to who will undertake the research and how will it be carried out must be made.

(ix) Statistical analysis may involve using manual techniques, computer techniques or a combination of both.

(x) Findings will need to be presented and a formal report submitted.

(b) **Specific research objectives and method of conducting research**

(i) **Research objectives**

Separate objectives are needed for the two groups of customers, those using Electronic Data Interchange (EDI) and those not using it.

(1) **Customers using EDI**

- To establish how they rate current distributive and logistics processes
- To identify areas where improvements can be made
- To establish to what extent perceived customer service levels can be improved by better distributive and logistics processes

(2) **Customers not using EDI**

- To establish reasons for non-use of EDI
- To identify incentives to encourage non-users to invest in EDI technology
- To quantify the likely benefit in improved customer service

(ii) **Conducting the research**

The most cost-effective way to undertake the research is likely to be a combination of in-house and external agency resource. My proposal is as follows.

(1) Draw up a research brief internally

(2) Short list and then commission a specialist marketing research agency

(3) Ask the agency to compile questionnaires (one for EDI customers, one for non-EDI users)

(4) Use the company's sales representatives to collect questionnaire data

(5) Await questionnaire analysis and presentation of findings by the agency

The questionnaire format should be such that the sales team can conduct semi-structured interviews. This would facilitate the collection of quantitative data (tick box, pre-coded choices) and qualitative data (views and opinions recorded from open-ended questions). Probing questions, such as 'What other factors are there?' can also be used to clarify responses or gather additional information. They are also useful for triggering further responses. More skill is required in conducting semi-structured interviews, but these should be within the capabilities of the sales team, provided that they are given an adequate brief.

19 RESEARCH FOR PRODUCT LAUNCH

The following report outlines the market research plan to be conducted prior to the launch of our new magazine aimed at teenage females.

Research conducted last year revealed the UK female teenage market as a viable new market for our magazine publications. The secondary research carried out at this time has defined a demographic and psychographic profile of our target market.

The following plan has been developed for **pre-launch research** into the market to define the most successful product characteristics, pricing and advertising support. As a wealth of secondary research has already been gathered, this plan will focus entirely on primary sources of information.

The plan is structured to cover each stage in the standard research process. Sections therefore cover the following areas.

- Define the research objectives
- Ascertain the best methods for obtaining the information
- Collect the data
- Process the data

- Make recommendations
- Implement the recommendations

Research objectives

Research objectives must be devised to be specific, measurable, actionable, reasonable and timescaled (ie SMART). Suggested objectives for the research are as follows.

- To investigate attitudes to magazine content and layout styles amongst the target group, to discover the most appropriate product mix
- To investigate attitudes to advertising message and content amongst the target group to discover the most appropriate advertising mix
- To quantify media consumption of the target group
- To investigate attitudes to magazine pricing amongst the target group

Methods for obtaining information

There are a two appropriate primary research methods which could be used to obtain qualitative data of this type. These methods are discussed in the sections below.

Focus groups

This is a research method which should be given consideration. In this method, a group of six to ten respondents from the target group is engaged in a group discussion with a moderator. Typically, the sessions are recorded or videoed through a two way mirror for later analysis. This format of research allows props to be used, such as advertising visuals and magazine layouts.

Hall tests

The usual format of this method is to recruit respondents from the target group on the street and to invite then to a nearby research room to view material and test their reactions. This could also be combined with a short interview. This method, would allow props to be used and appropriate qualitative data could be obtained.

The recommendation is to use focus groups for this research for the following reasons.

- It is a more cost-effective way of gathering respondent data, leading to larger number of respondents being involved within the budget
- The recording of focus groups allows more in depth analysis of the discussion
- The target group is more likely to 'open up' in a group
- There are potential legal and/or moral implications surrounding street recruitment of this target group

Collect the data

The first issue to consider is that of sampling. Although we have defined demographic and psychographic profiles of the target group, it is recommended that we address geographic considerations for the sample. Previous research projects have used specific city locations in the North, Midlands and South East of the UK to mirror the UK population. It is suggested that this research uses the same locations.

Respondents will be recruited through snowballing techniques which could be achieved through schools and colleges within the target areas. We must also consider the legal and moral implications of respondent recruitment. We will need to gain parental permission and possibly parental accompaniment for the respondents.

Process the data

Discussions will be captured on video. Transcripts of discussions will be produced and qualitative analysis techniques applied to the results.

Recommendations

The results will be written into a report format and a presentation given to company directors and marketing management.

Resource/Costs/Timing issues

We do not have the in-house expertise to conduct a research project of this type. A research brief will be written and submitted to two external marketing research companies. Previous experience would suggest that the budget of £30,000 will finance recruitment, data collection, analysis and reporting of 15 focus groups. The likely timescale for this project is 2 months from the awarding of the contract.

List of key concepts and Index

These are the terms which we have identified thoughout the text as being KEY CONCEPTS.

BPP PUBLISHING

CIM Order

To BPP Publishing Ltd, Aldine Place, London W12 8AA
Tel: 020 8740 2211. Fax: 020 8740 1184
email: publishing@bpp.com
online: www.bpp.com

Mr/Mrs/Ms (Full name)

Daytime delivery address

Postcode

Daytime Tel

Date of exam (month/year)

POSTAGE & PACKING

Study Texts

	First	Each extra	
UK	£3.00	£2.00	£
Europe*	£5.00	£4.00	£
Rest of world	£20.00	£10.00	£

Kits/Success Tapes

	First	Each extra	
UK	£2.00	£1.00	£
Europe*	£2.50	£1.00	£
Rest of world	£15.00	£8.00	£

	7/01 Texts	9/01 Kit	Success Tapes
CERTIFICATE			
1 Marketing Environment	£18.95 ☐	£9.95 ☐	£12.95 ☐
2 Customer Communications in Marketing	£18.95 ☐	£9.95 ☐	£12.95 ☐
3 Marketing in Practice	£18.95 ☐	£9.95 ☐	£12.95 ☐
4 Marketing Fundamentals	£18.95 ☐	£9.95 ☐	£12.95 ☐
ADVANCED CERTIFICATE			
5 The Marketing Customer Interface	£18.95 ☐	£9.95 ☐	£12.95 ☐
6 Management Information for Marketing Decisions	£18.95 ☐	£9.95 ☐	£12.95 ☐
7 Effective Management for Marketing	£18.95 ☐	£9.95 ☐	£12.95 ☐
8 Marketing Operations	£18.95 ☐	£9.95 ☐	£12.95 ☐
DIPLOMA			
9 Integrated Marketing Communications	£18.95 ☐	£9.95 ☐	£12.95 ☐
10 International Marketing Strategy	£18.95 ☐	£9.95 ☐	£12.95 ☐
11 Strategic Marketing Management: Planning and Control	£18.95 ☐	£9.95 ☐	£12.95 ☐
12 Strategic Marketing Management: Analysis and Decision (9/01)	£25.95 ☐	N/A	£12.95 ☐

SUBTOTAL £

Grand Total (Cheques to *BPP Publishing*) I enclose
a cheque for (incl. Postage) £ ☐
Or charge to Access/Visa/Switch
Card Number

Expiry date   Start Date

Issue Number (Switch Only)

Signature

We aim to deliver to all UK addresses inside 5 working days. A signature will be required. Orders to all EU addresses should be delivered within 6 working days.

All other orders to overseas addresses should be delivered within 8 working days.

* Europe includes the Republic of Ireland and the Channel Islands.

REVIEW FORM & FREE PRIZE DRAW

All original review forms from the entire BPP range, completed with genuine comments, will be entered into one of two draws on 31 January 2002 and 31 July 2002. The names on the first four forms picked out on each occasion will be sent a cheque for £50.

Name: _____   Address: _____

_____

_____

How have you used this Text?
(Tick one box only)

☐ Home study (book only)

☐ On a course: college _____

☐ With 'correspondence' package

☐ Other _____

Why did you decide to purchase this Text?
(Tick one box only)

☐ Have used companion Kit

☐ Have used BPP Texts in the past

☐ Recommendation by friend/colleague

☐ Recommendation by a lecturer at college

☐ Saw advertising

☐ Other _____

During the past six months do you recall seeing/receiving any of the following?
(Tick as many boxes as are relevant)

☐ Our advertisement in the *Marketing Success*

☐ Our advertisement in *Marketing Business*

☐ Our brochure with a letter through the post

☐ Our brochure with *Marketing Business*

Which (if any) aspects of our advertising do you find useful?
(Tick as many boxes as are relevant)

☐ Prices and publication dates of new editions

☐ Information on Text content

☐ Facility to order books off-the-page

☐ None of the above

Have you used the companion Practice & Revision Kit for this subject?   ☐ Yes   ☐ No

Your ratings, comments and suggestions would be appreciated on the following areas.

	Very useful	Useful	Not useful
Introductory section (How to use this text, study checklist, etc)	☐	☐	☐
Setting the Scene	☐	☐	☐
Syllabus coverage	☐	☐	☐
Action Programmes and Marketing at Work examples	☐	☐	☐
Chapter roundups	☐	☐	☐
Quick quizzes	☐	☐	☐
Illustrative questions	☐	☐	☐
Content of suggested answers	☐	☐	☐
Index	☐	☐	☐
Structure and presentation	☐	☐	☐

	Excellent	Good	Adequate	Poor
Overall opinion of this Text	☐	☐	☐	☐

Do you intend to continue using BPP Study Texts/Kits?   ☐ Yes   ☐ No

Please note any further comments and suggestions/errors on the reverse of this page.

Please return to: Kate Machattie, BPP Publishing Ltd, FREEPOST, London, W12 8BR

REVIEW FORM & FREE PRIZE DRAW (continued)

Please note any further comments and suggestions/errors below.

FREE PRIZE DRAW RULES

1   Closing date for 31 January 2002 draw is 31 December 2001. Closing date for 31 July 2002 draw is 30 June 2002

2   Restricted to entries with UK and Eire addresses only. BPP employees, their families and business associates are excluded.

3   No purchase necessary. Entry forms are available upon request from BPP Publishing. No more than one entry per title, per person. Draw restricted to persons aged 16 and over.

4   Winners will be notified by post and receive their cheques not later than 6 weeks after the relevant draw date. Lists of winners will be published in BPP's *focus* newsletter following the relevant draw.

5   The decision of the promoter in all matters is final and binding. No correspondence will be entered into.